Goethe's

FAUST

Its Genesis

and

Purport

Goethe's
FAUST
Its Genesis
and
Purport

by

Eudo C. Mason

UNIVERSITY OF CALIFORNIA PRESS
BERKELEY AND LOS ANGELES   1967

University of California Press
Berkeley and Los Angeles, California

Cambridge University Press
London, England

Copyright © 1967, by The Regents of the University of California

Library of Congress Catalog Card Number: 67-14969

Designed by Pamela F. Johnson

Printed in the United States of America

To the Memory of
Esther

Preface

I HAVE AIMED in this study at giving not only my own interpretation of Goethe's *Faust*, but also a representative survey of critical opinion, especially during the last eighty years or so, and of the most influential trends of Faust scholarship and research, so far as they affect the actual text of the play, the history of its composition, its style and form, Goethe's sources, and the autobiographical elements that can be supposed to underly it.

It emerges that *Faust*, in a greater degree perhaps than any other outstanding literary work of the modern world, lends itself to the most varied and contradictory interpretations. This is due not only to each individual critic having his own axe to grind, but also to a certain intrinsic ambiguity of the work itself. It reposes on the great polarities of Goethe's own life and on his efforts to unite them in a higher synthesis—on the polarities of realism and idealism, of the sensual and the spiritual, of the amoralism of genius and a quasi-Christian ethical austerity. We are all of us inevitably tempted to interpret *Faust* in terms of the particular poles of this manifold dualism that appeal most to us personally, but its true significance lies in the tension between them.

I have been reluctantly forced to the conclusion that far too much academic scholarship and research on *Faust* is concerned with factitious solutions of factitious problems, and particularly that the "Higher Critics" have made complex and obscure what is often comparatively simple and clear, thereby setting up artificial barriers between the reader and Goethe's work. In challenging some of the sacrosanct dogmas of *Faust* criticism I have tried always to give a fair statement of the arguments on both sides of the question.

It is sometimes rightly enough claimed that we have the advantage of knowing a good deal more purely factually and historically about the processes by which *Faust* was produced than Goethe himself could, either in his earlier years, when the future was unforeseeable for him, or in his later years, when he had only his memory to rely upon. But all this documentary knowledge still tells us little about what he was getting at with his work. That is what matters most, and it is something that Goethe alone knew and never fully revealed, probably never could fully have revealed to anybody. The answer to that question, so far as it can be answered at all, is to be found less in the documentary evidence about the writing of *Faust*, important though that is, than in the text of the drama itself, in Goethe's other works, and in the totality of his character as a poet and a human being. I have frequently had occasion to protest against the too common assumption that Goethe himself did not know or care what he was getting at in *Faust* or that he was even not getting at anything in particular at all. Amongst the critics to whom I owe most in my attempts to reconstruct and elucidate the visionary conception or "inner fairy tale" that shapes itself in Goethe's *Faust*, I would particularly name six who, widely though they differ from one another in their conclusions, have in common a fine amplitude of outlook and a refreshing sense for essentials: Konrad Burdach, H. A. Korff, Max Kommerell, Emil Staiger, Wilhelm Emrich, and the too little known Karl Wollf.

It would have been impossible within the compass of the present volume to deal with the second part of *Faust* anything more than cursorily. The reader is referred here to the relevant chapter in Emil Staiger's great book on Goethe and to the valuable special studies by Karl May, Max Kommerell, and Wilhelm Emrich.

For all the English versions of German and occasional French and Latin quotations, I am myself responsible.

There are many to whom I owe a debt of gratitude for help and encouragement of various kinds, without which this book could not have been completed. In particular I would name here Professor K. G. Knight, Dr. Hugh B. Nisbet, Mr. David A. Dushkin, Dr. Margarete Zehnder, Miss Sheila Millar, and my late wife. My special thanks are due also to the University of California Press for the patience, understanding, and courtesy that they have shown to me.

Eudo C. Mason

Edinburgh

Contents

1. Sources

THE CONCEPTION of the magician as a man endowed with occult knowledge and capable of performing supernatural feats through mysterious agencies is found all over the world from the earliest times. Individuals of exceptional spiritual powers have often tended to live on in the popular imagination as magicians, the fantastic legends that accumulated around their names all displaying a certain family likeness. This process continued unabated with the advent of the Christian Era and throughout the Middle Ages, the magician being seen now, however, predominantly as one who can only have obtained his mysterious powers by entering into league with the devil and thus incurring damnation. Witchcraft, which according to some authorities was originally quite distinct from magic, came thus to be more and more closely associated with it, as did also the comparatively lawful and respectable sciences of astrology and alchemy. The Middle Ages knew indeed the more innocuous type of magician, as represented by Merlin, for example, and Shakespeare sets before us in Prospero a magician who is at the same time a model of virtue and wisdom. But these are phenomena that do not concern us. We are interested in the other aspect of these old legends, above all in the pact with the devil, which was not, however, necessarily conceived of as always terminating disastrously for the magician: sometimes the devil was outwitted by a cunningly devised clause in the treaty, sometimes the magician was saved by the intervention of the Virgin Mary.[1]

The belief in magic and witchcraft, far from declining with the coming of the Reformation, as one might expect it to have done,

flared up with greater intensity than ever and with a scarcely prec-
edented ponderous literalness, especially in Germany, where the
new humanism, for all its enlightened tendencies, was powerless
against it and sometimes indeed allowed itself to be infected with
it. Luther, in particular, thought more medievally on this subject
than the Middle Ages themselves. Goethe himself, though a great
admirer of Luther, inveighed against "die verfluchte Teufelsimagi-
nation unseres Reformators, der die ganze sichtbare Welt mit dem
Teufel bevölkerte und zum Teufel personifizierte" (the accursed,
devil-ridden imagination of our Reformer, which was always seeing devils, peopled the entire visible world with devils and personified it as the devil).[2] It was in this devil-ridden world of Luther's
that the historical Faust[3] lived, a shadowy figure of whom little
more is definitely known than that he was probably born at Knitt-
lingen in Würtemberg about 1480 and probably died under sinister
circumstances at Staufen near Freiburg in Breisgau about 1540 or
1541. Even his name is uncertain. He has gone down to posterity as
Johannes Faustus, but it seems likely that his real Christian name
was not Johann, but Georg, and there is even some slight doubt
whether his real surname was not Sabellicus. He arrogated to himself the academic titles of "Magister" and "Doctor," without ever
having really studied at any university. Such evidence as there is
suggests that there was much of the braggart and charlatan in him,
and that he mastered all the tricks for imposing on the credulity of
the masses as a quacksalver and a practitioner of astrology and all
the other arts of soothsaying. He was constantly roving about from
one part of Germany to another and possibly further afield still,
and was regarded by the authorities of at least two cities as an undesirable person, whom they refused to harbour in their walls.
Humanists like Trithemius and Mutianus spoke of him with contempt, theologians like Luther and Melanchthon with abhorrence.
Some of the records, such as they are, point to his having been a
scoffer at religion, which may in part account for the rumours cir-
culating soon after his death that he was a necromancer in the
most abominable sense of the word, with a familiar spirit in the
form of a black dog, Praestigar. How far he himself really believed
in or tried to practise black magic cannot be determined. Possibly
he was killed by an explosion in the course of an alchemistic ex-

periment, this giving rise to the belief that the devil had come to bear him off to Hell. Authentic records were soon submerged in legendary accretions, and less than fifty years after his death he had been metamorphosed into Dr. Johannes Faustus, Professor at Wittenberg and heir to all the magicians of previous centuries. In 1587 Spies published in Frankfort the first of the Faust chapbooks, in its own crude way a powerful literary performance, which, while incorporating much grossly farcical old anecdotal material, is essentially a deadly earnest warning against all human pride and striving after forbidden knowledge. In particular the theme of Faust's pact with the devil and his subsequent damnation is treated with an abundance of matter-of-fact, circumstantial detail and with uncompromising Lutheran fervour.

A translation of this Frankfort chapbook appeared shortly afterwards in England and was dramatized in 1592, if not earlier, by Christopher Marlowe as *The Tragical History of Dr. Faustus.* Marlowe certainly ennobles the conception of Faust's character and invites us to regard him not only with horror, but also with admiration and sympathy:

> Cut is the branch that might have grown full straight,
> And burned is Apollo's laurel bough,
> That sometime grew within this learned man . . .

But there is no substantial foundation for the claim sometimes made[4] that Marlowe was consciously or even unconsciously out to challenge the religious postulates of the chapbook, or to represent Faustus as anything but a culpable character, the justice of whose fate is not to be questioned. There are no traces within this play of those audaciously heterodox and blasphemous sentiments which Marlowe is reported to have expressed sometimes in private conversation. One or other of the troupes of English actors who went to Germany during the Shakespearean period took Marlowe's *Dr. Faustus* with them in their repertoire, and there are records of their performing it in Graz in 1608 and in Dresden in 1626. Out of this a German Faust drama gradually evolved; for the theory of Bruinier and Höfer that Marlowe himself based his tragedy in part on a still earlier German play is so dubious and has found so little support that it may here be disregarded. Translated, adapted, and much garbled and debased in the process, it was still recognisably Marlowe's *Dr. Faustus* that enjoyed such great popularity on the stage in Germany throughout the seventeenth and the greater part of the eighteenth century, and from the later seventeenth century onward also as a puppet-play. Amongst the most important changes it underwent were the addition of a Prologue in Hell, the substitution of the Duke of Parma for the German Emperor, and the large part assigned to the Clown ("Pickelhäring," "Hanswurst," "Kasperl," or "Lustige Person"), an indispensable figure in most German dramas of that age, whose speeches and action were largely improvised and who here appeared first as Faust's rascally servant and then as a night-watchman. There was no single, authorized text for this crude, popular German Faust drama, which never appeared in print and varied from troupe to troupe, from puppet-theatre to puppet-theatre, probably even from performance to performance. It has no serious literary pretensions, and such knowledge of it as we have is derived from contemporary diaries and letters, from old play-bills and from fragmentary manuscripts, out of which Simrock (1846), Carl Engel (1865), and E. Höfer (1914) have tentatively reconstructed composite texts. The popularity of the Faust story led to its being imitated from an early date in chapbooks and dramas showing the similar fortunes of Faust's "Famulus" Wagner, also a magician, with a familiar spirit called "Auerhahn."

Goethe cannot have been directly influenced by Marlowe's *Dr. Faustus,* because he did not come to know it till 1818, when he read it in Wilhelm Müller's translation. But indirectly it did exercise an important and recognisable influence on him through the crude German popular plays which were descended from it. It is usually and quite legitimately assumed that he first became acquainted with the name and story of Faust in early boyhood through one of these plays, probably performed by puppets, though we have no direct evidence for it. The only mention of Faust in the three passages in which Goethe recalls his childhood enthusiasm for the puppet-theatre is in *Wilhelm Meisters theatralische Sendung* ("Wilhelm Meister's Theatrical Mission"), where Wilhelm's grandmother reminds his father of his own early days: "ihr habt mich um

manchen Batzen gebracht, um den Doktor Faust und das Mohren-
ballett zu sehen" (You children wheedled many pennies out of me
to see Dr. Faust and the Moorish Ballet). Goethe's earliest reference to Faust is in his comedy *Die Mitschuldigen* ("The Companions in Guilt") of winter, 1768–1769, where Söller, finding
himself in a tight corner, exlaims:

> Es wird mir siedend heiss. So war's dem Doktor Faust
> Nicht halb zu Muth, nicht halb war's so Richard dem dritten.*

The coupling of Faust with Richard III here suggests that Goethe
was thinking of some kind of stage performance, either by puppets
or by living actors.

The point of time when Goethe did at last come to know the
traditional Faust drama in its original, authentic form, as Marlowe
had written it, was far too late for him to be in the least influenced
by it or even more than moderately impressed by it,[5] and he seems
to have had as little suspicion as anybody else at this time that here
was nothing less than the source from which the crude German
popular plays were ultimately derived. Only later research was to
reveal the links of this connexion. His knowledge of the Faust
chapbook tradition was equally vague and defective, a circumstance
that is in itself not to be deplored or wondered at, and would hardly
be worth remarking on at all, if certain mistaken conceptions on the
subject had not gained wide currency, confusing and sometimes
even falsifying important critical issues. He never so much as
suspected the existence of the original, authentic Faust chapbook,
as Spies published it in 1587, for the good reason that it survived
in extremely few copies and was not rediscovered till after his death.
Nor did he know Georg Widmann's intolerably tedious expansion
of Spies to a tome of 671 pages, with its uninspired commentaries,
produced in 1599. What he did know was Nikolaus Pfitzer's somewhat retrenched but still excessively bulky and wearisome revision
of Widmann, published in 1674, which he must have been in a
position to consult before 1776, as appears above all from certain

---

* I feel boiling hot. Neither Dr. Faust / Nor Richard III felt half so bad as
I do.

motifs in the "Auerbachs Keller" scene, and which he borrowed
from the Ducal Library in Weimar in 1801. Hermann Schneider
(1949) falls short of the insight and reliability which he so often
elsewhere displays, when he asserts: "Goethe . . . war von früh
auf ein gründlicher Kenner dieser ganzen [Faust-] Überlieferung,
der dramatischen wie der romanhaften" (Goethe was from an
early age a thorough master of the entire Faust tradition, alike in
its dramatic and in its narrative forms).[6] Schneider attributes to
him explicitly a knowledge of Spies and Widmann, as well as
Pfitzer. Goethe regarded Pfitzer as the earliest Faust book. If he
had known anything about Spies and Widmann, he could never
have written as he did on November 20, 1829, to Zelter: "der
Ursprung [der Faust-Legende] scheint ins sechzehnte, die Aus-
bildung ins siebzehnte Jahrhundert zu gehören" (The Faust legend
seems to belong in its origins to the sixteenth century and to have
been brought into shape in the seventeenth century). The bringing into shape of the Faust legend had taken place before 1600,
and the seventeenth century can be said rather to have brought it
out of shape again.

Towards the end of the seventeenth century the spread of the
new Enlightenment mentality led advanced thinkers to regard
the story of Faust with increasing scepticism, and in 1683 it was
submitted to a stern critical examination by Johann Georg Neumann in his *Disquisitio Historica prior de Fausto Praestigatore*,
in the course of which he expressed the opinion: "Zudem ist der
Kerle mit alle nicht werth, dass man so viel Wesens von ihm
machen sollte" (What is more, the fellow is in any case not
worth making so much fuss about). In the general rationalistic
onslaught on ancient superstitions and absurdities during the following decades Faust was again and again singled out as a target;
Gottsched, the acknowledged spokesman of these tendencies, inveighed on various occasions against the fooleries ("Alfanzereien")
of "das Märchen von D. Fausten" (the fairy-tale of Dr. Faustus),
and declared in 1728: "Nur der Pöbel schleppet sich noch mit D.
Fausts und andern dergleichen Büchern herum, die man ihm aber
mit der Zeit auch aus den Händen bringen wird" (Only the mob
still cling to Dr. Faustus and similar books, which will in the course

of time be taken away from them). By 1750, Faust seemed to have been relegated once and for all to the category of those things that anybody with the least pretensions to education and culture would be ashamed of taking seriously. In 1755, Moses Mendelsohn declared in a letter to Lessing: "Eine einzige Exklamation—o Faustus, Faustus! könnte das ganze Parterre lachen machen" (One single exclamation, "O Faustus! Faustus!" could make the entire pit in a theatre roar with laughter). In the following year Johann Friedrich Löwen ridiculed Faust in a long satirical poem, *Die Walpurgisnacht* ("The Walpurgis Night"), which showed him involved in the annual revelries of the witches on the Brocken—an innovation in the Faust legend later taken over by Goethe, who records in Book VI of *Dichtung und Wahrheit* ("Poetry and Truth") that he knew and admired this poem in his early Frankfort years, before he was sixteen. Even the strolling players, who catered chiefly for the masses, yielded to the modern, enlightened trend of opinion and dropped the Faust drama from their repertoires: the last recorded performances[7] of it seem to have taken place in 1770, in Hamburg and Strasburg, in which latter city it may have been seen by the young Goethe. From that time it was confined to the puppet-theatre, as a mere absurd fairy-tale, which could only interest children. As a puppet-play it has survived to our own day.

The surprising point is that Faust was no sooner thus contemptuously flung out of the front door of the temple of German literature and culture than the younger generation of writers set about bringing him in again at the back door. This paradoxical process began indeed with no less a person than the greatest of all representatives of the Enlightenment amongst German men of letters, Lessing, who as early as 1755 planned a sentimental domestic tragedy on the Faust theme, "ohne alle Teufelei, wo ein Erzbösewicht gegen einen Unschuldigen die Rolle des schwarzen Verführers vertreten sollte" (without any diabolical machinery, in which an arch-villain was to take over the part of the black tempter against an innocent man). Nothing came of that project of Lessing's, but in 1759 he published his remarkable seventeenth *Literaturbrief* ("Letter on Literature"), where he deceptively appears, as in nothing else he wrote, to be just a precursor of the Storm and Stress movement of which he was to disapprove so strongly on its efflorescence some fifteen years later. The seventeenth "letter" is an energetic attack on Gottsched and his efforts to reform the German theatre on French classical lines. Lessing argues that the truer model to be followed is Shakespeare and goes on:

> Dass aber unsere alten Stücke wirklich sehr viel Englisches gehabt haben, könnte ich Ihnen mit geringer Mühe weitläufig beweisen. Nur das Bekannteste derselben zu nennen: *Doktor Faust* hat eine Menge Szenen, die nur ein Shakespearsches Genie zu denken vermögend gewesen. Und wie verliebt war Deutschland und ist es zum Teil noch in seinen "Doktor Faust!"*

Lessing then sets before the reader as the work of "one of his friends" a specimen scene (in reality not at all Shakespearean) from his own Faust drama, which, unlike the originally planned domestic tragedy, now conforms fairly closely in its external outlines with the old tradition. This Faust drama of Lessing's constitutes one of the major mysteries of German literature. It is supposed to have been completed and ready for publication by December, 1776, and then shortly after that to have disappeared without leaving any traces behind except one brief scenario and two reports made from memory some years after Lessing's death by his friends, v. Blankenburg and Engel. There is one connexion in which we shall have occasion to refer again to these vestigiary remnants of Lessing's *Faust*, though they are really only of secondary interest to us, since they were not made public before 1784 and therefore cannot have been known to Goethe before that year at the earliest. Here once more, as in the case of his earliest knowledge of the puppet-play and in so many other cases, we find ourselves, in spite of the immense body of material that has come

---

* I could with little trouble demonstrate to you at length that our older plays really have very much of the English manner in them. To name only the best known of them: *Doctor Faustus* contains a number of scenes which can only have been conceived by a Shakespearean genius. And how enamoured Germany used to be and in part still is of its *Doctor Faustus!*

down to us on nearly every aspect of Goethe's work on *Faust*, left tantalizingly in the dark about a point of capital importance. Not one single allusion by Goethe either to the posthumously published remnants of Lessing's Faust drama or even to the seventeenth *Literaturbrief* is recorded, and we therefore cannot be certain that he ever so much as glanced at either of them, still less that he was impressed or influenced by them. What can, however, be fairly assumed is that Lessing's defence of Faust in 1759 was, directly or indirectly, in a considerable measure responsible for the astonishing way in which from about 1770 onward so many younger writers, especially of the Storm and Stress generation, adopted Faust as the hero for ambitious literary plans of their own, treating the legend, of course, no longer naively and literally, but symbolically. Goethe was only one of quite a number who more or less independently of one another hit on some scheme of this kind, most noteworthy amongst the others being "Maler" Müller, Lenz, Klinger, and—because of certain motifs introduced into their by no means inspired work—Paul Weidmann and Johann Friedrich Schink. Lessing is rumoured to have withheld his own *Faust* from the press until some of the others which were expected to appear shortly, above all Goethe's, should be published, in order that he might out-Faust them all. "Meinen Faust holt der Teufel; aber ich will Goethes seinen holen" (The Devil carries off my Faust, but I intend to carry off Goethe's),[8] he is on not unimpeachable authority supposed to have said. The curious rehabilitation of Faust, just at the time when he seemed to have been discredited beyond all hope, was perhaps in part due to his having, through the very invective of Gottsched and other spokesmen of the Enlightenment, acquired a quasi-symbolical significance. Once the reaction against the Enlightenment, at least in its more rigid and dogmatic forms, had fairly set in, it was quite natural that Faust should for many assume a similar role to that of the stone the builders rejected, which in spite of that became the chief cornerstone.

In 1725, when the fortunes of Faust had already fallen very low, a drastic abridgement of Pfitzer's unwieldy tome to the compass of a pamphlet of forty-one pages was published by an anonymous writer under the *nom-de-plume* "ein Christlich Meynender" (a man with a Christian outlook). The writer touches in his Preface on the controversy regarding the credibility of the Faust legend and agrees in the main with the enlightened sceptics, but he is still fascinated by Faust and, leaving the issue more or less open, contents himself with giving the actual narrative in succinct form as a legend that is at least curious and may even have something in it. This fourth and last chapbook, though it falls far short in literary quality of the original one of 1587, is an immense improvement on Widmann and Pfitzer. It continued to be reprinted down to the end of the eighteenth century, and was the most important of Goethe's sources. He must have owned a copy and had it constantly at hand, whereas Pfitzer was only accessible to him in libraries. When he first came across it we do not know for certain. It is usually assumed that one of the later reprints of it must have been amongst the humble chapbooks he read in early childhood, though it is missing in the list of seven titles given in his only account of these chapbooks, in *Dichtung und Wahrheit*, Book I. The absence of *Faust* from this list may mean that Goethe did not come across the Faust chapbook until later, but it is quite as likely to be due to his love of mystification, to the way in which he sometimes enjoyed keeping his readers in the dark on points he knew were bound specially to interest them. It is certainly not a merely accidental silence, any more than his silence on the equally important question of the popular Faust plays is merely accidental. We can be certain that he must have come across the Faust book of the "Christlich Meynender" by 1770 at the latest. In all probability he knew it very much earlier.

The critics differ considerably on the questions, how thoroughly Goethe knew the traditional Faust chapbooks and dramas, what his attitude towards them was, and how much his own *Faust* owes to them. We are here to some extent in the dark, because we know so little for certain not only about his earliest acquaintance with them, but also about when he first seriously decided to write a Faust drama of his own—a point to which we shall have to return later. Hermann Schneider, who, as we have already seen, unwarrantedly attributes to Goethe a knowledge of the Spies and Widmann chapbooks, says: "Der junge Goethe muss ein unverdrossener Leser gewesen sein, und so nahm er . . . auch den masslos öden geistlich-gelehrten Erläuterungswust aus Pfitzers Feder in sich auf" (The youthful Goethe must have been an indefatigable reader and so he even ploughed through the unspeakably dreary theological expository rubbish from Pfitzer's pen).[9] Schneider assumes this because he also assumes that it was Goethe's intention, "vor allem, die überkommene Faustgeschichte szenisch [zu] bearbeiten. Die Arbeit begann . . . mit der Dramatisierung der Historie" (above all to produce a stage version of the traditional Faust story. His work began with the dramatization of the chronicle).[10] Hermann Hefele (1931) attributes to Goethe a similar deference for and dependence upon the historical traditions and sources: "Er begriff sie [die Faustidee] . . . nur . . . als Geschichtsbild des Mittelalters. . . . die mittelalterliche Geschichtssubstanz des Faust hat er nirgends preisgegeben" (He conceived of the idea of Faust only as a historical picture of the Middle Ages. He has at no point violated the medieval historical essence of Faust).[11] This leaves out of account Goethe's own statement in a letter to Zelter of November 20, 1829: "Nur dürfen wir sie [die Faustische Legende] nicht wohl ins Mittelalter setzen" (We hardly ought to place the Faust legend in the Middle Ages). It is doubtful whether Goethe, even from the first beginnings of his work on *Faust,* ever saw in the old legend anything more than a point of departure for a free creation of his own, and whether he therefore ever felt obliged to study the old Faust literature anything more than cursorily, with an eye only to the general outlines and to effective particular motifs which he could adapt to his own private purposes. Most of what he needed he could find in the book of the "Christlich Meynender," without ranging further afield. He said himself to Eckermann on February 16, 1826: "Beim Werther und Faust musste ich . . . in meinen eigenen Busen greifen, denn das Überlieferte war nicht weit her" (In writing *Werther* and *Faust* . . . I had to draw upon by own heart, because the sources did not amount to much). There is no reason to suppose that Goethe at any stage felt occasion to take his sources for *Faust* half so seriously as many of his critics do, still less to go in for regular research on the subject. They were important for him, indeed, but only as raw material, not as authorities, and the most interesting thing about them for us is the freedom with which he treated them. We should not expect to be able to trace back everything in Goethe's *Faust* to these sources, or believe that by doing so we can solve any of the major problems of interpretation. Schiller records in a letter of July 20, 1801, to Körner, how Goethe had said to him, "dass er zu seinem Faust gar keinen Trost in Büchern gefunden habe." (that in writing his *Faust* he had found no help at all in books).

A legend of such wide currency as that of Faust inevitably leaves its mark at many different points in literature and elsewhere: it was dealt with in popular ballads and miscellaneous poems, imitated in such works as the Wagner chapbooks and dramas, and alluded to in the most varied contexts by writers of the most divergent schools of thought. Some of this odd, scattered material came Goethe's way. In 1801 he is known to have consulted Neumann's *Disquisitio* of 1683, in which, however, he can have found nothing suitable for his purposes. Far more important for him was Löwen's *Walpurgisnacht*, with which he was, as we have seen, familiar before he was sixteen. During his years as a student in Leipzig, 1765 to 1768, he regularly frequented Auerbachs Keller, where he must have been impressed by the crude early seventeenth-century frescos depicting Faust carousing with students and riding on a barrel, the chief inspiration for his own "Auerbachs Keller" scene. Of capital importance for him was, however, an extensive body of literature which has, indeed, no direct bearing on the Faust legend, but which he brought into relationship with it: those mystical, "pansophical," alchemistic, and generally occult writings with their curious cosmogonies, which, going back to the Gnostics and Plotinus, flourished so exuberantly in sixteenth- and seventeenth-century Germany and were represented in Goethe's own period above all by the Rosicrucians and Swedenborg. Goethe is known to have taken a very lively interest in such cabbalistic writings in 1769 and the first half of 1770, that is to say during the long interval of convalescence between his years as a student in Leipzig and Strasburg. It is indeed only in one single passage of about one hundred lines that a decisive influence of these early cabbalistic studies of Goethe's can be clearly recognized; but this is one of the most important and also of the most problematic in the entire *Faust*, and much else depends on it. It takes up the greater part of Faust's opening monologue, from the lines:

> Flieh! Auf! Hinaus ins weite Land!
> Und dies geheimnisvolle Buch,
> Von Nostradamus' eigner Hand,
> Ist dir es nicht Geleit genug?*

Its theme is the contemplation of the sign of the Macrocosm and the invocation of the Earth-spirit. We shall deal with it at length later on. It is enough for the present to note that Goethe has here radically modified the original Faust legend by substituting for uncompromisingly diabolistic black magic the far more respectable conceptions and practices of the cabbalists, thereby creating, as will be seen, some very difficult problems for himself and for us. There has been endless research and speculation on this cabbalistic element in Goethe's *Faust*, rival theories jostling one another thick and fast, one critic claiming that the decisive influence on Goethe here can only have been Iamblichus, another Paracelsus, another Helmont, another Welling, another Swedenborg, etc. More important, however, than these particular questions are certain seldom fairly faced questions of a more general nature, some of them similar to those arising with regard to Goethe's direct sources for the actual Faust story, others even more complicated. One would like to know how systematically and in what spirit Goethe studied these cabbalistic writings, what they meant to him, and whether his attitude towards them underwent any far-reaching changes. One would like to know whether they from the outset attracted him solely or chiefly because of certain close affinities he saw between them and the Faust theme and because of the use he could make of them in his own Faust drama, or whether he was interested in them to begin with for quite other reasons, and only later thought of fusing them with his Faust plans. The direct

---

* Flee! Away into the open country! / And is not this mysterious book, / Written by Nostradamus' own hand, / All the companionship you need?

evidence on all these questions is so scanty and inconclusive that
they can at best only be answered hypothetically, and many critics
tend here to rely simply on their own *a priori* intuitions and assumptions, with the most divergent results. Some, like Ernst
Grumach, maintain that it is impossible really to understand
Goethe's *Faust* without detailed knowledge of his cabbalistic
sources, that in them and in them alone the solution of nearly
all the major problems of interpretation, indeed the central secret
of the entire work, is to be found. My own view is that Goethe
would have been no true artist if his creative freedom had not
asserted itself in the face of these admittedly important cabbalistic
sources, just as it asserted itself in the face of the traditional Faust
dramas and chapbooks. It is good that we should know something
about that occult reading of his and be able to take it into account
whenever a genuine occasion to do so arises, but we should also
be on our guard against the danger of overestimating its significance, reading it into everything, and explaining in terms of it what
is susceptible of a less esoteric, more universally human and natural
explanation. It is an artistic defect in a work of art only to be
intelligible in its totality by reference to its sources, unless it belongs to a period far remoter from our own than Goethe's, or to
a completely alien cultural tradition.

There is something else to be considered in our survey of the
sources of Goethe's *Faust*, namely, what may be called the autobiographical element. He himself said, as has already been noted,
that in writing *Faust* he had to draw upon his own heart ("in
meinen eigenen Busen greifen"), because the traditional sources
did not amount to much. Many critics devote most of their exertions to tracing back the characters, situations, and emotions in
Faust to the particular private experiences of the author which
may be supposed to have inspired them. The identity of Faust with
Goethe himself being taken for granted, something corresponding
to each of Faust's moods, each of his aspirations, each of his
adventures, each of his developments is sought in Goethe's own
biography, and it is assumed that such and such a passage or scene
could not have been written, such and such a situation could not
have been devised, before or after some particular date when Goethe

had not yet gone through the underlying experience or had already outgrown it. Similar themes of debate are, how much Mephistopheles owes to Herder, how much to Merck; how much Gretchen owes to the Frankfort "Gretchen," how much to Friederike Brion, how much to Susanne Margarethe Brandt, how much perhaps to Lotte Buff. Precedents for this biographical approach can be found in Goethe himself, who described all his works as "Bruchstücke einer grossen Konfession" (fragments of a great confession), and in *Dichtung und Wahrheit* assigns a not always convincing autobiographical origin to nearly every work mentioned. "Das Benutzen der Erlebnisse ist mir immer alles gewesen," he said to Laube in 1809; "das Erfinden aus der Luft war nie meine Sache, ich habe die Welt stets für genialer gehalten, als mein Genie" (The utilization of my experiences has always been everything to me; inventing things out of the air was never in my line; I have always thought the world had more genius than I myself have). Goethe often, however, spoke in a very different tone about the relationship between poetic creation and personal experience. Thus Caroline Herder tells her husband in a letter of February 9, 1789, how Goethe had said to her:

> "Der Dichter nehme nur so viel von einem Individuum, als notwendig sei, seinem Gegenstand Leben und Wirklichkeit zu geben; das übrige hole er ja aus sich selbst, aus dem Eindruck der lebenden Welt." Und da sprach gar viel Schönes und Wahres darüber. Auch, dass wir den Tasso, der viel Deutendes über seine eigene Person hätte, nicht deuten dürfen, sonst wäre das ganze Stück verschoben.*

In fact, the same Goethe who, more perhaps than anyone else, inaugurated and gave countenance to the nineteenth-century biographical method of interpreting literature, was also one of the

---

* "The poet only borrows from an individual so much as is needed to give life and verisimilitude to the presentation of his subject; the rest he draws from himself, from the impression of the living world." And he said much that is fine and true on this theme. Also that, although there are many hints of his own person in *Tasso*, we ought not to interpret it as a self-portrait, because if we did, the entire play would be distorted.

earliest and most penetrating critics of that method. He can even at times hyperbolically dismiss the personal experience of the poet as of very little moment or as a positive nuisance:

> Denn da der Dichter durch Antizipation die Welt vorweg-
> nimmt, so ist ihm die auf ihn losdringende wirkliche Welt
> unbequem und störend; sie will ihm geben, was er schon hat,
> aber anders, das er sich zum zweitenmale zueignen muss.*[12]

In a conversation of February 26, 1824, Goethe further developed this idea of "anticipation," applying it particularly to *Faust*:

> So hatte er mir vor einiger Zeit gesagt (writes Eckermann),
> dass dem echten Dichter die Kenntnis der Welt angeboren
> sei, und dass er zu ihrer Darstellung keineswegs vieler Erfah-
> rung und einer grossen Empirie bedürfe. . . . Überhaupt hatte
> ich nur Freude an der Darstellung meiner innern Welt,
> [sagte er], ehe ich die äussere kannte. Als ich nachher in der
> Wirklichkeit fand, dass die Welt so war, wie ich sie mir
> gedacht hatte, war sie mir verdriesslich, und ich hatte keine
> Lust mehr, sie darzustellen . . . Die Region der Liebe, des
> Hasses, der Hoffnung, der Verzweiflung und wie die Zustände
> und Leidenschaften der Seele heissen, ist dem Dichter ange-
> boren, und ihre Darstellung gelingt ihm . . . So konnte ich im
> Faust den düstern Zustand des Lebensüberdrusses im Helden
> sowie die Liebesempfindungen Gretchens recht gut durch An-
> tizipation in meiner Macht haben.†

---

* Since the poet knows the world in advance by anticipation, the powerful impact upon him of the actual world disconcerts and disturbs him; it wants to give him what he already possesses, only in another form, so that he has to assimilate it a second time.

† Not long before he had said to me that the genuine poet has an inborn knowledge of the world and does not at all need a great deal of experience or a large stock of empirical observations in order to be able to depict it. "Alto-gether," he said now, "I only took pleasure in the presentation of my inner world, before I came to know the outer world. When I afterwards discovered that the world was in reality as I had imagined it, it was irksome to me and I no longer felt any wish to portray it. The sphere of love, hatred, hope, despair, and all the other states and passions of the soul is innate in the poet, and he

When Eckermann demurred that nobody could ever believe Goethe had written *Faust* without the amplest concrete observation and experience of the world, Goethe rejoined:

> Mag sein . . . ; allein hätte ich nicht die Welt durch Antizipation bereits in mir getragen, ich wäre mit sehenden Augen blind geblieben, und alle Erforschung und Erfahrung wäre nichts gewesen als ein ganz totes und vergebliches Bemühen.‡

In view of such utterances as these one should be more cautious than most critics are about tracing the themes and motifs of *Faust* back to particular experiences of the poet. Even Konrad Burdach, admirably though he as a rule writes on *Faust*, insists: "Goethe *bleibt stets* . . . Gestalter und Deuter seiner Ichheit" (Goethe *always remains* the poetic fashioner and interpreter of his own ego), and says he could not make up his mind whether Faust was to end disastrously or not, until he was able to foresee more clearly whether his own life was likely to end disastrously or not.[13] We shall encounter various other examples of the kind of thing that is involved. Of course Goethe's own concrete experiences were important; we need to know about them, so that we can take them into account when occasion arises. But we should bear in mind that he was ultimately no more dependent upon them than he was upon his traditional and cabbalistic sources. The biographical approach is only reliable when we understand and apply it in a more extensive sense, seeing in *Faust* less a conglomerate of Goethe's various concrete, private experiences, deposited so to speak in fossilized form, than a comprehensive reflection of his sensibility and his vision of life in their entirety, of what he was and went through not only empirically, but also imaginatively, by "anticipation." In this sense the *Faust* drama as a whole—but not

---

succeeds in depicting it. Thus in *Faust* I could very well have the hero's gloomy state of *mal-de-siècle* and Gretchen's feelings of love within my power by anticipation.

‡ It may be, but if I had not already contained the world within me by anticipation, I should have remained blind with seeing eyes, and all inquiry and experience would have been nothing but completely dead and fruitless exertion.

any single character in it, not even Faust himself—can legitimately
be regarded as an expression of Goethe's "personality." We find
here, transfigured, heightened, and invested with a no longer simply
private, but universal validity, what we find also in his life and
in his mind. We find here in particular—and at this point Goethe
departs fundamentally alike from the letter and the spirit of the
original Faust legend—that fervent preoccupation with and metaphysical exaltation of the love of the sexes which is so characteristic
of Goethe. It is more fruitful to apprehend this central phenomenon in its paradoxical, variegated totality, than to tick off one by
one on lists the heroines of his works, as one matches them with
their presumable models amongst the many real women he is
known to have loved through all gradations of the sensual and
spiritual during the course of his long life. He himself said on this
question to Eckermann on October 22, 1828:

> Die Frauen . . . sind silberne Schalen, in die wir goldene
> Äpfel legen. Meine Idee von den Frauen ist nicht von den
> Erscheinungen der Wirklichkeit abstrahiert, sondern sie ist
> mir angeboren, oder in mir entstanden, Gott weiss wie!
> Meine dargestellten Frauencharaktere sind daher auch alle
> gut weggekommen, sie sind alle besser, als sie in der Wirklich-
> keit anzutreffen sind.*

An integral component of that no longer merely biographical,
empirical personality of Goethe which finds expression in *Faust*
is the age in which he lived; for, as he himself wrote: "ein jeder,
nur zehn Jahre früher oder später geboren, dürfte, was seine eigene
Bildung und die Wirkung nach aussen betrifft, ein ganz anderer
geworden sein" (each one of us, if he had been born only ten years
earlier or later, would, so far as his own culture and the effect
he produces upon the external world is concerned, probably have
become somebody entirely different).[14] With all his unique greatness, Goethe is still very much a man of his own age, which was

---

* Women are dishes of silver in which we lay apples of gold. My idea of
women is not derived from the phenomena of real life, it is something that was
born with me or has sprung up within me, God knows how. That also is why
the female characters in my works have all of them come off favourably; they
are all of them better than the women who are to be met with in real life.

in some respects different from our age. This also should be taken into consideration in our attempts to understand *Faust*. It was significant for Goethe that he was born and lived his formative years at one of the great transitional periods in the history of the European mind, when the triumphal advance of Enlightenment rationalism came up against its own limits and began to suffer its first great débâcle: the supernaturalism of Christianity, which had seemed irretrievably doomed, was afforded a fresh lease of life, but —more important—intoxicating vistas of new, modern and individualistic forms of mysticism were opened up, which centered no longer upon the transcendental God, but upon nature, or upon humanity, or upon art, and emancipated alike from the restraints of sober, matter-of-fact, consistent reason and of traditional religion with its conceptions of sin and of the nothingness of the creature in face of the creator. This was the spiritual ground-pattern of the age of Goethe as a whole, and it was eminently congenial to him. He stood out within it by the uniqueness of his genius and largely helped to determine it, but not without its largely helping to determine him in turn, from the outset and all along the line. It was an age that hovered with divided mind at the brink of the self-deification of the human individual and the abrogation of good and evil, that was ready now to reject traditional Christianity far more radically than the Enlightenment deists had done, now to cast itself once more almost unconditionally into its arms, now to reinterpret it symbolically in terms of its own modern, Pelagian aspirations and uneasinesses. All this is found in peculiarly intense, subtle, and paradoxical forms in Goethe as the supreme representative of his age, and it is all of the greatest importance for the understanding of *Faust*—certainly of greater importance than the old chapbooks and popular plays, or than his cabbalistic studies, or even than the particular private experiences upon which he drew to "give life and verisimilitude to the presentation of his subject."

2. The Chronology and Unity of FAUST

IT IS IMPOSSIBLE to discuss Goethe's *Faust* adequately without taking into consideration the chronology of its composition and the problems this raises. Many of these chronological problems are comparatively trifling and need only concern the specialist. But some of the knottiest of them are fundamental.

We have exact evidence as to when *Faust* was completed. Goethe put the finishing touch to the second part in January, 1832, a few weeks before his death and when he was in his eighty-third year. The evidence as to the date when he began it is, as will be seen, vague and contradictory, but it cannot have been later than 1772, and some scholars would put it appreciably earlier. The two parts of *Faust* therefore span between them the entire sixty or so years of Goethe's effective literary career, if that is regarded as commencing about 1771. *Faust* was begun by a young man who was just finding his feet as a poet; it was completed by an old man with one of those feet in the grave. Thus *Faust* accompanied Goethe through all the changing phases of his development from his first Storm and Stress years onward; and all the varieties of his poetic language, all the prosodic forms he ever employed, rhymed or unrhymed, Germanic and classical, except the hexameter and the elegaic couplet, virtually all the contradictory ideological and emotional aspirations, interests and tendencies that successively swayed

him, are manifested in it. He was not, indeed, uninterruptedly occupied with *Faust* from 1772 or earlier till 1832. There were long
intervals in which he laid it on one side, particularly from 1775 to
1788 and again from 1806 to 1825, but in each one of the six
decades from 1771 to 1830 he turned his attention to *Faust*; even in
the decade 1811–1820, of which there is least to report, an important draft outline for Part II was written on December 16, 1816.

Only at the very beginning of the sixty years in question, up to
1775, and at the very end, from 1825 onward, did Goethe work at
Faust whole-heartedly and with the clear conviction that he was
engaged on something quite congenial and worth while. In the
intervening half century, from 1776 to 1825, his feelings towards
Faust were mixed, and there predominated in them a certain re-
pugnance, a certain hopelessness even. *Faust* seemed to him then
destined to remain a fragment: it seemed to him impossible that
he should ever finish it; it seemed to him a waste of time to try to
finish it; he disliked it as "barbaric," "grotesque," formless, nebulous, and unclassical; he had to goad himself on artificially to work
at it, by promising it to his publisher, or he had to be goaded on
to it by Schiller. It was under such conditions as these, and with
such misgivings as these, that he unsuccessfully tried to round off
the fragmentary initial version abandoned in 1775, and now usually known as the "Urfaust," during the years 1788–1789 in Rome
and Weimar, producing the first printed version, *Faust, ein Fragment*, published in 1790. It was under the same conditions and
with the same misgivings that he in the years 1797–1806 completed
Faust, I. Teil, published in 1808. His own references to *Faust* in
these years are often impatient and hostile. The first thing he
wrote on resuming work on it in June, 1797, was the poem in
ottava rima stanzas, "Zueignung" (Dedication), the purport of
which can be summed up in the words: I am really old enough to
know better than to engage on this crazy task, which goes completely against all the classical convictions and standards so painfully acquired since my immature Storm and Stress years. In the
valedictory companion *ottava rima* stanzas ("Abschied"), written
perhaps in the following May, but excluded from the final text,
this theme is further developed: Goethe thinks of the relief it
would be to have this uncongenial task behind him at last, so that

he could devote the rest of his life undistractedly to the entirely different, classical ideals in which he now alone really believes, and evokes what he conceives would be his state of mind in putting the finishing touch to *Faust*:

> Am Ende bin ich nun des Trauerspieles,
> Das ich zuletzt mit Bangigkeit vollführt,
> Nicht mehr vom Drange menschlichen Gewühles,
> Nicht von der Macht der Dunkelheit gerührt.
> Wer schildert gern den Wirrwarr des Gefühles,
> Wenn ihn der Weg zur Klarheit aufgeführt?
> Und so geschlossen sei der Barbareien
> Beschränkter Kreis mit seinen Zaubereien!*

How uncertain Goethe's hopes were of ever being able to reach the consummation here so longingly evoked appears from the fragmentary verses of the same years:

> In holder Dunkelheit der Sinnen
> Konnt' ich wohl diesen Traum beginnen,
> Vollenden nicht.**

Even in the final stage, when he was working at the second part of *Faust* with more or less undivided eagerness, he could, on February 16, 1826, say to Eckermann:

Das Teufels- und Hexenwesen machte ich nur einmal; ich war froh, mein nordisches Erbteil verzehrt zu haben, und wandte mich zu den Tischen der Griechen. Hätte ich aber so deutlich wie jetzt gewusst, wieviel Vortreffliches seit Jahrhunderten und Jahrtausenden da ist, ich hätte keine Zeile geschrieben, sondern etwas anderes getan.†

---

* Now I have reached the end of the tragedy, / Completing it finally with misgiving, / No longer affected by the stress of human turmoil / Or by the power of darkness. / Who likes to describe the chaos of emotion, / When his path has led him through to clarity? / And so let the confined circle of these barbarities / And magical goings-on be rounded off and done with!

** In the gracious darkness of my senses / I could indeed begin this dream, / But not complete it.

† I went in for the business of devils and witches once and once only; I was glad to have consumed my Nordic portion, and turned to the tables of the

That he should really be able to write the second part of *Faust* and so bring the work to a conclusion seemed to Goethe almost an impossibility right up to the eve of his embarking upon the task in 1825. He thought rather of publishing at some date the fragments that already existed, together with an explanatory synopsis of the unwritten remainder.

The piecemeal, jerky, and long-protracted way in which *Faust* was produced is conspicuous enough when one reads it, especially when the so disparate first and second parts are juxtaposed. One of the chief problems of *Faust* is its unity. That it has not in any strict sense unity of form is obvious. This also troubled Goethe's artistic conscience, particularly at the so important juncture already touched upon, when, in June, 1797, less than two months after completing the most perfect and extensive of his works in the classical taste and manner in which he now believed, *Hermann und Dorothea*, he was visited by the unaccountable urge to devote himself to *Faust* once more. The aesthetic unity of *Faust* is the central theme of the "Vorspiel auf dem Theater" (Prelude on the Stage), which follows in the text upon the opening dedicatory stanzas and was in all probability written immediately after them. This Prelude, usually supposed to have been modelled upon the similar introductory scene to Kalidasa's *Sakuntala*, takes the form of a dispute between the Theatrical Manager, the Poet, and the Comedian about what kind of play is to be performed. It is throughout, like the bulk of the actual *Faust* drama, in so-called "Madrigal" verses, of which there will be more to say later. But the first speech of the Poet falls, as it can do, without infringing the very labile laws of the protean Madrigal verse, inconspicuously into the exact form of two *ottava rima* stanzas, so closely linked in sentiment, phrasing, and tone with "Zueignung" that they could even be supposed to have belonged to the original draft of it. In this way the "Vorspiel auf dem Theater" mediates prosodically between "Zueignung" and the main body of *Faust*. Here, however, we are already brought up against one of the innumerable textual problems that complicate *Faust* scholarship and criticism. It was maintained in 1949 by

---

Greeks. But if I had known as clearly as I do now how much that is excellent has been there for hundreds and thousands of years, I would not have written one line [of *Faust*], but done something else instead.

Oskar Seidlin[1] that nobody has ever succeeded in establishing any clear relationship between this "Vorspiel auf dem Theater" and *Faust*, that it is altogether inappropriate to it, and must originally have been written in 1795 for Goethe's projected, but never completed, sequel to the *Magic Flute* of Mozart and Schikaneder, and only at a much later date transferred to its present unwarranted position. Such hypotheses are on principle always to be regarded with suspicion. Seidlin's chief argument, that the "Vorspiel" is too frivolous to fit in with so earnest and weighty a work as *Faust*, does not take into account the characteristic and refreshing irony with which Goethe regularly spoke of his greatest undertakings, especially of *Faust*. Similarly unsound is the argument of Momme Mommsen that the "Vorspiel" could not have been written before 1798 because in it Goethe treats his *Faust* with an "astonishing, cool, ironical" detachment inconceivable till long after the summer weeks of 1797, when the deeply earnest and inward "Zueignung" poem was produced: "Das V*orspiel* in das Jahr 1797 datieren, hiesse Goethe zumuten, sein Dichten am *Faust* von aussen statt von innen begonnen zu haben" (To date the Prelude in 1797 would mean assuming that Goethe began work on *Faust* from outside instead of from within).[2] There is plenty of this same by-no-means astonishing irony and detachment in Goethe's references to *Faust* in his letters to Schiller of summer, 1797, nor is the "Vorspiel" written anything like so much "from outside" only as Mommsen for controversial purposes postulates. Its very real bearing on *Faust* is clear enough, once one recognizes, what both Seidlin and Mommsen fail to recognize, that its central theme is, as has been stated, the problem of the drama's unity. The Theatrical Manager and the Comedian, who care only for box-office returns and applause, browbeat the Poet into abandoning the puristic ideals of unity, harmony, and form which he eloquently upholds, and producing instead the kind of heterogeneous, loosely strung-together farrago that they demand of him. He boggles indeed at the Theatrical Manager's cynical request:

> Besonders aber lasst genug geschehn! . . .
> Die Masse könnt Ihr nur durch Masse zwingen,
> Ein jeder sucht sich endlich selbst was aus.
> Wer vieles bringt, wird manchem etwas bringen;

Und jeder geht zufrieden aus dem Haus.
Gebt Ihr ein Stück, so gebt es gleich in Stücken!
Solch ein Ragout, es muss Euch glücken;
Leicht ist es vorgelegt, so leicht als ausgedacht.
Was hilft's, wenn Ihr ein Ganzes dargebracht,
Das Publikum wird es Euch doch zerpflücken.*

But the Poet becomes more yielding when the "Lustige Person"
puts the question on a slightly higher, though still far from aesthetically unimpeachable, plane by suggesting that he should content
himself with the haphazard, approximate unity of a casual love-
affair, by which Goethe clearly means what is nowadays called a
"slice of life":

Lasst uns auch so ein Schauspiel geben!
Greift nur hinein ins volle Menschenleben!
Ein jeder lebt's, nicht vielen ist's bekannt,
Und wo ihr's packt, da ist's interessant.
In bunten Bildern wenig Klarheit,
Viel Irrtum und ein Fünkchen Wahrheit,
So wird der beste Trank gebraut,
Der alle Welt erquickt und auferbaut.†

Goethe's own sympathies are by no means exclusively with the
Poet, who is treated with gentle irony and gets the worst of the
dispute, the last word remaining with his adversaries. Even the
Theatrical Manager's cynical indifference to artistic standards was

* But above all see to it that enough happens! / It is only with mass that you
can impress the masses; / Each one in the end picks out what suits him. / He
who brings much will bring something for Tom, something for Dick, something
for Harry— / And each of them will leave the house satisfied. / If you give a
piece, then give it in pieces, and have done with it! / Such a ragout shouldn't
cause you any difficulties; / It is as easily served up as it is thought out. / What
is the good of offering a united whole? / The audience will only pull it to bits
for you anyhow.

† Let us produce that kind of play! / Simply plunge into the fulness of
human life! / Everybody lives it, but there are not many who know what it
really is, / And wherever you take hold of it, it is always interesting. / Brightly
coloured pictures with a little clarity in them, / Much error and a little spark
of truth, / That is how the best drink is brewed, / Which delights all the
world and does its heart good.

not quite alien to Goethe, who knew well, from his own disagreeable experiences of these very years in his capacity as theatrical manager in Weimar, how impossible it is to run a theatre successfully without concessions to the crude tastes of the public. In principle, however, the Poet is represented as being in the right, as though there were no alternative to his lofty aesthetic ideals but the obviously baser *commedia dell'arte* or, at best, the popular opera. If Goethe had wanted to, he could have raised the entire issue to a far higher level by making the Poet's adversaries appeal to one of the greatest possible precedents, the precedent that had actually inspired him in the earliest stages of his work on *Faust*, Shakespeare himself. But Goethe's own aesthetic convictions had now become emphatically classical, and greatly though he still admired Shakespeare, he no longer altogether approved of him, least of all as a model for the modern dramatist. He had become, alike in practice and, as appears particularly in his correspondence with Schiller, in theory, a stickler for correct, austere, unmixed form, and according to his present standards the sort of thing he was doing in *Faust* was at most to be exceptionally condoned and tolerated, not aesthetically vindicated. This comes out especially clearly in the words originally put into the mouth of the Theatrical Manager, but excluded from the final text:

Nur heute schränkt den weiten Blick mir ein,
Nur heute lasst die Strenge mir nicht walten.
Lasst unser Stück nur reich an Fülle sein,
Dann mag der Zufall selbst als Geist der Einheit schalten!*

The point of the "Vorspiel auf dem Theater" is that in it Goethe comes to terms, as best he can, with his classical conscience on the worrying problem of the dramatic unity of *Faust*, and he is likeliest to have felt the need to do that when he resumed work on the play in summer, 1797.

It is natural for us to reflect here that the traditional ideas of form and unity derived from Aristotle are, after all, not the only possible ones, and that the Faust theme itself, especially as Goethe

* Just for to-day only, to please me, limit your extensive vision, / Just for to-day only, to please me, relax your severity. / Let our play only be rich in abundance, / Then chance itself may preside as the spirit of unity.

envisages it, affords legitimate scope for an extreme variety of style, incident, and interest. By its very nature this dramatic poem renounces all claims to be a perspicuous presentation of one single action, or even of a connected series of actions on one and the same plane. It is rather a cosmic vision or dream, and as such can indulge in every kind of freakish fancy, in wild combinations and excrescences. Such a composition, we feel, can still have a peculiar, polyphonic unity-in-diversity, of the kind we recognise in Shakespeare's plays; and in theory it would be difficult to set any limits to what might be done in the way of mingling heterogeneous elements under the sanction of such a unity in diversity, independent of official, established standards of form. Joyce's *Ulysses*, T. S. Eliot's *Waste Land*, and similar extreme modern experiments have familiarised us with the idea of an esoteric unity of form underlying what appears at first sight to be sheer chaos, and such esoteric, polyphonic unity is in our eyes every bit as valid as the more obvious and simple unity of classical aesthetic tradition, perhaps even more valid. Goethe himself, however, especially the classical Goethe of the 1790's, did not think on these lines. For him, so far at least as the drama is concerned, the validity of traditional aesthetic theory was not relative, but absolute; he felt, indeed, the need to reinterpret it on modern, liberal, philosophical lines, largely disregarding the artificial unities of time and place, but he did not entertain the possibility of any legitimate alternative principle. Drama that flouted the essential principles of the classical tradition was in his eyes, however great its merits might be in other respects, artistically formless—even Shakespeare's work, and even his own *Faust*. He said to Boisserée in August, 1815: "Die Einheit des Gedankens, die lebendige Gliederung durch den Gegensatz zur Identität, das ist es, was allen Kunstwerken zugrunde liegen muss. Das ist, was die Franzosen mechanisch ergriffen haben in ihrem Schauspiel, und was Shakespeare nicht hat, und warum seine Stücke in dieser Hinsicht bei aller Poesie nichts taugen" (Unity of idea, vital organisation from contrast to unity, that is what should be at the bottom of all works of art. That is what the French mechanically realized in their drama and what Shakespeare has not got, and that is why his plays, in spite of their poetic qualities, are in this respect worthless).

In his Storm and Stress days, when he had rebelled against established principles of poetic form, he had seen Shakespeare as formless and praised him for it in the words: "Shakespeares Theater ist ein schöner Raritätenkasten" (Shakespeare's theatre is a raree-show),[3] and that is how he continued to see Shakespeare later, when formlessness had become for him something to be deprecated. The idea of an "inner" form which he advanced in 1775 (*Aus Goethes Taschenbuch*) is not really aesthetic, but rather psychological; he understood by it simply the unifying effect of the poet's personality upon his work, and it stands in a line with the "raree-show" of 1772 and with the principle of "plunging into the fulness of human life" and allowing "chance to preside as the spirit of unity," formulated in the "Vorspiel auf dem Theater." The idea of a polyphonic unity in diversity as a possible legitimate alternative to the stricter classical standards of dramatic form was indeed already being formulated and discussed during Goethe's earlier years by Samuel Johnson, Gerstenberg, and Herder in their interpretations of Shakespeare, but Goethe himself took no cognizance of it. He felt that he had to choose not between two different, equally defensible principles of formal unity, but between form and formlessness. Thus, in writing to Schiller on December 6, 1797, he referred playfully to *Faust* as a "Tragelaph"—a fabulous animal, half goat, half stag. "Ich werde wohl zunächst an meinen Faust gehen, teils um diesen Tragelaphen los zu werden, teils um mich zu einer höheren und reineren Stimmung . . . vorzubereiten" (First of all I shall probably set to work on my *Faust*, partly to get rid of this Tragelaph, partly to prepare myself for a loftier and purer poetic mood). On September 16, 1800, he finds ironical consolation in the idea suggested to him by Schiller, that *Faust* may at least be "ein nicht ganz verwerfliches poetisches Ungeheuer" (a not altogether objectionable poetic monstrosity); and in some fragmentary verses of the same years he says of *Faust*:

> Des Menschen Leben ist ein ähnliches Gedicht:
> Es hat wohl einen Anfang, hat ein Ende,
> Allein ein Ganzes ist es nicht. (*Abkündigung*)*

---

* Human life is a similar poem; / It has indeed a beginning and an end, / But it is not a totality.

Although Goethe himself saw it as a regrettable but necessary condition of his attempting to complete *Faust* in 1797 that he should, in this one exceptional case, jettison the only standard of artistic unity that he acknowledged in great drama, it still remains possible that he was unconsciously guided by some such feeling for paradoxical unity-in-diversity as we recognise in Shakespeare's work, and that *Faust* may therefore after all, in this sense, have far more unity of form than he claimed for it. Only to a limited extent, however, can any conceivable esoteric principle be thought of as holding *Faust* together aesthetically and establishing a satisfying higher correspondence or harmony between the disparate elements, as between the different movements of a musical symphony. In particular Part II is, aesthetically considered, so different from Part I that it gives the impression of being an entirely separate work, to which one responds, if at all, in quite another way. Goethe himself insisted again and again on this difference in character between the two parts of *Faust*—for example, in conversation with Eckermann on February 17, 1831: "Der erste Teil ist fast ganz subjektiv, es ist alles aus einem befangeneren, leidenschaftlicheren Individuum hervorgegangen . . . Im zweiten Teil aber ist fast gar nichts Subjektives, es erscheint hier eine höhere, breitere, hellere, leidenschaftslosere Welt" (The first part is almost entirely subjective, it has all emerged from a more confused and passionate individual. In the second part, however, there is hardly anything subjective, here a loftier, wider, brighter, more dispassionate world appears). This is shown quite practically by the circumstance that, while *Faust I* is and always has been one of the most popular, *Faust II* is and always has been one of the least popular of Goethe's works. *Faust I* is for the many, for everybody, whether they really understand it or not; *Faust II* is for the few, for the specialists and highbrows, whether they really understand it or not; nor is it thinkable that this should ever become otherwise. *Faust I* makes an immediate appeal; it has all the advantages of undiminished natural vitality. *Faust II*, even in its most inspired passages, several of which were written contemporaneously with the last stage of Goethe's work on *Faust I*, that is to say before 1806, is remote from the common levels of experience, and it makes very exacting demands on the attention, erudition, and intellectual agility of the reader, and long stretches of Acts I and IV are linguistically inert and would hardly appeal much to anybody, if it were not for the larger context to which they belong. That Goethe should, at the age of over seventy-six, have completed the second part at all is one of the most impressive and moving phenomena in the annals of literature, but the fact remains, in spite of everything the critics say, that he was too old to be able to infuse genuine poetic life into the whole of it. The wonder is that he was able to do it at all, and that it has in parts—especially in the "Classical Walpurgis Night," the "Helena Tragedy," and the final act—as much life as it has. One thing that no underlying esoteric principle can do, however, is to fuse the vital and the comparatively moribund, the inspired and the laborious, together into a convincing aesthetic unity; it is like the experiment of putting new wine into old bottles. In this respect, if in no other, the unity of the two parts of *Faust* remains a hypothetical rather than an actual unity, a matter, so to speak, of faith, not of direct aesthetic experience. Goethe himself, it may be noted, was mercifully unconscious of this stylistic un-evenness of the second part of *Faust*, and thought of it as being qualitatively all of a piece. On March 17, 1832, only five days before his death, he wrote to Humboldt: "ich lasse mich keine Furcht angehen: man werde das Ältere vom Neuern, das Spätere vom Frühern unterscheiden können . . ." (I have no fears that anybody will be able to distinguish between what is older and what is newer, what is earlier and what is later). He had said much the same thing forty-four years earlier, on the occasion of his unsuc-cessful attempt to complete *Faust* during his Italian journey. "Auch was den Ton des Ganzen betrifft, bin ich getröstet; ich habe schon eine neue Szene ausgeführt, und wenn ich das Papier räuchere, so dächt' ich, sollte sie mir niemand aus den alten herausfinden" (So far as the tone of the whole work is concerned I also feel re-assured; I have already written one new scene, and if I were to smoke the paper, I don't think anybody would be able to dis-tinguish it from the old ones).[4] It must be admitted that Goethe often succeeded in recapturing something of the tone of the "Urfaust" in his later work upon *Faust I* between 1788 and 1806, and that doubts, differences of opinion, and errors can arise about the dating of individual passages, where there is no definite docu-mentary evidence to go by, and the style alone has to serve as our guide. But the discrepancies in tone and in vital intensity within each of the two parts of *Faust,* and still more between them both, corresponding roughly to the three chief stages in Goethe's development—his youthful Storm and Stress years, his classical middle period, and his old age—are so far-reaching and conspicuous that a total impression of artistic heteronomy cannot be escaped. The hope he expressed in a letter to Heinrich Meyer of July 20, 1831, "es soll mir gelungen sein, allen Unterschied des Frühern und Spätern ausgelöscht zu haben" (that I have succeeded in obliterating every distinction between what was earlier and what was more recent), proved delusory.

What may be looked for instead of the aesthetic unity, which can only be claimed with considerable reservations for Goethe's *Faust,* is a thematic unity, a unity of philosophical purport, a central idea running through the whole work and unifying all its so disparate parts, if not for the sensuous imagination, then at least for the reflecting intellect. Goethe's own declarations on this possibility are interesting but contradictory. On the one hand he vigorously denied in a conversation with Eckermann of May 6, 1827, that in writing *Faust* he had been animated by any desire to express an idea.

> Die Deutschen sind übrigens wunderliche Leute!—Sie machen sich durch ihre tiefen Gedanken, die sie überall suchen und überall hineinlegen, das Leben schwerer als billig. Ei, so habt doch einmal endlich die Courage, euch *den Eindrücken hinzugeben* . . . aber denkt nur nicht immer, es wäre alles eitel, wenn es nicht irgend abstrakter Gedanke und Idee wäre! Da kommen sie und fragen mich, welche Idee ich in meinem Faust zu verkörpern gesucht. Als ob ich das selber wüsste und aussprechen könnte! . . . Es hätte auch in der Tat ein schönes Ding werden müssen, wenn ich ein so reiches, buntes und höchst mannigfaltiges Leben, wie ich es im Faust zur Anschauung gebracht, auf die magere Schnur einer einzigen durchgehenden Idee hätte reihen wollen!*

---

* The Germans, by the way, are queer people! / With their profound thoughts and ideas, which they seek everywhere and read into everything, they make life unreasonably difficult. Ah! have the courage at last *to surrender yourselves to impressions* . . . but don't always believe that everything is worth-

On the other hand Goethe was indignant some twenty years earlier, when the young History professor, Heinrich Luden, in discussing with him *Faust, ein Fragment,* which was all that had at that point been published, questioned whether the scenes constituting that *Fragment* had ever been conceived as organic parts of a larger dramatic whole with an underlying idea, and whether the poet would ever be able to supplement them in such a way as to make them look like organic parts of such a dramatic whole. Goethe who had only a few weeks before this delivered the completed manuscript of *Faust, I. Teil* to his publisher, protested:

> Wie aber haben Sie ich denn die Entstehung des Faust gedacht? Habe ich Sie recht verstanden, so sind Sie der Meinung gewesen, und sind noch der Meinung, dass der Dichter gar nicht gewusst hat, was er wollte, als er die Dichtung begann, sondern dass er auf das Geratewohl, dass er in das Blaue hinein gedichtet und sich nur des Namens Faust wie einer Schnur bedient habe, um die einzelnen Perlen aufzuziehen und vor der Verstreuung zu bewahren.†

The true interest of *Faust,* Goethe told Luden in the same conversation, lay not in the individual episodes and passages, but in the "Idee, welche den Dichter beseelt hat, und welche das Einzelne des Gedichtes zum Ganzen verknüpft, für das Einzelne Gesetz ist und dem Einzelnen seine Bedeutung gibt" (the idea which animated the poet, and which links the single elements together to a whole, governing them as a law and conferring their significance upon them).

---

less, unless it is somehow an abstract thought and idea! There they come and ask me what idea I have tried to embody in my *Faust!* As though I knew that myself and could put it in so many words! It would indeed have been a pretty business, if I had wanted to string so ample, varied, and extremely multifarious a life as I have presented in *Faust* upon the meagre thread of one single connecting idea.

† How do you suppose that Faust was written? If I have understood you rightly, you were of the opinion and still are of the opinion that the poet did not in the least know what he was driving at when he began the work, but wrote at random, just as it came to him, merely using the name of "Faust" as a thread on which to string the single beads and keep them from being dispersed. (August 19, 1806).

The contradiction between these two declarations is not quite so great as it at first appears to be. It is to be accounted for in part by the circumstance that at the time of the conversation with Luden, Goethe had, chiefly under the influence of Schiller, come to be a believer in the "idea," whereas in his last years, when the conversation with Eckermann took place, he had largely turned against it once more. We can take it for certain that there is indeed what we should call an "idea" at the back of *Faust*, although the old Goethe, in his dislike of abstract philosophical speculation, preferred not to designate it by that particular term. Even in the course of his impatient outbreak of 1827 against the "idea," Goethe actually gave to Eckermann, in words which we shall have to consider later, some indication of what the idea at the back of *Faust* is—namely, that it turns upon Faust's salvation. In another important conversation with Eckermann of February 13, 1831 Goethe spoke of Act 3 of *Faust, II. Teil* (commonly referred to as "Die Helenatragödie") as having "einen ganz eigenen Charakter, so dass er, wie eine für sich bestehende kleine Welt, das übrige nicht berührt und nur durch einen leisen Bezug zu dem Vorhergehenden und Folgenden sich dem Ganzen anschliesst" (a character altogether of its own, so that, like a little world existing by itself, it does not impinge upon the rest and is only connected with the whole work by a tenuous rapport to what precedes and follows it). Eckermann, taking up the image he had heard Goethe use before in these questions, suggested that this was true of all the rest of Faust too, that it consists of so many separate episodes ". . . die, in sich abgeschlossen, wohl aufeinander wirken, aber doch einander wenig angehen. Dem Dichter liegt daran, eine mannigfaltige Welt auszusprechen, und er benutzt die Fabel eines berühmten Helden bloss als eine Art von durchgehender Schnur, um darauf aneinanderzureihen, was er Lust hat." (which are complete in themselves and affect one another indeed, but have little to do with one another. The poet is out to give expression of a multifarious world, and employs the story of a famous hero simply as a kind of connecting thread, on which he can string whatever he likes). Goethe said then: "Sie haben vollkommen recht; . . . auch kommt es bei einer solchen Komposition bloss darauf an, dass die einzelnen Massen bedeutend und klar seien, während es als ein Ganzes immer

inkommensurabel bleibt, aber eben deswegen gleich einem un-
aufgelösten Problem die Menschen zu wiederholter Betrachtung
immer wieder anlockt" (You are quite right; all that matters in
such a composition is that the individual sections should be significant and clear, while in its totality it remains incommensurable, but
for that very reason, like an unsolved problem, entices men again
and again to contemplate it afresh). "Incommensurable" is a favourite word of Goethe's during the last years of his life for char-
acterising the *Faust* drama in its totality, especially the second part.
Only for the single sections does he occasionally claim some degree
of formal unity, particularly for the Helen of Troy section, of which
he writes to Knebel on November 14, 1827:

> Daher denn die Masse von Erfahrung und Reflexion um
> einen Hauptpunkt versammelt, zu einem Kunstwerk anwach-
> sen musste, welches, ungeachtet seiner Einheit, dennoch
> schwer auf einmal zu übersehen ist . . . die Hauptintention
> ist klar und das Ganze deutlich; auch das Einzelne wird es
> sein und werden, wenn man die Teile nicht an sich betrachten
> und erklären, sondern in Beziehung auf das Ganze sich
> verdeutlichen mag.*

Goethe was concerned indeed to work out the first two acts of the
second part as far as possible in such a way that they should lead
up to the episode of Helen of Troy in an "ästhetisch-vernunft-
gemässer Folge" (aesthetic and rational sequence), so that it might
no longer appear "phantasmagorisch und eingeschoben" (as an
interpolated phantasmagoria) (January 24, 1828 to Zelter), and in
this he largely succeeded. These are, however, still only sporadic
approximations to unity in what remains essentially "incommensurable." In attempting to interpret *Faust* either aesthetically or
philosophically we find ourselves at every hand brought up against
this problem of unity in one or other of its many aspects.

The problems of unity which arise from the intrinsic character
of Goethe's *Faust* and from the long-protracted, piecemeal way in

---

* This accumulation of experience and reflection around one dominant point
was bound to grow into a work of art which, in spite of its unity, is still difficult to take in at one glance. The chief intention is clear and the whole perspicuous; the details will be so, or will become so, too, if one can look at and
interpret the parts not by themselves, but in their relationship to the whole.

which it was written are aggravated by the circumstance that our purely factual knowledge about it is defective and uncertain. There is indeed a great body of manuscript material available, including many rough drafts and "paralipomena." Innumerable, often very ample and valuable declarations of Goethe himself about *Faust* in his letters, diaries, and conversations have come down to us, together with an abundance of contemporary references to it. Gräf's systematic compilation of such data in his *Goethe über seine Dichtungen*[5] comprises over six hundred pages and is still not exhaustive. But despite this plethora of material and information, we find ourselves again and again without any direct documentary evidence at all, or only with vague, ambiguous, or contradictory evidence, on major points, especially where the all-important earlier stages of Goethe's work on the drama are concerned, so that we might almost lament in Faust's own words:

> Was man nicht weiss, das eben brauchte man,
> Und was man weiss, kann man nicht brauchen.*

This is due in considerable part to Goethe's secretiveness. He carefully destroyed the manuscripts that would have been most illuminating for us, he kept quiet on points of the greatest importance, and when people interrogated him too searchingly about his intentions in *Faust* he would as a rule either put them off with evasive or misleading answers, or refuse to give any answer at all, as he did when Luden asked him for more information about the underlying "idea" of the drama:

> Mit diesem Aufschlussgeben wäre die ganze Herrlichkeit des Dichters dahin. Der Dichter soll doch nicht sein eigener Erklärer sein und seine Dichtung in alltäglicher Prosa fein zerlegen; damit würde er aufhören Dichter zu sein. Der Dichter stellt seine Schöpfung in die Welt hinaus; es ist die Sache des Lesers, des Ästhetikers, des Kritikers, zu untersuchen, was er mit seiner Schöpfung gewollt hat.†

---

* The things one doesn't know are just those one could do with, / The things one does know one cannot do anything with.

† It would be all over with the poet's grandeur, if he gave such information. It is not for the poet to be his own interpreter and analyse his work minutely in everyday prose; if he did so, he would cease to be a poet. The poet exposes

How little Goethe was disposed to help the critics in these attempts, especially so far as *Faust* was concerned, emerges from what he wrote to Reinhard on June 22, 1808: "Soviel habe ich überhaupt bei meinem Lebensgange bemerken können, dass das Publikum nicht immer weiss, wie es mit den Gedichten, sehr selten aber, wie es mit dem Dichter dran ist. Ja, ich läugne nicht, dass, weil ich dieses sehr früh gewahr wurde, es mir von jeher Spass gemacht hat, Versteckens zu spielen" (This much I have been able to observe in general during the course of my life, that the public does not always know where it is with poetic works and very seldom knows where it is with the poet. Yes, I don't deny that, as I perceived this very early, it has always amused me to indulge in mystification).

Perhaps Goethe would have been more communicative if he could have foreseen that by his secretiveness and love of mystification he was providing the practitioners of "Higher Criticism" with ideal conditions for using *Faust, I. Teil* as one of their happy hunting grounds, much to the detriment of "the poet's grandeur." By employing their favourite device of detecting supposed discrepancies and contradictions in action, thought, or language, the critics of this type attempt to demonstrate that Goethe's entire conception of *Faust* must have undergone a whole series of drastic changes, and that the final text of Part I is just a sketchily co-ordinated patchwork of mutually contradictory fragments—many of them very brief fragments—produced at all of these various stages. This disintegrating method of interpreting *Faust*, indeed, has, at least in its extremer forms as represented by Gustav Roethe, now fallen into discredit. But it continues to be employed, many of its contentions are generally accepted, and no serious scholar can afford simply to ignore it. There is, as will be seen, at least one very obvious major discrepancy affecting the relationship between Mephistopheles and the Spirit of Earth which it is almost universally acknowledged can only be accounted for by the hypothesis that Goethe materially modified his earlier plan about 1797; nor is this the only case in which even a scholar who otherwise strongly distrusts the principles and practices of "Higher Criticism" may

---

his creation to the view of the world; it is for the reader, the aesthetician, the critic to try to find out what he was aiming at with his creation. (August 19, 1806)

feel himself compelled to resort to such hypotheses. It is one thing, however, to resort thus to such hypotheses only reluctantly and with caution in face of acute major problems where no alternative is to be found, and another to indulge in them irresponsibly in and out of season for their own sake. Everything turns here upon the question, whether the same kind and degree of consistency may legitimately be demanded of a work of the imagination, as is to be demanded of a purely factual, mathematical, scientific, or philosophical document. Many of the "contradictions" the disintegrating critics present as so "insoluble" are due only to Goethe's having been concerned to evoke in *Faust* a fantastic dream-world not subject to the causal laws of everyday reality, and others are simply manifestations of the inherent dialectical processes of the human psyche. Goethe himself was sceptical of the "Higher Criticism," which had already made considerable progress during his lifetime. He believed that those who applied it to the Homeric poems did not sufficiently take into account "die gewaltsame Tendenz der poetischen und kritischen Natur zur Einheit" (the powerful tendency to unity of the poetic and critical nature) (April 28, 1797 to Schiller), and even thought it better to stick to the text of the New Testament just as it stands, without attempting a historico-critical examination of it.[6] Luden, in his already quoted conversation with Goethe of August 19, 1806, was one of the first to attempt, if only on a small scale, to apply the new methods of textual criticism to *Faust,* and what Goethe said to him, he would probably have said to all his successors down to the present day:

Alles, was Sie da vorbringen, kann nichts gelten. In der Poesie gibt es keine Widersprüche. Diese sind nur in der wirklichen Welt, nicht in der Welt der Poesie. Was der Dichter schafft, das muss genommen werden, wie er es geschaffen hat. So wie er seine Welt gemacht hat, so ist sie. Was der poetische Geist erzeugt, muss von einem poetischen Gemüt empfangen werden. Ein kaltes Analysieren zerstört die Poesie und bringt keine Wirklichkeit hervor. Es bleiben nur Scherben übrig, die zu nichts dienen und nur inkommodieren.*

* Everything you advance is beside the point. In poetry there are no contradictions. They exist only in the real world, not in the world of poetry. What

What Goethe here condemns is the pedestrian literal-mindedness of such critics as Luden. He frequently discussed the problem of contradictions in works of art, justifying them under some circumstances as legitimate means towards a higher aesthetic end. One well-known example to which he appealed in this connexion was that of Lady Macbeth's children. On July 5, 1827, he with a certain pride drew the attention of Eckermann to a contradiction in the third act of *Faust II* which even the "Higher Critics" might have overlooked. " 'Mich soll nur wundern,' sagte Goethe lachend, 'was die deutschen Kritiker dazu sagen werden. Ob sie werden Freiheit und Kühnheit genug haben, darüber hinwegzukommen . . . Wenn durch die Phantasie nicht Dinge entständen, die für den Verstand ewig problematisch bleiben, so wäre überhaupt zu der Phantasie nicht viel' " ("I wonder what the German critics will say about it," he said with a laugh, "and whether they will have enough freedom and boldness not to let it disturb them . . . If through the imagination things did not arise which remain eternally problematic for the understanding, the imagination would not amount to much"). Far too few of Goethe's critics in Germany or in any other country have displayed the kind of "freedom and boldness" he here demands of them; they have, instead, displayed freedom and boldness of exactly the opposite kind and at just the wrong points. We should always, in face of an apparent or even a real inconsistency in *Faust,* be on our guard against concluding, with the "Higher Critics," that we know better what Goethe was getting at than he himself did. Our first endeavour should be to accept this poetic world of Goethe's as he created it, in the conviction that it is in the main as consistent as he intended it to be, or saw any need for it to be.

---

the poet creates must be accepted as he has created it. His world is as he has made it, and that is that. What the poetic mind engenders must be received by a poetic temperament. A cold analysis destroys the poetry and does not produce any reality. All that remains is broken pieces, which serve no purpose and are only a nuisance.

3. The Problem
of the
Göchhausen Transcript

*Aber eben weil es Bruchstücke sind, müssen sie zu einem
Ganzen gehören, und im Ganzen poetisch aufgefasst werden.**
(Goethe in conversation with Luden, August, 1806)

ON SEPTEMBER 17, 1775, Goethe wrote to Auguste von Stolberg,
"ich machte eine Szene an meinem Faust"—that he had that very
morning "made a scene" of his *Faust*. This is the first occasion on
which he mentions the Faust drama by name in his letters that have
come down to us, though he must have begun work on it some years
earlier. About three weeks after this he wrote to Merck, "Hab'
am Faust viel geschrieben" (that he had been doing a lot of work
on *Faust*). Before another month had elapsed he had left his native
Frankfort for Weimar, where he was to remain for the rest of his
life. This decisive turning-point brought with it the first great interruption in his work on *Faust*. To begin with he was too much
engrossed with the practical business of finding his feet in an entirely new environment to be able to do any sustained literary work,

* But just because they are fragments they must belong to a whole and
should be poetically apprehended as parts of that whole.

and by the time he had settled down in Weimar his outlook on
life, and with it his taste and poetic ideals, had radically altered;
he had outgrown the recklessness of his Storm and Stress years, and
the chaotic world of *Faust* was superseded by the classically dis-
ciplined world of *Iphigenie*. He frequently gave readings from his
fragmentary *Faust* manuscript in the Weimar court circles, especially in his early years there, but it was out of the question for
him in his new frame of mind to resume the work where it had been
abruptly broken off in autumn, 1775.[1]

The old manuscript of *Faust*, which Goethe took to Weimar
with him in November, 1775, and which seems still to have been
in existence as late as 1816, has not survived. It is to be presumed
that Goethe destroyed it in order that nobody might be able to
distinguish the earlier parts of *Faust I* from the later additions. But
he gives us a description of it in his *Italienische Reise*[2] in the form
of a quotation from a letter dated "Rome, 1 March 1788":

> Das alte Manuskript macht mir manchmal zu denken,
> wenn ich es vor mir sehe. Es ist noch das erste, ja in den
> Hauptszenen gleich so ohne Konzept hingeschrieben; nun ist
> es so gelb von der Zeit, so vergriffen (die Lagen waren nie
> geheftet), so mürbe und an den Rändern zerstossen, dass es
> wirklich wie das Fragment eines alten Kodex aussieht.*

The original of this letter has not been preserved, and its authenticity is sometimes disputed—partly because Herder, to whom alone
it could have been addressed, must have known the old manuscript
too well to need any description of it, partly because it is thought
to conflict with other accounts of Goethe's early Faust manuscript
that have come down to us. It is known that Goethe, in compiling
the *Italienische Reise*, did sometimes doctor the old letters and
other papers he utilized, and perhaps even invented some of
them. It is not inconceivable that he is here throwing dust in
the eyes of his readers and critics, as we know he sometimes tended

---

* The old manuscript often sets me thinking, when I see it before me. It is
still the original one, indeed the principal scenes stand in it just as they were
first written, without any rough drafts; now it is so yellow with age, so tattered
and torn (the sections were never stitched together), so brittle and crumpled
at the edges, that it really looks like the fragment of an old codex.

to do, especially where *Faust* is concerned. Intrinsically, however, his own description of the pre-1776 Faust manuscript is likely to be quite as authentic as any descriptions of it that have come down to us at second or third hand. The most important point about it is that it contains the only explicit indication we have from Goethe himself about the way in which the principal early scenes of *Faust* were written, namely, like most of his other work of these Frankfort Storm and Stress years, *at one stroke*—"ohne Konzept." That is something that the "Higher Critics," who insist on regarding *Faust* as an extremely complex and multiple palimpsest, refuse to believe. Goethe also says that this was still the *first, original manuscript*—"Es ist noch das erste"—which clearly enough implies that there had been no yet earlier versions, such as many influential scholars feel impelled to postulate. Those who refuse to take Goethe's word on these points do not indeed go so far as to suggest that he is making deliberate misstatements; they assume rather that "his memory is deceiving him." That is, however, a possibility that can be ruled out where issues of such importance not only for the reader, but also for Goethe himself are concerned. If what he here says about the early manuscript of *Faust*, and about the way in which he worked on the drama before 1776, is not substantially accurate, then he must be quite deliberately misleading us. It would be a pointless pious fiction to assume that he, who liked to indulge in mystification, was incapable of doing that.

These problems would be a good deal simpler if Goethe had not seen fit to destroy the old manuscript, except for one or two single sheets which, so far as they go, fit in well enough with his description of it in the *Italienische Reise*. We are, however, not quite so much in the dark about it as Goethe would have preferred us to be. Through a lucky chance we possess the next best thing to the original manuscript itself: a transcript of it. In the late Frankfort and early Weimar years Goethe frequently lent the manuscript, or parts of it (it is important to note that "the sections were never stitched together"), to his friends, and about 1776 one of these friends, Luise von Göchhausen, a lady of the Weimar court, took advantage of the opportunity to make—one can be pretty sure, surreptitiously—a copy of it, which remained undiscovered till 1887, when it was published by Erich Schmidt under

the title: *Goethes Faust in ursprünglicher Gestalt* (Goethe's Faust
in its original form). This document, usually referred to as the
"Urfaust" (that is, "the original Faust"), is of immense value,
though it by no means solves all our problems. It disappointed the
practitioners of higher critical methods by not differing anything
like so much from *Faust, ein Fragment* of 1790 or from *Faust I*
of 1808 as, according to their theories, it should have done. In fact
there is very little in it, and nothing of any moment, that was
not embodied in the final text—sometimes with very slight, sometimes with more far-reaching, changes of diction and form, designed
to give it a less extremely unruly and overweening character. It
confirmed some of the more cautious and reasonable hypotheses
of the higher critics and refuted once and for all some of their
more arbitrary ones: passages they had argued could, on grounds
of purport or style, not possibly have been written before 1788,
were now shown uncontrovertibly to have been written before
1776. Thus the passage in "Trüber Tag. Feld" from "Bring mich
hin!" to "Mord und Tod einer Welt über dich Ungeheuer!"
(Take me there! Murder and death of a world upon you,
monster!), which according to Scherer[3] must have been a "nicht
sehr glücklicher Zusatz" of 1808, "ein Versuch des fast sechzig-
jährigen Goethe, den Jargon seiner Jugend zu sprechen" (a not
very felicitous addition . . . an attempt of the nearly sixty-year-old
Goethe to speak the jargon of his youth), turned out to belong to
the original text, as also did the forty-two lines of the opening
monologue beginning with "O sähst du, voller Mondenschein . . . "
(Ah, would that light of the full moon . . .), which Scherer[4] was
strongly inclined to assign on grounds of style and metre to the
years 1788–1789. But although the "Higher Critics" were at least
compelled to admit that nothing in Luise von Göchhausen's transcript could have been written later than October, 1775, they were
unwilling to admit anything more than that, and everything has
been done to belittle the importance of that transcript and to
minimize such objective certainty as it has brought into the vexed
problems of Faust scholarship and criticism. As a result, matters
remain much as they were before that momentous discovery; the
most diverse wiredrawn hypotheses and farfetched constructions,
which convince nobody but their own originators, still inconclusively jostle one another, the one point of general tacit agreement

being that in this field direct factual evidence is on principle to be suspected as probably untrustworthy, and straightforward common sense to be dismissed as unscholarly, or, in the words of Gustav Roethe,[5] as "skrupelloser Dilettantismus" (unscrupulous amateurishness).

Whether the Göchhausen transcript was made, as some maintain, from an intermediate copy that has not survived, or, as seems more probable, from Goethe's own working manuscript, matters comparatively little. That we have in it, apart from a few slight clerical slips, a substantially faithful reproduction of the old manuscript described by Goethe in the *Italienische Reise* scarcely anybody has had the hardihood to deny. It proves at least that such a manuscript must have existed, whatever inaccuracies there may be in Goethe's own account of it. A more serious point made by some of those who are out to belittle the value of the Göchhausen transcript is that we have no guarantee for its being complete. This is, of course, true. Ernst Grumach makes out a strong though not unchallengeable case for there having originally been an early "Wollustszene" (scene of lust) in *Faust*,[6] which made a deep impression on Wieland and Einsiedel when they heard Goethe read the play in his first winter in Weimar, but which is missing alike in the Göchhausen transcript, in *Faust, ein Fragment*, and in *Faust I*, and must have been suppressed and destroyed by Goethe himself —because of its extremely indecorous character—about 1776 or soon after. In this connexion Goethe's statement that the "Lagen" (sections) of the old manuscript were never stitched together is important. It is to be assumed that the scenes were at this stage not written down continuously, one after the other, as in a completed work, but that each began on a new double sheet, so that Goethe could, if he wanted, easily change their order, add to them or remove one or the other of them. It is conceivable that he may early in 1776 have seen fit to remove and destroy one scene in this way, on grounds of decorum, as Grumach suggests. One cannot, however, admit this much, without at least theoretically also admitting the further possibility, which Grumach deduces from it, that the Göchhausen transcript may represent only a comparatively small selection from what Goethe had written of *Faust* up to 1775, and therefore has no right to be designated as the "Urfaust." But although this is possible, the question still remains, how probable it is. If there is quite a lot missing from the Göchhausen transcript which it ought to have contained, had it been as complete as it in 1776 might have been, then that missing early material must have consisted either of scenes and passages that were never incorporated in the final text at all and most of which, like the supposed "scene of lust," Goethe destroyed, or of scenes and passages that did eventually find their way into the final text, but have hitherto been almost universally looked upon as products of the years 1788–1789 and 1797–1801. Grumach maintains that there was material of both these kinds, but it is the latter possibility that particularly interests him. He would, as we shall see, antedate the "Prolog im Himmel," which has hitherto always been on the strongest grounds assigned to the years 1797–1801, by some thirty years. That is a case that will have to be considered later on its own merits. Goethe's *Faust* presents innumerable minor points of dating which are of importance to the critic only in so far as he is concerned not with the drama itself as a work of art, but with what can be read between or above and below the lines of it. Such problems do not interest us here; they can be left in that eternal uncertainty that is the congenial element of those to whom the devising of abstruse, inconclusive hypotheses is an end in itself. There are, however, a few genuinely important dates—and that of the "Prolog im Himmel" is one of them—on which, in the nature of things, a great deal depends in our efforts to understand Goethe's *Faust*, and the issue before us now is, whether there is really so little objective evidence for these dates too, that they must remain at the mercy of the esoteric critics with their inexhaustible ingenuity. In face of such a work as *Faust* and of such a poet as Goethe a greater measure of good will, of trustfulness, of—one might almost say—faith is called for on the part of the reader than the disintegrating critics are prepared to accord. Such critics seem to be unaware how insulting their fundamental postulates often are to Goethe's integrity as an artist and even to his intelligence. There is room in literary criticism and scholarship for an aesthetic principle analogous to the juridical principle of British law that a prisoner must be assumed to be innocent until he has been proved guilty. On the analogy of this same juridical principle it is here proposed that the Göchhausen transcript should be regarded as in the main a faithful and also a substantially complete reproduction of Goethe's original Faust manuscript until something weightier has been proved against it than anybody has so far succeeded in proving, and that it is therefore entitled to be called the *Urfaust*.

One thing we can be certain of is that Goethe all along kept by him, in addition to his actual Faust manuscript, which consisted only of completed or nearly completed scenes, a considerable number of loose sheets, many of them probably only little scraps of paper, on which he had jotted down odd lines and ideas as they occurred to him from time to time, with a view to incorporating them in still unwritten sections of the play or to working them up into whole scenes. Over two hundred unutilized odd jottings of this kind have come down to us, chiefly from the later stages of his work on *Faust*, especially on the second part; they are technically referred to as the "Faust-Paralipomena." Those that had been utilized Goethe normally destroyed. It can be assumed that there was already a considerable number of such odd jottings, or "Splitter" (splinters), as they are commonly called, in existence before November, 1775, in addition to the actual completed scenes, and that most of them found their way later into the scenes written in 1788–1789 and 1797–1801, where nobody will ever be able to pick them out from the rest of the text. These "splinters" were, however, no part of Goethe's manuscript proper, and therefore they do not appear in the Göchhausen transcript. He seems to have kept them in some kind of a bag; whether the actual manuscript was also kept in this bag or separately we cannot be certain, but very likely it was. After 1797, with the help of his secretary, he filed his Faust splinters according to an elaborate system. But in his happy-go-lucky Storm and Stress years he was apparently contented to jumble them all together in a bag.

When the business of these splinters is properly understood, one of the chief arguments advanced against the authenticity of Goethe's own description of his old Faust manuscript is found to be without substance. At the end of September, 1775, Goethe was visited in Frankfort by Johann Georg Zimmermann (1728–1795) and read to him a few fragments of *Faust*; as Zimmermann recorded in a letter to Reich of January 25, 1796: "Er hat mir einige Fragmente davon in Frankfurt vorgelesen, die mich bald entzückten und bald wieder halb tot lachen machten"—parts of it "ravished" him, while others made him "laugh himself half-dead." In 1832,

thirty-seven years after Zimmermann's death, A. W. Schlegel re-
counted in a letter to Hayward an anecdote Zimmermann was
evidently fond of telling about this meeting of his with Goethe,
which also appears in Rehberg's *Goethe und sein Jahrhundert,* published in 1835. The two versions differ from one another at various
points. Schlegel makes the gross blunder of giving Weimar instead
of Frankfort as the scene of Zimmermann's visit to Goethe, but his
version, which is the more picturesque and sensational of the two,
is the one usually preferred. According to Schlegel, "Goethe apporta
un sac, rempli de petits chiffons de papier. Il le vida sur la table
et dit: Voilà mon Faust!" (Goethe fetched a bag full of little
scraps of paper and tipped it out on the table, saying: "There is
my Faust!") From this Gustav Roethe argues that up to the end
of September, 1775—that is to say, up to the very eve of Goethe's
departure for Weimar—there was still no connected manuscript of
Faust in existence: "Der Faust, den Zimmermann sah, war nicht
auf Lagen zusammenhängend niedergeschrieben, sondern bestand
aus Blättern, ja Fetzen Papier" (The *Faust* that Zimmermann saw
was not written down connectedly in sections, but consisted of
loose sheets or rather scraps of paper).[7]

Not till after Zimmermann's visit, and perhaps during the
first weeks in Weimar, did Goethe, according to Roethe, at last
prepare from these scraps a "Reinschrift" of *Faust,* chiefly because
he needed it for his semi-public readings there, and even then this
"fair copy" was, according to Roethe, nothing but a "vorläufige
Sammlung und Redaktion solcher Fetzen" (provisional collection
and redaction of such scraps): "So zweifle ich nicht daran dass
jener Reinschrift des Urfaust auf ungehefteten Lagen der 'sac rempli de petits chiffons de papier' vorhergegangen ist, dessen Inhalt
erst nachträglich . . . zu ein paar Gruppen notdürftig zusammen-
hängender Szenen geordnet worden ist" (I do not doubt that the
fair copy of the *Urfaust* in unstitched sections was preceded by the
"bag full of little scraps of paper," the contents of which were only
subsequently arranged in a few groups of sketchily connected
scenes).[8] Goethe's work on *Faust* throughout the entire phase up
to October, 1775, consisted, according to Roethe, exclusively of
"Fetzenproduktion"[9] (production in scraps), very few of these
scraps exceeding one hundred and fifty lines and most of them being

under one hundred lines in length: "Der Urfaust zerlegt sich uns in eine grosse Zahl von Fetzen" (The *Urfaust* falls apart for us into a large number of scraps).[10] Roethe claims to be able to distinguish these scraps from one another by their style and contents, sorts them out into three different, unrelated groups, and in the process drastically dismembers nearly all the longer scenes. Roethe accepts the Göchhausen transcript indeed as a trustworthy reproduction of Goethe's "fair copy" of late autumn, 1775, but regards it for that very reason as a document of comparatively little value, which can only mislead us on the important question of how Goethe conceived of and worked on the Faust drama in those early years. If the so-called *Urfaust* is, however, as Roethe would have us believe, only a patchwork of scraps, sketchily and provisionally given a bare semblance of coherency for merely ephemeral, practical purposes, without any comprehensive vision of a poetic whole being involved, then the same must be true also of *Faust I*, in so far as in it Goethe only amplified that *Urfaust* without undertaking anything to make it less sketchy and provisional, or seeing any necessity to do so. One is reminded here of Goethe's already quoted words to Luden: "How do you suppose that Faust was written? If I have understood you rightly, you were of the opinion and still are of the opinion that the poet did not in the least know what he was driving at when he began the work, but wrote at random, just as it came to him." That is indeed what such critics as Roethe, Scherer, Niejahr, Schuchardt, Burger, and the rest of them take for granted. The real issue here is simply, how far Goethe himself knew what he was driving at when he began work on *Faust*. Admittedly the *Urfaust* is fragmentary; so, for that matter, is *Faust I*, as Goethe himself declared; and so is *Faust II*. The entire Faust drama is fragmentary; in its essence it had to be fragmentary and was meant to be so. But just as much conscious and comprehensive formative power is needed for the production of a successful fragmentary work as for the production of such rounded-off classical compositions as *Iphigenie* or *Tasso*, and this conscious and comprehensive formative power manifests itself already in the *Urfaust*.

Roethe's arbitrary procedure illustrates particularly well in an extreme form the kind of thing that very many critics and scholars have long been doing and still are doing in their dealings with

Faust, and the kind of thing that it is indeed difficult for anybody who dives only a little below the surface in these matters not to do. It may seem to us intellectually, psychologically, and aesthetically impossible that the *Urfaust* should have been produced in brief incoherent scraps, but what are we to say in reply to the arguments of Roethe and his fellows? What, above all, are we to do about Zimmermann's anecdote? Some allowance is obviously to be made for its having lost nothing in the telling. Rehberg, in his version of the anecdote, says only that Goethe *"zeigte . . .* Zimmermann *einen Haufen Papiere* mit den Worten: da ist mein Faust" (*showed* Zimmermann *a heap of papers* with the words: "There is my *Faust"*). It is, however, conceivable that Goethe shook out a bagful of papers before Zimmermann, many of them little scraps, inscribed not with fragments of the Faust drama proper, but with odd jottings or "splinters" towards it, and with his love of mystification, perhaps also in an impulse of youthful braggadoccio, proclaimed to him: "Da ist mein Faust!" without drawing his attention to the fact that amongst all these jumbled papers there was a number of unstitched sections containing complete scenes. It is intrinsically more probable that Zimmermann was not so observant as he might have been, that the anecdote lost in accuracy what it gained in piquancy, or that Goethe was drawing the long bow, than that the manuscript described in the *Italienische Reise* and reproduced by Luise von Göchhausen was not already in existence by the end of September, 1775. The jumble of odd scraps of paper was undoubtedly also then in existence, but it was not on them that the actual *Urfaust* was written; they were merely "splinters."

Another piece of evidence sometimes appealed to in support of the theory that Goethe's pre-Weimar work on *Faust* was only a "production in scraps" without any over-all plan at the back of it, is a letter written by Knebel on December 23, 1774, to Bertuch, some eleven days after his first visit to Goethe: "Ich habe einen Haufen Fragmente von ihm, unter andern zu einem 'Doktor Faust', wo ganz ausnehmend herrliche Szenen sind. Er zieht die Manuskripte aus allen Winkeln seines Zimmers hervor" (I have a heap of fragments from him, amongst others some belonging to a Dr. Faust drama, with extraordinarily fine scenes in it. He pulls out manuscripts from every corner of his room). There is no suggestion here, however, that the manuscripts Goethe pulled out from the different corners of his room all of them belonged to *Faust*; and if that were what Knebel meant, it would conflict with Schlegel's version of the Zimmermann anecdote, according to which Goethe kept all his Faust manuscripts (if "little scraps of paper" can be dignified with the name of "manuscripts") together in a bag. It is to be supposed rather that Knebel is referring here to the manuscripts of different works—he speaks of *Faust* "amongst others." It furthermore emerges from Knebel's letter that Goethe was, nine months before Zimmermann's visit, in a position to set before his friends and even lend to them in manuscript a number of complete scenes of *Faust*—such as could not, according to Roethe, have existed at that stage. We cannot imagine Goethe handing over to Knebel a wad of little scraps of paper with disconnected fragments on them. What he lent him was probably a number of the unstitched sections of his own original manuscript. He wrote to him shortly afterwards (presumably on December 28, 1774): "Geben Sie meine Sachen nur nicht aus Händen. Es wäre nichts dran gelegen, wenn nicht gewisse Leute was draus machten" (Whatever you do, don't let those manuscripts of mine out of your hands. It wouldn't matter so much, if there were not certain people who might get up to tricks with them). The Faust manuscript lent to Knebel in December, 1774, was evidently one that a piratical publisher could have printed just as it stood.

The *Urfaust* consists of some twenty unnumbered scenes[11]—two of them, the fourth and nineteenth, extremely short (four and six lines, respectively), and one, the seventeenth ("Strasse vor Gretchens Türe") obviously incomplete. It has been plausibly suggested by Enders and Sarauw that Goethe may have been at work on this scene in October, 1775, when the great interruption came with his summons to Weimar. The last sixteen scenes comprise the entire "Gretchen tragedy," substantially as it stands in the final text, except for certain comparatively minor points to be discussed later. These scenes hang together in as close and organic a concatenation at least in the *Urfaust* as they do in *Faust I*, some would maintain indeed even more closely and organically. The four scenes that precede them, on the other hand, are in no way linked up with one

another or, except at one point, with the Gretchen tragedy; and
the second one, Mephisto's conversation with the young student,
has, as it stands in the Göchhausen transcript, no recognisable
bearing on Faust, who is not so much as mentioned in it. Not
until 1788–1789 did Goethe, in revising this scene and retrenching
it at one point and making additions to it at another, also supply
at the beginning and end of it the necessary passages to integrate
it in the action of the Faust drama proper; and we cannot be
absolutely certain that it was not originally intended to be introduced in some other way. The first scene consists of Faust's opening monologue with the conjuration of the Erdgeist, followed by
the conversation with Wagner—all substantially as in the final text.
The third scene is "Auerbachs Keller," but almost entirely in prose
and differing also in other respects considerably from the final version. The fourth scene, "Landstrasse," which immediately precedes
the Gretchen tragedy, consists only of a stage direction and four
lines of dialogue, the first two spoken by Faust, who asks Mephisto
why he casts down his eyes in passing a wayside cross, the other two
being Mephisto's reply:

> Ich weiss es wohl, es ist ein Vorurteil,
> Allein genung, mir ist's einmal zuwider.*

This is the only scene of the Göchhausen transcript that completely
disappeared from Goethe's final text of *Faust*, but it is significantly
also the only passage from his own original manuscript that is
preserved. In removing it from the body of the play he deleted the
scenic directions and kept the actual dialogue as a "splinter," presumably for possible use in some other context, covering the
remainder of the sheet on which it stood, pretty certainly in the
years 1788–1789, with various other "splinters," now found amongst
the Faust "Paralipomena." This circumstance, so far as it goes,
suggests that fewer of Goethe's early *Faust* papers were totally
destroyed than such critics as Grumach would have us believe.

Not only in its action, but also in every other respect the *Urfaust*
presents—and this has been a great opportunity for the "Higher

---

* I know indeed that it is only a prejudice, / But the long and short of it is
that I just loathe it.

Critics"—a remarkably heterogeneous character. Its dramatic appeal ranges from darkest tragedy to the most caustic satire and the most boisterous hilarity, from subdued pathos to lurid violence; its language ranges from extreme emotional and imaginative intensity, subtlety and dignity to sometimes almost crude stridency or bluntness. The question arises, whether this marked unevenness of tone, which often manifests itself even within the individual scenes, is due simply, as critics like Scherer and Roethe would have us believe, to passages produced by Goethe at different stages in his advance from comparative immaturity to comparative maturity standing here side by side, or whether there may not be some other explanation for it.

A similar heterogeneity, which also presents great opportunities to the disintegrating critics, is to be observed in the formal media employed in the *Urfaust*. The "Auerbachs Keller" scene (except for the first eight lines) and the three final scenes are in highly varied prose, that of scene nineteen ("Nacht. Offen Feld") having, however, so pronouncedly rhythmical a character with its six short lines that it might also be regarded less as prose proper than as a kind of free verse. The sixteenth scene ("Dom") is quite definitely in the kind of free verse that Goethe often employed in his lyrical poetry during the years 1772–1775, as are also three important passages in the first, tenth, and thirteenth scenes. The rest of the *Urfaust* is in rhymed verse, chiefly in a combination of the old German "Knittel" verse, which is known to us above all from the work of Hans Sachs (1494–1560), with the so-called "Madrigal" verse-form, which was developed in German poetry from Italian and French models in the seventeenth and eighteenth centuries and much used by such writers of the generations preceding Goethe's as Gellert and Wieland. Both these verse-forms are characterized by great freedom—the Knittel verse in respect of actual metre, in so far as it consists of four-beat rhyming couplets in which the number of unaccented syllables can be varied *ad libitum* (this is known as the principle of "freie Füllung," or "free filling"); and the Madrigal verse not indeed in respect of the metre, which must remain fairly strictly iambic, with regularly alternating unaccented and accented syllables, but in respect of the length of the lines and the disposition of the rhymes, both of which can, as in its principal model, older French *vers-libre*, be varied without restriction. It was Goethe's brilliant achievement to combine these two labile verse-forms for the purposes of his *Faust*, thereby producing a highly flexible and adaptable prosodic medium, capable of the most comprehensive scale of modulations and in this respect comparable with Elizabethan blank verse. This Goethe had already fully achieved in the *Urfaust*, and in all his later work on both parts of *Faust* this blending of Knittel and Madrigal verse remains the dominant prosodic form.

Up to comparatively recently it occurred to nobody that the central prosodic form of Goethe's *Faust* was anything but the traditional Knittel verse of Hans Sachs, and even now, when, thanks chiefly to Andreas Heusler, the equally or still more important Madrigal component in it has at last come to be recognised, this older, erroneous assumption is still often to be met with. The pure Knittel verse was just the right thing for many of the various purposes Goethe pursued simultaneously in his *Faust*, especially for evoking an antiquated, sixteenth century or, as he himself put it "woodcutlike" atmosphere appropriate to the Faust legend. But for some of his other, subtler, more passionate and subjective purposes, Knittel verse would have proved too stiff and primitive, if he had not supplemented and blended it with the more musical, supple, and lyrical Madrigal verse. This he does so effectually that the naive reader or listener is as a rule not conscious whether it is Knittel verses or Madrigal verses that he is responding to, or of the transitions from the one to the other. It is not indeed intended that he should be conscious of this difference, nor is there any need for him to be so. The Faust verse is not just a mixture of these two verse-forms, but a genuine synthesis of them. Even the academic counters of syllables can sometimes be in doubt, to which of the two categories a particular verse should be assigned.

It remains to be mentioned that four songs are introduced as such into the *Urfaust*, those of the Rat and of the Flea in the third scene, that of the König von Thule in the sixth scene, and the fragmentary song "Meine Mutter, die Hur . . ." in the twentieth scene. Gretchen's monologue scenes, the twelfth and fifteenth, also take the form of songs in stanzas. The passage in the first scene in which the Erdgeist reveals its essence ("In

Lebensfluten . . .") is also no longer either Knittel or Madrigal verse, but rather an excursion into pure lyrical form; and the same might be said of the corresponding passage in the same scene in which the essence of the Sign of the Macrocosm is disclosed ("Wie alles sich zum Ganzen webt . . ."). The four songs proper create, of course, no such problems as the abrupt juxtaposition within the actual dramatic text of Faust verse, prose and scenes or passages in free verse or lyrical stanzas, since they are not presented as the spontaneous expression of the feelings and thoughts of the singer forming themselves on his or her lips in the moment of utterance. These songs are supposed to have existed in the singer's memory independently of and anterior to the given situation, and so form no part of the specifically dramatic texture. They could have been introduced into a work of absolutely homogeneous dramatic and stylistic texture without in the least impairing its homogeneity, just as the Song of the Fates ("Parzenlied") remembered and sung by Iphigenie does not in the least impair the formal homogeneity of *Iphigenie*. But the characters in the *Urfaust*, when they are expressing themselves in their own persons, speak (some would say indifferently) in Knittel verse, Madrigal verse, rhymed stanzas, free verse, and prose. According to Petsch's statistical analysis,[12] one third of the *Urfaust* is in prose, while a little over 32 percent of the verse is Knittel verse, a little over 56 percent Madrigal Verse, 6 percent is free verse, the remaining 5 percent taking the form of songs. The most interesting point here is the marked preponderance of Madrigal over Knittel verse.

This formal heterogeneity of the *Urfaust* tends to be the point of departure of the disintegrating critics in their ingenious exertions to take the work to pieces and demonstrate that those pieces never originally belonged together and have only been patched into a semblance of coherency. In the light of this formal heterogeneity all the other real or apparent disparities and contradictions observable in the work, and all the scanty objective or semi-objective evidence we have in the form of statements made by Goethe and his acquaintances, of possible sources, influences, parallels, and presumable inspirations from Goethe's own private experiences, are interpreted as proving that the *Urfaust* was produced in two or three different stages, each in all respects entirely distinct from the others—one characterised by the use of prose, one by the use of Knittel verse, and perhaps an intermediate one characterised by the use of free verse—and that the text we have is only a pastiche of fragments from these disparate phases. It is the same kind of method as that by which it is proved that such productions of the remoter past as the Homeric poems, the books of the Bible, or *Piers Plowman* incorporate, in the form in which we know them, the work of many different writers remote in period, antecedents, and outlook from one another. The pioneer here was Wilhelm Scherer (1846–1886), who died one year before the *Urfaust* transcript of Luise von Göchhausen was discovered. In 1879, in his article "Faust in Prosa," Scherer propounded the theory, which in modified forms still underlies all speculation on these questions, that Goethe's original intention was to write *Faust* throughout in prose, and that the prose scenes we have are survivors from this projected and in part executed original prose version of winter, 1771–1772, as are also the four free verse passages, which are to be regarded simply as prose cut up into short lines to look like verse.

One of the favourite arguments employed in this field is that Goethe did not know anything about Knittel verse until he discovered Hans Sachs in spring, 1773, and that therefore no part of the *Urfaust* that is in Knittel verse can have been written, at least in its present form, until after that date, everything not in such verse being pretty certainly earlier. The bottom has long since been knocked out of this argument, which however still continues to flourish without any bottom. For one thing, Goethe is found using Knittel verse with much virtuosity in a letter of January 4, 1773, well before the presumed date of his discovery of Hans Sachs, about which we really know very little, but which in all probability took place as early as summer or autumn 1772. For another, Knittel verse is not employed anything like so consistently in the *Urfaust* as in the various works produced about 1773 under Hans Sachs' influence, the most notable of which is the fragmentary *Ewiger Jude* ("Wandering Jew"); and the Madrigal verse, which, as has been seen, is now recognised as being every bit as important for *Faust*, was certainly familiar to Goethe as early as November 6, 1768, when he wrote a long letter to Friederike Oeser in it. It has furthermore been shown that Goethe must have known quite a lot about Knittel verse as early as 1766, during his first years as a student in Leipzig, from Gottsched's *Kritische Dichtkunst* ("Critical Art of Poetry") (1730), of all the most unexpected sources. Of this publication Goethe writes: "Sie überlieferte von allen Dichtungsarten eine historische Kenntnis, so wie vom Rhythmus und von verschiedenen Bewegungen desselben" (It conveyed to us a historical knowledge of all the poetic *genres* and also of prosody and its different movements).[13] Gottsched, notwithstanding his classico-rationalistic limitations, gives a circumstantial account of Knittel verse, illustrated by two specimens of his own production, and in 1765 he also reprinted various old German plays in this verse-form, notably by Scherenberg (1480) and Rosenplüt (mid-fifteenth century), which are thought by some to have exercised a direct influence on Goethe in his *Faust*.[14] Goethe's own declaration in *Dichtung und Wahrheit*, Book VII, that he wrote a skit on Clodius' *Medon* in August, 1767, "in Knittelversen" is perhaps more reliable than used to be supposed, when he was believed not to have known anything about Knittel verse before 1773. These discoveries have, however, as will be seen, only discredited one set of hypersubtle and quite unnecessary hypotheses, in order to make room for another.

Just as there is no objective evidence that Goethe might not very well have devised and employed the synthesis of Knittel and Madrigal verse as it is found in the *Urfaust* much earlier than 1773, so also there is no objective evidence that he could not have written one or other of the prose scenes or free verse passages that occur in it as late as October, 1775. The mere circumstance of a scene or passage being in one or the other of these three media, or in lyrical stanza form, then, as such, is no criterion for determining whether it was written earlier or later within the three and a half years or so preceding his departure for Weimar in November, 1775. If we look at his other quite copious, though in many cases fragmentary, work in dramatic form of these three and a half years, we find no evidence at all of his having at any point once and for all abandoned one medium in favour of another—for example, prose in favour of some kind of verse, or vice versa. On the contrary, he is by and large seen using all these media side by side throughout these years, just as the particular occasion demanded. Thus in the fragmentary *Mahomet* drama of 1773 he mingled verse and prose. The convenient rule of thumb which the critics have tried to establish here is not only far too mechanical, but also downright fallacious. In the case of many scenes and passages in the *Urfaust* it matters very little, or not at all, in what order they were first written. But there are a few, above all the opening monologue and the scene "Trüber Tag. Feld," in connexion with which this question is of immense importance. Such cases cannot be decided by any rule of thumb; they need to be examined individually and in all their bearings, though this is seldom done.

We are not on much firmer ground when we try to clarify these issues solely or chiefly by the criterion of comparative maturity or immaturity. For one thing, there can be differences of opinion as to what does or does not constitute maturity. It is not a question on which the judgment of the average academic critic is to be trusted. We shall see how Scherer in 1879 set up a demonstrably nonsensical rule of thumb in this matter which has remained unchallenged to the present day. For another thing, Goethe does not in the period of rather less than four years with which we are concerned advance so steadily and unremittingly in maturity that he cannot, even to the very end of it, again and again still indulge in comparative sentimentality, bombast, and crude farce of a kind that he might theoretically be supposed long since to have left behind him—as appears in *Stella, Erwin und Elmire, Claudine von Villa Bella,* and *Hanswursts Hochzeit,* all written in 1775. "Auerbachs Keller" is the only scene in the *Urfaust* for the dating of which there is any objective documentary evidence: in the same letter of September 17, 1775 to Auguste von Stolberg, in which he says he has that very morning "made a scene of his *Faust*" he goes on almost immediately to compare himself in his love quandaries on account of Lili Schönemann with a poisoned rat, reproducing the substance and some of the phrasing of the "Song of the Rat" which Frosch sings in the "Auerbachs Keller" scene. This, of course, by no means *proves* that the scene written that day was the "Auerbachs Keller" one; but it does at least make it seem probable. In any case it matters very little in itself when that particular scene was written. What does matter is that so many critics, amongst them Hefele, Max Morris, H. Schneider, Roethe, and Enders, feel entitled to dismiss the documentary evidence, such as it is, out of hand, with no further argument than that the scene is in their judgment crude and "immature," or that it is in prose at all. On such grounds they maintain that it cannot have been written later than spring, 1772; Roethe[15] makes the characteristic qualification that the "Rattenlied mit allem, was dazu gehört," is a "späterer Einschub" (*Song of the Rat*, with all that belongs to it, [is a] later interpolation) of September, 1775, while some of them, following in the footsteps of the egregious Luden in his conversation with Goethe of 1806, are confident that it must have been the very first part of *Faust* to be written[16] and would even date it in Goethe's student years in Leipzig, that is to say before 1768. In reply to all this it may be said in the first place that the "Auerbachs Keller" scene is crude because, as a rollicking drinking scene, it is meant to be so and could not be anything else—whenever it was written; in this appropriate crudity, which Goethe preserved when he rewrote it in verse about 1788–1789, lies its point and its beauty. Secondly, Goethe was still just as capable of such crudity—or "immaturity," if it must be so termed—in autumn, 1775, as he had been in winter, 1771–1772, or in his Leipzig years. We have his own word for it that there was much in the no longer surviving original version of the first acts of *Egmont*, also written in autumn, 1775, that he later saw fit to eliminate, because it was "allzu aufgeknöpft und burschikos" (all too free and easy and full of student slang)[17]—just those qualities which the critics shake their heads over as crude and "immature" in the "Auerbachs Keller" scene. Whether the "Auerbachs Keller" was written in 1775 or, as seems less probable, very much earlier, the curious circumstance of its beginning with eight lines of Knittel verse and continuing in prose is not easily controvertible evidence that Goethe employed these two media not in successive phases of his work on the *Urfaust*, but simultaneously.

Equally unreliable are arguments for the dating of passages from parallels in phrasing. Those who know how often authors—and particularly Goethe—can inexplicably come back to a phrase coined by themselves or encountered in the work of another writer, twenty, thirty, or more years earlier, will be well aware how little such parallels prove when they remain within a range of less than four years. Numberless striking parallels to passages in all parts of the

Urfaust are to be found scattered throughout Goethe's writings of the years 1771–1775, and none of them ultimately prove anything more than that it is always one and the same mind that we have before us. The so popular type of argument based on relationships between motifs and passages in the *Urfaust* and the private experiences of Goethe which may be supposed to have inspired them is equally inconclusive, because, even when the postulated relationship is convincing, as it by no means always is, the possibility should be allowed for, though it hardly ever is allowed for, that a considerable interval of time may lie between the experience in question and its crystallization in poetic form. The common assumption that the youthful Goethe always expressed his experiences in artistic form immediately after undergoing them is quite without foundation, and reposes only on a mistaken, over-literal interpretation of some of his own statements on the question, especially in *Dichtung und Wahrheit*. We can be certain, of course, that a work or a passage in a work cannot have been written before the experience that inspired it, but that is all we can be certain of. It may have been written the very next day, or not till years afterwards.

In considering whether or not the heterogeneity of the *Urfaust* is due merely to fortuitous and external causes, as the disintegrating critics would have us believe, one should note that Goethe in his later work on the drama did nothing to make it less heterogeneous, but rather went out of his way to make it more so. He did indeed rewrite the prose "Auerbachs Keller" scene in mixed Knittel and Madrigal verses in the years 1788–1789, and the "Kerker" scene in May, 1798, and it may be supposed that about the same time he thought of similarly versifying the only remaining prose scene of any length, "Trüber Tag. Feld." But eventually, in March, 1806, he decided after all to leave it, and so it appears, lightly revised here and there, but still in prose, in the final text of *Faust I*. Meanwhile he increased the heterogeneity of *Faust* in 1788–1789 by introducing a monologue of thirty-four lines in blank verse (in the new scene, "Wald und Höhle") and a large number of rhyming two-beat lines in the "Hexenküche." The additions of 1797–1801 bring further passages in two-beat and three-beat rhyming lines and, in the "Walpurgisnacht" scene and its appendage, many quatrains and other prosodic varieties. In *Faust II* we find, amongst a multitude of other new prosodic forms, Dantesque *terza rima* and extensive sections in iambic trimeters and in alexandrines. We must recognise here, on the part of the fully mature Goethe, who quite certainly knew what he was getting at, a deliberate cultivation of heterogeneity as a stylistic principle. It may be noted, by the way, that no real analogies to this extreme cult of heterogeneity can be seen anywhere in Goethe's work outside *Faust*; for the hybrid form of his ballad operas, of the sequel to the *Magic Flute*, and of his many "Fastnachtspiele" (carnival plays), "Maskenspiele" (masques), and similar ephemeral compositions is merely a concession to the demands made upon him as an entertainer, and has little to do with his more serious poetic productivity; while the more ambitious "Festspiele" (pageants)—*Pandora* and *Des Epimenides Erwachen* ("The Awakening of Epimenides")—aim at a degree of uniformity in tone and diction such as is found at most in some individual sections of *Faust*, not in the Faust drama as a totality. But the question arises, when and how Goethe arrived at the stylistic principle of heterogeneity which he beyond doubt quite deliberately cultivates in his work on *Faust* from 1788 onward. It could, of course, be so that he was simply in his maturer years making the best of the bad job of his chaotic immaturity, in the feeling that he might as well be hanged for a sheep as a lamb, that there was nothing for it now but to go on trudging doggedly and defiantly along the labyrinthine paths into which he had inadvertently blundered as a harumscarum young man. The disparaging way in which he talks about *Faust* in the "Zueignung" stanzas, in the "Vorspiel auf dem Theater" and elsewhere suggests that he may sometimes have seen things in this light. But there is more to it than that. If we look at the *Urfaust* responsively and appreciatively as a work of dramatic and poetic art, it must strike us that, whether Goethe is employing prose or one or another of the various forms of verse available to him, the medium is always admirably appropriate to the particular situation or sentiment to be presented, and we may well ask ourselves whether that is not the true reason why Goethe uses that medium on that occasion, rather than because it is the only medium at his disposal in that given phase of his development. And if this were the true explanation of the heterogeneity in the actual media employed in the

Urfaust, might it not be true also of the various other heterogeneities that characterise the *Urfaust,* and not only the *Urfaust,* but also the final text of *Faust I* and *II?* The higher critics naturally refuse to admit that the *Urfaust* may be as heterogeneous as it is, not because Goethe produced it with only the vaguest and most fluctuating ideas about what he was getting at, but because he from the outset quite deliberately intended it to be heterogeneous. Such an admission would quite undermine their fundamental assumptions and invalidate their methods. Accordingly we find Scherer denying "dass die stilistischen Verschiedenheiten aus der Verschiedenheit der Gegenstände fliessen"(that the stylistic differences arise from the differences between the subjects dealt with),[18] and Roethe petulantly dismissing as "eine grosse, ja mystische Überspannung des Bogens" the notion that "jede Szene des Urfaust habe durch ihre besondere Aufgabe auch ihre Form erzeugt, so dass die Verschiedenheit der äusseren Form nicht für sich betrachtet werden dürfe, sondern nur als der notwendige Reflex des Inhalts" (It is a great, indeed mystical extravagance to suppose that each scene of the *Urfaust* generated its own form through its own special function, so that differences in external form ought not to be considered by themselves, but only as a necessary reflection of the contents).[19] But we shall find nothing farfetched or improbable in the idea of Goethe's freely varying his medium from scene to scene and even from passage to passage, according to the requirements of the given situation or sentiment, if we remember that he had before him in 1771 an excellent precedent for such practices in Shakespeare, with his alternation of blank verse, prose, and various types of rhyming verse. The legendary Faust theme afforded—and Goethe may well be supposed to have felt this—legitimate scope for a much more extensive adoption of this Shakespearean heterogeneity than the historical themes of *Götz von Berlichingen* and *Egmont.*

In versifying the "Auerbachs Keller" scene in 1788–1789 Goethe was probably animated in good part by the will to comparative uniformity of medium, at least to the extent of eliminating prose from *Faust,* although in the "Wald und Höhle" scene of the same years he introduced a far greater anomaly in the form of a long soliloquy in his then newly acquired blank verse, immediately followed by dialogue in Faustian Knittel and Madrigal verse—the most startling anomaly of style in either part of the final *Faust* text. Where his motives for versifying the "Kerker" scene in May, 1798, are concerned, we are not dependent on guesswork only; from the letter he wrote to Schiller on this occasion it emerges that considerations of comparative stylistic uniformity for its own sake played at most a secondary part in this decision: "Ein sehr sonderbarer Fall erscheint dabei: Einige tragische Szenen waren in Prosa geschrieben, sie sind durch ihre Natürlichkeit und Stärke, in Verhältnis gegen das Andere, ganz unerträglich. Ich suche sie deswegen gegenwärtig in Reime zu bringen, da denn die Idee wie durch einen Flor durchscheint, die unmittelbare Wirkung des ungeheuern Stoffes aber gedämpft wird" (A very curious case arises: some tragic scenes were written in prose; through their naturalness and force they are, by comparison with the rest, quite unendurable. Therefore I am at the present moment trying to versify them, so that the idea shimmers through a veil, as it were, while the immediate effect of the fearful theme is toned down).[20] What troubles Goethe here about his original version is less its stylistic heterogeneity as such than its intensity and realism. While the "Kerker" scene, the only one of the three in question which he actually did versify, gained in some respects through this toning-down process, it lost in what matters still more—in "naturalness and force," in "immediate effect." Decisive was the older Goethe's elsewhere attested dread of the genuinely, unadulteratedly tragic. Nothing that Goethe here says about the tragic prose scenes in the *Urfaust* supports the view that they could not, either because they are in prose at all or for any other reason, have been written later than 1772. On the contrary, if Goethe had really, as so many scholars still maintain, originally intended to write *Faust* in prose throughout, and then later decided to use verse instead, he could hardly by 1798 so completely have forgotten such a radical change of plan as to be surprised at finding those three prose scenes in his old manuscript.

The disparities in the *Urfaust*, which the critics make so much of and depict as inexplicable except by elaborate, tangential, and un-

verifiable hypotheses, present no problems at all if we admit that
Goethe knew from the outset what he was getting at. So far as
that is admitted, these disparities will appear to us natural, necessary, and admirably appropriate to the Faust theme as Goethe
envisaged it, and only in so far as it is not admitted shall we feel
that it very much matters in exactly what order the individual
scenes or passages were written or what particular private experiences of the poet may have inspired them. There is, however, one
very real major disparity in the *Urfaust* which does not trouble
most of the critics in question and which few of them seem even
to be aware of. It is a disparity that will only strike those who
are prepared to see and accept the work in its totality, to consider its detailed aspects not merely in isolation, but in their full
relationship to one another and to this totality. The difficulty is
that this *Urfaust* has so extraordinarily little to do with Faust.
That is to say, there is so very little in it of what is demanded
not simply by the legendary and traditional sources empirically
considered, but by the intrinsic idea of Faust's person and destiny.
For although a writer, in undertaking the full-scale poetic presentation of a well-known mythical, legendary, historical, or otherwise traditional figure, is free to carry out the task on his own lines
with whatever personal reinterpretations and symbolical undertones he chooses, there is always a certain basic narrative sequence
that he must in one way or another adhere to, a certain basic minimum of events, situations, and motifs that he must in one way or
another bring in, if there is to be any point in his using the name
of that figure at all. There is no objection to his fulfilling these
conditions as esoterically and impishly as James Joyce does in his
Ulysses; if he, however, fails to fulfil them at all, he may indeed
produce an excellent piece of work, as Brecht, for example, does
in his *Mutter Courage*, but we shall be entitled to complain that
he has cheated us with his choice of name for his hero or heroine.
Now the basic narrative sequence, the staple of events, situations,
and motifs demanded of any large-scale work that calls itself
"Faust" is that the hero should embrace the study and practice
of magic; that he should conjure up the devil and conclude a pact
with him, staking his soul in return for the devil's services over a

limited period of time; that he should after this embark on a series of fantastic travels and adventures involving his magical powers and bringing him in contact with all sorts of people, including the great ones of the earth; that the spirit of Helen of Troy should become his paramour; that at the end of his time he should perish in some strange and terrible way and that the devil should claim his soul under the terms of the pact. One or the other of these motifs can, of course, be omitted, all of them can be reinterpreted or given a strange, symbolical twist: how far an author can legitimately go in remodelling the legendary data, Thomas Mann's *Dr. Faustus* shows. But unless this ground-pattern is recognizable, we must say that the work in question, however good it may otherwise be, simply is not *Faust* and has no business to call itself *Faust*.

Now whereas all these elements are found in the final text of Goethe's *Faust I* and *II*, considered together, there are very few traces of them in the *Urfaust*, except in the opening scene, where Faust is shown dedicating himself to the study and practice of magic and invoking the Erdgeist, which can be accepted as a legitimate substitute for the traditional invocation of the devil. This promising start is not followed up. Mephistopheles appears indeed later as Faust's companion, and it is indicated that some kind of pact exists between the two, but how he comes to be there and what the nature of Faust's pact with him is—points of the greatest importance for the Faust legend—remains unknown. Instead we are given the tragedy of Gretchen, which, impressive though it is, simply does not belong to the intrinsic idea of Faust, in whatsoever spirit and by whomsoever that idea may be treated. In fact, when Goethe abandoned work on Faust for some thirteen years in autumn, 1775, he had still not done more than barely begin to deal with the Faust theme proper, but had expended the greater part of his time and energies on something else instead, and when he dropped the work again for almost another thirty years, on putting the finishing touches to *Faust I* in 1806, he had still not progressed much beyond the preliminary stages of the essential Faust story. The Gretchen tragedy, just because it is in its own way so excellent, creates really the greatest problem,

so far as the unity of Goethe's *Faust* is concerned. If it were eliminated and the action went on immediately from the "Hexenküche"
or even from the "Auerbachs Keller" scene to the scenes at the
Emperor's Court in Act I of the second part, we should have no
such serious difficulties about apprehending the work as a unity.
Nobody in his senses would, of course, think for this reason of
regretting that Goethe wrote the Gretchen tragedy or did not
cancel it. But it still remains an erratic block in the drama as a
whole. One might exaggeratedly and grotesquely illustrate the kind
of incongruity that faces us here by imagining that Shakespeare had
shown Macbeth, immediately after his encounter with the witches,
falling in love with and seducing the Porter's daughter, and filled
up the remaining acts of the tragedy with that theme, reserving
the murder of Duncan and what arises from it for treatment years
later in a second part.

Goethe has made the Faust theme so peculiarly his own, and
it is so much better known to most readers in his presentation of
it than in any other form, that the Gretchen tragedy is generally
taken for granted as normally and necessarily belonging to it, especially amongst those critics who are eternally on the look-out for
minutest inconsistencies and discrepancies in matters of detail. A
laudable exception here is Hermann Schneider, who writes:

> Es mag wunderlich klingen: Ein Gretchendrama in Wett-
> bewerb mit dem Faustdrama—, wo ja alle Welt Faust *und*
> Gretchen als einhelliges Hauptpaar dieser Dichtung im Be-
> wusstsein trägt! Und doch hat es seine Richtigkeit: die Hand-
> lung des Magiers Faust ist der Natur der Sache nach
> männlich. Sie kannte die Buhlschaft mit der selbst noch halb
> dämonischen Helena, erlaubte wohl auch einmal eine kleine
> Episode irdischer Erotik . . . aber sie duldete kein Gretchen,
> keine für Faustgestalt und Faustgedanken tödliche Konkur-
> renz. Goethe aber kennt nun an zweierlei Helden des wer-
> denden Dramas, zweierlei Interessen, zweierlei Handlungen:
> Gretchen und den Magus. Man sage nicht, dass dieser die
> Gretchenhandlung bestimmt. *Das* ist ja gerade unser Vor-
> wurf: Dieser Liebhaber ist nicht *Faust*. . . . Für die ganze

Gretchenhandlung . . . gibt es keinen Faust, bedarf es keines Faust, ja ist die Faustnatur völlig fehl am Ort . . . Es bleibt dabei: die Gretchenhandlung hat die Fausthandlung erstickt, ja, die Gretchengestalt . . . die Faustgestalt an die Wand gedrückt.*[21]

Similarly Burger points out in 1942, "wie wenig die Gretchen-tragödie ihrem Ursprung und ihrer Ausführung nach zu dem Faust-titanismus passt" (how little the story of Gretchen by its origin and its execution accords with the titanism of Faust).[22] Goethe never thought that the choice of an established theme like that of Faust did not impose on an author such obligations as have here been outlined, or that even a man of such exceptional genius as he felt himself to be could afford to ride roughshod over those obligations. When the Gretchen tragedy is dealt with in detail, it will be seen that he was from the outset conscious of these difficulties and did what was in his power to overcome them. The question at present, however, is how Gretchen found her way into the Faust drama at all, and this is bound up with the further questions, when and how Goethe began work on *Faust*, and what his original plan for the work, if he may be supposed to have had any, was like.

Those critics who think that what matters most is to find a literary "source" for everything in Goethe's *Faust* trace the Gret-chen tragedy to the following passage in the chapbook of the

---

* It may sound strange to speak of a Gretchen drama in competition with the Faust drama—when the whole world thinks of Faust and Gretchen to-gether as perfectly matched in the two leading parts of this work! And yet it is quite right. The story of Faust is by its very nature masculine. It knew of the amour with Helen of Troy, who is in any case herself a half daemonic being; it admitted just once in a way a little interlude of earthly love, but it did not tolerate any Gretchen, any rivalry fatal to the figure of Faust and the idea of Faust. From now onward, however, Goethe knows two distinct heroes in his germinating drama, two distinct kinds of interest, two distinct plots: Gretchen and the Magus. Let no one assert that it is the latter who determines the course of the Gretchen plot. *That* is just our objection: this lover is not *Faust*. Throughout the Gretchen plot there is no Faust, there is no need for any Faust, indeed the nature of Faust is entirely out of place. The fact remains: the Gretchen plot has strangled the Faust plot, indeed the figure of Gretchen has thrust the figure of Faust to the wall.

"Christlich Meynender" of 1725, for a proper understanding of which it must be remembered that under the terms of his pact with the devil Faust had renounced matrimony:

> Faust musste wider sein Versprechen einen Appetit auf Weiberfleisch bekommen. Er verliebte sich auch in eine schöne doch arme Magd, welche bei einem Kramer in seiner Nachbarschaft dienete, die ihm aber ausser der Ehe nichts erlauben wollte, weswegen er sie zu verehlichen willens war und darüber mit dem Geiste [Mephistophilis] hart zusammen kam, und doch noch mit seinem Kopfe durchzudringen vermeinte.*

Lucifer himself has to intervene with all his terrors to bring Faust to his senses, and then, by way of compensation, gives him Helen of Troy as a concubine. In 1952, Hans Albert Maier proclaimed that he had discovered in the same chapbook a more likely source for the Gretchen tragedy, namely the passage: "In Gotha verunreinigte er [Faust] Valentin Hohenweyers Ehebette, und als der Wirt ihn deswegen das Haus zu räumen nötigte, so verbannete er einen Poltergeist in dasselbige" (In Gotha, Faust polluted the marriage-bed of Valentine Hohenweyer, and when the landlord forced him on account of that to quit the house, he caused it to be haunted by a poltergeist). The name "Valentin," given by Goethe to Gretchen's brother, and with it the entire conception of the Gretchen tragedy, can only, Maier argues, be derived from this passage in the 1725 chapbook. He writes:

> Im Volksbuch . . . bleibt Valentins Weib ebenso gesichtslos, wie es namenlos bleibt. . . . Natürlich ist es höchst bezeichnend für den schöpferischen Dichter und Psychographen Goethe, dass er gerade diese Episode und sie nur in ihrer rein menschlichen, nicht in ihrer magischen Seite aufgriff. Ob-

---

* In spite of his promise Faust could not help feeling an appetite for female flesh. He fell in love too with a beautiful but poor serving-girl in the employment of a shopkeeper hard by, who would not, however, allow him anything outside wedlock. Therefore he wanted to marry her and embroiled himself with the Spirit [that is, Mephistophilis], still thinking that he might contrive to get his own way.

gleich also die Episode im Volksbuch und in Drama ganz verschiedene Funktionen zu erfüllen hat, so beweist der Name Valentin doch, dass Goethes Phantasiearbeit vom Volksbuch ausging. Neben der völligen Akzentverschiebung und Auftreibung von drei Zeilen zu einem halben Drama besteht der kühne Schritt Goethes darin, dass er aus dem Ehepaar ein Geschwisterpaar Valentin und Gretchen machte.*[23]

In fact, one must ignore every feature and aspect of the Gretchen tragedy, except the completely irrelevant circumstance that Gretchen's brother happens to be given the name "Valentin" and the very obvious circumstance that Gretchen herself is "beautiful" and comparatively poor, in order to establish the slightest, most peripheral, and insignificant relationship between it and the old chapbooks. The two passages in question are the only ones anybody has so far been able to point out in the entire body of traditional Faust literature[24] as possible "sources" for the Gretchen tragedy, and all they really prove is how utterly alien to that old tradition Goethe's Gretchen tragedy is. If either of these passages was Goethe's point of departure, then he left it with the least possible delay in seven-league boots; and those boots alone can be of interest to us.

The more general and sensible view is that the Gretchen tragedy has nothing to do with the old Faust books, but arises out of Goethe's own personal feelings and experiences. The mysterious Gretchen belonging to the fringe of the Frankfort underworld, whom Goethe represents himself in Book V of *Dichtung und Wahrheit* as having loved at the age of about fifteen, used, because of her name, to be regarded as the real-life model of the Gretchen

---

* In the chapbook, Valentine's wife remains as featureless as she is nameless. It is, of course, highly characteristic of the creative poet and psychograph Goethe, that he seized upon just this episode, and dwelt only upon the purely human, not on the magical side of it. So, although the episode has to fulfil quite different functions in the chapbook and in the drama, the name Valentine still proves that the chapbook was here the point of departure for the work of Goethe's imagination. In addition to the complete shifting of the emphasis and the expansion of three lines into half a drama, Goethe's bold step consists in transforming the married couple into a brother and sister, Valentine and Gretchen.

in *Faust*, but there is something apocryphal about the whole episode, and it is now as a rule rightly passed over in this connexion.
The far more obvious and almost universally accepted model for
Gretchen is the country pastor's daughter, Friederike Brion of
Sesenheim, with whom Goethe had a highly important love-rela-
tionship during his years as a student in Strasburg, and whom he
deserted in summer, 1771. His remorse on this occasion was one
of the decisive experiences of his life and mirrors itself in much
of his writing of the Frankfort years 1771–1775. The only specific
instances of this that he mentions in *Dichtung und Wahrheit*
(Book XII) are Maria and her faithless lover Weislingen in *Götz
von Berlichingen* (written in autumn, 1771), and Marie Beau-
marchais and her faithless lover Clavigo in *Clavigo* (written in
spring, 1774). But it is clear that the variations on the same theme
in *Stella* (written in spring, 1775) have their roots in Goethe's
desertion of Friederike Brion, and the same may be reasonably
postulated of the Gretchen tragedy, which nobody would think
of dating before that desertion, that is to say before Goethe's return to Frankfort in August, 1771. Since 1940, however, these
issues have been in part simplified, in part complicated through
the discovery made by Ernst Beutler and published in that year
of the probable source of the actual tragic fate of Gretchen. From
the eighth to the twelfth of October, 1771, the trial took place in
Frankfort of the twenty-five-year-old Susanna Margarethe Brandt,
a servant at one of the inns of that city, for the crime of infanticide; the death sentence was formally passed on her on January 9,
and she was beheaded on January 14, 1772. The suggestions already
variously made that there might be some connexion between this
case of Susanna Brandt and Goethe's Gretchen tragedy were materially strengthened by Beutler's discovery of an eight-page précis
of the trial prepared at the instructions of Goethe's father and
bound up in his vast twenty-one-folio-volume collection of miscel-
lanea bearing upon the institutions and history of Frankfort from
1343 to the most recent times. This was not the first attempt to
identify Goethe's Gretchen with a particular historical figure. In
1914, Otto von Boenigk in his *Das Urbild von Goethes Gretchen*
had tried to demonstrate that the original of Gretchen was the
shoemaker's daughter Maria Flint, who was beheaded for infanti-

cide at Stralsund in 1765. There is a certain sameness about all these trials for infanticide, but Beutler draws attention to the one Goethe is likeliest to have known about from first-hand observation not long before the inception of the Gretchen tragedy. There is felt by many to be a significant relationship between the circumstance that Susanna Brandt attributed the power her seducer obtained over her to his having put something into her wine, and that Goethe's Gretchen unintentionally poisons her mother by secretly putting a sleeping-draught into her drink; that Susanna Brandt laid the chief blame for her downfall and crime directly upon the devil, and that the devil plays a certain part in Gretchen's downfall; and that both Susanna Brandt and Gretchen have a brother who is a soldier. What is made most of, however, is that Susanna Brandt was consoled by her sister and a friend with the words: "Sie wäre die erste nicht" (She would not be the first), that is to say, not the first girl to have been seduced, and that Mephisto, in scoffing at Faust for allowing Gretchen's fate to prey on his conscience, uses the phrase: "Sie ist die erste nicht" (She is not the first). Beutler expressly declares[25] that Susanna Brandt has nothing to do with Goethe's conception of Gretchen's personality.

That the trial excited the sympathy of the Goethe family may well be assumed, though the fact of Goethe's father having a record made of it proves little one way or another in this matter, since he regularly preserved records of anything out of the way that happened in Frankfort. One thing that worries Beutler is that, although his lines of inquiry lead again and again to close associates and kinsmen of Goethe, they all break off just too short. At no point in contemporary records or in *Dichtung und Wahrheit* is any reference to Susanna Brandt's trial and execution by Goethe himself to be found, and the one passage in *Dichtung und Wahrheit*, Book IV, which Beutler does appeal to, where Goethe speaks of having attended "verschiedene Exekutionen" (various executions) in his early life and gives as an example the public burning of an immoral French novel, belongs to the period before the Imperial Coronation of 1764. It is just conceivable that Goethe at the tender age of nine witnessed the beheading in 1758 of an earlier Frankfort infanticide, Anna Maria Frölich, or that he at least knew Kolbele's pamphlet of 1765 about this case, which presents some interesting

analogies to the Gretchen tragedy.[26] Beutler ingeniously explains
the absence of any references to the Susanna Brandt case by Goethe
as typical of his "Art, den Nachtseiten des Lebens gegenüber aus-
weichend zu schweigen und nur mittelbar im Widerschein der
Dichtung zu enthüllen, wie sehr er ergriffen war" (tendency to keep
out of the way of the seamy side of life and remain silent about it,
only revealing indirectly in the mirror of his poetic work how
shattered he was by it).[27] So far as this characteristic tendency of
Goethe's can be supposed to have existed as early as 1771, it is
likely to have led him to take as little notice as possible of the trial
of Susanna Brandt and certainly to keep well out of the way of her
execution. Presumably he could not, however, help taking some
notice at least of the trial. This was bound to interest him considerably, as one of the fifty-six theses that he had undertaken to
dispute upon only two months previously, in his juristic examination in Strasburg on August 6, 1771, had been: "An foemina partum
recenter editum trucidans capite plectenda sit? quaestio est inter
Doctores controversa" (It is a moot point amongst doctors of law
whether capital punishment should be inflicted on a woman who
kills her new-born child). In 1783, when the ruling Council of
Weimar considered abolishing the death penalty for infanticide in
the Duchy, Goethe voted for its retention.[28] The question was
touched upon on February 19, 1831, in the course of a conversation
with Hofrat Karl Vogel, whom Goethe greatly admired as a doctor
and administrator and who attended him in his last illness. Goethe
had been inveighing against the way in which modern "Schwäche
und übertriebene Liberalität" (softness and exaggerated liberality)
led to the laws not being enforced as severely as they should be,
and it was agreed amongst the interlocutors that doctors were often
much to blame for so laxly enabling criminals to escape the punishment they deserved on grounds of diminished responsibility: "Bei
dieser Gelegenheit (Eckermann reports), lobte Vogel einen jungen
Physikus, der in ähnlichen Fällen immer Charakter zeige und der
noch kürzlich bei dem Zweifel eines Gerichts, ob eine gewisse
Kindesmörderin für zurechnungsfähig zu halten, sein Zeugnis dahin
ausgestellt habe, dass sie es allerdings sei" (In this connexion Vogel
praised a young physician who always displayed strength of character in such cases and who shortly before, when a court had been

in doubt whether a certain infanticide should be regarded as responsible for her actions, had testified that she indeed was so).[29] If Goethe had any comment to make upon this, it is not recorded by Eckermann. We have no conclusive evidence, either in the relevant scenes of the *Urfaust* or elsewhere, that even the twenty-two-year-old Goethe necessarily disapproved on principle of the death penalty for infanticide in any and every case—for example, in the case of Susanna Brandt, which differs materially from that of his own Gretchen—though we can regard it as very probable; nor is it a question about which we really need to know anything. A movement in favour of humaner views on crime and punishment, especially in this matter, was characteristic of that age and manifested itself at many points in contemporary German literature.

Beutler is confident that everything in the later scenes in the Gretchen tragedy was "geboren aus dem Erbarmen, dem Grauen und persönlichsten Erschüttertsein durch die Tragik, wie sie das Leben dem Dichter vorgespielt hatte" (born of the compassion, the terror and the most personal agitation of the poet's soul by the tragedy which life had enacted before him),[30] in the fate of Susanna Brandt. He is certain that Goethe must have been an "Augenzeuge" (eye-witness) of the execution and opines that on this occasion he felt the fear of death "vielleicht zum ersten Mal in aller Schwere" (perhaps for the first time in his life in all its oppressiveness).[31] The passage which Beutler quotes as evidence for this view, it is interesting to note, is Gretchen's anticipatory vision of the execution as Goethe versified it in May, 1798, not the briefer and less detailed original prose version of it, as it stands in the *Urfaust*. Hermann Schneider in 1949 visualizes how in the January days of 1772 Goethe "so oft um jenes Gemäuer herumgestrichen sein mag, das die Betrogene, Verlassene barg" (may so often have prowled around the walls that concealed the betrayed and forsaken girl), and writes also: "Die Kerkerszene . . . ist in eben jenem Turm spielend zu denken, an dem Goethe damals so oft mit Grauen und Mitgefühl vorübergegangen sein muss. Hier sass Gretchen gefangen, bangte ihrem Urteil entgegen . . . Nicht weniger mag der Dichter gelitten haben, bis die Gestaltung der Szene 'Kerker' ihn vom ärgsten befreite" (The *Dungeon* scene is to be thought of as taking place in that very tower which Goethe

must at that time so often have passed with terror and pity. Here
Gretchen was sitting as a prisoner, awaiting her sentence full of
fear. The poet himself may not have suffered much less, until the
writing of the *Dungeon* scene had relieved him of the worst).[32]
Again Schneider says of Susanna Brandt: "Das beklagenswerte
Wesen . . . scheint im Weltenplan seine Aufgabe erfüllt und die
Unsterblichkeit verdient zu haben. . . . Ihr dankt die Menschheit
den entscheidenden Impuls zur Erschaffung einer ewigen Dichtung" (The lamentable creature seems to have fulfilled her mission
in the cosmic plan and earnt immortality. To her, mankind owes
the decisive impulse for the creation of an eternal poetic work).[33]
There is surely something wrongheaded about this attempt to co-
ordinate art and real life at the very point where they remain most
intransigently separate from one another. Just as hard words break
no bones, so also the tenderest and most inspired words even of the
greatest poet heal no bones. That for anybody in the terrible plight
of Susanna Brandt there might be some kind of compensation,
redemption, or consolation in the fact of his after all having given
occasion to a great work of art is the thought rather of an academic
critic than of a poet.

It is hardly one of the necessary or legitimate tasks of the critic,
to attempt thus rashly with the aid only of his own imagination
to reconstruct the innermost processes of such a mind as Goethe's,
who has "an inborn knowledge of the world," especially of the
"sphere of love, hatred, hope and despair, and all the other states
and passions of the soul," by "anticipation." For such a mind a
very little experience can go a very long way. It can even sometimes
happen that a poet's experience is as much inspired by his work as
his work by his experience; something of the kind seems to have
happened to the youthful Goethe himself between the moment
when he first conceived of *Werther*, on hearing of the suicide in
Jerusalem in November, 1772, and the time when he actually
wrote it nearly a year and half later. More important than the
particular private experiences that may have helped to inspire the
Gretchen tragedy is the fact that it would in any case have been
impossible for him in those Storm and Stress years to go on working
at *Faust* for long, without bringing in "love" as he understood it,
that is to say a conception of love alien to the spirit of the Faust

legend and anachronistic in the early sixteenth-century world of the historical Faust—just as he brought such love into *Götz von Berlichingen* and *Egmont* and even into the fragmentary Prometheus drama of 1773. The Faust tradition did indeed afford one legitimate opportunity for the unfolding of some kind of love interest, in the Helena episode, and we can accept as reliable Goethe's repeated declarations during the last years of his life that he had from the outset intended to deal with that episode, and to deal with it moreover in a way not so very dissimilar to that which we actually find his adopting in 1800 and in 1825–1826. But this Helena motif was too remote and fantastic to give proper scope for that realistic, warm-blooded, and tender treatment of love which was alone truly congenial to the still youthful Goethe, and it was inevitable that he should either deliberately or involuntarily supplement it with something more after his own heart, however intrinsically incongruous with the idea of Faust it might be. Once he had, it matters little under the influence of what particular private experiences, grafted such a problematic scion on the Faust theme, in the form of the story of Gretchen, it threatened to flourish like a parasite at the expense of the parent tree. The task of finding his way backward and forward from the brilliant digression of the Gretchen tragedy to the Faust legend proper was still not even attempted when Goethe left Frankfort for Weimar in 1775, but this does not prove that at that time Gretchen was in his eyes, as is sometimes maintained, a valid substitute for Helen of Troy, still less that the Gretchen tragedy was in his eyes, as is sometimes also maintained, a valid substitute for the Faust tragedy, so that there was no need for anything else to follow upon it.

Certain vestigiary rudiments of the authentic Faust theme are indeed already present in the first four scenes of the *Urfaust*, above all in the opening one, but we cannot set about estimating or interpreting them without making up our minds whether they were produced before or after Goethe allowed himself to be diverted from that authentic Faust theme into the *cul-de-sac* of the Gretchen tragedy. Here, however, during the last twenty-five years or so, the Higher Critics and the hunters after autobiographical sources of inspiration with their theories, which could otherwise be disregarded as at least innocuous, have in a loose but formidable alliance with one another made themselves masters of the field. For anybody who looks at the *Urfaust* openmindedly in all its bearings, that is, in its relationship to the Faust legend and idea and to what we know of Goethe as a personality and an artist, it must seem extremely improbable that he should have embarked on the Gretchen tragedy before he had written the opening scene with the invocation of the Erdgeist. It is in that scene alone of the entire *Urfaust* that Faust really does appear as Faust; here and here alone, the youthful Goethe is, so to speak, truly on the rails in his treatment of the Faust theme, and he had to be on them, before he could go off them. This is the view of Emil Staiger, who wrote in 1952 with special reference to Beutler's discoveries about Susanna Brandt: "Mit welchem Faust hat Goethe begonnen? Biographische Dokumente scheinen auf die Gretchentragödie zu deuten. Die Gretchentragödie ist aber durch das Volksbuch und das Puppenspiel gar nicht vorbereitet. Faust heisst zunächst der Mann, der am Pult unruhig auf seinem Sessel sitzt und alle vier Fakultäten verwünscht. Wer dies bedenkt, erklärt: zuerst hat Goethe den Monolog . . . verfasst" (With which Faust did Goethe begin? Biographical documents seem to indicate that it was with the Gretchen tragedy. But the Gretchen tragedy is something for which there is no precedent at all in the chapbook and marionette play. Faust means, to begin with, the man who sits restlessly in his armchair cursing all four Faculties. He who takes this into consideration will declare: the first thing Goethe wrote was the [opening] monologue).[34] Similarly Burdach, writing some eight years before Beutler's revelations, maintained that the opening monologue was our "sicherer Massstab für Wertung des frühesten Faustplans" (our reliable criterion for estimating the earliest Faust plan).[35] Staiger, as one of the greatest living critics, can afford thus simply to defy the academic disintegrationists; but not even his authority can empower the rest of us to do so. If we do, we shall have such taunts levelled at us as that "die vornehmste Beweisführung des Philologen, die philologische nämlich," seems to us "bedeutungslos oder ungangbar zu sein" (the paramount line of reasoning of the scholar, namely the scholarly line, [seems to us] meaningless or impracticable),[36] or that we are "unscrupulous amateurs."[37] Unless these disintegrationists can be met and coped with fairly on their own ground, even an Emil Staiger is theoretically in danger of being dismissed as unscholarly and amateurish. For though they differ very much amongst themselves as to which section of *Faust* was written first, they unanimously declare that it cannot (with the possible exception of lines 1–32) have been the opening scene, which few of them regard as much more than a particularly eligible object for the exercising of their arts, or value highly for its own sake, though it is the finest thing in the entire *Urfaust*, superior in its own way to the Gretchen tragedy. Most of them are inclined to see it as a mosaic of passages of widely differing dates, but in its main substance as the last part of the *Urfaust* to be written. Herein they remain true to their worthy forerunner, Luden, who said with reference to *Faust, ein Fragment* in his memorable conversation with Goethe of 1806: "Zuletzt von Allem schien mir der Monolog gedichtet zu sein, mit welchem Faust das Fragment eröffnet. Der Hans Lüderlich sollte zu Ehren gebracht, es sollte ihm ein Empfehlungsschreiben an die Welt mitgegeben werden, damit man ihn zuliesse, auch in honnete Gesellschaft" (The last part of all to be written seems to me to be the monologue with which Faust opens the Fragment. It was a matter of whitewashing the debauchee and giving him a letter of recommendation to the world, so that he could be admitted even in respectable company). Hermann Schneider (1949) indeed believes that the first thirty-two lines of the opening scene are one of the earliest parts of *Faust* to be written, though still not the very earliest, and would date them almost to a day, about Easter, 1770, shortly after Goethe's arrival in Strasburg, when there was an opportunity for him to see the old popular Dr. Faustus drama performed in that city by Ilgner's troupe: "Und man mag sich ausmalen, dass Goethe, von der Aufführung heimkehrend, in dem edlen Trieb des Bessermachens sich Gedanken und Bau des Eröffnungsmonologs durch den Kopf gehen liess und zuhause alsbald am Schreibtisch sass oder nach kurzem Schlaf um Mitternacht 'wie ein Toller' aus dem Bette fuhr, um den neuen Faustprolog zu Papier zu bringen" (One can imagine Goethe on his way back from the performance, pondering in a noble urge to emulation over the ideas and structure of the opening monologue and then, on arriving home, sitting straight down at his desk or jumping out of bed at midnight "like a madman," after a brief sleep, in order to commit to paper his own new Faust prologue).[38] Of course one can imagine such things; the point is whether one has any business to do so. In any case Schneider, who is a good example of the way in which a fundamentally sound critic can allow himself to be intimidated by the superspecialists into accommodating his penetrating ideas to their theories and discoveries, not only dates the first thirty-two lines of the opening monologue too early, but also the rest of it, with the all-important invocation of the Erdgeist, long after the inception of the Gretchen tragedy, which is too late.

There will be more to say in another connexion about this constant and still flourishing practice of dismembering the opening monologue, which goes back always to the microscopic mind of Scherer, some of whose arguments are, however, anticipated as early as 1806 by Luden. Those who maintain that the opening scene of the *Urfaust* was the last to be written have, it must be admitted, one interesting piece of external evidence to which they can appeal in support of their higher-critical deductions and intuitions. In 1854 a certain Gubitz published in a biographical sketch of Knebel, who had died some twenty years previously, an anecdote communicated to him by a relative of the latter: "Merkwürdig ist, dass ihm (Knebel) Goethe schon damals (that is, in December, 1774) eine der letzten Szenen des Faust vorlas, und die ersten Szenen gar noch nicht vorhanden waren" (A curious thing is that Goethe at that early date read to Knebel one of the last scenes of *Faust*, and that the first scenes were still not in existence).[39] Knebel certainly seems to have laid claim to some special inside knowledge about the genesis of *Faust*. This emerges from Luden's statement that, immediately after his memorable conversation with Goethe of August 19, 1806, Knebel said to him: "Sie haben vielleicht nicht ganz unrecht mit Ihrer Konjektur über die Entstehung des Faust. Ich glaube fast, und nicht aus schlechten Gründen, Ihre Vermutung könnte so ziemlich richtig sein" (Perhaps you are not so wrong with your conjecture about the genesis of *Faust*. I almost think, and not without good grounds, that your supposition might be more or less correct).[40] In 1928, however, a far more reliable piece of evidence turned up, which throws new and unexpected light on this whole question, namely a letter written by Knebel himself on January 11,

1775 to F. H. von Einsiedel from Strasburg. Here Knebel says: "Um Ihnen noch den Inbegriff von meiner und unser aller Weisheit mitzuteilen, so hab' ich Ihnen den Anfang der ersten Szene aus Göthens Doktor Faust abgeschrieben, den Sie sogleich Wieland mitteilen müssen" (To give you the quintessence of my wisdom and of the wisdom of us all I have copied out for you the beginning of the first scene of Goethe's Dr. Faust, which you must at once communicate to Wieland).[41] Knebel's words: "den Inbegriff von meiner und unser aller Weisheit," can only refer to Faust's opening monologue: "Hab nun ach die Philosophei . . ." Knebel and Karl August had not remained more than three days in Frankfort in December, 1774. It must have been on December 11 that Goethe read "one of the last scenes" to Knebel, and on the same day, or at most one day later, he entrusted him with the manuscript of *Faust* containing, according to Knebel's own contemporary testimony, the opening scene. We can only assume either that Knebel's memory deceived him at a remove of some thirty years after this event, or that Luden and Gubitz's informant both misunderstood him and gave garbled accounts of what he said. Heinrich Spiess, who maintains that the invocation of the Erdgeist was not written till autumn, 1775, tries to get round the evidence of Knebel's letter by suggesting that the "erste Szene" communicated to Knebel was still incomplete, breaking off after line sixty-four:[42] this is a typical example of the flimsy hypotheses resorted to in such cases. What is most likely still to have been missing in the manuscript entrusted to Knebel is the "Auerbachs Keller" scene, which can on cogent linguistic and other grounds hardly be dated before Goethe's Swiss journey of summer, 1775, and possibly also the scene between Mephisto and the Student.

The years in which we can be absolutely certain that Goethe was working on the *Urfaust* are 1773–1775. Its close resemblance in language, tone and sentiment to his known other writings of these years would alone be sufficient evidence of this. But we have also external documentary testimony for it. For the year 1775 there are the letters of September and October to Auguste von Stolberg and Merck quoted above. For the year 1774 there is this important statement to Eckermann, which is also of interest for the light it throws on the original *Urfaust* manuscript: "Der Faust entstand

mit meinem Werther; ich brachte ihn im Jahre 1775 mit nach
Weimar. Ich hatte ihn auf Postpapier geschrieben und nichts daran
gestrichen; denn ich hütete mich, eine Zeile niederzuschreiben, die
nicht gut war und die nicht bestehen konnte" (*Faust* was written
about the same time as my *Werther*; I brought it with me to
Weimar in 1775. I had written it on post paper and deleted nothing
in it; for I had taken care not to write down a line that was not
good and fit to stand unaltered).[43] About autumn, 1774, indeed,
rumours began to circulate in German literary circles that Goethe's
Faust was "fast fertig" (almost completed) and on the point of
publication. For the year 1773 we have the declaration in a letter
of Goethe's to Zelter of May 11, 1820 that "ein wichtiger Teil des
Faust" (an important section of *Faust*) was written about the same
time as *Satyros* and the fragmentary Prometheus drama, which can
be fairly reliably dated in late summer and autumn of that year.
The documentary evidence that Goethe was already working on
Faust in the preceding year, 1772, is less conclusive, but there are
intrinsically no objections on grounds of language, tone and sentiment to the view that he may very well have done so, since no
radical turning-point in his development separates the two years,
or the work he is known to have produced in them, from one another. The one document we have to go by here is the letter in
Knittel verse written to Goethe in summer, 1773, by Gotter in acknowledgment of the just published drama, *Götz von Berlichingen*,
and concluding with the words:

Schick mir dafür den Doktor Faust,
Sobald Dein Kopf ihn ausgebraust!*

Gotter here, for the sake of a grotesque rhyme, humorously uses
the word "ausgebraust," which implies a violent process of composition, in an unprecedented transitive way, and this has led to
disputes as to exactly what he means. It was only in summer, 1772,
in Wetzlar, that Gotter had been together with Goethe, and the
most natural, though not the only possible interpretation of his
words is that Goethe had during those Wetzlar months at least

* Send me in return your Dr. Faust, / As soon as your head has "extrava-
sated" it!

spoken to him about his Faust plans and perhaps even read to him some already existing scenes or passages. Our other piece of documentary evidence for the year 1772 is more problematic. In Book XII of *Dichtung und Wahrheit* Goethe writes with reference to his first visit to Darmstadt in March of that year: "*Faust* war schon vorgerückt, *Götz von Berlichingen* baute sich nach und nach in meinem Geiste zusammen" (Some progress had already been made with *Faust*; *Götz von Berlichingen* was gradually taking shape in my mind). Goethe's memory was certainly deceiving him when he stated, at a remove of over forty years, that *Götz von Berlichingen* was only beginning to take shape in his mind in March, 1772, as the first version of that drama had been completed three months before that. The possibility must therefore be reckoned with that his memory was also deceiving him, when he spoke in the same sentence of "some progress having been made with Faust" by March, 1772. The passage is indeed sometimes appealed to as evidence that Goethe had begun work on *Faust* before he began work on *Götz von Berlichingen* in October, 1771, but it obviously only betrays that he had in 1813 but vague, inexact recollections about the commencement of the latter and perhaps also of the former drama. Hanna Fischer-Lamberg is certainly right when she says that the statement about *Faust* in *Dichtung und Wahrheit*, Book XII does not apply to the very beginning of Goethe's association with the Darmstadt circle, but to the later phases as well, and has no precise chronological significance.[44]

The most explicit and specific evidence we have as to when Goethe began work on *Faust* is largely negative, but none the less valuable for that. In the tenth book of *Dichtung und Wahrheit* Goethe writes with reference to the Strasburg years 1770 and 1771:

Am sorglichsten verbarg ich ihm [Herder] das Interesse an gewissen Gegenständen, die sich bei mir eingewurzelt hatten und sich nach und nach zu poetischen Gestalten ausbilden wollten. Es war *Götz von Berlichingen* und *Faust* . . . Die bedeutende Puppenspielfabel des andern klang und summte gar vieltönig in mir wieder. Auch ich hatte mich in allem Wissen umhergetrieben und war früh genug auf die Eitelkeit desselben hingewiesen worden. Ich hatte es auch im Leben auf allerlei Weise versucht und war immer unbefriedigter und gequälter zurückgekommen. Nun trug ich diese Dinge, so wie manche andere, mit mir herum und ergetzte mich daran in einsamen Stunden, ohne jedoch etwas davon aufzuschreiben.*

The close analogy postulated here by Goethe between his own twenty-one-year-old student self and the middle-aged professor and magician Faust is indeed, like many other such all too schematic attempts in *Dichtung und Wahrheit* to explain his works auto-biographically, far from convincing. Such disillusionment as he occasionally felt in those years was very different in intensity and duration and also in its objects from that which he bodies forth by "anticipation" and "inborn knowledge" in the character of Faust. In other respects, however, this passage makes a more reliable impression, and entitles us to believe that Goethe only in the Strasburg years seriously began to contemplate writing a Faust drama of his own, and that he only actually began to write it after his return to Frankfort. This fits in with his remark in the letter to Salzmann of October, 1771, that during the Strasburg months he had "mehr gedacht als getan" (thought more than he had performed). The balance of probabilities also seems in favour of his not having made a proper start on *Faust* until he had finished the first version of "Götz von Berlichingen," which must have engrossed all his powers, that is to say not before 1772.

This is the most widely, but by no means universally, accepted view. There are still many who would date the beginnings of *Faust* very much earlier than 1772. They appeal above all to Goethe's frequent declarations during the years 1826–1832 that the second part of *Faust*, on which he was then working, particularly the

---

* I was particularly careful to conceal from Herder my interest in certain subjects which had taken roots within me and were gradually seeking to unfold themselves in poetic figures. They were Götz von Berlichingen and Faust. The notable puppet-play of the latter murmured and reverberated within me in a multitude of tones. I too had engaged in the pursuit of all kinds of knowledge and had discovered early enough how futile it is. I too had launched out into life in the most various ways and always come back more and more dissatisfied and tormented. I now ruminated on these things, and on many others too, taking my delight in them during my hours of solitude, but without committing anything to paper.

Helena episode, almost exactly corresponded to his "älteste Konzeption," and that the earliest conception was sixty years old. Thus he wrote to Nees von Esenbeck on May 25, 1827 of "der dreitausendjährigen Helena, der ich *nun schon sechzig Jahre* nachschleiche" (the three-thousand-year-old Helen of Troy, on whose trail I have been creeping *for sixty years now*); and five years later, on March 17, 1832, he similarly wrote to Humboldt: "Es sind *über sechzig Jahre*, dass die Konzeption des *Faust* bei mir jugendlich, von vorne herein klar, die ganze Reihenfolge hin weniger ausführlich vorlag" (*Over sixty years ago* the conception of *Faust* stood clearly before my youthful eyes from the outset, the entire sequence less in detail). These statements are immensely important as evidence that Goethe did not, as so many critics postulate, begin writing *Faust* at random, without knowing what he was getting at, but had from the outset a "conception" of the whole work before him, and moreover a conception which, if we can take his word for it, tallied substantially with what he ultimately made out of it. We learn from them, if they are trustworthy, as they probably are, something about the lines on which Goethe's mind moved when the Faust legend was "murmuring and reverberating through it in a multitude of tones" during the Strasburg years, and we recognize that they are just the lines on which we should, in view of the existing tradition and the intrinsic idea of Faust, have expected it to move. But how worthless these same statements are for the exact dating of the beginnings of Goethe's work on *Faust* emerges from the fact of his having told Kraukling on August 31, 1828, that the Helen of Troy episode was "eine *fünfzigjährige* Konzeption" (a *fifty-year* old conception); and of his having said to Eckermann on December 6, 1829: "Da die Konzeption so alt ist und ich *seit fünfzig Jahren* darüber nachdenke" (as the conception is so old and I have been pondering on it for *fifty* years), and continuing, "Die Erfindung des ganzen zweiten Teiles ist wirklich so alt, wie ich sage" (The invention of the entire second part really is as old as I have said). And less than four months before writing to Humboldt that the conception of *Faust* was "over sixty years old" he had informed him in a letter of December 1, 1831, that the second part had been "seit *fünfzig* Jahren in seinen Zwecken und Motiven durchgedacht" (thought out in its aims and motives for *fifty* years). These are, as

was pointed out by Minor in 1901,[45] simply round figures to which
no exact chronological significance attaches; whether he says "sixty"
or "fifty" years makes no difference. The same is true of the much
quoted phrase in the letter to Zelter of June 1, 1831: "Es ist keine
Kleinigkeit, das, was man im *zwanzigsten* Jahre konzipiert hat, im
82. ausser sich darzustellen" (It is no trifle to bring forth in one's
eighty-second year what one had conceived in one's *twentieth*).
This was not the kind of occasion on which Goethe could have
been expected to stop and ask himself: Now exactly how old was
I when the old Faust puppet-play began to murmur and reverberate
within me in Strasburg? It can actually not have been till after his
twenty-first birthday. None of these general utterances with their
round figures—in another letter to Zelter, of September 4, 1831, he
merely says "seit *so vielen* Jahren" (for *so many* years)—is inconsistent with the preciser statement in *Dichtung und Wahrheit* that
he meditated much on the Faust theme and how he should treat
it when he was a student in Strasburg, without committing anything to paper until somewhat later. But the round figures *"sixty
years"* (not, of course, the more frequently occurring "fifty") and
"in one's *twentieth* year" are again and again interpreted literally as
evidence that *Faust* was planned and even begun as early as 1769
or still earlier. These same round figures may also have been in part
responsible for the dates 1769–1808 given by Riemer and Eckermann in 1836 for the commencement and conclusion of *Faust I* in
their by no means throughout reliable chronological list of
Goethe's works. The year given for the conclusion, 1808, is patently
a false date: *Faust I*, though published in that year, was completed
in 1806 or rather, as will be seen, for practical purposes in 1801.
And 1769 is just as likely to be false for the commencement. Riemer
and Eckermann may also have been misled by the circumstance
that Goethe in his *Annalen* treats the year 1769 as the beginning
of the new epoch of his development which terminated with his
departure for Weimar in 1775, the epoch now usually referred to
as his Storm and Stress years, to which the *Urfaust* belongs. But
that new epoch did not really begin until he met Herder in Strasburg in September, 1770. In the year 1769 he was still marking time
in a much subdued and comparatively unproductive state of mind
after the breakdown of his first venture into the world as a student

in Leipzig, and the one work he did then complete, the comedy in Molière's manner, *Die Mitschuldigen* ("The Companions in Guilt") remains with its alexandrines, and in all other respects, well within the Gallican and Gottschedian convention of Enlightenment classicism, as do all his other known dramatic projects of that year. He was still in this subdued state of mind during the first weeks in Strasburg, in spring, 1770, when Schneider imagines him leaping out of bed like a madman to write the first thirty-two lines of Faust's opening monologue. The sort of thing Goethe was really writing in those very days was: "Wie ich war, so bin ich noch, nur dass ich mit unserem Herre Gott etwas besser stehe, und mit seinem lieben Sohn Jesu Christo. Draus folgt denn, dass ich auch etwas klüger bin und erfahren habe, was das heisst: die Furcht des Herrn ist der Weisheit Anfang" (I still am as I was, except that I am on a somewhat better footing with our Lord God and with his dear Son Jesus Christ. It arises from this that I am also a little more sensible and have discovered the meaning of the words: The fear of the Lord is the beginning of wisdom).[46] It can hardly have been in this frame of mind that Goethe penned Faust's defiant sneers at theology and all traditional Christian beliefs. Before not much more than a year had elapsed Goethe had obtained for himself in Strasburg the reputation of being "ein wahnsinniger Religionsverächter" (a crazy despiser of religion),[47] and shocked Professor Metzger by maintaining "que Jésus Christ n'était pas le fondateur de notre religion, mais que quelques autres savants l'avaient faite sous son nom; que la religion chrétienne n'était autre chose qu'une saine politique etc." (that Jesus Christ was not the founder of our religion, but that certain other *savants* had devised it in his name; that the Christian religion was nothing more than sound politics, etc.).[48] Here in Strasburg, between Easter, 1770, and summer, 1771, lies the real turning point in the youthful Goethe's development, before which he cannot reasonably be imagined to have begun or even to have planned his *Faust* drama. Yet this one great, obvious dividing line is regularly disregarded by the microscopic Faust interpreters, who set up instead various quite arbitrary dividing lines of their own within the comparatively homogeneous period from 1771 to 1775. To distinguish on internal grounds alone between what Goethe could or could not have writ-

ten before or after 1773 or 1774 within that period is an impossible
task, as is demonstrated by those who so assiduously and dictatori-
ally claim to be able to do it. Not to be able to distinguish on
internal grounds alone between what he could or could not have
written before or after 1771, on the other hand, is to convict oneself of intellectual myopia. There is, in fact, not a word of truth
in the favourite postulate on which the hypotheses of the "Higher
Critics" about the Urfaust all depend, that, to quote Enders,
Goethe "sich doch sonst zu keiner Zeit im Stil so energisch und
periodisch entwickelt" (Goethe's style at no time develops so energetically and in distinct phases)[49] as in the years 1772–1775.

Those who seek the solution of the knottiest Faust problems in
old cabbalistic and alchemistic texts tend often to assert that the
year 1769, when Goethe is known to have studied such texts, must
also have been the year in which he at least planned and perhaps
actually wrote not only certain sections of the Urfaust, but also
much else that either appeared for the first time in the Fragment
of 1790 and in Faust I in 1808, or has completely vanished and can
only be reconstructed from the Paralipomena and similar indirect
evidence. Thus Agnes Bartscherer would date the bulk of the opening monologue and also part of the Spaziergang vor dem Tor (first
published in 1808) in 1769 or in the first three months of 1770,
and Grumach, writing in 1952–1953, similarly dates even the
"Prolog im Himmel" and works out in considerable detail a hypothetical scheme of Faust as Goethe must originally have planned
it in 1769 on the basis of Welling's Opus mago-cabbalisticum. According to Agnes Bartscherer, Goethe, on the strength only of
having read Paracelsus, "habe die Eingangsszene . . . auch schreiben
können, hätte er Faustbuch, Puppenspiel und Volksdrama nie
gekannt" (could have written the opening scene of Faust without
ever having known the Faust chapbook, puppet-play or popular
drama).[50] Producing one parallel that seems to her conclusive, she
exclaims: "Dann schwindet auch der Hauptanlass, die Konzeption
des Dramas im Jahre 1769 in Zweifel zu ziehen. Goethe brauchte
nicht erst unter den Einfluss Herders zu geraten, brauchte nicht
erst Stürmer und Dränger zu werden" (Then the chief ground for
questioning 1769 as the date of the conception of Goethe's Faust
disappears. There was no need for him to come under the influence

of Herder first, or to become a Storm and Stress poet first).[51] But the "chief ground" for questioning 1769 as the date of Goethe's embarking on *Faust* is not a matter of parallels, but of his poetic development. There are far too many parallels to the opening monologue of *Faust*; one stumbles upon them right and left in the literature of all ages and all countries. Since men first learnt to write books, they have regularly tended to turn away from them in disgust. There was no need for Goethe to encounter either Herder or Paracelsus to discover *that*.

The distinction of being the very first scenes of the *Urfaust* to be written is claimed also for the dialogue between Mephisto and the Student and for the "Auerbachs Keller" scene, both of which are on the ground of their crudely boisterous humour often assigned to the Leipzig university years 1767 or 1768. Here again the pioneer is Luden, who said to Goethe in August, 1806:

> Die Szene in Auerbachs Keller schien mir zu allererst geschrieben zu sein. Sie ist so frisch, so lebendig, so jugendlich, so burschikos, dass ich geschworen haben würde, sie sei in Leipzig von dem Dichter-Studiosus geschrieben oder gedichtet worden. Die zweite Szene, die nach dem Auftritt im Keller gedichtet worden, schien mir der Auftritt zwischen dem Schüler und Mephistopheles. Diese Szene ist gleichfalls so frisch, so lebendig und wahr, dass sie nur aus der unmittelbaren Anschauung des Lebens und Treibens auf der Universität . . . hervorgegangen sein muss.*

Hermann Hefele, writing in 1931, similarly asserts that "Auerbachs Keller" is "zweifellos der älteste Bestandteil der Urfaustdichtung" (undoubtedly the oldest section of the *Urfaust*), and expressly argues, as do also Max Morris and Roethe, that the style is too immature for the year 1775, to which, as has already been seen,[52] the external evidence points. In 1926 Schuchardt revived the theory

---

* This scene in Auerbach's Cellar appeared to me the very first to have been written. It is so fresh, so full of life, so youthful, so free and easy, that I could have sworn it was written in Leipzig by the student-poet. The next scene to be written after "Auerbach's Cellar" seemed to me the dialogue between the student and Mephisto. This scene too is so fresh, so full of life and truth, that it can only have proceeded from firsthand observation of university goings-on.

already propounded in 1891 by Seuffert that the dialogue between
Mephisto and the Student is the oldest part of *Faust* and a product
of the Leipzig years, probably written at first only as a self-contained
farce to satirize university life in general and then later adapted to
the theme of the *Faust* drama, which somehow arose out of it, by
the transforming of what was originally just the caricature of a
professor, perhaps Gottsched, into Mephisto masquerading as
Faust. Amongst those who accept this intricate theory of Schuchardt's is Hermann Schneider, who asserts in 1949 that, even if
the student scene itself was not actually written in Leipzig, a
precursor of it most certainly must have been. Schuchardt's most
powerful argument in defence of his hypothesis is a by no means
convincing parallel between a couplet in Gottsched's specimen
Knittel verses and two lines in the Student scene, which belong,
however, to the additions made by Goethe to that scene in 1788
or 1789 and are not present in the *Urfaust* version. The circumstance that the Student scene, as it stands in the *Urfaust*, contains one of the finest Storm and Stress passages in the entire
work, Mephisto's ironical encomium on the study of logic, is
accounted for by Schuchardt with the characteristic higher critical
hypothesis that the best part of that encomium must be a later
interpolation. Burger[53] would treat the entire passage on logic as
a later interpolation, while Hermann Schneider,[54] on the strength
of another supposed parallel, this time to Scherenberg's *Spiel von
Frauen Jutten* (1480), demonstrates that just this passage must
have been written in the Leipzig years, and concludes that Goethe's
work on his great tragedy must have begun with the "heiterer
Fremdkörper" (extraneous *jeu d'esprit*) of the Student scene:
"Das war ein würdiger Auftakt für das Faustdrama eines jungen
Aufklärers" (That was a worthy point of departure for the Faust
drama of a youthful Enlightenment poet). This quite leaves out
of account the stridently anti-Enlightenment character of the
entire scene, especially of the encomium on logic. One grave objection to this early dating of the Student scene, that Goethe in
some draft notes for *Dichtung und Wahrheit* speaks of his experiences at the University of Strasburg in the years 1770 and 1771
as having helped to inspire it, is hushed up or brushed on one
side by such critics as Schuchardt, Burger, and Hermann Schneider.

Schuchardt in particular, who intimidates us by presenting his great discovery as "eine unabweisbare Tatsache" (an irrefutable fact), is a worthy partner of Luden, Scherer, and Roethe in the mysteries of higher criticism.

One of the first postulates of these critics would seem to be that no validity attaches to such utterances of Goethe himself as: "Bei jedem Kunstwerk, gross oder klein, bis ins Kleinste, kommt alles auf die *Konzeption* an" (In every work of art, great or small, down to the very smallest, everything depends upon the *conception*). (*Maximen und Reflexionen*) They assume that nothing at all depends upon the conception, that Goethe produced the entire *Urfaust* piecemeal, without having or needing to have any conception, beginning at the least important point. They can indeed appeal on this issue to Goethe himself, who seems sometimes to contradict his own declaration about the all-importance of the "conception," as, for example, when he said to H. Meyer on March 21, 1806: "Von allen seinen poetischen Werken sei keines mit klarem Verstande dessen, was gemacht werden solle und müsse, sondern bloss durch ein Gefühl, eine Ahndung, das sei das Rechte, entstanden, ohne weiteres Räsonnement darüber" (Not a single one of his poetic works was produced with a clear understanding of what should and ought to be done, but only through a feeling, an intuition that it was the right thing, without any further ratiocination about it). This, though not literally, is no doubt substantially true. No intelligent critic would suggest that Goethe's original conception of *Faust*, as it took shape in his mind during the Strasburg years, was a carefully thought-out and constructed plan on paper such as is recognisable at the back of all Lessing's and Schiller's dramas; it was rather a matter of "feeling," of "intuition," of an imaginative vision, with little of "dramatic algebra" about it. But as such it must have been a comprehensive vision, the sense of an organic whole. To begin with the parts and then to combine them to a whole is the practice of the "clear understanding" rather than of the intuitive imagination, which tends usually, as Goethe himself again and again says in his scientific writings, to proceed in the opposite way. The original conception may indeed be, and often is, modified almost out of recognition before the work is completed; but it must be there, and unclear though it may be in points of detail, it will always be the conception of a coherent totality. A due sense of this leads Burdach to regard sceptically all theories that would make Goethe begin work on *Faust* during the Leipzig years, long before he can be supposed to have had any conception of the Faust drama as such: "Die vage Möglichkeit, (writes Burdach in 1932) dass Goethe ganz früh, vielleicht schon in der Leipziger . . . Studienzeit . . . die Szene des Tischzaubers gedichtet hätte, besteht natürlich, rein theoretisch betrachtet . . . Aber schon die Szene zwischen Mephistopheles und dem Schüler setzt den Plan eines *Faustdramas* voraus, weil sie allein in einem solchen Sinn hat." (Theoretically considered, the vague possibility exists of course that Goethe may very early, perhaps in his Leipzig student years, have written the *Auerbach's Cellar* scene. But even the scene between Mephisto and the Student presupposes the plan for a Faust drama, since it would only have any meaning within such a context).[55]

Schuchardt's supreme achievement in conjectural architectonics is his contention, also in the article of 1926 referred to above, that various scenes of the Gretchen tragedy were written in the Leipzig years as fragments of what was originally intended to be a light-hearted, more or less salacious, erotic comedy of student life: "Ein paar Jahre weiteren Wachstums und Vertiefung seines Gemüts, und der Dichter wird aus dem, was er zunächst als eine lustige Posse gesehen hatte, eine ergreifende Tragödie machen" (After a few years of further development and deepening of his spiritual life the poet will transform what he had originally envisaged as a jolly farce into a heart-rending tragedy).[56] One might in the same way argue that *Romeo and Juliet*, because it begins light-heartedly and has many salacious passages, was originally intended to be an improper comedy, and that Shakespeare only later decided to make a tragedy out of it. Schuchardt bases this theory of his largely on prosodic arguments, which quite leave out of account the possibility that Goethe may in the years 1772–1775 deliberately have cultivated metrical heterogeneity as the appropriate medium for the particular aim he had set before him in the Gretchen tragedy, namely to evoke synoptically "all Erden Weh und all ihr Glück" (all the woe of earthly life and all its bliss). Minds which can see any inconsistency between the more frivolous passages in the Gretchen tragedy and its essential purport would presumably also find it inconsistent that a man diving from a springboard walks away from the water before he runs towards it.

Although the critics who would date the beginnings of *Faust* long before 1772 have found a considerable following, and few have ventured to challenge their theories outright, the generally accepted view nowadays is that the first scene Goethe produced was "Trüber Tag. Feld," which, it is assumed, must have been inspired by the execution of Susanna Brandt on January 14, 1772 and written, if not on that very day, then immediately before or after it, and that it was followed not much later by the two remaining final scenes of the Gretchen tragedy, "Nacht. Offen Feld," and "Kerker." This is commonly regarded as an incontestable certainty and as the only possible point of departure for all discussion of the chronology of the *Urfaust*, and therefore too of the question, how Goethe first envisaged and set about writing the drama. It is here that the inquiries of the biographical interpreters, as represented by Beutler, and of the textual critics, as represented by Scherer and Roethe, converge and seem completely to corroborate one another. For long before Beutler's discoveries regarding Susanna Brandt, Scherer had argued that "Trüber Tag. Feld" must, on linguistic grounds, but above all because it is in prose at all, have been written in winter, 1771–1772, about the same time as or shortly after the first version of *Götz von Berlichingen*.

For minds exclusively dominated by higher critical principles the view that the last three scenes of the *Urfaust* were the first ones to be written is in no way problematic; it is indeed for them an eminently satisfactory result, just the kind of result they always hope and expect to find. But for others there is something disconcerting, if not spurious about it. If nothing more were involved than the possibility that Goethe may, so to speak, have written the Gretchen tragedy backwards, no serious problems would arise. For the Gretchen tragedy considered by itself, is, whatever anybody may say to the contrary, as coherent and rounded-off a work of art as it was intended to be; and it can be fully understood and appreciated as such without there being any real need for us to know what private experiences may have helped to inspire it or how long it took Goethe to produce it or in what exact order the scenes composing it were written. Such questions are only really important, and the answers to them are only really illuminating and relevant, in those frequent enough cases where an author has obviously wavered in or radically modified his original poetic intention, overshot it or fallen short of it, or allowed something extraneous to divert him from it; and there is no sound reason for supposing that any of these things happened to Goethe in respect of the Gretchen tragedy, once he had fairly embarked upon it. We happen to know that he must have worked on it intermittently for about three years, but it is aesthetically as much of a piece as if he had completed it within not much more than three months. This was achieved, however, at the expense of the Faust theme and the Faust idea proper. Goethe's very success with the so congenial Gretchen tragedy meant a *débâcle* with the actual Faust drama, a *débâcle* which he was still unable to retrieve in 1788 and 1789, which he only partially retrieved in the years 1797–1801 and did not completely retrieve till 1831. So, while it matters very little whether the opening or the closing scenes of the Gretchen tragedy were written first, it is disturbing to be called upon to believe, or rather to be peremptorily forbidden to doubt that Goethe began work on the Gretchen tragedy before he had done anything about the *Faust* drama proper. Yet that is precisely what we are at the present juncture of scholarship and criticism forbidden to doubt, namely, as Hans Albert Maier puts it, that "Goethe plante seinen Faust, als er vom Schicksal der Brandt erschüttert wurde." (Goethe planned his Faust when he was shattered by the fate of Susanna Brandt).[57] It is not easy to see how the idea of a *Faust* drama could ever have arisen out of that particular experience, the obviously natural and appropriate expression of which would have been in the form of the more or less realistic domestic tragedy. There are some who see no problems here at all and even ignore Goethe's own statement that he had at least been intensively meditating upon the Faust theme while he was still a student in Strasburg. Those who do see serious difficulties here have devised the most varied, elaborate, ingenious, but not convincing, theories to get round them. One of the troubles about all these theories is that they pile hypothesis upon hypothesis about things we do not know, can never know, and should resign ourselves to not knowing, and take us further and further away from what we actually possess and can be sure of—the text of the *Urfaust*. This affects above all the interpretation of the opening scene, which is regarded as not corresponding to any definite intention that Goethe ever had, but rather as the mere detritus of a number of successive intentions that he failed to carry out. One feels impelled to question whether the dating of the scene "Trüber Tag. Feld" in January, 1772, which has given rise to so many uncertainties, is really itself so certain as it is claimed to be. The fact that the Gretchen tragedy may well have been partly inspired by the fate of Susanna Brandt is not in itself evidence that that scene or any other scene in it must have been written immediately after her execution. The early comedy *Die Mitschuldigen* was not written till about a year after Goethe's distressing experiences with Käthchen Schönkopf, which are known chiefly to have inspired it. Some of the most important and vivid sections of the essay on the Strasburg Minster (*Von deutscher Baukunst*) were not written till over a year after Goethe had left Strasburg. Nearly two years elapsed between the experiences underlying *Werther* and the actual writing of the novel. Such a period of gestation between an experience and the large-scale poetic transfiguration of it is normal with the youthful Goethe, as it is with most poets. It remains to be seen what other arguments are advanced for Goethe's having begun the Gretchen tragedy with "Trüber Tag. Feld" in January, 1772, before he had made a start on the Faust theme proper.

4. *"Trüber Tag. Feld"*

THE DATING OF "Trüber Tag. Feld" is of special importance because it alone of all the sixteen scenes composing the Gretchen
tragedy contains certain definite allusions to Faust's adventures
before his meeting with Gretchen, particularly to the opening
monologue with the invocation of the Erdgeist. It thereby constitutes the sole link that holds together the two so disparate divisions into which the *Urfaust* falls, and, however sketchily, unites the
extraneous Gretchen story with the Faust theme proper. Infuriated
with Mephisto for having concealed from him the disaster that has
befallen Gretchen with the birth and killing of her child and with
her consequent flight, trial, and condemnation to death, Faust
bursts out:

> Hund! abscheuliches Untier! Wandle ihn, du unendlicher
> Geist, wandle den Wurm wieder in die Hundsgestalt, in der
> er sich nächtlicher Weile oft gefiel vor mir herzutrotten, dem
> harmlosen Wandrer vor die Füsse zu kollern und dem Um-
> stürzenden sich auf die Schultern zu hängen! Wandle ihn
> wieder in seine Lieblingsbildung, dass er vor mir im Sand
> auf dem Bauch krieche, ich ihn mit Füssen trete, den
> Verworfnen!*

* Dog! Abominable monster! Transform him, you infinite Spirit, transform
the worm back into the shape of a dog, in which he often liked to trot along
before me at night, rolling on the ground at the feet of the harmless wayfarer
and clinging to his shoulders when he tumbled over. Transform him back into
his favourite shape, so that he may crawl before me on his belly in the sand
and I may kick the wretch!

Mephisto, in the course of his reply, says jeeringly:

> Warum machst du Gemeinschaft mit uns, wenn du nicht
> mit uns auswirtschaften kannst? Willst fliegen und der Kopf
> wird dir schwindlich. Eh! Drangen wir uns dir auf oder du
> dich uns?†

Faust then once more apostrophizes the "infinite Spirit," this time
in the words:

> Grosser, herrlicher Geist, der du mir zu erscheinen würdig-
> test, der du mein Herz kennst und meine Seele, warum
> musstest du mich an den Schandgesellen schmieden, der sich
> am Schaden weidet und am Verderben sich letzt?‡

For the understanding of the *Urfaust*, which must necessarily be
the basis for our understanding of the entire Faust drama, everything depends on what we make of this last passage. As the text
stands—and it was, after all, put together by Goethe himself with
a full sense of poetic responsibility—it is impossible to see in the
"infinite, great and glorious Spirit" whom Faust here apostrophizes
anything other than the Erdgeist whom he invokes in the opening
monologue and who there appears before him. The natural assumption is that the opening monologue with the invocation of
the Erdgeist was already in existence when the scene "Trüber
Tag. Feld" was written, or at least that the two scenes, whichever
was the earlier of them, were written with no great interval of time
between them, that they belong together, have a common conception underlying them and therefore throw light upon one
another. Only on these assumptions, which were generally accepted
up to thirty or so years ago, can the *Urfaust* be seen as a genuine,
though fragmentary work of art, with a comprehensive intention
at the back of it, and not as a mere patchwork of disjointed
"scraps." But these are just the assumptions modern Goethe schol-

---

† Why did you enter into association with us, if you cannot stand the pace?
You want to fly, and your head swims. Eh! Did we force ourselves upon you,
or did you force yourself upon us?

‡ Great, glorious Spirit, you who deigned to appear before me, you who
know my heart and my soul, what made you chain me to the depraved companion who rejoices in mischief and revels in havoc?

arship almost unanimously forbids us to make, dismissing them as "naive" and "amateurish." It insists that, as Hans Albert Maier puts it, "die Erdgeistszene . . . sicher erst Jahre nach der Prosaszene ['Trüber Tag. Feld'] niedergeschrieben wurde" (the Spirit of Earth scene was certainly not written till years after the prose scene ["Dull Day. Field"]), and that therefore "bei der Niederschrift der Prosaszene die Erdgeistszene . . . in der uns bekannten Form gewiss *noch nicht konzipiert* war" (when the prose scene was produced the Spirit of Earth scene had assuredly . . . *not yet been conceived of* in the form in which we know it).[1] It assumes that Goethe's mental outlook, and with it his idea of Faust, had completely changed during the four or so years intervening between the two scenes, and that therefore the Spirit apostrophized by Faust in "Trüber Tag. Feld" can have nothing to do with the Spirit invoked by him in the opening scene. It assumes that the conceptions underlying the two scenes are entirely different from one another, indeed mutually contradictory, and is inclined to regard the invocation of the Erdgeist as a mere isolated episode which was never intended to have any further consequences for the action of the play. In fact, it has been ruled that the two scenes do not in any way hang together or throw any light on one another; the apparent connexion between them is dismissed as fortuitous, delusory, and misleading.

Some of the most important grounds for, and consequences of, this modern view will only become apparent when we consider the Erdgeist and the problems it raises. For the present it is to be noted that there is a real difficulty here, in face of which every thoughtful reader is compelled, whether he likes it or not, to resort in some measure to hypotheses of the kind so beloved by the "Higher Critics." For there is no denying that the passages quoted above from "Trüber Tag. Feld" and still retained with only a few insignificant verbal changes in the final text of *Faust,* as it was established in 1806, do betray remnants of an early plan that Goethe must at some point have abandoned and replaced with another. The reference to Mephisto often trotting before Faust at night in the form of a dog and playing tricks on "the unsuspecting wayfarer" presupposes a scene either actually presenting this or at least describing it, which was in all probability never written but only planned, and which, if it was indeed written, has not survived. What in some measure, but still only remotely, corresponds to it is Mephisto's first appearance before Faust in the form of a black poodle, at the end of the scene entitled "Spaziergang vor dem Tor," and there is no reason for believing that this was written before 1798, that is to say not till well over twenty years after "Trüber Tag. Feld." Nowhere, except in that scene, is there any suggestion throughout Goethe's drama of Mephisto's reappearing in dog-form after his first encounter with Faust. This is a motif from the old chapbooks, in which Mephisto regularly accompanies Faust in the guise of the black dog Praestigar, and seldom appears in any other shape, though he is not there represented as playing tricks on "the unsuspecting wayfarer." Similarly the very much more important reference to Faust's having been "chained" to his "depraved companion," Mephisto, by a "great, glorious Spirit" presupposes one or more scenes that Goethe in all probability only planned, and which, if they were indeed written, have not survived. All these postulated but non-existent scenes, it should be noted, can only be thought of as occupying positions somewhere between the opening scene and the beginning of the Gretchen tragedy, that is to say in what Goethe was himself regularly to refer to as "die grosse Lücke" (the great gap), a gap which the Student scene and "Auerbachs Keller" merely stood about in like two small, uncemented bricks, without in any way helping really to fill it, and which was not ultimately filled till after 1797. The first hypothesis these facts force us to adopt is that the extremely important point in the Faust story where Mephistopheles makes his initial appearance presented peculiar difficulties for Goethe, and that he was in doubt as to the best way of treating it, at least so far as the details were concerned, and, it would seem, went on putting off the writing of it till long after the years in which the *Urfaust* was produced. Once we realise this, we shall find it quite conceivable that he may have written the Student scene or "Auerbachs Keller," or even both, as late as 1775, in order at least to have something specifically Faustian to put in the baffling "great gap" and to counterbalance the Gretchen tragedy.

But to admit this much is also to admit the possibility that the "great, glorious Spirit" itself, who had "deigned" to appear before

Faust and who "knows his heart and soul" may be an entirely different spirit from the Erdgeist, and that what is referred to in "Trüber Tag. Feld" may not be the opening invocation scene known to us in the *Urfaust*, but some other scene of quite another character, either merely planned by Goethe but never written, or else perhaps actually written, but later replaced by the Erdgeist scene, which alone has survived. That this is theoretically possible is not to be denied. The only question is, as in all such cases, what necessity there is for assuming that it really is so. Only when every more simple, natural, and straightforward explanation has been demonstrated to be untenable is it legitimate to resort to complex, far-ranging hypotheses; and even then, any hypothesis more complex than the problem it is designed to solve or ranging far beyond it, should be regarded with suspicion. That is to say, if we find ourselves (as we indeed do) forced to postulate that Goethe's original plan for *Faust* did not remain unchanged, we should on principle satisfy ourselves that the assumption of *one* such change of plan will not adequately account for all the data, before we can legitimately assume, as so many critics do, that he changed it two, three, four, five, or many more times, or that he never had any definite plan at all. And just as the number of changes in plan we postulate should be kept down to the minimum required for a satisfactory explanation of all the data, so also should the extent of each individual change postulated. There may, indeed, as in the case of Goethe's *Tasso*, be compelling documentary grounds for assuming that an author has completely reversed his original intention, but where there are no such compelling grounds, we should assume that he has probably not altered his initial plan more than he had to. This is a restraint in the use of hypothesis dictated to us by the nature of reality, the economy of art, and the respect due to such a mind as Goethe's. We should remember that an artist never alters his original conception more often or more radically than he has to; it is not the sort of thing that even a Hölderlin does haphazard every five minutes, just for the fun of it. There is never any pleasure, but rather always much vexation for him in having to do it, as is testified by Goethe himself in the case of his already mentioned *Tasso*, about which he constantly complains in such terms as: "*Tasso* muss umgearbeitet werden; was da steht, ist zu

nichts zu brauchen; ich kann weder so endigen noch alles wegwer-
fen. Solche Mühe hat Gott den Menschen gegeben." (*Tasso* must
be recast; what there is of it cannot be utilized; I can neither complete it on the same lines nor simply scrap the lot of it. Such toil
does God impose on us mortals!)[2]

Representative modern *Faust* scholarship refuses to recognize
this principle of restraint in the devising and multiplying of hypotheses. What it believes in instead is, as Roethe puts it, "kühne
Konjekturalkritik grossen Stils" (bold conjectural criticism in the
grand style),[3] indulged in for its own sake, and the bolder and the
more conjectural the better. Neither qualitatively nor quantitatively
can such critics postulate enough changes in Goethe's *Faust* plans,
and they consequently make things far too easy for themselves in
their attempts to demonstrate that the difficulties and problems
arising out of the scene "Trüber Tag. Feld" are quite insoluble
in any natural, simple, straightforward way. They attach no importance to the circumstance that Goethe himself in 1806 incorporated that scene in the final text of *Faust*, without seeing any
need to eliminate from it allusions to events that have never occurred in the preceding parts of the play, and some of which are
even inconsistent with what does occur in it. They would apparently prefer to assume that Goethe only acted as he did on that
occasion because he was too indolent or too bored to do anything else, hoping nobody would notice anything amiss, or even
that he was too muddleheaded to notice anything amiss himself,
rather than that he knew what he was about. They do not admit
that what was evidently consistent enough for Goethe should be
consistent enough for us. They do not take into consideration
that the world of Faust is—by Goethe's own definition—a "Nebel-
welt" (a nebulous world),[4] a "Traum" (a dream),[5] and that in
such a nebulous dream-world the strict laws of consistency and
cause and effect, which dominate such a clearly focussed waking
world as that, say, of *Hermann und Dorothea*, do not obtain and
would indeed be out of place. Nine tenths of the "contradictions"
in *Faust* so triumphantly exposed by the "Higher Critics" are due
simply to Goethe's being engaged on a work that was meant by its
inmost laws to have something of the incoherency and inconsistency of dreams. Until this is realized, we shall still have people

writing, as Max Morris does, after he has reconstructed some five different plans he supposes Goethe to have had successively for the pact between Faust and Mephisto: "Goethe verzichtet also in diesem letzten Stadium darauf, irgend einen der bisherigen Pläne konsequent durchzuführen. Er stopft die Lücken, so gut es gehen will, in resigniert-ironischem Anschluss an das Volksbuch" (So Goethe at this last stage abandons the idea of carrying out any of his previous plans consistently. With ironical resignation he stops the gaps as best he can on the lines suggested by the chapbook).[6]

Another, more specific point to which the critics will not attach due importance is that Goethe had demonstrably in 1788 still not abandoned the plan adumbrated in "Trüber Tag. Feld" for filling the "great gap," although he was to abandon it some nine years later. For in that year he took the most important of the relevant passages in "Trüber Tag. Feld" and expanded it to Faust's blank verse soliloquy with which the new scene then produced, "Wald und Höhle," commences:

> Erhabner Geist, du gabst mir, gabst mir alles,
> Warum ich bat. Du hast mir nicht umsonst
> Dein Angesicht im Feuer zugewendet . . .
> . . . O dass dem Menschen nichts Vollkommnes wird,
> Empfind' ich nun. Du gabst zu dieser Wonne,
> Die mich den Göttern nah und näher bringt,
> Mir den Gefährten, den ich schon nicht mehr
> Entbehren kann, wenn er gleich, kalt und frech,
> Mich vor mir selbst erniedrigt, und zu Nichts,
> Mit einem Worthauch deine Gaben wandelt.*

If Goethe had in 1788 still not abandoned the plan of having Mephisto "given" or "chained" to Faust as a base companion by a great and noble Spirit that had deigned to appear before him,

---

* Sublime Spirit, you gave me, gave me everything / That I asked for. Not in vain did you / Turn your countenance towards me, encompassed with fire / . . . Oh now I feel that perfect fulfillment / Is not the lot of man. In addition to this joy / Which brings me nearer and nearer to the gods / You gave me also the companion, whom I can / No longer get on without, although he coldly and insolently / Debases me in my own eyes, and with a breath of words / Turns all your bounties into nothing.

it is reasonable to suppose that he had also not abandoned it in 1775, the year in which the modern critics usually declare the invocation of the Erdgeist to have been written. In fact, it looks as though this way of bringing Faust and Mephisto together may well have belonged to a plan which Goethe envisaged perhaps even as early as 1771 in Strasburg, or not much later, not finally rejecting it as unsatisfactory until 1797, and as though the scenes "Beschwörung des Erdgeists," "Trüber Tag. Feld," and "Wald und Höhle" all three had this one, still substantially unmodified original plan underlying them. Goethe indeed goes out of his way in 1788, in the versification of the passage from the old prose scene, to identify the Spirit there referred to with the Erdgeist, by bringing in the phrase "im Feuer," which clearly alludes to the stage direction in the Invocation scene: "der Geist erscheint *in der Flamme*" (the Spirit appears *in the flame*). Nevertheless ingenious—far too ingenious—arguments are advanced, for example by Rickert, to prove that the "erhabne Geist" of the "Wald und Höhle" scene cannot possibly be the Erdgeist. Particularly interesting here is the case of Hans Albert Maier who, finding himself compelled to admit that in the "Wald und Höhle" monologue the Spirit who had appeared to Faust is indeed identified with the Erdgeist, hits on the explanation that Goethe "sich erst durch das Missverstehen der alten Prosaszene zu der Annahme von Mephistopheles Erdgeistsendlingsschaft entschloss" and thereby "sich . . . selbst überinterpretierte" (that Goethe only as a result of his having misunderstood the old prose scene decided to assume that Mephisto was an envoy of the Spirit of Earth, [thereby] overinterpreting himself)[7] and misleading his readers and critics.

There is one piece of evidence for the dating of "Trüber Tag. Feld" which, though by no means conclusive, deserves to be taken more seriously than it is by the modern critics who are bent on assigning that scene at all costs to January, 1772. It is usually agreed that the scene "Kerker" must have been written if not *immediately* after "Trüber Tag. Feld," then at least *fairly soon* after it, because of the close connexion in purport between the two. It is here that the brief and otherwise comparatively unimportant scene "Nacht. Offen Feld," which links the two together, takes on a special significance. Faust and Mephisto, having in the

previous scene spoken about Gretchen's terrible predicament and
made plans to rescue her, are here shown galloping past a place of
execution in the open countryside at dead of night. Faust sees
certain mysterious creatures hovering around the place of execution, and in answer to his questions about them is told by Mephisto
that they are a covey of witches. It has since 1809 been generally
admitted that this scene must have been inspired by the stanza
in Bürger's *Lenore* where the heroine is borne by her demon lover
on a black horse past a place of execution surrounded by a "Luft-
gesindel" (airy rabble) of dancing spirits; indeed, it is to be assumed that Goethe intended his readers to recognize a kind of
allusion to Bürger's *Lenore* here. But *Lenore* was not published
till autumn, 1773, and therefore Goethe's scene "Nacht. Offen
Feld" cannot have been written before that date. The presump-
tion arising from this that the other two prose scenes, which
immediately succeed and follow it and are so closely linked with
it, can also not have been written before autumn, 1773, is naturally
unwelcome to those who would date them a year and a half
earlier. Accordingly Roethe denies that the scene was inspired by
Bürger's *Lenore* at all, and proposes the characteristically ingenious
interpretation that Mephisto is lying and that the figures hovering
above the place of execution are in reality not witches at all, but
angels who have come to receive Gretchen's soul.[8] It is, of course,
just possible that "Nacht. Offen Feld" was only written as an afterthought, much later than the two other prose scenes, and inserted
between them.

More valid in the eyes of the representative modern critics than
Goethe's own sufficiently clearly indicated intention that the Invocation scene and "Trüber Tag. Feld" should be regarded as having
one and the same conception at the back of them is the stylistic
difference between the two scenes, that is to say above all the
circumstance that the former is in verse and the latter in prose.
Great ingenuity has been devoted to proving on linguistic grounds
that "Trüber Tag. Feld" could not possibly have been written
later than February, 1772—first of all by Scherer in 1879, then by
Carl Enders in 1905. This view has been corroborated by the
mediumistic method of "Schallanalyse" (Tone-Analysis) and will
no doubt also sooner or later be corroborated by the judiciously

programmed use of computers. The technique here involved is complex and can only be fully explained and criticized by detailed examination of the texts concerned in the original German. But everything turns upon Scherer's contention that linguistically the prose of "Trüber Tag. Feld" tallies exactly with the first version of *Götz von Berlichingen,* as Goethe wrote it in the last three months of 1771, just in all those characteristics that he eliminated in his radical revision of it in February, 1773. From a comparison of these two versions of *Götz von Berlichingen,* it is claimed, a reliable criterion can be established for distinguishing between Goethe's use of language before and after spring, 1772, and by this criterion "Trüber Tag. Feld" cannot possibly have been written later than that date. Like the first version of *Götz,* it belongs unquestionably to "jener kurzen Shakespearisierenden Gärungsepoche, . . . in welche Goethe zu Strassburg erst verfiel und *aus der er sich zu Anfang 1772 schon wieder herauszuarbeiten begann"* (that brief "Shakespearising" epoch of fermentation which Goethe only entered upon in Strasburg and *which he was already beginning to work himself out of again by the commencement of 1772).*[9] Everything depends upon this contention of Scherer's that it is possible to distinguish a short, clearly delimited stage in Goethe's early development, beginning about 1770 or 1771 and not extending much beyond the first two months of 1772, during which *alone* he wrote the kind of prose that is found in "Trüber Tag. Feld" and, many would now add, in the original "Kerker" scene. Scherer's word is taken for this, and his formula is echoed in innumerable variations. Thus Enders writes in 1905 of the "Genieprosa" (genius-prose)[10] of that supposed brief epoch, using the word "Genie" here in the traditional German sense as synonymous with Storm and Stress. Roethe speaks of the "hyperbolischer Kraftstil" and of the "knappere, gehacktere Flüche und Klagen" (hyperbolical style of strength . . . terser, abrupter curses and lamentations),[11] which distinguish the writings of that phase from everything Goethe produced after spring, 1772. Beutler in 1940 speaks of the "wildeste Shakespeare-Prosa" (wildest Shakespearean prose) of that epoch, characterizing it as "erratisch-vulkanhaft" (erratic and volcanic).[12] Burger in 1942 describes it as "ungebärdig und ungebändigt" (unruly and unsubdued).[13] Günther Müller in 1947 calls it "naturalistische Ausdrucksprosa" (naturalistic, expressionistic prose);[14] Hermann Schneider in 1949, "lebensnahe" (close-to-life) prose.[15] Hanna Fischer-Lamberg in 1957 echoes these phrases, and speaks of "die Heftigkeit der Diktion, die Nachahmung Shakespearescher Manier, das Bedürfnis nach Übertreibungen" (the violence of the diction, the imitation of Shakespeare's manner, and the urge to exaggerations).[16] All these epithets are apt enough as characterizations of the prose of "Trüber Tag. Feld" and "Kerker," but they apply just as well to the second version of *Götz von Berlichingen* as to the first, indeed to most of Goethe's Storm and Stress writing down to autumn, 1775, and to the entire Storm and Stress movement as it is represented also by Goethe's contemporaries. Scherer's pretty well universally accepted contention is, however: "zwischen der ersten und zweiten Fassung des Götz liegt *eine Stilveränderung Goethes*, und jene Szene ['Trüber Tag. Feld'] . . . steht auf Seite der ersten Fassung" (between the first and second versions of *Götz von Berlichingen* there lies *a change in Goethe's style*; and that scene ["Dull Day. Field"] stands on the side of the first version).[17]

Scherer, who thus inaugurated this idea of a decisive revolution in Goethe's style between 1772 and 1773, was, it should be noted, very much less interested in the youthful Storm and Stress Goethe for his own sake than we nowadays are, and also thought very much less highly of him than we do. In fact, he estimated him quite negatively. According to Scherer it was not until Goethe went to Italy that he attained "die höchste Stufe seines Stiles" (the highest phase of his style): "So scheint alles Frühere nur eine Vorbereitung gewesen zu sein . . . Mit dem Jahre 1788 scheint das eigentliche Können zu beginnen; was voranging, war nur Versuch und Lernen" (So everything earlier appears only to have been a mere preparation . . . In the year 1788 his real ability seems to begin; what preceded it was only experiment and apprenticeship).[18] In particular, Scherer is out of sympathy with the supposed brief Shakespearean epoch to which he would assign "Trüber Tag. Feld," deprecating it as an epoch of "krasser Naturalismus" (crass naturalism),[19] and his contention that it did not last much beyond spring, 1772, amounts really to an effort to demonstrate that Goethe's Storm and Stress phase was already over at a time when we now see it as only just having properly begun. Scherer's attitude here is simply that of his generation, which still saw and estimated Goethe's Storm and Stress years substantially as the more than sixty-year-old Goethe himself had somewhat unjustly and misleadingly presented and estimated them in *Dichtung und Wahrheit*. The rediscovery, intensive firsthand study, and new appreciation of that youthful phase of Goethe's development were still in their beginnings at the time when Scherer wrote, and they made no impact on him. Curiously enough, however, these postulates of Scherer's about the Storm and Stress Goethe, the inadequacy of which would at once be recognised in any other connexion, are still accepted as absolutely valid and unchallengeable in the one question of dating "Trüber Tag. Feld."

A disinterested examination of Goethe's procedure in rewriting *Götz von Berlichingen* in February, 1773, shows beyond dispute that he was above all concerned not to make the language *less* "crassly naturalistic," less "Shakespearean," less "hyperbolical," "terse," "abrupt," "wild," "erratic," "volcanic," "unruly," "unsubdued," "expressionistic," or "close to life," as Scherer and his disciples maintain, but to make it *more* so. What dissatisfied him about the language of the first version of *Götz von Berlichingen* was, as we know from his letter of July, 1772, to Herder, that too much in it was "nur gedacht" (merely thought out), instead of being the immediate sensuous expression of sheer feeling and vitality. The vast, representative bulk of the innumerable stylistic changes he made in the text of that drama in February, 1773, were uniformly dictated by this will to greater immediacy, intensity, abruptness, and sensuousness of expression. The best known and most striking example of this is the substitution of the coarse, pithy interjection, "Bist doch krepiert, du Memme!" (You have died like a dog after all, you poltroon!) for the abstract, rhetorical generalization originally put into the mouth of the Imperial Lansquenet: "So lauert der Tod auf den Feigen, und reisst ihn in ein unrühmlich Grab" (Thus death lies in wait for the coward and plunges him into an inglorious grave). It is not, as—according to Scherer, Roethe, and all the others—it ought to be, the *earlier* version of this passage that is the more terse, abrupt, volcanic, expressionistic, etc., but the *later* version, that of 1773. Nor is this

an isolated, exceptional case; it is typical of the relationship between the two versions throughout; scores of similar examples
could be cited, and they all of them show that Goethe at this
stage, far from renouncing the "crass Shakespearean naturalism"
of 1771, was rather governed by the will to intensify it and to
eliminate anything incompatible with it. Scherer, who had no
use for such naturalism, was blind to this glaringly conspicuous
aspect of Goethe's revision of *Götz von Berlichingen* in 1773 and
to the principle underlying it, and his great prestige as an expert
has similarly blinded the critics of later generations to it.

What made it possible for Scherer and his followers thus to
ignore so striking a phenomenon was the circumstance that Goethe,
while pursuing his general principle of intensifying the naturalistic
and expressionistic language of *Götz* in 1773, and of eliminating
from it everything that was "nur gedacht," did also frequently
tone down individual hyperboles, and completely suppressed certain passages and scenes, usually indeed not on linguistic grounds,
but because they made the action altogether too straggling and
diffuse or were in other respects unsatisfactory. These alterations
and deletions constitute, however, no contradiction or betrayal of
that will to Storm and Stress immediacy and intensity of expression which was his true guiding principle in the recasting of *Götz*.
Most of what he thus altered or eliminated had to go, not because
it was wildly Shakespearean as such, but simply because it was intrinsically bad by *any* standard, including the wild Shakespearean
standard. It is one thing to reject a stylistic ideal altogether, and
quite another to recognise that one has here and there made it
ridiculous by overdoing it and running the risk of lapsing into mere
bombast. The successful use of an extravagant, tumultuous style
demands some capacity for self-criticism and self-discipline, no
less than the successful use of a restrained, classical style does. Nor
is the procedure of an author in revising an older piece of work in
every respect a reliable clue to what he may or may not do in the
months and years to come when he is engaged in the very different
task of original composition. The conditions are entirely different
in the two cases. Although Goethe in February, 1773, in addition to eliminating from *Götz* what was "nur gedacht," also at
several points toned down the extravagance of the language, he

continued to employ the same extravagances without any restraint in *Clavigo* in 1774, in *Stella* in 1775, pretty certainly also in the no longer extant original opening acts of *Egmont* written in the same year, and quite certainly again and again in his letters down to and beyond the end of the Frankfort years; nothing could be more staccato and volcanic than the letters to Auguste von Stolberg of 1775.

The great, infallible test established by Scherer for distinguishing Goethe's dramatic prose of the years 1771–1772 from that of the years 1773–1775 turns out to be completely fallacious. He draws attention to the hyperbolical "grosse Zahlen" (big numbers) in which the original text of *Götz* abounds, such as "Das würd ein *Jahrtausend* vergangner Höllenqualen in einem Augenwink aus meiner Seele verdrängen" (That would in an instant remove a *thousand years* of past hell-torments from my soul), asserts that all such "big numbers" were eliminated on the revision of that text in February, 1773; and then triumphantly points to the two phrases in "Trüber Tag. Feld": "Du grinsest gelassen über das Schicksal von *Tausenden* hin!" (You sneer complacently over the fate of *thousands*), and "Den entsetzlichsten Fluch über dich auf *Jahrtausende!*" (The most fearful curse upon you for *thousands* of years), proclaiming: "Das entscheidet. Es ist unmöglich, dass ein Dichter, der an einem Werke mit sich einig ist, solche Übertreibungen wegzuschaffen, sie an einem anderen sollte neu gemacht haben" (That decides the matter. It is impossible that a poet, once having made up his mind to eliminate such exaggerations in one work, should indulge in them all over again in another one).[20] This is Scherer's one great definite and impressive argument, and it certainly does prove something, though not what it is meant to prove and is widely accepted as proving. It proves that Scherer was not only incapable of really appreciating the Storm and Stress Goethe, but also that he had nothing more than a superficial knowledge of him. If he had studied him only a little more carefully, he would have known that, although the hyperbolical "big numbers" were much pruned in the 1773 revision of *Götz von Berlichingen*, they were by no means completely eliminated, that Goethe allowed them to stand in no fewer than eight cases, and that he went on employing them with no restraint at all in his

work and correspondence of the succeeding years, particularly in
Werther and *Clavigo* in 1774 and in *Stella* in 1775. Thus Werther
"netzt" Lotte's hand "mit *tausend* Tränen" (bedews [Lotte's hand]
with a *thousand* tears), and "küsst ihre Hand mit *tausend* Freuden" (kisses her hand with a *thousand* ecstasies), and Stella says
that "ein *Jahrtausend* von Tränen und Schmerzen" (a *thousand*
years of tears and sufferings) could not counterbalance the first
happiness of love, and describes how she fell into the arms of
the nurse of her dead child "mit *tausend* Tränen" (with a *thousand* tears). Countless examples of these hyperbolical "big numbers" could be cited from Goethe's writings of the years 1773–1775,
when he had, according to Scherer, forsworn the use of them for
ever. So much for the keystone of Scherer's demonstration that
"Trüber Tag. Feld" must have been written in winter, 1771–
1772. This is an excellent example of the fallibility of experts and
of the impossibility of solving delicate problems in such infinitely
complex fields as the language of genius by professorial rules of
thumb.

Equally inconclusive are the various parallels in phrasing—not
more than two or three of them striking—between "Trüber Tag.
Feld" and the first version of *Götz* accumulated so assiduously by
Scherer and his successors, most notably Enders. Apart from the
notorious unreliability of such parallelisms as chronological evidence under all circumstances, it may be noted that just as striking
resemblances to some of the most distinctive phrases in "Trüber
Tag. Feld" occur in Goethe's writings of the years 1773–1775 and
even later, as in the original version of *Götz*. It will no longer seem
so significant to us that the word "Elend" (misery) occurs frequently in "Trüber Tag. Feld" and in one of the suppressed scenes
of *Götz*, when we know that it also runs as a kind of *leitmotif*
through *Stella*; similarly Goethe's way of using the words "böse
Geister" (evil spirits) and "schmieden . . . an" (to link together
with chains) can be paralleled not only in the original version of
Götz, but also in his writings after 1773. The phrase "unwieder-
bringlich verloren" occurs not only in both versions of *Götz von
Berlichingen*, but also in the second act of *Clavigo* in 1774. It was
a fixed expression of the day. Furthermore, if it is to be admitted
at all that any of these parallelisms of phrasing prove anything

more than that Goethe, within the comparatively homogeneous four years' span of his development from 1771 to 1775, sometimes tended when dealing with similar themes to express himself in similar terms, they are quite as likely to have been occasioned by his intensive work on the original *Götz* manuscript in February, 1773, as by contemporaneity of composition. A far more convincing case could be made out for "Trüber Tag. Feld" having been written at the same time as or shortly after the original *Götz von Berlichingen*, if it were possible to demonstrate that it contains striking examples of that frequent "merely thought-out" abstractness and cerebrality which, more than anything else, distinguishes the earlier from the later version of that drama, and which so much disturbed Herder and Goethe himself. This is a line of inquiry, however, which, thanks to Scherer's opacity, nobody has thought of pursuing and which, if it had been pursued, could only have led to the conclusion that "Trüber Tag. Feld" is too free from this distinctive weakness of the original *Götz* to have been written as early as winter, 1771–1772. It is, for what it is meant to be and for what it, in the dramatic context of the Gretchen tragedy, needed to be, an excellent piece of work, perfect of its kind, so that Goethe himself in 1806 found nothing of moment to alter in it. It is "crass," because it deals with a crass situation, and presupposes a no lesser degree of maturity than any other parts of the *Urfaust*.

In fact, Scherer's argument that "Trüber Tag. Feld" must have been written about the same time as the first version of *Götz von Berlichingen* proves as ill-founded as his argument that the opening Invocation scene could not have been written in the form known to us before spring, 1773, because it was not till then that Goethe came to know the Knittel verse of Hans Sachs.[21] All that remains of the vast complex of higher critical hypotheses based upon these arguments of Scherer's, if we do not allow the prestige of the experts to deter us from scrutinizing it open-mindedly, is the obvious fact that the one scene is in prose and the other in verse, which in itself proves nothing. Even if Scherer's argumentation were sounder than it is, it would at most prove that the prose scenes were written some time before February, 1773, possibly as late as autumn, 1772; Beutler himself would date the "Kerker"

scene much later than "Trüber Tag.   Feld," not till after September, 1772.[22] By then, at the latest, however, Goethe must have
begun experimenting with Knittel verse for serious poetic purposes,
and the two supposed distinct phases of Goethe's early work on
Faust, that in which he employed prose and that in which he
employed Knittel verse, instead of being separated by an interval
of about a year, turn out, even by higher critical postulates, to
overlap and merge indistinguishably into one another. The balance
of probabilities is in favour of Goethe's having, after a prolonged
period of gestation, actually begun to write *Faust* some time in
1772, rather in the latter than in the former half of that year, and
of his having already then envisaged it as a composition in which,
on the analogy of Shakespeare's procedure, Knittel verse mingled
with Madrigal verse should be used freely side by side with prose
and free verse, just as seemed fittest for the scene or passage in
question. This view covers the known facts with a minimum of
hypothesis, leaving open those more detailed chronological problems to which we should like to have, but can never hope to have,
and do not really need to have final answers; and it accords best
with the idea we should have of how such a poet as Goethe works—
that is to say, as an artist who knows what he is about.

   Inconclusive though the magisterially advanced and docilely accepted linguistic and biographical arguments for the dating of
"Trüber Tag.   Feld" in January, 1772, are, it still remains theoretically possible that it may indeed have been written then, before
any other part of *Faust*, and that the Invocation of the Erdgeist
was not written till October, 1775, as is maintained by Spiess and
Krogmann.[23] But it is equally possible and intrinsically more likely
that the Invocation was written in autumn, 1772, and that "Trüber
Tag.   Feld" was not written till autumn, 1775, or that both scenes
were written almost simultaneously at some unspecifiable point of
time between these two dates. None of the elaborate hypotheses
of the experts have brought us or ever will bring us any nearer to
genuine certainty on this issue. That is something to which we
should resign ourselves. It would after all not matter if "Trüber
Tag.   Feld" could be proved to have been written as early as 1766
and the Invocation scene as late as 1832, so long as it is admitted
that the same conception lies at the back of them both and that

they are to be interpreted in the light of one another. Scherer himself, who was responsible for the entire higher critical wild goose chase, far from denying this, postulated that Goethe wrote the Invocation scene shortly before "Trüber Tag. Feld," in winter, 1771–1772, but in prose, turning it into Knittel verse (except for a few sentences of the original preserved in the guise of free verse) some time after spring, 1773, without changing its purport. It weighs nothing with him that, according to Goethe himself, the most important scenes of the *Urfaust*—and none is more important than this opening scene—were all written directly as they stand, "ohne Konzept" (without any rough draft).[24] Certainly the opening scene makes the impression of having been from the first written in its present metrical form and not transposed into it from a prose original. It is totally different in this respect from the only two scenes known to be versifications of prose originals, "Auerbachs Keller" and "Kerker."

There is nothing then in all the arguments and constructions of modern criticism that need deter us from assuming at least tentatively that we have before us in the opening scene of the *Urfaust* Goethe's inward point of departure, anterior to the irruption of the extraneous Gretchen theme, and quite possibly also the first scene to be written in point of time. It will be our business to see whether this scene, interpreted in the light of "Trüber Tag. Feld" and of "Wald und Höhle," may not disclose to us some of the most important features of the earliest plan for *Faust* Goethe can legitimately be presumed to have made.

5. The Erdgeist
and Mephisto

THE OPENING SCENE of the *Urfaust*, although it is appreciably longer than any of the others, still amounts only to 248 lines. The first 168 of these lines comprise Faust's actual monologue, the remaining eighty his conversation with Wagner. Some twenty-seven of the first 168 lines are indeed spoken by the Erdgeist whose five utterances towards the end of the monologue do not, however, annul its intrinsically monologistic character. This monologue has been particularly savagely mauled by the Higher Critics.

The first thirty-two lines are more Hans-Sachs-like—or, as Goethe himself would have put it, more "holzschnittähnlich" (woodcut-like)—with their jerky, irregular metre, their archaisms and their naive tone, than any other passage of comparable length in the whole of *Faust*, except the dialogue between Mephisto and the Student in its original form. They adhere closely to the pattern of Faust's traditional opening monologue, as it was inaugurated by Marlowe and reproduced in the popular German stage and puppet plays. It is the type of exposition that has still not moved far in the direction of realistic illusionism or psychological subtlety from the practice of mediaeval biblical and allegorical drama, where the characters ingenuously inform the audience in so many words about who they are and what the situation is. Faust says that he has learnt all there is to be learnt in the four faculties of the university, but is dissatisfied with such mere sterile book-knowledge and with the kind of life to which it restricts him, and has decided to study magic instead, in the hope of arriving at a more immediate and genuine insight into the mysteries of the universe:

> Dass ich erkenne, was die Welt
> Im Innersten zusammenhält,
> Schau alle Würkungskraft und Samen
> Und tu nicht mehr in Worten kramen.*

The following thirty-two lines show a marked change in manner. Faust apostrophizes the moon that shines in dimly through the small panes of his study window, dwells bitterly on the contrast between the confined, dusty world of books, anatomical specimens, and scientific apparatus to which his academic profession condemns him, and the free, open, healthful world of nature with its mountains and meadows. The metre becomes more regular, with far fewer cases of "free filling"; the tone becomes more modulated, lyrical, inward, subtle and modern; the diction, richer and more vivid. The primitive woodcut of the first thirty-two lines gives way to something less angular and stiff; colour enters, and we have before us something more like an oil-painting.

In the succeeding twelve lines Faust returns to the theme of magic, seizes from his library one single volume, "—dies geheimnisvolle Buch / Von Nostradamus' eigner Hand" (this mysterious book / by Nostradamus' own hand), as the only one of any value, and resolves to flee with it "hinaus ins weite Land" (into the open countryside), that being the only appropriate place to peruse it.

The remaining eighty-eight lines, up to the point where Wagner is heard knocking at the door, show Faust actually employing this magical book, which he at once proceeds to open and contemplate in his study, instead of taking it out into the open countryside with him as he had at first designed. The only thing we learn about this book, apart from the fact that it was written by Nostradamus, who is to be considered as standing generically for all the cabbalistic and occult writters from the Neo-Platonists and Gnostics through Paracelsus to Swedenborg, is that it contains a number of "heilge

---

* That I may know what holds the world / Together at its innermost core, / Seeing all operative power and all the seeds of things / And no longer dabbling in mere words.

Zeichen" (holy signs or emblematic diagrams); whatever expository
text it may also contain is apparently of no interest to Faust, who
has rejected all mere words and who has also to be displayed in
greater animation than would be possible if he were merely to
read, either out loud or to himself. The kind of mystical signs that
Goethe here has in mind are well known from old cabbalistic books;
they have chiefly an astrological or cosmogonic character. They are
the "Lines, circles, scenes, letters and characters," of which Marlowe's Dr. Faustus speaks. We hear only about two of them by
name—that of the Makrokosmus and that of the Erdgeist, both of
which produce a deep effect on Faust, culminating in the actual
invocation, appearance, and disappearance of the Erdgeist.

Between the knocking of Wagner and his entrance Faust speaks
four further lines, which terminate the monologue.

Scherer, in his *Betrachtungen über Faust* of 1884, treats this
monologue as a patchwork of mutually contradictory fragments
written at widely separated periods and belonging to three or more
entirely different plans, not one of which was carried out. He finds
it an "unlösbaren Widerspruch" (irreconcilable contradiction)
that Faust should only now speak of dedicating himself to the
study of magic, if he has already some time since been in possession
of a magical book; that he should resolve to employ this book out
in the open countryside and then after all employ it in his study;
that when he does open it he seems to be seeing its contents for the
first time, although the Erdgeist subsequently says that he has "an
seiner Sphäre lang gesogen" (long been sucking at its sphere), and
Faust's own words imply that he has "besought" (*"erfleht"*) it
previously. Scherer asserts that, on the analogy of one of the old
puppet-plays, at least two intervening scenes must originally have
been planned, in one of which Faust would have been shown
coming into possession of the magical book and in the other of
which we should have been informed that he has long before this
been striving to conjure up the Erdgeist. The most important and
influential of Scherer's contentions is, however, that the second
section of the monologue was not originally written as a continuation of the first thirty-two lines, but as an entirely fresh and very
much later substitute for them, because Goethe felt them to be a
"kindliche, vom Standpunkt einer verfeinerten Technik undrama-
tische Exposition" (a childish and, from the point of view of a

refined technique, undramatic exposition).[1] The second section
seemed to Scherer so very much maturer than the first that he was
inclined to date it as late as 1788,[2] an untenable hypothesis of
which nothing more has been heard, since the discovery of the
Urfaust transcript a year after Scherer's death proved that the
passage in question must have been written before November,
1775, at the latest. Scherer's explanation of how so many incoherent
fragments came to be sketchily patched together to form the monologue as we now know it is that Goethe "gewiss darauf rechnete, dass
das Publikum es nicht so genau nehmen würde" (certainly counted
on the public's not being so particular about it).[3] Thanks to Scherer
it is still very widely assumed that the first thirty-two lines, because
they are so primitive and comparatively prosaic, must have been
written very much earlier than the rest of the monologue, with
which they have no essential connexion, and that they probably
belong to some early plan of Goethe's, in which he would have
adhered closely to the puppet play and aimed at little more than
a dramatization of the chapbooks. Hermann Schneider, who (as
we have seen)[4] would date the first thirty-two lines as early as April,
1770, says of them:

> Diese 32 Verse stehen in der Tat ganz für sich. Denn das
> spüren wir—im weitesten Sinne: jeder Leser!—dass die grosse
> Soloszene unmöglich aus einem Guss sein kann. . . . Mit den
> Versen: "O sähst du, voller Mondenschein—" ergreift ein
> ganz anderer Faust das Wort. Dort körniger Archaismus,
> echter Fauststil vom Volksdrama her, hier die melancholische
> Schwärmerei eines Sohnes der empfindsamen Zeit . . . Der
> Faust (und der Goethe) der ersten 30 Verse ist wirklich ein
> ganz anderer als der des weiteren Monologs und der Erdgeist-
> szene.*[5]

---

* These thirty-two verses stand indeed quite by themselves. For we—and by
that I mean in the most comprehensive sense every reader—feel that the great
monologue cannot possibly have been produced at one stroke. With the verses:
"Ah! would that, light of the full moon . . ." an entirely different Faust begins
to speak. On the one hand we find rough-and-ready archaism, the genuine
Faust style of the popular dramas, on the other the melancholy reverie of a
son of the age of sensibility. The Faust (and the Goethe) of the first 30 verses
is really an entirely different person from the one of the rest of the monologue
and the Spirit of Earth scene.

Scherer is too intelligent not to foresee some at least of the objections that can be raised to his drastic disintegration of the
opening monologue, and tries in the course of his exposition to
discredit them highhandedly in advance by the characteristic device of treating all his possible adversaries as though it were they
who were indulging in far-fetched, unverifiable hypotheses. The
one objection which Scherer did not foresee and would certainly
have scouted contemptuously, if he could have foreseen it, is that
the criterion of dramatic art underlying all his arguments does not
apply to the opening monologue of Goethe's *Faust* or to any other
part of it. The realistic convention on which most serious, sophisticated drama, be it classical or naturalistic, reposes, is absolutely
valid in all cases, according to Scherer, and any failure to conform
to it is evidence that the dramatist either does not know his job or
has, for some reason or other (carelessness, vacillation or self-
estrangement) bungled it. Now it may readily be conceded to
Scherer and his many present-day followers that Goethe fails to
conform to the realistic convention in the opening monologue of
Faust, and indeed throughout the drama; and it may furthermore
be conceded that even in a drama or narrative involving supernatural agencies and events the realistic convention can still be
adhered to: Stevenson's *Dr. Jekyll and Mr. Hyde* and Henry James's
Turn of the Screw are evidence of this. What is not to be conceded,
however, is that Goethe's failure to conform to the realistic convention in the opening monologue is due to immaturity, incompe-
tence, carelessness, self-estrangement or to any other such fortuitous
causes. In particular it must be protested that what is condemned
by Scherer as "prosaic," "childish" and "undramatic" in the first
thirty-two lines of the monologue cannot possibly be due to
Goethe's having written them before he had acquired a "refined
technique" in the matter of exposition. Long before the earliest date
to which anybody would think of assigning those lines Goethe had
proved himself a virtuoso of illusionistic, realistic dramatic technique in his juvenile rococo comedies *Die Laune des Verliebten*
("The Moodiness of the Lover") and *Die Mitschuldigen* of 1768
and 1769, and the first scene of *Götz von Berlichingen,* as it was
written in autumn, 1771, is a masterpiece of exposition within
the realistic convention. The exposition of *Faust* is unrealistic,

"childish," "prosaic," and "undramatic" then, not because Goethe was at the time of writing it too unskilled and inexperienced to make anything more sophisticated out of it, but for some other reason, and that other reason can only be because that is how he wanted it to be. It is moreover easy enough to see why he wanted it to be like that. The primitive and artless appealed to him just because he was trying to emancipate himself from the sophistication, artificiality, and intellectuality of Enlightenment culture; it appealed to him in the folksong and ballad, in Hans Sachs and sixteenth-century woodcuts, and it seemed to him that his *Faust* drama should at least begin in the old traditional, primitive way, however much he proposed to modernize the theme and make it his own in the sequence. It was like the traditional first move in the game of chess, which betrays nothing of how skilful or unskilful the player is or of what kind of game he intends to play. Those first thirty-two lines are excellent of their kind and absolutely appropriate where they stand; it is vandalistic to think with Scherer that Goethe might have done better to scrap them and begin the play with Faust's apostrophe to the moon, about which there is so little to make us realise that the figure we see before us is meant to be *Faust*. Furthermore Goethe even within these thirty-two woodcut-like lines skilfully works up to something that goes beyond the limited mentality of the old chapbooks and puppet plays, and he shows how far he was, when he wrote them, from designing merely to dramatize the traditional Faust legend without transforming it into something characteristically modern and his own: Faust's aspiration to "know what holds the world together at its innermost core," instead of "dabbling in mere words," is purest Storm and Stress and has a most intimate bearing upon the invocation of the Erdgeist that follows and upon what distinguishes Goethe's own conception of Faust from the traditional conception of him. Nor is this the only evidence that the first thirty-two lines from the outset hung integrally together with the rest of the scene.

The "contradictions" made so much of by Scherer in the main body of the monologue must indeed appear as genuine, serious contradictions, if the action is considered as taking place according to realistic conventions at a historically fixed point of time. But that is not how Goethe himself envisaged it or intended it to be

understood. Time and external circumstance are here largely symbolical. Everything essential about Faust up to the moment of his
invoking the Erdgeist and thereby embarking upon his specifically
Faustian destiny is here brought together succinctly and simultaneously, without the deference to minuter details of time, place,
causation and motivation demanded in a realistic drama. If Ibsen
had been the author, we should rightly have expected to be informed exactly how and when Faust came to be in possession of the
book of magic, whether he was able to use it successfully at the first
attempt or not, why he talks of taking it out into the open country
without actually doing so, what his previous relationships to the
Erdgeist may have been, and so on. But for the particular purpose
that Goethe has here set before him all these questions are completely irrelevant, and the scenes desiderated by Scherer for dealing
with them would have been mere futile, operatic excrescences, con-
tributing nothing to the real meaning of the drama, but rather
obscuring and diluting it. Above all it would have been ruinous if
Faust had been represented, in conformity with the chapbooks and
puppet-plays, as having to cope with technical problems in learning
the know-how of magic and putting it into practice, especially in
the matter of invoking the Erdgeist, and it calls for a more than
usual degree of ponderous literal-mindedness to read any such
chronological meaning as that into the Spirit's words: "An meiner
Sphäre *lang* gesogen." Not only or for the first time by employing
specifically magical practices has Faust been "sucking at the sphere"
of the Erdgeist; he had been doing so by his discontent and by his
desire to penetrate the hidden mysteries of things, long before he
had decided to resort to magic, long before the name or conception of such an entity as the Erdgeist had presented itself to his
consciousness. In the symbolical time of this scene, which is not
measurable by any clock, the outward and the inward, the experiences of the instant and the gradual developments of years merge
indistinguishably into one another. A scene showing Faust actually
tramping out into the open countryside with Nostradamus' mysterious book under his arm could have added nothing to his inward
vision of himself doing all this, would indeed only have detracted
from it and trivialised it. It is to be borne in mind that Goethe
throughout his work on the first part of *Faust* envisaged it as a

drama to be read, not to be acted: thence much of the irony in the "Vorspiel auf dem Theater." The only stage he has in mind is the reader's imagination. If he had been governed by practical theatrical considerations he would pretty certainly have contrived to bring some other personages into his exposition beside the hero, and to provide for more action, variety and dialogue, as Marlowe does and as the puppet-plays do. As it is, however, he has given us, to adapt a phrase of his own coining, "die Summe von Fausts Existenz" (the sum of Faust's existence) in the form of an introductory monodrama, comparable with his *Proserpina* or his *Prometheus* poem.

Everything points to the opening monologue having been written within a comparatively short space of time—a few weeks at most—as a single, continuous piece of work with one and the same conception and inspiration underlying it. The change in tone between the first thirty-two lines and the succeeding passage, which is regularly adduced as evidence to the contrary, proves nothing. Sudden and extreme changes of mood are of the very essence of Faust's character, as they are of the character of the youthful Goethe, who likens himself in his fifteenth year to a chameleon, and in his eighteenth and twenty-second years to a weathercock; and who wrote to Auguste Stolberg in August, 1775, "Hundertmal wechselts mit mir den Tag" (I change a hundred times a day), and in the following month, "Gott! so in dem ewigen Wechsel, immer eben der selbe" (God! in this eternal change I am still always the same). "Wie oft sah ich ihn schmelzend und wütend in einer Viertelstunde" (How often I have seen him languishing and furious within the same quarter of an hour!), Stolberg records of him on June 8, 1776. Barker Fairley writes admirably on this question: "The unexpected darting of Faust's mind from his study to the moonlit landscape and back again is simply Goethe's mind darting in its usual way, and the text must be interpreted accordingly."[6] Equally discerning is Hanna Fischer-Lamberg's comment: "Das Undisziplinierte, Sprunghafte, das man oft als Kompositionsfehler angesehen hat, den man nur durch häufige Unterbrechungen der Arbeit am Monolog zu erklären vermöchte, gehört zu Faust wie zu Goethe" (The undisciplined, erratic quality which has often been looked upon as a fault in composition, to be accounted for only by frequent interruptions in the work on the monologue, is characteristic of Faust and Goethe alike).[7] Such "Sprünge und Würfe" (sudden jumps and abrupt transitions) were theoretically advocated and deliberately cultivated as an integral part of the poetic programme of Storm and Stress, with its belief in sensuous immediacy of expression; one can read much about them in the early writings of Herder, particularly in the *Auszüge aus einem Briefwechsel über Ossian und die Lieder alter Völker* (*Extracts from a Correspondence about Ossian and ancient Folk-Songs*); Goethe was completely at one with Herder on this issue, as we can see especially from his letter to him of July, 1772.

The critics who insist that Faust's opening thirty-two lines could not possibly have been written on the same day as his address to the moon would, if they adhered consistently to their own principles, also be forced to assume that the extremely fine poem *Auf dem See* ("On the Lake"), with its remarkable twofold change of mood and metre, was composed on three quite different and widely separated occasions, whereas we know from the manuscript that the whole of it was jotted down within an hour or so on June 15, 1775, and that immediately before and after it two quatrains totally different in character from it and from one another were also produced, the one boisterous to the point of grossness, the other languishingly tender. That is characteristic of the youthful Goethe. The point of the lyric *Auf dem See* is not in one or the other of the three contrasting moods with their distinctive metrical patterns, considered separately, but in their juxtaposition, in the transitions between them, in the scintillating spiritual restlessness which they symphonically express, "in eternal change still always the same." So it is also with the abrupt changes of mood, tone and cadence in Faust's opening monologue. Goethe would never have been able to conceive of or to write *Faust*, if he had had as one-tracked a mind as so many of his critics attribute to him and seem to have themselves.

Goethe conceived of his Faust as too noble-minded ever, for the sake of power, fame, wealth, happiness, pleasure or any other acquisition, even knowledge, deliberately and with open eyes to seek communion with or ally himself to the forces of evil as such. He might indeed be, or imagine himself to be, "beyond good and evil," but that alone would fundamentally distinguish him from the Faust of tradition, whose entire character and destiny depend upon there being no possibility for him of transcending good and evil, even in the imagination. Yet Goethe's Faust, though most of the time too titanic and spiritually emancipated to see in the conception of "evil" a reality to be taken seriously, looking down with contempt on those who still "fear Hell and the Devil," and though, so far as evil ever does seem to him a reality, he is too noble-minded ever deliberately to choose it, was somehow to be brought into the traditional Faust situation of being allied with the spirit of evil. He had recognizably still to be Faust. The radical transformation of the sources involved by this loftier conception of the hero's character cost Goethe considerable labour and thought, and created problems for him, some of which he found it extremely difficult to solve. Goethe indeed says hardly anything himself about his struggle with these problems, but even if we had not the *Urfaust* transcript and the *Fragment* of 1788–1790 to go by, with all that they reveal indirectly about the stages in which the drama was produced, *Faust I* alone, as it was published in 1808, would betray to us something of what these problems were and how and why Goethe was so long baffled by them. The fact that he so seldom expressly draws attention to the contrast between the original Faust legend and what he sets before us should not mislead us into assuming that that legend spontaneously transformed itself in such remarkable ways, without his having to rack his brain about it.

It is, as has already been seen, commonly assumed that Goethe originally intended merely to dramatize the old Faust legend, without changing its fundamental postulates or purport, and only gradually and unconsciously diverged from this plan, not completely jettisoning it in favour of a radical transformation of the sources until 1788 or 1797. Even the Gretchen tragedy is seen as only a first tentative and involuntary step towards this transformation, on which it has in any case little bearing one way or the other, since the Faust who appears as Gretchen's lover is hardly less remote from the lofty-souled magus seen in the rest of Goethe's drama than from the unprincipled sorcerer of the old legend. It is rather to the opening monologue that we should look for evidence as to how far Goethe, in writing the *Urfaust*, still adhered to the postulates and spirit of his sources, and how far he was already out to transform them.

One of the chief consequences of Goethe's ennoblement of Faust's character was that his Faust could never, like his traditional prototype, conjure up the devil, that some adequate substitute had to be found for that central, decisive motif of the old legend. This meant in turn that Goethe could not utilize the idea of magic upon which that legend reposed, but had to find some adequate substitute for that too. These are problems which Goethe had already faced and at least in part solved, when he wrote the opening monologue.

What Faust aims at in resorting to magic is to enter into communion with the world of spirits for the sake of the hidden knowledge they can impart to him. This runs as a *leitmotif* through all the sections of the opening monologue, linking them together and conferring upon them the unity so often denied by the critics. It occurs already in the first thirty-two lines.

> Drum hab ich mich der Magie ergeben,
> Ob mir durch *Geistes* Kraft und Mund
> Nicht manch Geheimnis werde kund.*

In the second section this motif is taken up again when Faust longs to hover by moonshine around mountain caves "mit *Geistern*" (with spirits). In the third section Faust expresses the hope that from contemplation of Nostradamus' mysterious book in the open countryside his soul may expand, "Wie spricht ein *Geist* zum andern *Geist*" (as one *Spirit* speaks to another *Spirit*); and then he becomes aware that there is no need for him to quit his study to experience this, for

> Ihr schwebt, ihr *Geister*, neben mir,
> Antwortet mir, wenn ihr mich hört!†

The contemplation of the Sign of the Makrokosmus leads Faust to exclaim in the words of some unidentifiable and probably only

---

* Therefore I have devoted myself to the study of magic, / To see if *through the power and mouth of Spirits* / Many secrets may not be revealed to me.

† You hover around me here, *you Spirits*, / Answer me, if you hear me.

putative[8] "Weise" (Sage): "Die *Geisterwelt* ist nicht verschlossen" (The *world of Spirits* is not shut off from us). The Erdgeist scornfully asks the overawed Faust what has become of his breast that "mit Freudebeben / Erschwoll, sich *uns, den Geistern,* gleich zu heben" (with joyous throbbing / Swelled to raise itself to the level of *us, the Spirits*). The same conception is expressed also in "Trüber Tag. Feld"—and this is one of the close links between that scene and the opening monologue—when Mephisto jeeringly asks Faust, "Warum machst du Gemeinschaft mit uns? . . . Eh! Drangen wir uns dir auf oder du dich uns?" (Why did you enter into association with us? . . . Eh! did we force ourselves upon you, or did you force yourself upon us?) The Erdgeist takes its leave of Faust at the end of the monologue with the mysterious, much discussed words: "Du gleichst dem *Geist,* den du begreifst, / Nicht mir!" (You resemble the *Spirit* that you can grasp, / Not me).

The conception of magic as communication "with Spirits" is, of course, traditional, and Goethe found plenty of precedents for it in his sources. Thus in Simrock's version of the puppet-play, Faust says that he wants "die Geister zu zitieren" (to invoke the Spirits), and again: "Nun will ich die Geister beschwören" (Now I will conjure up the Spirits), upon which the stage direction follows: "Eine Menge Geister erscheint" (A number of Spirits appear). In Höfer's version Mephisto says to Faust on one occasion: "So kannst du von uns Geistern keine Hülfe suchen" (You can seek no help from us Spirits). In the chapbook of the "Christlich Meynender," Faust begins his study of magic by reading in Zoroaster "von ascendenten und descendenten Geistern" (about ascending and descending Spirits) and discovers from his own horoscope "dass die Geister eine sonderliche Zuneigung zu ihm haben sollten" (that the Spirits should have a particular liking for him). In this chapbook Mephisto is usually referred to simply as "der Geist" (the Spirit). But though Goethe adheres verbally to the tradition of magic in general and of the Faust legend in particular with his use of the word "spirit" (*Geist/Geister*), he has inconspicuously modified its meaning. The sources all of them quite clearly indicate that the spirits involved are *evil* spirits, in fact devils, and that Faust is all along fully aware of this. Thus the Spies chapbook makes no bones about it that Faust "den Teufel vor sich fordern mochte" (desired to summon the Devil before him), or that he "also den Teufel . . . beschwor" (he conjured up the Devil). The "Christlich Meynender" says similarly that Faust "zitierte nicht ohne geringen Missbrauch Göttlichen Namens den Teufel" (with no slight profanation of the name of God invoked the Devil). In Marlowe's play, Faust is told on the best authority that his magical volume is a "damned book," and he speaks to himself of his intention to "try if devils will obey thy hest, / Seeing thou hast prayed and sacrificed to them." In Simrock's puppet-play Faust declares:

> Ich muss mich mit der Hölle verbinden, . . .
> Um die Geister zu zitieren . . .*

In Höfer's version he similarly says: "Deswegen habe ich mich resolviert, . . . die unterirdische Höllenmacht zur Hülfe anzurufen" (Therefore I have resolved to summon the aid of the subterranean might of Hell).

Through the total absence of anything corresponding to these unambiguous terms, the "spirits" envisaged, apostrophized, and invoked by Goethe's Faust take on a fundamentally different character from those of the chapbooks and puppet-plays. The possibility that any of them might be evil spirits is not touched upon: it simply does not interest Faust and is apparently not meant to interest us either. The one spirit that actually does appear, without in the full magical sense of the word being formally and deliberately conjured up, the Erdgeist, is something distinctly different from what is traditionally understood by an "evil spirit," still more by "the Devil." The only point where evil spirits are referred to by name in the *Urfaust* is in connexion not with Faust and his magical undertakings, but with Gretchen and her conscience: she has, as Faust says in "Trüber Tag. Feld" been "handed over to evil spirits" (bösen Geistern übergeben), and we see one of these evil spirits tormenting her in the scene "Dom" (Cathedral). Faust's assumption in the opening monologue appears to be simply that there is an invisible world of spirits which, just because it is spiritual, must be superior to the merely natural and human world, and that it is

---

* I must ally myself with Hell / In order to invoke the Spirits.

a noble and courageous enterprise to communicate with that spiritual world, an enterprise indeed that raises one to the level of a "superman" (Übermensch) or even of a "god." These are typical eighteenth-century sentiments, which Goethe himself may be supposed in considerable measure to have shared.

Many commentators find a solution of this problem in the conception of "white" magic, which, as opposed to "black" magic, confined itself to the conjuring up of beneficent, or at least neutral and harmless, spirits and was therefore widely regarded as more or less lawful. Certainly this is a relevant and helpful conception, and we know that Goethe was here influenced by writings that do in the main fall into the category of what goes by the name of white magic. But Goethe nowhere explicitly or even implicitly makes use of this distinction between white and black magic, and little reflexion is needed to see why he did not and could not do so. The idea of white magic as such is alien not only to the tradition but also to the essence of the Faust legend. Somehow, even if he does not deliberately practise black magic, Faust has got to find himself allied to the devil, if he is to be Faust at all. One could think of the situation in such a way that Faust, while only intending to practise white magic, finds out too late that he has after all, without knowing it, been practising black magic instead or as well. Such a formula comes near to what Goethe was evidently getting at, but there are still elements in it which are not warranted by the actual text. There is no indication that Faust is conscious of or worried by the distinction between white and black magic, nor would it be in keeping with his turbulent, high-vaulting soul, which is "not afraid of Hell or the Devil," to pick his steps in such a way. What he asks is not whether a spirit is good or evil, but whether it can "hear" him and will "answer" him, whether he can "grasp" it, whether— twice he uses this significant word—he feels it to be "near" to him. In other words he seeks amongst the spirits the one most congenial to himself, to his own needs and aspirations, leaving the issue of good and evil on one side as irrelevant. In excluding the idea of a specifically black magic Goethe has necessarily excluded that of a specifically white magic too. The Erdgeist, whom we should pretty certainly have to assign to the sphere of white magic, and Mephisto, whom we should quite certainly have to assign to the sphere of

black magic, belong together to the one undivided but heterogeneous world of spirits and are, so to speak, colleagues—this emerges
clearly enough from the way in which Mephisto, taking up the
Erdgeist's taunt at Faust for having aspired to "raise himself to
the level of us Spirits," asks Faust: "Why did you enter into association with *us?*" Goethe's *Faust* depends upon the distinction
between white and black magic being disregarded. In this sense
and in this connexion the work and the hero can both be said to be
beyond good and evil, or at least to aspire to that emancipated
condition. How far Goethe himself can also be said to be beyond
good and evil here, must be considered later.

There are many critics, however, who assume that the Erdgeist
was only an afterthought of Goethe's and that originally Faust
was represented as conjuring up the "Höllenfürst" (Prince of Hell),
Lucifer, instead; and there are many more who assume that Goethe
planned but failed to write a subsequent scene, in which Faust
would have invoked the Devil as such and that, in response to this
invocation, either Lucifer or Mephisto would have appeared. The
postulate underlying both these theories is that Goethe to begin
with had no thoughts of radically altering the purport of the traditional Faust legend and that he therefore originally based his
drama unambiguously on black magic. This is, as will be seen, an
unnecessary and misleading postulate, for which there is no really
valid evidence. One of the most significant features of Goethe's
drama is that *his* Faust never conjures up the Devil as such and
does not appear as the sort of man who could well be thought of
as doing so. The most convincing explanation of the invocation
of the Erdgeist and of the "grosse Lücke" which follows upon it
and which was only filled with such difficulty and delay, is that
Goethe was from the outset bent upon finding some fundamentally
different basis upon which to bring his Faust into the required
alliance with Mephisto from that of the old tradition with its
unambiguous black magic and diabolism. If he had not all along
had this intention, which was eventually fulfilled with much ingenuity after 1797, it is not easy to see why there ever should have
been any great gap or any invocation of the Erdgeist. The treatment
of the theme on traditional lines could have presented no problems;
if nothing more than that had been involved, Goethe would surely

have tackled it at once, unhesitatingly and with verve. But there is not the least trace of his having ever done so or intended to do so; on the contrary, the evidence of the *Urfaust*, and particularly of "Trüber Tag. Feld," which so many wrongly or rightly regard as the earliest scene to have been written, all shows Goethe departing on these essential points from his sources.

Apart from all other considerations, there are purely formal and technical reasons why Goethe is unlikely ever to have contemplated following up the invocation of the Erdgeist with another invocation scene in which Faust would have conjured up the Devil. Such a scene could hardly have been so devised or executed that it would not have seemed an anti-climax or a repetition detracting from the effectiveness of what had gone before. It would have been well nigh impossible and hardly desirable to adapt the conjuration motif to the Devil so impressively as to outshine the opening scene with the Erdgeist; it would also have been very difficult—and hardly worth attempting—to vary the conjuration motif so radically and extensively in applying it to the Devil that the resulting new scene could have constituted either a fitting dialectical counterpart to the Erdgeist scene, as the "Klassische Walpurgisnacht" does, for example, to the Nordic "Walpurgisnacht," or a production so different in character as no longer to challenge comparison with it. It will be found that Goethe never repeats a once successfully treated major motif within one and the same work, unless the second treatment of it can thus either transcend the first, supplement it dialectically at the same level of achievement, or differentiate itself from it fundamentally in tone, interest, and attendant circumstances. None of these possibilities would have been open to him in writing such a second invocation scene for *Faust* as many critics suppose him to have planned. The opening monologue had exhausted the invocation motif. It was a situation in which Faust could only be presented once. What we have in Faust's invocation of the Erdgeist is not something supplementary to a projected invocation of the Devil, but Goethe's substitute for the traditional invocation of the Devil. In any case Faust's own declaration in "Trüber Tag. Feld" that he has been "chained" to Mephisto by the "great, glorious Spirit," however it is interpreted, precludes the possibility of his having conjured Mephisto up of his own accord.

What has been said here of the unlikelihood of Goethe's ever
having planned a second invocation scene in which Faust would
have conjured up Mephisto, applies still more strongly to the theory
occasionally maintained that he intended Faust to invoke the
Erdgeist once more. If, however, the "grosse, herrliche, erhabene
Geist" referred to in "Trüber Tag.   Feld" and in the "Wald und
Höhle" scene of 1788 is the Erdgeist—and there is no justification
for assuming that it could be anything else—then it must have been
part of Goethe's early plan that that Spirit should, without needing
to be invoked once more, manifest itself again in some way and
play a further part, probably a central part, in the action of the
drama. In particular it is to be assumed that Goethe intended to
introduce some scene or passage that would have thrown more light
on Faust's statement that Mephisto had been "chained" or "given"
to him as a companion by the Erdgeist, and possibly also on his
feeling that the Spirit "knows his heart and soul." That seems to
have been a decisive factor in the earliest conception of the Faust
drama which we can reasonably suppose Goethe to have had and
which he still thought of carrying out as late as 1788. Eventually,
however, in 1797, he hit upon what seemed to him a better way of
bringing Faust and Mephisto together, and abandoned the earlier
conception, without thinking it necessary to eliminate the existing
traces of it or to tidy up the loose ends, as he quite easily could have
done, if he had in this case attached as much importance to strict
consistency as his critics do. It is possible, however, to recognise
fairly clearly what the essentials of that earlier, never executed conception must have been, without resorting to any of the intricate,
unverifiable hypotheses regularly indulged in on these questions.
Everything depends here upon how Goethe arrived at the idea of
his Erdgeist and what he meant by it.[9] Our point of departure
should be that Goethe evidently conceived of the Erdgeist in such
a way that it was in keeping with its nature to link Faust and
Mephisto together in companionship, and of Faust and Mephisto
in such a way that it was in keeping with their natures thus to be
linked together by the Erdgeist. Those many critics who maintain
that it is incompatible with the natures of all or any of the three
to stand in this relationship to one another would do well to ask
themselves whether they may not have formed *a priori* a mistaken

notion of the Erdgeist and perhaps also of Faust and Mephisto. It is intrinsically more likely that they should have done this than that one of the most striking pieces of information given to us by Goethe twice, at an interval of some fifteen years, about the three figures in question, should be spurious.

It is at this point that Goethe's occult and pansophical studies of 1769 and the first months of 1770 are of major importance for the interpretation of *Faust*. For the idea of "magic" represented by the mysterious book of Nostradamus with its "holy signs" and by the unnamed sage, who is quoted as having declared that "the world of Spirits is not shut off from us," is indubitably derived from those studies. The question is only, in what way and in what degree it is derived from them, and that is a question on which there is much difference of opinion. The widely, though by no means universally accepted, view is that everything essential in the entire invocation scene is taken from the youthful Goethe's occult reading and can only be properly understood in the light of it. One difficulty is that we do not know so much about that reading as we should like to know. Our direct, documentary evidence on the subject is twofold. There are a few striking excerpts and book-titles noted down by Goethe in his commonplace book or *Ephemerides* in winter 1769–1770, and the theme is also touched upon, not without irony, in two paragraphs of Book VIII of *Dichtung und Wahrheit* which were written about 1811. In the first of these paragraphs Goethe records how, during the Frankfort months of convalescence between his university years in Leipzig and Strasburg, he consulted amongst other works Welling's *Opus mago-cabbalisticum* (1735), the anonymous *Aurea catena Homeri* (1723), and the writings of Paracelsus (1493–1541), the apocryphal Basilius Valentinus (1600), Helmont (1577–1644), and Starckey (died 1665). In the other he describes his own alchemistic experiments of the same months, especially his attempts to produce "Mittelsalz" (*sal-medium*) by treating "sonderbare Ingredienzen des Makrokosmus und Mikrokosmus auf eine geheimnisvolle wunderliche Weise" (by treating queer ingredients of the Macrocosm and the Microcosm in a mysterious and strange way). The spirit in which the youthful Goethe thus indulged in occult reading and alchemistic experiments was fundamentally different from that in which Faust is represented as devoting himself to magic and practising it. The background of Faust's magical venture is a radical scepticism with regard to Christianity, particularly with regard to Christian teachings about the destiny, powers, and limitations of the human soul and about "was die Welt im Innersten zusammenhält." Only for one who feels that he has seen through and outgrown Christian revelation can magic mean what it means for Faust. The youthful Goethe's occult studies and alchemistic experiments, on the other hand, were, strange though this may at first appear to us, part and parcel of his important though abortive pietistic conversion of 1769, when he came nearer to unconditional acceptance of Christian revelation that at any other stage in his long life, and his chief mentor and collaborator in these pursuits was the ultra-devout Susanna von Klettenberg. The point of them was that they seemed to provide some way of escape from the purely rationalistic, mechanical, and soulless conception of the universe inculcated by modern science, and thereby to make enthusiastic Christian belief still possible. Only within the framework of eighteenth-century pietism is such a strange alliance of fundamentally orthodox Christianity with ancient heterodoxies and fantasias thinkable. What for Faust is a decisive step away from Christian belief was for the youthful Goethe of the Frankfort interim months a decisive step towards it.

Faust's rejection of all established academic learning is indeed symbolic for Goethe's own Storm and Stress revolt against Enlightenment rationalism, but the impulses underlying that revolt were infinitely more vigorous, clear sighted, and independent than those that had led him two or three years earlier to dabble indiscriminately in occultism and pietism. All the indications are that, in adopting a detached and critical attitude towards pietism, as he did from summer, 1770, onward, Goethe also adopted a detached and sceptical attitude towards occultism, no longer devoting much of his time or energy to it, but waging the battle against Enlightenment mentality with the weapons of his own bold, fundamentally modern, and by no means unenlightened intellect. Only once after 1770, in the Storm and Stress years proper, does Goethe allude specifically to the occultist tradition, and that is in his review of Lavater's *Aussichten in die Ewigkeit* (*"Outlooks on Eternity"*) of

November 3, 1772, where he praises Swedenborg in terms reminiscent of the opening scene of the *Urfaust* as "der gewürdigte *Seher unsrer Zeiten*, rings um den die Freude des Himmels war, zu dem Geister durch alle Sinnen und Glieder sprachen, in dessen Busen die Engel wohnten" (the esteemed *visionary of our own days*, who was surrounded by the joy of Heaven, to whom Spirits spoke through all his senses and limbs, in whose bosom the angels dwelt). How thorough Goethe's study of Swedenborg or of the earlier cabbalistic writers was we do not know. What can be said is that, although certain cabbalistic conceptions, notably that of "das innere Licht" (the inner light), are to be detected in his thought and occasionally even have some importance for his scientific work, he nowhere gives the impression of being, as the anthroposophists would have us believe, spiritually dominated by occultism; and that from 1771 onward his attitude towards just these issues in which the occultists most strikingly differentiate themselves from the rest of mankind is nearly always sober and matter-of-fact. Even in his Storm and Stress years he is hardly ever on strained terms with what is known as "common sense," however hostile he may be to the Enlightenment cult of "Reason." In fact, such evidence as we have suggests that occultism was only a brief phase in Goethe's development, that it was nearly over, leaving few traces behind it, by the time that his so important Storm and Stress epoch properly began, and that even in 1769 and early 1770 he was interested in it rather than swept off his feet by it, retaining his critical faculties and his intellectual independence in face of it. To some extent and in some ways the cabbalists did indeed furnish his mind with imagery and with figures and patterns of thought, thereby helping to determine his intellectual life and development, as Ronald Gray shows in his *Goethe, the Alchemist* (1952). But it was nothing like to the same extent as many other less out-of-the-way phenomena, such as the ideas of Spinoza, Leibniz, Rousseau, and Herder, art and science in an infinite variety of forms, mediaeval and Hellenic culture, Shakespeare, his own immediate reactions to nature, his many experiences of love and friendship, and even orthodox Christian tradition. Goethe was not the man to re-interpret all these phenomena in terms of occultism, as though the key to them were to be sought there; it was more in accordance with his nature to re-interpret occultism, so far as his mind dwelt upon it, in terms of those phenomena, and that meant largely disregarding its claims as a body of sacrosanct, unchallengeable doctrine which must be accepted lock, stock and barrel on the authority of the masters' *ipse dixit.* For Goethe, so far as we can judge, the only way of taking the cabbalistic writings seriously was to take them figuratively, not literally; that was why he could ridicule them mercilessly in the very months during which he is known to have been doing some of his work on the *Urfaust,* in the farcical drama *Satyros* of 1773. It is unlikely that, with such an attitude, he ever studied the cabbalists anything like as systematically and laboriously as many critics suppose him to have done. By 1771 he must have been fully conscious of the difference between his own comparatively sophisticated, subjective, imaginative, and symbolical conception of "spirits" in nature, and the naive, mentally undisciplined and quite literally understood animism which runs riot in cabbalistic writings and which was the one element in those writings that attracted him enough for him to be able to borrow it and adapt it to his own poetic purposes in the early stages of his work on *Faust.*

When Faust opens his book of magic he does not, as we might well expect him to do, proceed immediately to invoke the Erdgeist. Instead he sinks into a long, intensive contemplation of the Sign of the Makrokosmus, about which no more is heard. Poetically this Makrokosmus passage is one of the finest in *Faust,* but it is widely regarded as only obscuring the purport of the play, without in any way furthering the action, and the question arises, how it comes to be there at all. Here too the favourite higher critical hypothesis of a later plan having been negligently superimposed upon an earlier one with which it is incompatible has been resorted to. Thus Roethe treats the entire Makrokosmus passage, comprising the thirty lines from "War es ein Gott, der diese Zeichen schrieb?" to "Schon glüh ich wie vom neuen Wein" (Was it a god who inscribed these signs? . . . Already I glow as with new wine), together with the two relevant stage-directions, as a retarding "Einschub" (interpolation), added much later, when Goethe's "Lebensgefühl" (sense of life) had become less turbulent, and maintains that originally only one sign or spirit was involved and that, whatever it was, it was certainly not the Makrokosmus.[10] Agnes Bartscherer also maintains that only one spirit is involved, but, unlike Roethe, she insists that this spirit must be that of the Makrokosmus.[11] She regards the verses and stage-direction referring to the Erdgeist not indeed as a later interpolation, but as an unfortunate, misleading digression, which should be ignored for purposes of interpretation. Her chief arguments are that the words addressed by Faust to the "great, glorious and sublime Spirit" in "Trüber Tag. Feld" and "Wald und Höhle" are more appropriate to the Makrokosmus than to the Erdgeist—a view maintained also by Rickert—and that nothing really corresponding to the invocation of the Erdgeist can be found in cabbalistic literature. The most commonly accepted view is that Faust finds himself unequal to grappling with the Sign of the Makrokosmus, which embraces the entire universe, and so, as a second best, resigns himself to invoking the less formidable and less comprehensive Erdgeist, which is more within his range; and that then, according to Goethe's original plan, finding even this inferior spirit too much for him, he is, in his frustration and despair, reduced (in a scene which, if it was ever written, has not survived) to invoking the devil.

Often, when the bewildering problem of the Erdgeist is debated, the Sign of the Makrokosmus is only perfunctorily touched upon or quite ignored as something irrelevant and superfluous. It is felt that there was not much point in Goethe's introducing two symbols for the pantheistic idea of nature, which differ from one another apparently only in degree (that is to say, in their magnitude and scope), where one might have served his purpose just as well or better. For that they are both pantheistic symbols is evident from their names and from the way in which they are presented; about that there can be no disagreement. What we have to decide is how Goethe came thus to duplicate the pantheistic principle here. Is one or the other symbol merely an accidental excrescence due either to his having temporarily lost control of his material, as Agnes Bartscherer assumes, or to his conception of nature having undergone a change, as Roethe assumes? Or did he, as so many others assume, simply wish to indicate within the pantheistic framework a descending scale of dignity and power? The far likelier possibility, which remains to be considered, is that the

Makrokosmus and the Erdgeist are meant to differ from one another not only in degree, but also and primarily in kind, that the relationship between them is one of contrast, of antithesis. This view has also occasionally been maintained, notably by Rickert; but it has found little support. In maintaining that the two symbols are indeed intended antithetically and that therefore both are necessary, and the one is only fully intelligible in the light of the other, we must from the outset admit that Goethe has not brought this antithesis out clearly enough and that it can easily be overlooked. The very names that he employs suggest a difference of degree, of greater and less (as earth is obviously less than the whole universe), rather than one of kind. Verbally considered, the opposite of the Makrokosmus would be Man as microcosm, and that of the Erdgeist would be the "Himmelsgeist" (the Spirit of Heaven)—presumably the transcendent God; but of these palpable antitheses there is no real trace in the invocation scene with its consistently pantheistic postulates. Nevertheless it will be seen that everything does indeed here turn on a genuine, all-important, though not clearly enough worked out, antithesis.

For generations now, endless labour and ingenuity have been expended upon attempts to find a solution of the Erdgeist problem in cabbalistic literature. Paracelsus, Welling, and Swedenborg are usually singled out as the authors of this type who probably influenced Goethe most, but various others, such as Iamblichus and Helmont, have also found keen supporters. One difficulty is that the common stock of cabbalistic ideas, terms and symbols recurs again and again in different combinations in all these writings, so that there is seldom a compelling reason to suppose Goethe derived such knowledge of it as he had from one of them rather than from another. The innumerable "parallels" in thought and phrasing detected between the cabbalists and Goethe's *Faust* seldom really prove anything; so far as they are not merely fortuitous, they usually turn out to be due to Goethe's having, like the cabbalists, been very familiar with the Bible and having employed scriptural phrases and allusions as frequently as they did. But disappointing though this line of research proves to be, so far as its own avowed aims are concerned, one or two not always fully appreciated negative conclusions of great value arise from it. While the Makrokos-

mus is one of the most prominent conceptions in all these cabbalistic writings, it has proved impossible to find anything in them
that really corresponds to Goethe's Erdgeist. The sort of thing
that is found instead is Paracelsus' *archaeus terrae*, which may
indeed have helped to suggest the name of Goethe's spirit, but
of which Paracelsus himself explicitly declares that it is "not a
spirit and also not a person." *Archaeus* appears in fact to be rather
a pseudo-scientific than a magical or mythical concept in this
period of transition from mediaeval magic to modern science, and
to denote a "force," in much the same way as that in which gravita-
tion and electricity are termed "forces." In speaking of the archaeus
terrae Paracelsus was thinking of the "force" of earth as one of the
four elements. Ernst Grumach, who is particularly pertinacious in
attempting to trace everything in Goethe's Faust back to Welling's
Opus mago-cabbalisticum, comes to the remarkable conclusion
that the Erdgeist is really not a spirit of earth at all, but a spirit of
the air, and can only account for Goethe's calling it "Geist der
Erde" by describing it as "dieser irdischste und niedrigste aller
Geister" (this earthiest and basest of all Spirits).[12] A conception
which often occurs amongst sixteenth-century cabbalists is that
of an *anima terrae*, where Earth is thought of not as one of the four
elements, but as a heavenly body with a kind of soul or vital principle at its centre. This vital principle comes a good deal nearer to
Goethe's Erdgeist, but, as Agnes Bartscherer says, it was never
regarded as a kind of spirit that could be invoked;[13] it played a very
subordinate part in cabbalistic speculation and Goebel speaks of
it as leading "eine traurige philosophische Schattenexistenz" (a
gloomy, philosophical pseudo-existence).[14] It was simply supposed
to be there, in the depths, but never to manifest itself in any other
way than through the bare existence of the earth as such. More to
our purpose is the old conception of tutelary spirits governing the
motions of the planets from without and above, and keeping them
in their "spheres." Goethe's Erdgeist is sometimes interpreted as
such a planetary spirit, particularly by Shelley, and its own words
to Faust, "Du hast . . . An meiner Sphäre lang gesogen,"[15] are seen
as supporting this view. But the belief in planetary spirits stood and
fell with the Ptolemaic system, for which the Earth was not a
planet, but the fixed centre around which everything else revolved,

and therefore had no "sphere" and no corresponding spirit. Once the Copernican conception of the earth as one of the planets established itself, the old idea of revolving spheres with their tutelary spirits was superseded, and it was not easy to adopt the Copernican position and at the same time to remain a cabbalist. The original, representative cabbalistic writers knew no planetary Spirit of Earth analogous to those tutelary spirits which they ascribed to the other planets and to the sun and the moon, nor did Swedenborg. It may be noted, however, that Herder, in a not really characteristic and later deleted draft passage in his study on "Plastik" (sculpture), written in 1769, raises the question, "ob es nicht einen Gott der Erde, des Jupiters, des Saturns gebe. Einen Gott des Monds; einen Gott der Sonne, der stärker ist, als alle Planeten" (whether there may not be a God of the Earth, of Jupiter, of Saturn, a God of the Moon, a God of the Sun, stronger than all the planets). He goes on:

—die Philosophie macht uns aber abergläubisch? Sie giebt uns einen Genius der Erde? Nein! nicht abergläubisch, der Genius hört auf mich so wenig, als ich auf das Schreien eines Wurms! Er ist zu gross dazu; er spricht nur mit dem Genius des Monds, der Sonne! Ich bin ihm zu klein! Ich bin ein Gott auf seinem Rücken und zugleich eine Laus, ein Wurm darauf; also nicht anbeten, nicht rufen, nichts . . .*[16]

It is highly probable that Goethe knew this unpublished manuscript of Herder's or at least that Herder expressed similar ideas in conversations with him in Strasburg about 1770–1771, and that we therefore have here one of the sources of the Erdgeist.

What is found at every hand in the old cabbalistic writings and does seem to correspond far more closely to Goethe's Erdgeist than their peripheral and shadowy ideas of an archaeus terrae or anima terrae is the *anima mundi* or *spiritus mundi*, the World Soul or

* But does philosophy make us superstitious? Does it give us a Genius of the Earth? No! not superstitious, for that Genius pays as little attention to me as I do to the crying of a worm! It is too great for that; it speaks only with the Genius of the Moon or the Sun! I am too small for it! I am a god on its back, and at the same time a louse, a worm on it; therefore there can be no question of worshipping it, of invoking it or of anything else of that sort.

World Spirit, "world" in this context being conceived of always as signifying not just earth alone, but the whole universe. The difficulty, however, is that Goethe, by distinguishing between his spirit and the Makrokosmus, and by explicitly designating it as the "Geist der Erde," has made it clear that it is something other than the World Spirit as such, or that it is the World Spirit with a difference, in some special sense. For the World Spirit in the usually accepted sense would obviously correspond to the Makrokosmus. That is why Agnes Bartscherer would pass over all specific mentions of the Erdgeist as something irrelevant and without real validity, maintaining that the spirit that does appear can after all only be the Spirit of the Makrokosmus, the World Spirit. A similar tendency is shown also by Rickert in his interpretation of the "Erhabner Geist" monologue of 1788 in "Wald und Höhle," which, he says, must be addressed to the Makrokosmus, not to the Erdgeist. Goethe himself in his later years sometimes (as we shall see) referred to the Erdgeist simply as the "Weltgeist" (World Spirit). But the distinction, which had ceased to be important to him then, certainly was highly important to him in the years when the *Urfaust* was written.

Whatever share such cabbalistic conceptions as the archaeus terrae and anima terrae may have had in suggesting the name of the Erdgeist to Goethe, it is essentially, as Niejahr says, something that Goethe himself freely invented,[17] and—it may be added— something that he invented specially for the purposes of his Faust drama and would probably otherwise never have thought of. The word he uses for his own personal purposes is "Weltgeist" or "Weltseele" (World Spirit or World Soul); only once does he refer to the "Erdgeist" outside *Faust*.[18] The real meaning of the Erdgeist, wherever else it is to be found, is certainly not to be found in the cabbalistic writings, which were for Goethe ultimately only material to be freely moulded and transformed by his own imagination in keeping with his own experiences and reflexions. He did not indeed invent the actual German word "Erdgeist" or "Erdengeist," but he gave to it a meaning which it had never had before. So far as it is recorded before his time, it signifies either, when applied to human beings, a base, materialistic disposition, or, in folklore, a usually malevolent, goblin-like being inhabiting particular caves and rocks, sometimes thought of as existing solitarily and being of more than human dimensions, but more often as dwarfish and swarming in great numbers—in fact, a kind of gnome. Earth spirits in this sense are often mentioned in cabbalistic literature, where they are given by Paracelsus such names as "Gnomi," "Pygmeae," and "Mani," and in the final stage of his work on *Faust I*, in 1800, Goethe himself alludes to them under the names "Kobold" and "Incubus." That his Erdgeist has nothing to do with such small fry of folklore, but is to be thought of as a unique mythical being of remarkable stature and dignity, is obvious. The technical terminology of the cabbalists was always Latin or Greek, but the natural connotation of the German word "Erdgeist" from the cabbalistic point of view and on the analogy of cabbalistic ways of thinking would have been, as we have found, a personification either of Earth as one of the four elements or of Earth as one of the heavenly bodies. We shall see, however, that neither of these conceptions has any relevancy to the most important aspects of Goethe's Erdgeist, which turn not upon cosmogonic, but upon ethical and psychological issues.

In *Faust, I. Teil*, as Goethe completed it after 1797, no causal relationship is indicated between the conjuration of the Erdgeist and that most important motif dictated by the intrinsic character of the legend and idea of Faust, the first appearance before him of Mephisto. It is unthinkable, however, that when Goethe first wrote the conjuration scene he did not envisage some such causal relationship, that the invocation of the Erdgeist was not specially intended and designed to lead up to and in some way to motivate Mephisto's first appearance. Mephisto was originally to have come to Faust *as a result of* his having conjured up the Erdgeist; that is clearly enough indicated by Faust's own statement that Mephisto has been "chained to him as a companion by the great and glorious Spirit." That conjuration was to be the great, decisive deed by which Faust is launched upon his specifically Faustian destiny, and therefore everything depends upon the frame of mind in which he performs that deed, whether or not he performs it as an absolutely free agent, with his eyes open and his head erect and with a full sense of responsibility and of his own powers.

If he sees in the Erdgeist nothing but a kind of inferior, smaller-scale substitute for the Makrokosmus, a second best that he must put up with, because the genuine Makrokosmus is too mighty for him, then his frame of mind in invoking it can only be one of resignation, frustration, discouragement and defeat, and his deed is determined less by his own will than by external agencies; he is doing not what he would really have preferred to do, if he had the choice, but what the hampering circumstances in which he finds himself alone allow him to do. That is the view we are compelled to take, so long as we recognize only a difference of *degree* between Makrokosmus and Erdgeist, and it is the view proclaimed without any misgivings by many critics, for example by Karl Wollf, who writes: "Fausts ursprüngliches Verlangen war schöpferisches Eins-werden mit dem All-Leben, mit der Gottheit selbst. Dann war er bereit, *sich mit dem irdischen Bereich zu begnügen*" (What Faust originally desired was union with the life of the universe, with the godhead itself. Then he was *ready to content himself* with the earthly sphere).[19] This same expression, *"sich begnügen"* (to content himself) is used also in the same connexion by Muschg.[20] But is it appropriate that Faust, whose most essential characteristic it is never to content himself with anything, should, on the first occasion when he appears before us, and in the moment that is to decide his destiny for all eternity, be shown to us as "ready to content himself" with a mere second best? If nothing more than that is involved in his appeal to the Erdgeist, then he is less aspiring and venturesome than the older Faust of the popular dramatic tradition, who is always represented in the opening scene as being faced with a choice and freely making that choice, not as simply sliding into his destiny resignedly from frustration to frustration. Marlowe took over a primitive allegorical device from the old moralities to project this existential choice of Faust's into concrete, visible action upon the stage; Faust's Good Angel appears on one side of him, warning him against the pursuit of magic, while on the other side his Bad Angel encourages him in it, and it is the Bad Angel whose advice he follows. This feature in Marlowe's drama recurs regularly in the German Faust puppet-plays and must have been known to Goethe from them. It was not, of course, a device that he could use unmodified in his own Faust drama, which was evidently conceived from the first not on orthodox

Christian, but on pantheistic lines, in keeping with the bent of his own mind since 1771 and with the dominant tendency amongst the advanced minds of his generation, and in which Faust was not unambiguously to choose "evil" as such. But some sort of corresponding existential choice Goethe's Faust too had, *mutatis mutandis*, to make, and the possibility suggests itself that the sign of the Makrokosmus and the Geist der Erde may be so to speak pantheistic equivalents or substitutes for the Christian Good and Bad Angels of the Marlovian tradition or may at least fulfil a similar dramatic function; that the pantheistic principle may have been duplicated here, in order that Faust may be faced with two alternatives to choose between. This can, however, only be so, if there is some fundamental *qualitative* difference between the two, compared with which their merely *quantitative* difference in magnitude and cosmic status counts for very little, so that Faust, in turning from the Makrokosmus to the Erdgeist, is not resigning himself and making the best of a bad job, but spontaneously and actively giving the preference to the Erdgeist and deciding in favour of it, in fact making the momentous existential choice which is to be expected of him. We should remember here that Goethe had by October, 1771, already largely emancipated himself from traditional morality; for he wrote in that month, in his "Rede zum Schäkespears Tag" (Speech for Shakespeare's Day): "Das, was wir böse nennen, ist nur die andere Seite vom Guten" (What we call evil is only the other side of good). It is therefore out of the question that the Makrokosmus should be simply "good" and the Erdgeist simply "evil"; but there may nevertheless be a qualitative antithesis between them corresponding at a considerable remove and in an emancipated, heterodox way to the primitive old antithesis of good and evil. Are there any legitimate grounds for regarding the Erdgeist not indeed as an Evil Spirit in the traditional sense of the word, but still as sinister, ambivalent, ruthless and dangerous, so that in turning to it Faust is taking an imprudent, temerarious, ominous, reprehensible step, as he would not be doing, if he adhered to the Makrokosmus instead? The Erdgeist so impressively bodies forth what we know to have been Goethe's own exuberant pantheistic sense of life that the idea of its possibly also having certain disconcerting or even sinister aspects occurs to very few readers. One cannot indeed suggest that Goethe deliberately invested the Erdgeist with such problematic aspects, without at the same time suggesting that he sometimes had serious misgivings about his own vitalistic pantheism. That is, however, just the suggestion that is here made, in full awareness that it is bound to meet with scepticism and opposition in many quarters.

The best point of departure in investigating these problems is the passage in which Faust turns away from the Sign of the Makrokosmus and addresses himself to the Erdgeist. This is indeed the key-passage of the entire invocation scene, the pivotal point on which everything else turns, although Agnes Bartscherer and Roethe would, as has been seen, dismiss it as an irrelevant digression or interpolation of no real validity. Faust breaks off his contemplation of the Sign of the Makrokosmus with the words:

> Welch Schauspiel! aber, ach, ein Schauspiel nur!
> Wo fass ich dich, unendliche Natur?
> Euch Brüste, wo? Ihr Quellen alles Lebens,
> An denen Himmel und Erde hängt,
> Dahin die welke Brust sich drängt—
> Ihr quellt, ihr tränkt, und schmacht ich so vergebens?

> (Er schlägt unwillig das Buch um und erblickt das Zeichen des Erdgeistes.)

> Wie anders wirkt dies Zeichen auf mich ein!
> Du, Geist der Erde, bist mir näher;
> Schon fühl ich meine Kräfte höher,
> Schon glüh ich wie vom neuen Wein.*

There is nothing to be detected in these verses of that resigned acceptance of a second best, which they are commonly interpreted as expressing, nor does Faust anywhere in the course of them sug-

---

* What a spectacle! but alas! only a spectacle. / Where can I grasp you, infinite Nature? / Where grasp you, breasts? You well-springs of all life, / At which Heaven and Earth hang, / Towards which my parched bosom yearns, / You gush, you give suck, and I languish thus in vain. / (He turns over the page angrily and sees the sign of the Earth-Spirit.) / How differently this sign affects me! / You, Spirit of Earth, are nearer to me. / Already I feel my powers mounting higher, / Already I glow as with new wine.

gest that the Sign of the Makrokosmus is too mighty for him. All
he says is that it cannot give him what he desires, and that he must
therefore seek that elsewhere. What it can give him is a "Schauspiel" (a spectacle), by which we are here to understand a purely
spiritual, inward vision, and that spectacle Faust has received to
the full in his contemplation of it. There is no suggestion that it
could have given anything else or anything more, if Faust had
been mightier than he is. He has exhausted its possibilities and
turns away from it not resignedly, but "angrily" (unwillig). It is
not Faust who proves unequal to the Sign of the Makrokosmus
and is rejected by it; on the contrary, the Sign of the Makrokosmus
proves unequal to Faust and is rejected by him. Beautiful though
the inward vision that it affords him is, it still does not give him
that intimate, sensuous, tactile union with the overflowing breasts
of "infinite Nature" after which he yearns. It is important to note
here that the question is throughout only of the Sign of the
Makrokosmus, not of the Makrokosmus itself or of a Spirit of the
Makrokosmus. There is no indication that the spiritual principle
embodied in the sign of the Makrokosmus could have manifested
itself in any other more palpable and objective way than in Faust's
inward vision, which is nothing less than a kind of *unio mystica*,
such as the contemplative ascetics experience. The way of the
ascetic, who austerely renounces all sensual gratification, all en-
tanglement in the particular and many, in order to devote himself
to undistracted contemplation of the One-and-All, is open to Faust
if he chooses to take it, but he does not choose to do so. To be so
strongly endowed with the inward, visionary gifts of the mystic as
Faust proves himself to be in his contemplation of the Sign of the
Makrokosmus is to have, in some measure at least, a vocation to
the ascetic life; and then to resolve in spite of that to plunge quite
unrestrainedly into the rough-and-tumble of worldly existence, as
Faust does when he turns to the Erdgeist, is to fly in the face of
that partial vocation and to ask for trouble. Faust can only do this
because he feels an equally strong or rather an even stronger urge
or "vocation" (if one may call it that) to the worldly life with its
excitement, adventures, and sensual gratifications. Faust is in fact
torn between these two urges or vocations, the one spiritual and

ascetic, the other worldly and sensual. Or as Goethe was to formulate it later in much quoted words, "zwei Seelen wohnen in seiner Brust" (he has two souls residing in his breast), and it is to the loftier of these two souls that the Sign of the Makrokosmus, to the lower that the Erdgeist appeals. Here at the outset, in turning to the Erdgeist, he decides in favour of the worldly, sensual side of his nature. When the Spirit appears Faust does indeed prove unequal to it and is rejected by it, but that is almost the exact opposite of the experience that he had gone through with the Sign of the Makrokosmus. The idea that Faust "glaubt, das Zeichen des Makrokosmus *oder* den Erdgeist wählen zu müssen" (thinks he has to choose between the Macrocosm and the Spirit of Earth) is touched upon by one of the best recent interpreters of Goethe, Emil Staiger, who goes on, however, to say that Faust could, if he had known, have had both together. What sinister aspect is there to the Erdgeist that could make Faust's choice of it so ominous as it needs to be to involve him in an alliance with Mephisto?

There is one fairly obvious contrast between the Sign of the Makrokosmus and the Erdgeist which has often been pointed out, notably by Rickert, and is widely acknowledged: the former embodies the principle of contemplation and evokes the contemplative element in Faust's nature, the latter embodies the principle of activity and evokes the active element in Faust's nature. In fact, we see under these symbols the *vita contemplativa* confronted with the *vita activa*—a dualism adumbrated in the gospel narrative of the sisters Mary and Martha and of central importance to the Middle Ages, which gave the preference to the contemplative life, but of equal importance to the eighteenth century, which just as resolutely gave the preference to the active life. Goethe and most of his eminent contemporaries, particularly Fichte, return again and again to this theme, insisting almost unanimously on the higher value of action as against a contemplative attitude towards existence. This is indeed a central theme of Goethe's Faust drama, for his Faust only is Faust in so far as he is a man of action in the sense of being committed to the principle of activity. But he has first to become a man of action, and only in doing so does he really become Faust in the essential meaning of the name. Previously, throughout his long years spent amongst books as a scholar and professor, he has led a contemplative life, and it is in the opening monologue, above all in the passage now before us, where he decides in favour of the Erdgeist and against the sign of the Makrokosmus, that he breaks violently with his past and his own former contemplative self, dedicating himself to the life of action that is the specifically Faustian mode of existence. The dualism of contemplation and action was, however, also conceived of by the Storm and Stress writers and especially by Goethe and by Herder, who so strongly influenced him in these years, as a dualism of mere dry theory and sensuous experience, of mere words and actual things, of mere ideas and palpable realities, of mere reason and immediate feeling, of mere thought and life. The view that this dualism of contemplation and action is symbolized by the Sign of the Makrokosmus and the Erdgeist is indeed rejected by Franz Koch and F. J. Schneider as irreconcilable with the "für die Jugenddichtung Goethes bezeichnende Gleichsetzung von Logos und Leben, Geist und Kraft" (identification of Logos and Life, of Mind and Power which characterizes Goethe's early work).[21] But enough evidence will be produced to show that this objection is quite unfounded and that the dualism in question runs all through Goethe's work from about 1771 onward, when he wrote in the first version of *Götz von Berlichingen*: "Überlegung ist eine Krankheit der Seele und hat nur kranke Taten getan" (Reflexion is a sickness of the soul and has only performed sick deeds).

One of the grounds for regarding the Sign of the Makrokosmus as representing the contemplative principle is that, after initially arousing in Faust—much as the Sign of the Erdgeist does—a "Wonne" that flows "auf einmal ihm durch *alle seine Sinnen*" (joy [that flows] through *all his senses* at once), and filling him with a glowing, youthful feeling of life in all his nerves and veins, it almost at once tranquillizes this "innre Toben" (inner tumult) and suspends the activities of all his senses except that of sight, for which Goethe here employs the word specially associated in the German language with mystical contemplation and inward vision, "Schauen." This gives more point to the lament, "Welch Schauspiel! aber, ach, ein Schauspiel nur!" for the decisive component in the word *Schau*-spiel is also *Schauen*. Faust's vision of the Makrokosmus, which he thus dismisses as "ein Schauspiel nur," is characterized by perfect harmony, by the absence of all violence, effort, or suffering.

> Wie alles sich zum Ganzen webt,
> Eins in dem andern würkt und lebt!
> Wie Himmelskräfte auf und nieder steigen
> Und sich die goldnen Eimer reichen!
> Mit segenduftenden Schwingen
> Von Himmel durch die Erde dringen,
> Harmonisch all das All durchklingen!*

A certain cool clarity distinguishes this vision, which, based in part on Jacob's Ladder, gives so to speak a bird's-eye view of the cosmic processes from some lofty and distant vantage-point, *sub specie aeternitatis*, far from the heat of the *mêlée* and the stress of the moment, where all agitation, striving and conflict no longer count in the timeless harmony of pure being, where the disorder of earthly, fleshly, human existence is overarched and counterpoised by a higher spiritual order analogous to that of Christian theism with its Heaven and angels. This is a conception that may not at first strike us as characteristic of Goethe, but is nevertheless often encountered in his writings, notably in the Song of the Three Archangels belonging to the 1797–1801 phase of his work on *Faust* and in a brief poem of his old age concluding:

> Und alles Drängen, alles Ringen
> Ist ewige Ruh in Gott dem Herrn.†

Faust has here already found an answer, and in its own way a valid answer, to his question, "what it is that holds the world together at the innermost core?"—if he could accept it. But his

---

* How everything is woven together to form the Whole, / Each one working within the other! / Where celestial powers mount and descend, / Handing to one another the golden buckets! / With pinions redolent of blessing / Penetrating through earth from Heaven, / And all harmoniously resounding through the All.

† And all tumult, all struggle / Is eternal peace in God the Lord.

will refuses to accept it, his nature is incapable of accepting it, and in this non-acceptance, which is equally determined by necessity and free choice, lies at once his greatness and what may be called his tragic guilt, his "hybris."

The Erdgeist embodies a vision of existence seen not from above and afar, but from close up and at the heart of the turmoil; not from the perspective of eternity, but from that of the moment, where passion, pleasure, and pain still assert themselves in full intensity, with nothing to mitigate or counteract them. It impresses itself not only on sight, in isolation the sense of distance, detachment and serenity, but upon the other senses too, above all that of touch, the sense of nearness, involvement and precipitancy. In this connexion it is to be noted that Goethe in July, 1772, wrote to Herder giving the sense of touch the preference before that of sight on lines similar to though not identical with those here indicated. It cannot indeed have been much later than autumn, 1770, that he introduced into his fragmentary epistolary novel *Arianne und Wetty* Herder's dictum: "Der kälteste Sinn ist das Sehen" (The coldest sense is that of sight). Faust demands, instead of a "spectacle" for his eyes only, something that he can also "grasp," something that is "nearer" to him. He feels that he has found this in the Sign of the Erdgeist, which produces an effect upon him exactly opposed to that produced by the Sign of the Makrokosmus, intensifying his inner tumult instead of tranquillizing it, so that he cries:

> Ich fühle Mut, mich in die Welt zu wagen,
> All Erden Weh und all ihr Glück zu tragen,
> Mit Stürmen mich herumzuschlagen
> Und in des Schiffbruchs Knirschen nicht zu zagen.*

It is by uttering these words that Faust evokes the Erdgeist. They are not a formal magical incantation, but they have the efficacy of one, because they are so fully attuned to the Spirit's nature. "Answer me, if you hear me," Faust had called a little before to

---

* I feel courage to venture out into the world, / To undergo all the suffering of earth and all its happiness, / To buffet with tempests / And not to lose heart when the ship's timbers are ground against the rock.

the spirits in general, and these are words which the Erdgeist must hear and answer. It makes its presence felt by causing the light of the moon and of Faust's lamp to be extinguished, and red rays to emanate from his head. A mysterious haze spreads in the room, a tremor descends from the vaulted ceiling and communicates itself to Faust's frame. All that remains for him to do, in order to make the already present Spirit manifest itself visibly, is to speak in undertones the incantatory formula given in the book, and this he does, "though it should cost his life" (Und kostet' es mein Leben). That is the nearest he comes to practising magic in the conventional sense, and Goethe makes as little of it as possible. The Spirit itself sums up its essential character in a lyrical passage that is a pendant to Faust's Makrokosmus vision:

> In Lebensfluten, im Tatensturm
> Wall ich auf und ab,
> Webe hin und her!
> Geburt und Grab,
> Ein ewges Meer,
> Ein wechselnd Leben!
> So schaff ich am sausenden Webstuhl der Zeit
> Und würke der Gottheit lebendiges Kleid.*

The insistence here is upon life, activity, movement, change, time, transiency, as opposed to the harmony, stability, and permanency of pure being which characterized the hymn to the Makrokosmus. Where the earlier vision had been static and serene, the later one is dynamic and turbulent. This is at once perceptible in the contrasted rhythmical character of the two passages. But for such terms as "zum Ganzen," "das All," and the actual name "Makrokosmus," the earlier vision of nature permeated by celestial powers from above might almost be thought to presuppose the transcendental Creator-God of Christian tradition, rather than the immanent deity of pantheism, and certainly stands near to that tradition in spite

---

* In floods of life, in a storm of activity / I wander up and down, / Rove hither and thither! / Birth and the grave, / An eternal ocean, / An everchanging movement, / A glowing life! / Thus I work at the humming loom of time / And fashion a living garment for the deity.

of its impersonal character. No such doubts can arise about the deity whose very flesh, whose "lebendiges Kleid" is wrought by the Erdgeist at the humming loom of time.

The vision of the Makrokosmus leaves Faust no scope or incentive for the assertion of his own individuality: in face of such perfect harmony there is nothing for him to do but to remain absorbed in passive, depersonalized wonder and awe, as one who recognizes that anything splendid *he* might originate, aspire after, or perform has been forestalled by the divine cosmic order. The vision of the Erdgeist, on the other hand, arouses in him a maximum of individualistic energy and aspiration. This polarity between Faust's two visionary experiences is widely acknowledged, even by some of those critics whose interpretation of the Invocation scene otherwise differs very much from that here presented. Thus Grumach speaks of the relationship between the "mere spectacle" of the Makrokosmus vision and Faust's will to "grasp the breasts of Nature" and "comprehend" the Erdgeist as the antithesis between "einem nur theoretischen oder kontemplativen Erkennen" and "einem Begreifen, das . . . seinen Gegenstand in unmittelbarster Berührung umfasst und umschliesst" (an only theoretical and contemplative knowledge and a comprehension which embraces and encompasses its object in directest contiguity).[22] In the same connexion Roethe, although he regards the Makrokosmus as only a superfluous afterthought of Goethe's, nevertheless speaks of the felicitous "Gegensatz der beschaulichen Friedensstimmung zu der handelnden Tatenlust" (contrast between a mood of contemplative tranquillity and the active desire to be up and doing).[23] Even F. J. Schneider, who, as was seen, explicitly rejects Rickert's thesis of a "sharp contrast" between the two visions, would, in agreement with Petsch, explain "die Unbefriedigtheit des kontemplativen Magiers am theoretischen Ergebnis seiner Schau" as having its ground "im Erwachen seines voluntarischaktiven Menschentums, in seinem Wunsch, sich auch irgendwie am Weltgeschehen zu beteiligen" (The ground for the meditative magician's dissatisfaction with the theoretical results of his contemplation lies in the awakening of his volitional, active humanity, in his desire to play some part of his own in the cosmic process).[24] But for most readers and critics it still remains unthinkable that so active and individualistic a pantheist as Goethe should ever have seen anything sinister in the active Erdgeist or anything ominous in Faust's invocation of that spirit.

"Tätig zu sein ist des Menschen erste Bestimmung" (The first vocation of Man is to be active), writes Goethe in *Wilhelm Meisters Lehrjahre*; and again: "Der Geist, aus dem wir handeln, ist das Höchste" (The highest thing of all is the spirit which stirs us to activity). Many parallels to this sentiment could be cited from all phases of his development. The Erdgeist is "der Geist, aus dem wir handeln," and Faust's decision in favour of it is one which we can be sure Goethe sympathized with and approved of. He had himself, in his own way, come to a similar decision during his Strasburg years. There are difficulties indeed about the idea of Faust as a "man of action," since in practice he really performs comparatively little in the way of definite deeds. But he is dominated by a restless inner urge towards activity, for which Goethe regularly uses the word "Streben" (striving); that word, more than any other, sums up his specifically Faustian character. The important point that is not always taken into consideration here is, however, that Goethe sees in activity not only the first and highest vocation of man, but also something problematic. In his *Maximen und Reflexionen* he writes: "Der Handelnde ist immer gewissenlos; es hat niemand Gewissen als der Betrachtende" (The doer is always without a conscience; no one has a conscience except him who contemplates); and again: "Unbedingte Tätigkeit, von welcher Art sie sei, macht zuletzt bankerott" (Unconditional activity, of any kind whatsoever, leads in the long run to bankruptcy). He expresses these views even more forcibly in one of the drafts for *Dichtung und Wahrheit*: "Tat steht mit Reue, Handeln mit Sorge in immerwährendem Bezug" (There is a permanent nexus between the deed and remorse, between activity and care). Nor is this sense of the dangers of the active, self-assertive, individualistic principle confined to Goethe's middle and later years, as we might at first expect it to be. It is implied in the remarkable Storm and Stress definition of tragedy which he gives as early as October, 1771, when he says of Shakespeare: "—seine Stücke drehen sich alle um den geheimen Punkt, . . . in dem das Eigentümliche unsres Ichs, die prätendierte Freiheit unsres Wollens mit dem notwendigen Gang des Ganzen zusammenstösst" (all his plays turn upon that mysterious point where our individuality, the supposed freedom of our will, comes into conflict with the necessary course of the Whole). We may fairly assume that his own Faust drama was intended to turn upon this same "geheimen Punkt," as do his *Götz von Berlichingen*, his *Werther*, and his *Egmont*. An individualism that knows nothing of the grave dangers of individualism is only a vague, rhetorical gesture. We can legitimately recognise a certain analogy between the Sign of the Makrokosmus and the "notwendige Gang des Ganzen," between the Erdgeist and "das Eigentümliche unsres Ichs, die prätendierte Freiheit unsres Wollens." In so far as the Erdgeist embodies the principle of activity, it is indifferent to ethical distinctions and takes life and death in its stride. In choosing it Faust is inevitably estranging himself from his own conscience and heading sooner or later for "bankruptcy."

One way in which Goethe made it clear that there is something sinister about the Erdgeist was by a stage direction running: "Es zuckt eine rötliche Flamme, der Geist erscheint in der Flamme *in widerlicher Gestalt*" (A reddish flame flickers, the Spirit appears in the flame *in a repulsive form*). This revealing final phrase —which Morris would explain away as meaning nothing more than "unwillig abweisend"[25] (indignantly aloof)—Goethe suppressed, however, in preparing the text of *Faust, ein Fragment* for publication in 1790. He retained indeed the words "Schröckliches Gesicht!" (Terrible apparition!) with which Faust reacts to the manifestation of the Spirit, but explicitly declared in a letter of June, 1819, to Graf Brühl, who was planning a stage production of *Faust I*, that the word "schrecklich" here was to be regarded only as expressing Faust's own feeling and not as describing the actual lineaments of the Spirit, and went on to say that "überhaupt hier nichts Fratzenhaftes und Widerliches erscheinen dürfte" (nothing grotesque and repulsive ought to appear here). In the same letter he said that he had himself thought of representing the Erdgeist on the stage by some kind of magic lantern device with the head of the Zeus Otricoli enlarged to gigantic proportions, and in a rough sketch of the Invocation scene made about 1811 he shows it with the magnified head of an Apollo. But these were the years in which he had grown out of touch with the original conception of the Erdgeist and would sometimes—for example in a scenario of November, 1812—refer to it simply as the "Weltgeist." For the understanding of that original conception the deleted phrase "in widerlicher Gestalt" is of considerable importance.

One of the chief clues to the true point of the Erdgeist is its actual name, which we have become used to and take for granted, but which was calculated to disconcert Goethe's contemporaries. The metaphysical and emotional associations of the word "earth" (*Erde*) are very different from those of the word "world" (*Welt*), and this distinction is very strongly felt in the German language. The conception of a Spirit of Earth was novel, paradoxical and startling; it could not be seen as simply identical with that of the World Spirit. It made a deep impression when it was first put before the reading public with the appearance of *Faust, ein Fragment* in 1790, and many writers took it over, each interpreting it in his own way. There was a tendency, most strikingly represented by Schiller and Novalis, to assume that the *Erdgeist* must be an evil spirit, undoubtedly because "earth" was symbolically associated with the baser side of human nature. This is closely connected with one of the most important connotations of the word "earth" and its derivatives, when it is thought of as standing for *this* world as opposed to any other world, particularly to the other world of Christian tradition, but also to the purely spiritual, "higher" world postulated by idealistic philosophy with its heroic ethical standards and its aesthetic doctrines of a beauty which is all harmony, tranquillity, nobility, dignity, and perfection. Walt Whitman, Nietzsche, André Gide, Rilke, and many others expressed that disapprobation of all religious or philosophical other-worldliness that is so characteristic of the modern mind in the form of dithyrambic hymns to the Earth. The youthful Goethe was one of the most important initiators of this revolution in our attitude towards the earth and earthliness. He appears in his Storm and Stress years particularly as an ecstatic earth-worshipper, infecting many contemporaries with his chthonic sentiments and outraging others. The first faint hint of this devotion to earth is to be found about November, 1771, in *Götz von Berlichingen,* where the leader of the gipsies says: "Wir wohnen an der Erd und schlafen auf der Erd" (We live close to the earth and sleep on the earth). In *Wanderers Sturmlied* ("Wanderer's Storm Song"), written probably about March, 1772, Goethe invokes the Muses and Graces as he tramps through the mud:

> Umschwebt mich, ihr Musen!
> Ihr Charitinnen!
> Das ist Wasser, das ist Erde
> Und der Sohn des Wassers und der Erde,
> Über den ich wandle göttergleich.

> Ihr seid rein wie das Herz der Wasser,
> Ihr seid rein wie das Mark der Erde,
> Ihr umschwebt mich und ich schwebe
> Über Wasser und Erde
> Göttergleich.*

In a review of November 3, 1772 Goethe deplores the way in which the other-worldly Lavater "sich über das Irdische hinauf entzückt, Erden mit dem Fuss auf die Seite stösst" (works himself up into raptures above the earthly sphere and kicks earth on one side). In a letter to Kestner of February 5, 1773 he speaks of "die unendliche Erde" (the infinite earth), a phrase that recurs in the fragmentary Prometheus drama of the following autumn and also in a not exactly datable letter of the same year to Roderer. His writings of the years 1773–1775 are permeated with this devotion to earth, which accompanies him in modified forms throughout his life. He made repeated use of the myth of the earth-born giant Antaeus, who drew all his strength from contact with his mother, the Earth;

* Hover around me, you Muses! / You Graces! / This is water, this is earth / And the son of water and earth, / On which I rove like one of the gods. / You are pure as the heart of the water, / You are pure as the marrow of the earth, / You hover around me, and I hover / On water and earth, / Like one of the gods.

he often saw himself as such an Antaeus, and his Faust is also an Antaeus.

A particularly striking example of the this-worldly cult of the earth and earthliness which dominates Goethe from about 1772 to his first years in Weimar occurs in *Der ewige Jude* ("The Wandering Jew") of 1774, where Christ is shown returning to earth once more:

> Er fühlt im vollen Himmelsflug
> Der irdschen Atmosphäre Zug.*

It could be said similarly of Faust that in turning from the Sign of the Makrokosmus to the Erdgeist he "feels in full celestial flight the pull of the earthly atmosphere." Christ salutes earth ecstatically with the words: "Sei Erde tausendmal gegrüsst!" (A thousand greetings to you, Earth!) But earth is not seen by him as having no seamy side to it. In feeling the pull of its atmosphere he also feels

> —wie das reinste Glück der Welt
> Schon eine Ahndung von Weh enthält.†

In his salutation of earth he goes on:

> O Welt voll wunderbarer Wirrung,
> Voll Geist der Ordnung, träger Irrung,
> Du Kettenring von Wonn' und Wehe,
> Du Mutter, die mich selbst zum Grab gebar,
> Die ich, obgleich ich bei der Schöpfung war,
> Im Ganzen doch nicht sonderlich verstehe.‡

The contradictions and ambiguities of earthly existence are a theme to which Goethe recurs again and again, especially in these years.

---

* He feels in full celestial flight / The pull of the earthly atmosphere.

† How the purest happiness in the world / Contains within it already a foreboding of pain.

‡ O world full of strange confusion, / Full of the spirit of order and of dull error, / You ring of joys and sorrows linked together, / You mother who bore me that I might come to the grave, / You whom, although I had a hand in creating you, / I still on the whole do not very well understand.

"Dass es der Erde so sauwohl und so weh ist zugleich!" (That earth should feel so uproariously cheerful and so wretched at one and the same moment!) he writes in his Swiss diary of summer, 1775. But this very imperfection and uncertainty of earthly life only endears it all the more to Goethe, as it does also to the Christ of his *Ewiger Jude* and to Faust, who desires to experience to the full "all Erden Weh und all ihr Glück." There are moments indeed in which the darker aspects of this earthly life become unendurable. Such moments visit Werther (1774), who rejoices to see them "wirken und schaffen ineinander in den Tiefen der Erde, alle die unergründlichen Kräfte" (working and toiling, one within the other, in the depths of the earth, all the unsearchable powers), but before whose eyes nature sometimes transforms herself into the "Abgrund des ewig offnen Grabs" (abyss of the ever open grave), or, even more terrible, into "ein ewig verschlingendes, ewig wieder-käuendes Ungeheuer" (an eternally devouring, eternally regorging monster). So great, however, is Goethe's devotion to earth, to the adventure of this life in this world, that he regards all its tribu-lations, dangers, and shortcomings as worth while, as integral parts of it, not to be just stoically endured, but rather ecstatically welcomed. He exclaims in an epistolary poem of December, 1773:

> Erdennot ist keine Not,
> Als dem Feig' und Matten.*

The very sufferings of earthly life are to be preferred to the un-trammelled joys of heaven, which would leave no scope for the enterprise and activity of human nature, especially of genius; thus the Muse in *Künstlers Erdewallen* ("The Artist's Earthly Pilgrim-age") (1773) says: "Der Himmel kann einen auch verwöhnen, / Dass man sich tut nach der Erde sehnen" (Heaven can so spoil one / That one longs for the earth). The same rejection of the untroubled, harmonious bliss of heaven in favour of the stormy uncertainties of earth is expressed in the poem *Menschengefühl* ("Human Feeling"), written in the last Frankfort or first Weimar years:

* Earthly affliction is no affliction, / Except for the cowardly and spineless.

> Ach, ihr Götter! grosse Götter
> In dem weiten Himmel droben!
> Gäbet ihr uns auf der Erde
> Festen Sinn und guten Mut,
> O wir liessen euch, ihr Guten,
> Euren weiten Himmel droben!†

The same will to this-worldliness is sometimes expressed by emphatic use of the word "Here!" Thus in the Prometheus drama of 1773 the hero cries:

> *Hier* meine Welt, mein All!
> *Hier* fühl ich mich.
> *Hier* alle meine Wünsche
> In körperlichen Gestalten.*

One manifestation of Goethe's will to this-worldliness was that he coined such composite words as "Erdgefühl" (earth-feeling) and "Erdgeruch" (earth-smell), and that he identified himself in a letter to Frau von Stein of May 19, 1776, on spending the first night in his garden-house in Weimar, with the "Erdkühlein" (Earth-heifer) of an old fairy-tale. Under his influence the young Duke Carl-August coined the similar word "Erdsaft" (earth-juice), with which one may compare Goethe's own phrase "das Mark der Erde" (the marrow of earth), found in *Wanderers Sturmlied* of 1772, in *Hanswursts Hochzeit* ("Hanswurst's Wedding") of 1775 and in the "Wald und Höhle" scene in *Faust* of 1788. It was certainly also under Goethe's influence that Lenz in a letter to Johanna Fahlmer, probably of February, 1775, used the word "Erdgefühl" and that Wieland wrote in 1776, "Mir ist nirgends wohl, bis ich meinen Stab in die Hand habe, unter meinen Bäumen zu leben und zu walten und den unendlichen Erdgeist einzuziehen (Nowhere do I feel happy until I have my staff in my hand to

---

† Ah! you gods, you great gods / In your wide Heaven up there! / If you would grant us on this earth / A resolute mind and good courage, / O, we would leave to you, you good ones, / That wide Heaven of yours up there!

* *Here* is my world, my all! / *Here* I feel myself to exist! / *Here* are all my desires / In bodily forms.

live in my own way under my own trees, breathing in the infinite
earth-spirit). (Compare J. G. Gruber, *Wielands Leben mit Ein-*
schluss vieler noch ungedruckter Briefe, Vol. 52 of Wielands
Werke, Leipzig 1828, p. 175).

It is Goethe's own word "Erdgeist," as we discover it in
Faust, that Wieland uses here; he clearly understands by it the
exhalations of earth as perceived by the sense of smell, symbolizing
a natural life, close to the soil. Another contemporary who makes
great use of such compound words is Herder, though we must suppose that, to begin with at least, it was he who influenced Goethe
in this, as in so many other respects, rather than Goethe who
influenced him. Amongst the innumerable earth-compounds, many
of them coinages of his own, which Herder uses in these years are
"Erdgesetze" (earth-laws), "Erdeschranken" (earth-limitations),
"Erdebürger" (earth-citizens), "Erdgebilde" (earth-forms), "Erde-
natur" (earth-nature), "Erdenursprung" (earth-origin), and—particularly interesting for us—"Erd-Gott" (earth-god), by which
however, he means *mankind*.[26] It is likely that Goethe coined the
name "Erdgeist," exactly as he coined so many other earth-
compounds during the same years, and out of the same impulse,
to give emphatic expression to his this-worldliness, and that it
therefore had in its origins, unlike the Sign of the Makrokosmus,
very much less to do with the cosmogonies and demonologies of
the cabbalists than is universally assumed. The conceptions of the
heavenly body, earth, as distinguished from the other heavenly
bodies, and of the element of earth, as distinguished from the other
three elements, are, as we have seen, the only ones that could play
any part in the old cabbalistic systems. But both these conceptions
of earth are irrelevant to the essential character and purport of the
Spirit that appears before Faust, and help us very little to a proper
understanding of it. That Spirit would seem to stand rather for
earth as opposed to "Heaven," that is to say for "This World" as
opposed to the "Other World"—the Other World connoting here
not only the specifically Christian Heaven, but also quite as much
or perhaps even more the purely spiritual "higher" sphere beyond
time and space postulated by idealistic philosophy.

The kind of this-worldliness that the Storm-and-Stress Goethe
stood for was even more hostile to idealistic metaphysics, ethics,

and aesthetics, which deny the validity of physical reality as perceived immediately through the senses and subordinate it to some transcendental, purely spiritual principle, than it was hostile to Christian supernaturalism. Without, of course, ever being downright materialistic, it tended emphatically towards something very much like materialism. A necessary corollary of the stubborn this-worldliness of the youthful Goethe was that "heiterer Widerwille gegen erhöhte Gesinnungen" (jaunty aversion for all high-minded sentiments) which we read of in the Book VII of *Dichtung und Wahrheit*, and of which there is abundant evidence in his writings of the Storm and Stress years. In his impatience with all fastidious, high-minded idealism he again and again defiantly indulges in a certain almost brutal crudity, particularly drastically in *Hanswursts Hochzeit* of 1775, in which one can discover what he really means by "das Mark der Erde." A more quotable example of this is what he calls his "altes Evangelium" (old gospel) in the verse letters to Merck of December 4 and 5, 1774, where all recognized religious and philosophical doctrines are contemptuously dismissed as tough, unappetizing meat unfit for the palate of such a one as himself.

> Denn er blecket nicht mit stumpfem Zahn
> Lang Gesottnes und Gebratnes an,
> Das er, wenn er noch so sittlich kaut,
> Endlich doch nicht sonderlich verdaut;
> Sondern fasst ein tüchtig Schinkenbein,
> Haut da gut taglöhnermässig drein,
> Füllt bis oben gierig den Pokal,
> Trinkt, und wischt das Maul wohl nicht einmal.*

In the sequel to the same verses Goethe indicates more precisely what sort of thing this attitude involves in the phrase: "Doch Menschenfleisch geht allem vor, / Um sich daran zu wärmen" (But there is nothing to beat human flesh for warming yourself on). It

---

* For he does not grind blunt teeth / On what was boiled or roasted long ago / And what, however well-manneredly he might chew away at it, / He would still not in the long run be able to digest particularly well; / Instead he grabs hold of a huge gammon of bacon, / Gluts himself on it like a regular day-labourer, / Greedily fills his cup to the brim / And drinks without even wiping his chops.

was this earthly, sensual aspect of Goethe's genius, his "stolze philosophische Verachtung aller Spekulation und Untersuchung, mit
einem bis zur Affektation getriebenen Attachement an die Natur
und an seine fünf Sinne" (proud philosophical contempt for all
speculation and investigation, with a devotion to nature carried to
the point of affectation, and a confining of himself to the evidence
of his five senses), that principally struck and strongly repelled the
idealist Schiller, before the two poets became friends and Schiller
discovered to his surprise how much Goethe had meanwhile himself been developing on idealistic lines. Interpreted as symbolizing
such a this-worldly and anti-idealistic outlook upon existence, the
Erdgeist makes sense, but the kind of sense it makes belongs to
and is characteristic of the post-Enlightenment period in which
Goethe grew to maturity; there is nothing corresponding to it in
the mentality and writings of the old cabbalists, and it is fully
intelligible without them.

At this point it becomes possible for us to recognize more clearly
why Goethe duplicated the pantheistic principle in the opening
scene of the *Urfaust*. There is nature pantheism and nature pantheism, and the kind of devotion to nature that had become current
from the early years of the eighteenth century onward had been
decidedly contemplative, high-minded and fastidious, tending to
avoid any open breach with Christian theism or with traditional
philosophical and religious ethics. The nature it was prepared to
exalt was an idealized, moralized, humanized, and beautified nature,
as distinguished from mere vulgar, physical, empirical nature, which
it tended to look down upon or to hide from sight beneath a veil
of humanitarianism and propriety. It was not with such an ethe-
realized and bowdlerized nature as this that Goethe wanted his
Faust to enter into communion, but with nature as she really is,
in all her ruthlessness and all her disconcerting aspects. Though
unfortunately it does not come out as clearly as it was meant to do,
that is the point of the contemplation of the Sign of the Makrokosmus preceding the invocation of the Erdgeist. It was not just a
matter of Faust's seeking a pantheistic relationship to nature in a
quite unspecified way. That would, according to the postulates of
the age, have been a perfectly innocuous, indeed an unambiguously
highminded thing to do, and Faust could have done it and still re-

mained a respectable professor; it would not have made a Faust of him, not have involved him in companionship with the devil. It was a matter of his deciding in favour of a particular conception of nature, of a this-worldly and realistic, as opposed to an other-worldly and idealistic way of seeing her. That is why the Spirit that appears before him is not just the *World* Spirit of philosophical and mystical tradition, but the Spirit of *Earth*, of *this*-worldliness, and it is also why it appears "in widerlicher Gestalt."

Goethe's *Faust* then, like all other great works of the world's literature, turns not upon some hypersubtle, abstract, and abstruse metaphysical issue comprehensible only to professional philosophers, or upon some obscure, esoteric point of cabbalistic lore, but upon one of the central problems of universal human nature, envisaged, admittedly, in the light of and in terms of the mentality of Goethe's own age. It turns upon the antithesis between this-worldliness and other-worldliness, between realism and idealism, between the dynamic and the static, between what Mephisto in his conversation with the young student calls "des Lebens goldner Baum" and "graue Theorie" (the golden tree of life [and] grey theory). But though there can be no doubt that Goethe's own sympathy when he wrote the *Urfaust* was with the this-worldly, realistic principle, he was by no means undividedly committed to it; even at that early stage he knew that there is much to be said for the other side, and was at pains to indicate that both are justified and necessary and cannot exist independently of one another, that the relationship between them is ultimately not just one of blind opposition, but of polarity. There is evidence enough in his writings of the Storm and Stress years that the reaction which was to make of him, shortly after the move to Weimar, predominantly, though, of course, never exclusively, an adherent of the idealistic principle, was inevitable. One of the most important pieces of evidence for this is the *Urfaust* itself, the true point of which is that it is not written one-sidedly from the this-worldly point of view, but at once glorifies it and, by implication, criticizes it, just as *Werther* at once glorifies and by implication also criticizes the cult of sensibility. The sheer poetic quality of the Makrokosmus passage shows that there is in a way as much, or almost as much of Goethe himself in it as there is in the Erdgeist passage. The two passages stand in

much the same dialectical relationship to one another as *Ganymed*
with its surrender to the higher powers and *Prometheus* with its
defiance of them, two poems which we know must have been written within a few months of one another, about 1774. Later Goethe
was to see in all existence a rhythmical alternation of such states
of expansion and contraction, as in the motion of the lungs and
the heart.

In endless variations this same dualism manifests itself in the
life and work of Goethe and also of many of his distinguished contemporaries and successors. In the field of aesthetics it appears as
the opposition between "the characteristic" and "the beautiful,"
on which he writes so incisively about 1772 in his essay *Von
deutscher Baukunst* ("On German Architecture"); in his geological
studies at a very much later date it appears as that between Vul-
canism and Neptunism, in his momentous botanical argument
with Schiller of July, 1794, as that between "Erfahrung" (experience) and "Idee" (the idea). Something closely analogous to it
is to be seen in Lessing's famous choice between "alle Wahrheit"
(all truth) in God's right hand, and "den einzigen immer regen
Trieb nach Wahrheit, obschon mit dem Zusatze, mich immer und
ewig zu irren" (the sole, ever-active urge towards truth, even with
the proviso that I should eternally go astray) in God's left hand;
also in Schopenhauer's distinction between "the World as Will"
and "the World as Idea," in Nietzsche's dichotomy of the "Diony-
sian" and the "Apollonian," and in Klages' philosophy of "Der
Geist als Widersacher der Seele" (the mind as adversary of the
soul). At the highest level of metaphysical abstraction it appears
as the dualism of the finite and the infinite, at a slightly lower level
as that between "becoming" (*Werden*) and "being" (*Sein*), at a
still lower as that between "feeling" and "thought," and at the
level of the man in the street as that between the physical and
the spiritual. Goethe himself in 1798 almost too baldly made use
of this last very obvious and familiar dualistic conception to char-
acterize Faust in the much-quoted words: "Zwei Seelen wohnen,
ach! in meiner Brust" (Two souls, alas, reside within my breast);
and in the preceding year Schiller, with little but his reading of
Faust, ein Fragment to go by, formulated the idea upon which, as
he saw it, the entire drama must hinge, in terms of that same almost
trite and hackneyed conflict between the flesh and the spirit: "Die

Duplizität der menschlichen Natur und das verunglückte Bestreben, das Göttliche und Physische im Menschen zu vereinigen,
verliert man nicht aus den Augen" (The dualism of human nature
and the unsuccessful attempt to unite the divine and the physical
in man are never lost sight of).[27] For all its modernity and subtlety,
then, Goethe's *Faust* has in this respect after all not advanced so
much as one might have expected on St. Paul with his declaration:
"For the flesh lusteth against the spirit, and the spirit against the
flesh, and these are contrary the one to the other; so that ye cannot
do the thing that ye would."[28]

From this it is only one step to recognizing that there is at the
back of *Faust*, in very rarified and transmuted form, something of
that primitive conflict between good and evil, which, however
sophisticated and emancipated we may be, still tends to interest
us more and to have more reality for us than all other conflicts. In
this connexion Goethe made an illuminating remark in one of his
draft notes for the seventh book of *Dichtung und Wahrheit*:
"Konflikt des Bösen und Guten kann nicht ästhetisch dargestellt
werden: denn man muss dem Bösen etwas verleihen und dem Guten
etwas nehmen, um sie gegeneinander ins Gleiche zu bringen" (The
conflict between good and evil cannot be represented aesthetically:
for one must add something to the evil principle and take something away from the good principle, in order to bring them into
equilibrium with one another). This is exactly what he himself has
done in the opening scene of the *Urfaust* and does indeed in most
of his major works. For although the Erdgeist is quite certainly not
the principle of evil in an absolute sense, it is so relatively, by
comparison with the Sign of the Makrokosmus. In order to establish
between the two that parity or "equilibrium" which he needs for
his aesthetic purposes, Goethe evokes the Sign of the Makrokosmus
less amply, vividly, and circumstantially, with a marked *diminu-
endo*, the Erdgeist with far more sheer weight and in a prolonged,
overpowering *crescendo*. It may not be a "good" spirit, but to make
up for that it is a "great" and "glorious" one, which interests and
excites us and spurs us on to audacious enterprises and ambitions,
as the benign, orderly Sign of the Makrokosmus does not. Having
chosen it, Faust finds out too late that he has after all chosen evil,
for it gives him Mephisto as his companion.

Unlike Wordsworth, Goethe hardly ever sees nature as identical

with or harmonizing with the moral law, which at times, though by
no means all the time, is also of the highest importance and value
in his eyes. The moral law, he declares in his poem of about 1783,
Das Göttliche ("The Divine"), is, so far as can be known, exclusively the property and prerogative of man, and quite alien to
"unfeeling" nature. In 1827 he hesitantly admitted that he might
perhaps have been the author of the aphoristic hymn on *Nature* of
1780, which we now know to have been written under his influence
by Tobler, commenting that in it she is portrayed as "ein unerfor-
schliches, unbedingtes, humoristisches, sich selbst widersprechendes
Wesen" (an unsearchable, unconditional, capricious, self-contra-
dictory being); but Tobler was scarcely speaking for Goethe, least
of all for the Goethe of 1780, when he also designated Nature in
this hymn as "gütig" (benevolent) and "weise" (wise). Goethe
could even in his later years say contemptuously from the aesthetic
angle in a conversation with Chancellor von Müller of April 25,
1819: "Die Natur ist eine Gans, man muss erst sie zu etwas
machen" (Nature is a goose, one must first make something out
of her). Werther's description of nature as "ein ewig verschlingendes, ewig wiederkäuendes Ungeheuer" does not stand isolated in
Goethe's writings of the Storm and Stress years which chiefly concern us now. It was pretty certainly he who wrote the anonymous
review of Sulzer in 1772 in which the passage occurs:

> Was wir von Natur sehen, ist Kraft, die Kraft verschlingt,
> nichts gegenwärtig, alles vorübergehend, tausend Keime
> zertreten jeden Augenblick, tausend geboren, gross und be-
> deutend, mannigfaltig ins Unendliche; schön und hässlich,
> gut und bös, alles mit gleichem Recht neben einander ex-
> istierend. Und die Kunst ist gerade das Widerspiel, sie
> entspringt aus den Bemühungen des Individuums, sich *gegen*
> die zerstörende Kraft des Ganzen zu erhalten.*

---

* What we see in nature is force devouring force, nothing present, everything transient, thousands of seeds trodden to death every moment, thousands
born, great and significant, infinitely varied, beautiful and ugly, good and evil
all existing side by side with the same right. And art is just the opposite, it
arises from the exertions of the individual to preserve himself against the
destructive power of the whole.

But this very amoral ruthlessness of nature at times appealed strongly to the titanic, amoral urge that was so integral a part of Goethe's genius during his Storm and Stress years, and, in a subdued form, also throughout his later life. Nature would attract him very much less than she does, if he believed she were indeed as edifying and moral as the idealistic nature-worshippers made her out to be, if he were not aware of what he calls in one of the jottings for *Hanswursts Hochzeit*, "der unendliche Ausdruck von Geilheit im Verbiegen und Verschmiegen der ganzen Natur, Anbiegen und Anschmiegen" (the infinite expression of lustfulness in the twisting and twining of all nature, nuzzling and snuggling). Shortly after going to Weimar he repeated on a minor scale the gesture of Faust in turning from Makrokosmus to Erdgeist in one of his own letters to the pietistic Lavater: "Alle deine Ideale sollen mich nicht irre führen, wahr zu sein, und gut und böse, wie die Natur" (All your ideals shall not make me stray from being true and good and evil like nature).[29] Faust is certainly right in thinking that the amoral Erdgeist more truly represents the character of nature as it actually is than the Sign of the Makrokosmus does; but whether he is right in therefore dedicating himself to that Spirit and so taking it upon himself also to live beyond good and evil is another question.

As the incarnation of nature, the Erdgeist is essentially ambivalent. It appears to Faust "in a repulsive form," but remains in his memory as "glorious"; it rejects him with scorn, but it seems to him in retrospect to have "understood his heart and soul"; it overwhelms him with its supremacy, so that he recoils from it like "ein furchtsam weggekrümmter Wurm" (a worm writhing in fear), and fails dismally in his efforts to assert himself as its equal, and yet he feels that, as the "Ebenbild der Gottheit" (image of the godhead), he should be able to claim equality, perhaps even superiority to it, and cries: "Und nicht einmal dir?" (Am I not even your equal?) In this phrase, which Grumach uses in support of his questionable contention that the Erdgeist is in itself only a quite inferior being, "the basest of all spirits," Goethe is drawing on biblical tradition. It is not as an exceptional individual of genius, but simply as an ordinary human being, "created in the image of God," that Faust might fairly have been able to claim some ascendancy over the Erdgeist. But that claim resides above all in the acknowledgment of ethical responsibility, through which alone man distinguishes himself from nature, and Faust has forfeited it by venturing beyond the "limits of humanity" and trying to raise himself as a "superman" to the level of the spirits, that is to say, beyond good and evil. In aspiring above humanity he has sunk below it, and it is now too late for him to insist that he was "created in the image of God." For the rest, the words, "Ich bins, bin Faust, bin deinesgleichen" (I am what I claimed to be, I am Faust, am your equal) and "Nicht einmal dir," with which Faust tries to brave out his humiliation, are no more legitimate, objective evidence as to the real stature and rank of the Erdgeist than Brutus' words, "Away, slight man!" are as to the real stature and rank of Cassius. There can be no doubt about the immense superhuman dignity and power of the Erdgeist; it does quite certainly represent the whole of nature, envisaged from the this-worldly angle, and not just some obscure, minor, cabbalistic conception, as Grumach would have us believe. But it is ambivalent, as nature itself is. It has to be ambivalent, in order that it may serve so to speak as a liaison officer or intermediary between God and the Devil. For that is what Goethe needed it for. The same conception is found in his conversation of September 8, 1815 with Boisserée: "Die Natur . . . ist eine Orgel, auf der unser Herrgott spielt, und der Teufel tritt die Bälge dazu" (Nature is an organ on which God plays, while the devil works the bellows). This essential ambivalence of the Erdgeist is responsible for those apparent contradictions made so much of by the critics who deny that the Invocation scene and "Trüber Tag. Feld" have anything to do with one another, or who postulate radical changes within the Invocation scene itself. Most of what Goethe has to say in his later years about "das Dämonische" (the daemonic), especially "dass es sich nur in Widersprüchen manifestiere" (that it manifests itself only in contradictions), and is "nicht göttlich, . . . nicht menschlich, . . . nicht teuflich, . . . nicht englisch" (neither human nor divine, neither diabolical nor angelic) (*Dichtung und Wahrheit*, Book XX), applies also to the Erdgeist, which may fairly be designated as his first great poetic presentation of this daemonic force.

It is often maintained that the real reason why the Spirit rejects

Faust is because he makes a grave mistake by responding to its revelation of its own being with the words:

> Der du die weite Welt umschweifst,
> Geschäft'ger Geist, wie nah fühl' ich mich dir!*

In particular it is argued that Faust gives offence to the Spirit by applying to it the epithet "geschäftig" (busy). Thus Friedrich and Scheithauer write in their commentary:

> Faust sieht das Wesen des Erdgeists im Umherschweifen und Geschäftigsein. Er verkennt die Zielstrebigkeit, das Schaffende, Schöpferische seines Wirkens. Er verkennt es, weil sein eigenes Streben noch ziellos und daher nur ge- schäftig, betriebsam ist, und offenbart damit, wie weit er noch vom Erdgeist entfernt ist. Wohl darum wird er von ihm zurückgewiesen.†30

Similarly Böhm finds that Faust with his words, "trifft die Man- nigfaltigkeit allein, ohne die Einheit" (catches only the multi- plicity, not the unity).31 But such interpretations are too artificial. Faust's words do not betray any misunderstanding or underestima- tion of the Spirit. The supposed discrepancy between its own decla- ration and Faust's response to it is only a construction of the com- mentators. The idea of "purposefulness" or "unity" is not involved. Goethe himself about 1822, in his zoological essay on *Lepaden* (limpets), has no scruples about applying to nature the word "geschäftig," which is regarded by the commentators as so offen- sively inept, when he writes: "Hier bewundern wir die *Geschäftig- keit* der Natur!" (We marvel here at the busy activity of nature). The Spirit rejects Faust not because of any particular thing he says or does, but because of what he is, because of the entire situation.

---

* You who rove about the wide world, / Busy Spirit, how near I feel myself to you!

† Faust sees the essence of the Spirit in a roving about and being busy. He fails to recognize the purposefulness, the productiveness and creativity of its operation. He fails to recognize this because his own striving is as yet aimless and therefore only busy, only bustling, and herein he betrays how far he still is from the Spirit of Earth. This is presumably why he is rejected by it.

It is not a stickler for spiritual etiquette or terminological niceties. It sees that he is afraid and it sees through the spuriousness of his attempts to persuade it and himself that he has overcome his fear. It is too much for him, as it must be too much for any man or any superman.

When the Erdgeist vanishes, it cries to Faust: "Du gleichst dem Geist, den du begreifst, nicht mir" (You resemble the Spirit you can grasp, not me). In view of the distinctive way in which the word "Geist" is used throughout the scene, it is natural to assume that this phrase, "der Geist, den du begreifst," spoken itself by a Spirit, is not intended vaguely, non-committally, and metaphorically, but refers to some specific Spirit; and if so, the only Spirit it can reasonably be supposed to refer to is Mephistopheles. In fact these words seem to link up with Faust's declaration in the scene "Trüber Tag. Feld" that Mephisto has been "chained to him as a depraved companion" by the "great and glorious Spirit." It is in this sense that they are interpreted by Max Morris, Burger, and various other critics, but more often no particular importance is attached to them, as though they were merely a figurative, non-committal phrase, and it is sometimes maintained that whoever or whatever they may refer to, it cannot possibly be Mephisto. Thus Karl Wolff (1949) says, "dass eine schlechtere Wahl kaum denkbar wäre. Mephisto: das sollte der Geist sein, dem Faust 'gleicht' und den er als wesensverwandt 'begreift'?" (a worse choice could scarcely be imagined. Is it to be supposed that Mephisto is the Spirit whom Faust resembles and whom he can grasp as akin to himself?)[32] But Goethe's own text clearly enough indicates that this is just what we are intended to suppose. That he never managed to work the conception out and eventually abandoned it in favour of another quite different device for bringing Faust and Mephisto together is presumptive evidence that he himself had great difficulties with it. We need therefore not be surprised at its causing us difficulties too. But it is likely to have been on some such lines as these: The Erdgeist is indeed daemonic, ruthless, destructive, beyond good and evil, and consequently also sinister, but there is nothing base about it. It is not a person with a consciousness or a conscience or a sense of responsibility; it is nature, and does what it has to do in magnificent indifference. It is what Goethe in his

Geschichte meines botanischen Studiums ("History of My Botanical Studies") of 1817 calls "das ungeheure Geheimnis, das sich
in stetigem Erschaffen und Zerstören an den Tag legt" (the tremendous mystery, which manifests itself in ceaseless creation and
destruction). In all its contradictions it still remains at one with
itself. No human being can do this or be this, not even a man of
Faust's stature. There is always, at least potentially, a baser side to
his nature, which will insinuate itself into and degrade his most
heroic and generous aspirations beyond good and evil, causing them
to end in disaster and shame. It is to this potential baser side of
Faust's nature that Mephisto corresponds, and that is why he resembles Mephisto and can "grasp" him, as he cannot resemble or
grasp the Erdgeist. Goethe himself, in a conversation with Eckermann of May 3, 1827, praised the acumen of Ampère in having
observed that there was much of his own nature in Mephisto as
well as in Faust, and it can reasonably be maintained that Mephisto
is indeed Faust's grosser *alter ego*, to whose visitation he has exposed himself by being able to invoke the Erdgeist, but unable to
retain his hold upon it. Or one can conceive of it so, that the negative aspects of the Erdgeist, of this-worldliness and unconditional
activity, have become embodied in Mephisto. A similar idea underlies such different works as Dostoevski's *Crime and Punishment*
and Synge's *Playboy of the Western World*, with its conclusion:
"There's a great gap between a gallous story and a dirty deed."

The view that Goethe originally intended Mephisto to come to
Faust as an emissary from the Erdgeist has often been maintained
and widely accepted, but as a rule in a form that has aroused violent and not unjustifiable opposition, and at present it has comparatively few supporters. It used to be assumed that, since the
Erdgeist is the anima terrae or archaeus terrae of cabbalistic tradition, Mephisto must be one of the mischievous, minor elemental
spirits subject to that master spirit, and therefore not a real devil
at all, and that he was only later transformed into a devil proper—
in 1788, at the earliest, or perhaps not till after 1797. This view,
propounded as early as 1837 by Weisse, is found in varying forms
in the Faust interpretations of Kuno Fischer, Max Morris, Agnes
Bartscherer, Hefele, Beutler, Burger, and others. Amongst the
many who have attacked it, Minor (1901) is particularly violent:

"Ein Faust ohne den Bund mit dem Teufel ist ein Unding oder ein Unsinn, der Goethe nie eingefallen ist und nie einem Dichter einfallen konnte, er ist eine frostige Gelehrtentiftelei" (A Faust without a pact with the Devil is an absurdity or a piece of nonsense which never entered Goethe's head and never could enter the head of any poet; it is a bit of frigid, bookish hair-splitting).[33] Similarly, Graffunder (1891): "Das Verhältnis, in dem Mephistopheles zu Luzifer gedacht werden muss, macht seine Entsendung vom Erdgeist unmöglich. Das sei mit allem Nachdruck gesagt" (The relationship in which Mephisto must be thought of as standing to Lucifer makes it impossible that he should have been sent by the Spirit of Earth. Let that be said with the greatest emphasis). Ziegler, Enders, and Hans Albert Maier, who are in agreement with Minor on the main issue, admit, however, that the notion of Mephisto's being an emissary of the Erdgeist certainly does seem to have entered Goethe's head in 1788 when he wrote the opening monologue of the scene "Wald und Höhle," but they think that the passage in "Trüber Tag. Feld," of which that monologue is an adaptation, should be interpreted in some other sense. Minor sees it as meaning nothing more than that "der Erdgeist . . . ihn [Faust] so tief durch seine Ablehnung hätte sinken lassen—wäre er ihm weiter entgegengekommen, so hätte sich ja Faust dem Teufel nicht ergeben" (the Spirit of Earth had allowed Faust to fall so low by refusing him—if it had given him a better reception Faust would not have abandoned himself to the devil). (See also, Graffunder, pp. 714–715.)

The Erdgeist (in Minor's eyes, an entirely divine, ethically unimpeachable being) has only "chained" Mephisto to Faust in the sense that it *did not actively prevent* the league between the two: "Seinen Bund mit dem Teufel darf er [Faust] dem Erdgeist zuschreiben, weil alles, was auf Erden geschieht, durch ihn geschieht, . . . nicht weil er es getan hat, sondern weil er es hat geschehen lassen" (Faust can ascribe his pact with the devil to the Spirit of Earth because everything that happens on earth happens through it . . . not because it has actually brought it about, but because it has allowed it to happen).[34] In this interpretation, however, which would most questionably invest the Erdgeist with the character of a divine providence, Minor has found few followers. It is generally admitted that the words, "Warum musstest du mich an den Schandgesellen schmieden?" imply some quite specific action on the part of whatever Spirit they are addressed to. But since Roethe (1920), the view has come to be widely accepted that, if Mephisto is a "real" devil, and has, as Faust asserts, been chained to Faust by some higher spirit, that higher spirit can only be the Supreme Devil, the Prince of Hell, Satan or, as he is more commonly named in the old chapbooks and plays, Lucifer or Pluto. In support of this it is pointed out that in some of those old books and plays Mephisto is expressly presented as only a minor devil, who has to take his orders from above. Thus in Marlowe's *Dr. Faustus* Mephistophilis says, "I am servant to great Lucifer," and in the chapbook of the "Christlich Meynender" the Spirit invoked by Faust explains that it is "ein Fürst und kein Diener der Höllen" (a prince and not a servant of Hell), but promises to send him, and does send him a servant of Hell, Mephistophilis, to be his familiar spirit. When this Spirit has difficulties with Faust, Lucifer himself appears in person to bring him to his senses.

The hypothesis was set up in 1920 by Roethe and has since been further developed by F. J. Schneider (1949) and Hans Albert Maier (1952) that Goethe originally, in close adherence to his sources, showed, or intended to show, Faust in the opening scene invoking the "Höllenfürst" (Prince of Hell), Lucifer, and then only two or three years later changed this plan, bringing in the Erdgeist in Lucifer's place. The scene "Trüber Tag. Feld" is regarded as belonging to the earlier plan, when Goethe is supposed still to have based the drama, in accordance with tradition, on black magic, the Invocation scene to the later plan, when he had decided to base it on white magic instead. The "great, glorious Spirit," apostrophized by Faust in the former scene, is assumed to be not the Erdgeist, but the Höllenfürst, whom Goethe later eliminated. According to Hans Albert Maier, Goethe envisaged in 1771 (the year to which Maier would assign "Trüber Tag. Feld") "einen wie auch immer geadelten Höllengeist" (an in one way or another ennobled infernal Spirit), and his "kühner Schritt" (bold step) of that year "läge dann lediglich darin, dass er seinen Faust den Teufel als einen grossen verstehenden Geist ohne einen Ton bigotten Abscheus anerkennen und verehren lässt" (would merely con-

sist in his having caused his Faust to acknowledge and venerate
the Devil, without any tone of bigoted abhorrence).[35] The substituting of the Erdgeist for the Höllenfürst demanded, according
to Maier, more intellectual "audacity" than Goethe could be
credited with at so early a date as winter 1771–1772,[36] though one
might demur that it would have been less audacious than representing the devil himself as a "great, glorious, understanding Spirit"
deserving of Faust's veneration. One of Maier's chief arguments
for there being no connexion between "Trüber Tag. Feld" and the
opening scene in the form in which we know it, namely that
"Mephisto in der Erdgeistszene gar nicht erwähnt wird" (Mephisto
is not mentioned at all in the Spirit of Earth Scene),[37] leaves out
of account the possibility that Mephisto may indeed be mentioned
in it—and we would maintain, quite certainly *is* mentioned in it—
cryptically, as the "Geist, den du begreifst."

A curious variant of this theory was promulgated in 1953 by
Ernst Grumach, who would date the entire Invocation scene, much
as it now stands, about 1769, but asserts that it was meant to be
followed by a further, far more important invocation scene, in
which Faust would have conjured up Lucifer. This is part and
parcel of Grumach's contention that the Erdgeist is really the
"alle impressiones des irdischen Geschehens aufnehmende Geist-
Mensch der Luft" (the Spirit-Man of the Air, who receives all the
impressions of earthly happenings),[38] taken over from Welling's
cabbalistic system, and "der niedrigste aller Geister" (the basest
of all Spirits). "Makrokosmusschau, Erdgeist—und Luziferszene"
are, according to Grumach, "Teile eines einheitlichen Planes, . . .
der sich im Rahmen des Wellingschen Systems bewegt" (The
contemplation of the Macrocosm, the Spirit of Earth scene, and the
Lucifer scene [are] parts of a unified plan designed within the
framework of Welling's system), the first two "bilden . . . die
notwendige Voraussetzung des geplanten Luziferszene, die sie
schrittweise vorbereiten und motivieren. Der auch vom Erdgeist
zurückgewiesene Faust wird zwangsläufig auf den Weg zu Luzifer
geführt" (. . . form the necessary postulates for the projected
Lucifer scene, which they lead up to and motivate step by step. On
being rejected by the Spirit of Earth, Faust is inevitably led to seek
the way to Lucifer).[39] Grumach asserts categorically that "die

Gesamtkonzeption der äusseren und inneren Welten, in denen die älteste Fausthandlung spielt" (the entire conception of the outer and inner world, in which the action of Faust takes place from its first beginnings) is derived from Welling, and that it is "hoffnungslos, dieses Spiel verstehen zu wollen, ohne sich dieses Weltbild [Wellings] immer wieder vor Augen zu führen" (It is hopeless to try to understand this drama, without again and again bringing before one's eyes Welling's cosmogony).[40] In view of these assertions from so authoritative a quarter, it is worth while to see what Goethe himself has to say about Welling. This is to be found once more in the eighth book of *Dichtung und Wahrheit* of 1811:

Sie [Susanna von Klettenberg] hatte schon insgeheim *Wellings* opus mago-cabbalisticum studiert, wobei sie jedoch, weil der Autor das Licht, was er mitteilt, sogleich wieder selbst verfinstert und aufhebt, sich nach einem Freunde umsah, der ihr in diesem Wechsel von Licht und Finsternis Gesellschaft leistete. Es bedurfte nur einer geringen Anregung, um auch mir diese Krankheit zu inoculieren. Ich schaffte das Werk an, das, wie alle Schriften dieser Art, seinen Stammbaum in gerader Linie bis zur Neuplatonischen Schule verfolgen konnte. Meine vorzügliche Bemühung an diesem Buche war, die dunkeln Hinweisungen, wo der Verfasser von einer Stelle auf die andere deutet, und dadurch das, was er verbirgt, zu enthüllen verspricht, aufs genaueste zu bemerken und am Rande die Seitenzahlen solcher sich einander aufklären sollenden Stellen zu bezeichnen. Aber auch so blieb das Buch noch dunkel und unverständlich genug; ausser dass man sich zuletzt in eine gewisse Terminologie hineinstudierte und, indem man mit derselben nach eigenem Belieben gebarte, etwas wo nicht zu verstehen, doch wenigstens zu sagen glaubte.*

---

* She [Susanna von Klettenberg] had secretly studied Welling's *Opus mago-cabbalisticum*, but as the author at once himself obscures and annihilates the light that he gives, she was looking around for a friend to keep her company in this alternation of light and darkness. I obtained the book which, like all such writings, could trace back its ancestry in a direct line to the Neo-Platonic

This is all that Goethe has to say about Welling's *Opus* throughout his long life, except that he soon found his way from it to other somewhat more palatable and digestible writings, such as those of Paracelsus. It seems improbable that he should have based his *Faust* on a work that he is never known to have spoken of except on this one occasion, and then with such irony and impatience.

"Lucifer," as distinct in name at least from the more opprobrious "Satan," is not to be dismissed as irrelevant for the conception of Goethe's Erdgeist. We have to take into consideration here the private Lucifer myth, which Goethe tells us he worked out for himself about 1769, and of which nothing is known but what he records in connexion with the account of his cabbalistic studies of the same year at the end of the eighth book of *Dichtung und Wahrheit.* The essence of this Lucifer myth, in which the solution to the problems of the Erdgeist has variously been sought, is that Lucifer is responsible for the entire creation, in so far as it is determined (as it is in the first place) by the principle of "Konzentration" (contraction), and that the Elohim (a kind of cabbalistic equivalent to the Christian Trinity) are only responsible for it in so far as they counteracted this ultimately materialistic and destructive force of contraction with the necessary complementary force of "Expansion" towards themselves; and that man, as the battleground of these two opposed forces, is "zugleich das vollkommenste und unvollkommenste, das glücklichste und unglücklichste Geschöpf" (at once the most perfect and the most imperfect, the happiest and the unhappiest of creatures), obliged to alternate in regular pulsation between self-assertion ("sich verselbsten") and self-surrender ("sich entselbstigen"). One difficulty is that the terminology here employed, especially that of expansion and contraction, is so very much that of the later years, when *Dichtung*

---

school. My principal occupation with this book was to observe very carefully the obscure references where the author directs the reader from one passage to another, promising thereby to disclose what he is concealing, and to note down in the margin the numbers of the pages of such passages which were supposed to explain one another. But for all this the book still remained obscure and unintelligible enough; except that in the long run one laboriously acquired a certain terminology and, by employing it just as one fancied, believed one was, if not understanding anything, at least saying something.

und Wahrheit was written, and that there are no traces of Goethe having employed it or anything really equivalent to it as early as 1769. We can well believe—and this is important for us—that Goethe had at that early stage, before the *Urfaust* was begun, some strange, semi-Manichaean ideas—partly his own, partly derived from the cabbalists—about Lucifer as a spirit of greater dignity and status than the Devil of orthodox tradition, but *Dichtung und Wahrheit* gives us probably only a very much transformed and therefore hardly reliable account of those ideas.

F. J. Schneider (anticipated as early as 1891 by Graffunder) sees irrefutable evidence that Mephisto must originally have been sent to Faust by Lucifer, and not by the Erdgeist, in the brief monologue spoken by Mephisto at the end of the first scene of the Gretchen tragedy, "Strasse" in the *Urfaust,* and deleted by Goethe about 1788 or 1789, for no other reason, presumably, than because it is poetically not very satisfactory, to make room for four new, more accomplished verses of similar purport. Mephisto comments ironically on Faust's command that he should procure a present for Gretchen:

> Er tut, als wär er ein Fürstensohn.
> Hätt Luzifer so ein Dutzend Prinzen,
> Die sollten ihm schon was vermünzen;
> Am Ende kriegt' er eine Kommission.*

In reality this casual allusion to Lucifer is at most only an additional piece of evidence, if any more is needed, that Mephisto feels himself to be a devil; it displays the same incorrigible flippancy as all his other allusions to his own diabolical nature and affiliations. He finds it an immense joke that he should be the devil; it is a fact indeed, but a fact that he himself can never take seriously.

One of the most ingenious suggestions about the relationship between Mephisto and the Erdgeist is that of Hermann Schneider,[41] according to whom Goethe's original intention was that Faust himself should indeed believe Mephisto to be "ein Sendling des Erd-

---

* He behaves as though he were the son of a monarch. / If Lucifer had a dozen princes like that, / They would squander a mighty lot for him; / In the end his property would be sequestrated.

geists," a "Mittelding zwischen Tier und Teufel, aus dem Umkreis des hohen Elementargeistes zu ihm abgeordnet" (an emissary of the Spirit of Earth, a hybrid between animal and devil sent to him from the entourage of the lofty, elemental Spirit),[42] but that he should be quite mistaken in that belief. "Mephisto hat mit dem Geist der Erde in Wahrheit nichts zu tun und vermag nur irgendwie in Faust den Glauben zu erwecken, er sei der Bote dieses Grossen. . . . [Fausts] Schritt hinüber in die Welt des Teufels erfolgte wider seinen Willen" (Mephisto has in fact nothing to do with the Spirit of Earth, but only somehow contrives to arouse in Faust the belief that he is an envoy from that great one. . . . Faust's step into the world of the Devil is taken against his own will).[43] "Mephisto hatte sich in der Tat dem Faust aufgedrängt, nicht dieser ihm" (In reality Mephisto had forced himself on Faust, not Faust on him).[44] "Die Aufgabe: zu motivieren, wie dieser Irrtum [on Faust's part] zustande kommen und sich so hartnäckig halten konnte, ist ungelöst geblieben und war im Grunde unlösbar" (The problem of motivating how this misunderstanding came about and could maintain itself so stubbornly remained unsolved and was at bottom insoluble).[45] But Schneider interprets the very brief cancelled fourth scene of the *Urfaust, Landstrasse* ("Highway"), in which Mephisto turns down his eyes in passing a wayside cross, as showing Faust suddenly torn out of his delusion and recognizing Mephisto's true diabolical nature for the first time. H. Schneider presents this hypothesis of his as "einen geistvollen Einfall Goethes" (a brilliant idea of Goethe's).[46] One can, however, at most admire it as a brilliant idea of Schneider's own, and as an idea altogether too brilliant and unsupported by the available data to be convincing.

The notion that Mephisto, if he has been sent to Faust by the Erdgeist, can only be a minor elemental demon and not a true devil, rests upon the assumptions that Goethe was concerned to body forth a coherent, consistent cosmogony and demonology modelled upon the cabbalists, and that the Erdgeist in particular is derived from and conforms to cabbalistic lore. But neither of these assumptions is tenable. We find Goethe right to the end insouciantly and, we can be quite sure, deliberately mingling any and every kind of cosmogony, demonology and mythology, Pagan and Christian, exoteric and esoteric, Nordic and Hellenic, ancient, mediaeval and modern, cabbalistic, mystical and rationalistic, Ptolemaeic, Copernican and of his own free invention, without any attention to system or consistency. The true dimension of the work is that of the inner world of visions and dreams, not that of a coherent cosmogony such as we find in Dante, Milton, and Klopstock. In particular Mephisto is, for those who demand consistency, a highly problematic figure. That he is a "true" devil can indeed be taken for certain, whatever anybody may say against it. His name alone, with all its associations, and the entire weight of the Faust tradition sufficiently guarantee that. It is extraordinary to find Scherer[47] arguing, because Mephisto says he does not possess "alle Macht im Himmel und auf Erden" (all power in Heaven and earth) and cannot loose "die Bände des Rächers" (the bonds of the avenger) ("Trüber Tag. Feld"): "Er ist kein Teufel demnach" (He is therefore no devil); and to find Enders[48] similarly perturbed by this "Beschränkung der Machtsphäre des Teufels" (limitation in the range of the devil's power). It would be quite out of accordance alike with theological tradition and with folklore to suppose that the devil is omnipotent, or anywhere near to it.[49] But it is impossible to decide whether Mephisto is only a subordinate, perhaps a very subordinate devil (even, Faust's own private "guardian devil"), or the supreme Devil, Satan himself. When the Lord distinguishes him in the "Prolog im Himmel" from the other "Geister, die verneinen," (spirits of denial, or devils) as the "Schalk" (rascal), Mephisto certainly appears as one of subaltern hellish rank.[50] The same is implied too, when he describes himself to Faust as "keiner von den Grossen" (not one of the great ones) — not one of the principal devils. Similarly at the Walpurgis night celebrations, when Satan is giving audience on the summit of the Brocken, Mephisto is junketing with witches and warlocks on the lower slopes. On the other hand he is often referred to by Faust and himself not simply as "*a* devil," but as "*the* devil," and in the "Hexenküche" scene he reveals himself to the witch as Satan and is recognized and acclaimed by her under that name. Most of the evidence here adduced occurs admittedly in the additions made to the drama after 1787, but the ambiguity of Mephisto's diabolical status is already clearly to be seen throughout the *Urfaust*, and would seem to have belonged to Goethe's deliberate intentions from the outset. This after all fits in well enough with our general linguistic practice, which probably has a deep psychological foundation, of readily referring to any devil as "the devil," as though there were no others. Where devils are concerned, plurality and particularity are evidently not felt as so very distinct from the comprehensive, generic singular with the definite article. Mephisto has, so to speak, to represent the entire infernal legions single-handed. It is remarkable too, in view of the essential character of the story, how seldom, and then as a rule only figuratively, "hell" is mentioned, and how discreetly, sparingly and often ironically the idea of damnation, of "going to hell," is touched upon. All this fits in with Goethe's well-known unwillingness to admit the reality of evil.[51] Mephisto is, in fact, the devil of an author who—as far as possible—refused to believe in the devil, not only literally, but also even figuratively. That is why Mephisto, although within the framework of the drama he is, of course, a "real" devil, can hardly ever take himself seriously as a devil. It was characteristic of Goethe to make out of the devil one of the greatest comic figures in all literature.

If, as has here been argued, the Erdgeist is very much less an entity of the old cabbalistic systems than is usually assumed, but rather the symbolical embodiment of "this-worldliness," there is no reason why Mephisto should not be its emissary and still remain as true a devil as he ever appears to be in any part of the drama. After all, one of the titles given to Satan in the New Testament is "the God of this world."[52] And here an interesting point arises. In the chapbook of the "Christlich Meynender"—of all Goethe's sources, the one with which he was most familiar—Satan is referred to in the pact between him and Faust as "der irdische Gott, den die Welt den Teufel pflegt zu nennen" (the earthly God, whom the world usually calls the Devil), and the same curious designation, "der irdische Gott," occurs once more later in the pact. It is far from impossible that this phrase had quite as large a share in suggesting Goethe's Erdgeist as the archaeus or anima terrae of the cabbalists, and that that Spirit did not, as so many critics maintain, replace an earlier Lucifer in Goethe's original plan, but was there from the beginning as a kind of Lucifer incognito. That there is something Lucifer-like about the Erdgeist has variously been remarked upon—the circumstance of its appearing "in der Flamme" and originally also "in widerlicher Gestalt" is an obvious point of resemblance, and the element of ruthless destructiveness which we have recognized in its nature links it up with what we know of Goethe's own early Lucifer myth. If anybody should object that the Erdgeist cannot possibly at one and the same time be Lucifer and the genius of nature, it may be replied that, on the one hand, Lucifer was, as we have seen, in the eyes even of the twenty-year-old Goethe a figure appreciably superior in stature and dignity to the devil, as he is usually conceived of, and on the other hand that Goethe, in spite of his pantheistic fervour, sometimes in those years saw nature as "an eternally devouring, eternally regorging monster." A similar answer may be given to a similar objection raised by Minor, "dass es natürlich unmöglich ist, in dem Diener des Erdgeistes, der selber im Dienste Gottes steht, einen Teufel zu sehen" (that it is, of course, impossible to see in the devil a servant of the Spirit of Earth, who itself is a servant of the deity).[53] It is indeed true that the Erdgeist "fashions a living garment for the deity." But when we see, as we in the course of time shall do, that Goethe later made Mephisto the direct servant of God the Lord himself, we shall have no difficulty in believing that he could very well in the *Urfaust* have made of the Erdgeist an ambivalent being which, while labouring, perhaps in the main involuntarily, in the service of God, in its own turn, perhaps also in the main involuntarily, employs the services of the devil, Mephisto. In fact, once we recognize how much more Luciferian than cabbalistic the Erdgeist, as the "God of this world" or "the earthly God," is, the alleged contradictions between the Invocation scene and "Trüber Tag. Feld" vanish, and we no longer have any valid reason for supposing that the substitution of that Spirit for the Lucifer or Satan of the Faust legend was only an afterthought of Goethe's, and not an integral part of his original conception. It is only a question of how early Goethe can be supposed to have begun to think of good and evil as distinguished from one another not absolutely but only relatively, and therefore as merging into one another at some secret point where they can, so to speak, transact extremely important but also extremely confidential business together and even exchange their natures—for it is such a secret point as this that is symbolically evoked in the Erdgeist. This is certainly not too audacious a view for Goethe to have arrived at by winter, 1771–1772, the earliest date at which we can believe him to have begun work on the *Urfaust*. For we have found it already clearly adumbrated in the "Rede zum Schäkespears Tag" of October, 1771,[54] and a few weeks later, in the original version of *Götz von Berlichingen* he casually introduces such conceptions as that of "the devil hoping for salvation"[55] and "God gambling with the devil." For one with a mind open to such ideas as these, the distinction between black, satanistic magic and the white, "natural" magic of the cabbalists could no longer have any cogency, and it would be the obvious course for him to base a Faust drama undertaken at that juncture upon what might be called "grey" magic, which is what we do find in the *Urfaust*. Not for a moment is Hans Albert Maier's contention to be admitted that "Luzifer und Erdgeist wirklich zwei verschiedenen Welten angehören" (Lucifer and the Spirit of Earth really belong to two different worlds).[56]

What chiefly arises from all this is that there is enough of Lucifer about the Erdgeist for it to be the Spirit which has chained Mephisto to Faust as a companion, without our needing to assume either that Mephisto is no real devil or that Goethe was changing his plans radically every five minutes. The transformation of Lucifer into the Erdgeist is to be thought of as something about which Goethe had made up his mind before he actually began to write the *Urfaust* in 1772, and which was to serve as one of the basic postulates of the action, not as a motif to be further developed or exploited within it. That is to say, the Spirit was to remain all along, for the inner economy of the drama, what it purports to be, Luciferian indeed and therefore sinister and ominous, Lucifer transmuted, if one will, but not just Lucifer in disguise and destined later to unmask himself or to be unmasked. It can hardly have been any part of Goethe's intentions that his Faust should, either in the case of the Erdgeist or in that of Mephisto, have been as it were merely trapped under false pretences into relationships with diabolic forces, when he believed himself to be engaged only in highminded and innocuous pursuits. He does what he does with his eyes open, knowing that he is courting shipwreck and that it may cost him his life. He is the victim ultimately not of anything external to himself, but of his own titanic aspirations to transcend the limits of humanity, and that means not in the last place the limits of good and evil.

The antithesis of other-worldliness and this-worldliness, of idealism and realism, upon which, it has here been argued, the Invocation scene, and with it the entire *Faust* drama turns, was central to Goethe's own life and work. Against all those who would identify Goethe, especially the Storm and Stress Goethe completely with Faust, we would, however, advance that, whereas Faust makes an irrevocable decision in favour of this-worldliness and realism, Goethe himself never made such an irrevocable decision. It is one of the secrets of his genius that the two opposed urges always ultimately counterbalanced one another in his nature, emphatically though he from time to time swung in one or the other direction. In a conversation of April, 1818, with Kanzler von Müller and Karoline von Egloffstein, he made what is rightly regarded as one of his most solemn and valid pronouncements on the last questions of human existence:

> Das Vermögen, jedes Sinnliche zu veredeln und auch den totesten Stoff durch Vermählung mit der Idee zu beleben, ist die schönste Bürgschaft unseres übersinnlichen Ursprungs. Der Mensch, wie sehr ihn auch die Erde anzieht mit ihren tausend und abertausend Erscheinungen, hebt doch den Blick forschend und sehnend zum Himmel auf, der sich in unermesslichen Räumen über ihm wölbt, weil er tief und klar in sich fühlt, dass er ein Bürger jenes geistigen Reiches sei, woran wir den Glauben nicht abzulehnen noch aufzugeben vermögen.*

Even in his Storm and Stress years, when he wrote the *Urfaust*, and when he seemed nearest to committing himself once and for

---

* The capacity to ennoble everything sensual and to give life even to the deadest material by wedding it with the idea, is the finest warrant of our supernatural origins. Man, however much the earth attracts him with its thousands and thousands of phenomena, still raises his eyes to the heavens arched above him in immense space, because he feels deeply and clearly within himself that he is a citizen of that spiritual domain, the belief in which he can neither repudiate nor abandon.

all to this-worldly realism, such sentiments as these were by no means unknown to Goethe, as the Makrokosmus passage and the *Ganymed* poem testify. He could never have written *Faust*, if he had not, even in those early years, been both a this-worldly realist *and* an other-worldly idealist.

6. Wagner/
Student/
Auersbach Keller

FAUST'S CONVERSATION with Wagner, which completes the opening scene of the *Urfaust*, and the other three scenes that intervene between it and the beginning of the Gretchen tragedy, present only minor problems of interpretation and little needs to be added to what has already been said about them in passing. There is a marked resemblance between Faust's conversation with Wagner and Mephisto's conversation with the young student. Both are satirical, with a more earnest vein showing through, the satire being more lighthearted and boisterous, the earnestness less obvious in the second of the two. Both show an inferior mind pitted against and pulverized by an immensely superior one, the joke in each case turning in considerable measure upon the inferior partner being too unintelligent and too much out of his depth even to realize how contemptuously he is being treated, feeling himself indeed on the contrary highly edified and flattered by what seems to him the affability and condescension of the great man. Wagner is Faust's "Famulus," that is to say a kind of senior research student attached to him as a higher servant in return for certain privileges; his mental inferiority is constitutional; the secondrateness of his mind has only been increased by the considerable learning he has already acquired. The young student is a freshman; his mental inferiority is in the first place simply a result of ignorance, immaturity, and inexperience; but he does not look as though he had the makings of a Faust or anything equivalent in him. Thematically the two conversations both continue and vary Faust's attacks upon the futility of all mere academic book-learning and of university life in his opening monologue. In the Wagner conversation the issues are rhetoric, history, and philosophy—all of them studies to which Wagner is devoted, while Faust dismisses the first as mere humbug, the second as so complacently and unimaginatively prac- tised that it is not much better, and the third as only genuine and worth while when it is pursued in a dangerously heterodox, free- thinking manner undreamt of by the pundits of the schools. In the conversation between Mephisto, disguised as a professor, and the young student, the Faculty of Arts, as represented by Logic and Metaphysics, and that of Medicine, as a means to promiscuous erotic experiences, are ridiculed in a ribald manner, and there is also much sometimes very coarse buffoonery about university life in general, particularly about the worthlessness of lectures and note- taking, the wretchedness of typical student lodgings and the con- ceitedness and rapacity of professors. The crudely humorous and not intrinsically very valuable passages dealing with these two last themes Goethe eliminated in 1788–1789, introducing instead, be- tween Mephisto's onslaughts on the Faculties of Arts and Medicine, two additional, similar attacks on those of Law and Theology, so that all four Faculties are now covered, as in Faust's opening monologue. An important factor is that both Wagner and the young student, for all their mental inferiority, have in their own ways aspirations to universal knowledge, which make them appear as second-rate travesties of Faust himself; Faust is conscious of this in dealing with Wagner, and it intensifies his impatience with him. Each dialogue contains one memorable passage of the highest poetic value, in which the quintessential doctrine of Storm and Stress, the total worthlessness of everything else in comparison with the intuitive powers of genius, is incisively proclaimed: Faust's attack on Rhetoric beginning: "Wenn Ihrs nicht fühlt, Ihr werdets nicht erjagen" (If you don't feel it, you will never be able to achieve it by straining after it), and Mephisto's attack on Logic, where the intuitive processes of the mind are likened to the working of a loom. The two conversations are sufficiently differentiated for us to be able to feel them as genuine pendants to one another, with a certain aesthetic, though not ideological polarity between them, and not as mere random variations on one and the same old theme.

The close analogy between these two dialogues forcibly suggests that they did not originate quite independently of one another, but that one must have grown out of the other, probably at no great remove of time. To those who reject the arguments often advanced that the Mephisto-Student scene must, because of its crudity, have been written very early, perhaps as early as 1767–1768,[1] it may well appear possible that it germinated from some passages in the original draft of the Wagner scene which seemed to Goethe inappropriate to the fundamental dignity and earnestness of Faust's character and to the particular brand of philistinism typified by Wagner. We shall see how Goethe later, in rewriting the "Auerbachs Keller" scene transferred on such grounds as these what had originally been Faust's rôle to Mephisto, and he may well have done something similar with certain untractable paralipomena of the Wagner scene at some point of time before November, 1775. In much the same way the "Vorspiel auf dem Theater" was probably evolved in summer, 1797, out of two redundant but in themselves valuable stanzas of the *Zueignung* poem.[2] It is a common phenomenon for poets, especially for Goethe, to make a new, independent work or section of a work out of the paralipomena of one just completed: many instances of it could be given.

The Wagner and the Student scenes, together with the attacks on university learning in Faust's opening monologue, still sometimes disconcert academic critics who feel almost personally insulted by them, maintaining that there is much to be said in defence of such learning and that Goethe himself ought to have seen and even must have seen that too. It is evidently difficult for some professors to tolerate or believe that such a man as Goethe may not always have taken professors and their spheres of operation as seriously as they take themselves, and so the effort is made to dissociate the youthful Goethe, at least in this matter, as completely as possible not only from the views expressed by Mephisto, but also even from those expressed by Faust himself. An extreme example of this is Wilhelm Böhm, whose view of Faust as intended to be fundamentally wrong in everything he says and does was,

as he himself confesses, largely inspired by his "persönliches Bedürfnis, zu glauben" (personal need to believe)[3] that Faust could
only have saved himself by returning to his study and resuming his
academic profession, the rejection of which was his first great mistake. In his later book, *Goethes Faust in neuer Deutung* (Cologne,
1949), Böhm amplifies this opinion. Faust, he declares, badly over-
estimates himself in thinking he is so superior to all his academic
colleagues: "sind alle Doktoren, Magister und Schreiber in einen
Topf zu werfen? Hat keiner etwas zu sagen, was auch Faust
angeht?" (Are all the Doctors, Masters and Scribes to be lumped
together? Has none of them anything to say that might be of importance to Faust?)[4] As Böhm sees it, it is Faust himself who has
proved his inadequacy, in so far as "er dem Wissen aller vier
Fakultäten nichts abgewinnen konnte" (he was unable to profit by
the knowledge of all the four faculties).[5] Accordingly Böhm also
breaks a lance in defence of Wagner, who does at least try "mit
seinem bescheidenen Pfund nach Kräften zu wuchern. Man soll
doch nicht vergessen, dass Wagner in seiner Einfältigkeit ein
herzensguter Kerl ist . . . Ist alles, was Wagner will, 'schales Zeug'?
. . . Ist dieser Ärmlicher wirklich der Ärmlichste von allen Erden-
söhnen?" (. . . to trade to the utmost with his humble talent. One
should not forget that Wagner, for all his simplemindedness, is a
thoroughly decent fellow . . . Is everything that Wagner aims at
merely "shallow stuff"? Is this poor wretch really the most wretched
of mortals?)[6] Such sentiments are unimpeachably humane and
laudable, but they are quite out of place here. All satirists know, as
private individuals, that much might be advanced in defence or ex-
tenuation of the things they satirize, but it is a law alike for the
writing and for the true appreciation of satire that these redeeming
features should for the time being be left out of account. One of the
fundamental postulates of Goethe's *Faust* is that there is no substitute for genius—an idea characteristic not only of the Storm and
Stress movement but also, in a modified form, of Goethe throughout his life. Everything turns upon this uniqueness of genius and, of
course, also upon the problems and dangers peculiar to it. Certainly plodding academic learning is not, within the framework of
Goethe's *Faust*, to be regarded as a possible substitute for genius or
as differing from it only in degree, not in kind. All artistic creation

necessarily involves a certain temporary unfairness to the other side of the question, such as we find here, whether it be in Goldsmith's *Deserted Village* or in Crabbe's *Village*, and at least aesthetically this onesidedness must be accepted. Wagner and the Student have not got genius, and against that decisive deficiency all their estimable other qualities count for next to nothing, and we only miss the point of what Goethe is getting at, if we lavish uncalled-for sympathy or approval on them. They are just foils to their infinitely superior and brilliant partners, and we should not try to make anything more out of them than that.

As out of place as Böhm's championship for Wagner and for Faust's pedestrian colleagues is the extreme moral indignation voiced by such critics as Karl Wollf over the "infernalische" and "teuflische" way in which Mephisto, in his disguise as a professor, corrupts the mind of the young student.[7] For one thing, he has, as Mephisto, a perfect right to behave infernally and diabolically, but what he does here is to be seen as a comparatively harmless joke. The appeal is to our sense of humour, not to our moral indignation. Of course Mephisto corrupts what little mind the student has, and chuckles over it too. But a case could be made out for no higher education being worth anything at all, unless it at least temporarily and in some measure corrupts the student's mind. That was the view of so high-minded an educator as Cardinal Newman. It would not be a bad thing if more professors had a little of Mephisto in them. There can be no doubt that Goethe himself was on the side of Faust and even of Mephisto in the two dialogues.

It is usual, in speaking of the completed *Faust* drama, to regard the "Auerbachs Keller" scene not as the beginning of Faust's adventures after the pact with Mephisto (which is what it really is), but as the end of his academic experiences, that is to say of what is called the "Gelehrtentragödie" (Tragedy of the Scholar), upon which follow the Gretchen tragedy, and (in the second part) the Helena tragedy and the "Herrschertragödie" (Tragedy of the Ruler). In the interests of this neat classification the four drinkers in Auerbach's Cellar are usually designated as students, though there is nothing to support this view of them except the circumstances that the historical Auerbach's Cellar in Leipzig was always much frequented by students, amongst others, and had been frequented by Goethe himself in his own Leipzig student days. The drinkers never do a thing or say a word that might suggest they are meant to be students, and one of them, Siebel, is a fat old man with a bald pate, while Alten (later Altmayer) is married. Far-fetched, unconvincing attempts have been made to establish re-semblances between the names Frosch, Brander, and Alten and the regular designations for first year, second year, and older students respectively in German student slang. It must at least be admitted that if the first thing Mephisto did with Faust on delivering him from his detested university environment in Wittenberg[8] were to plant him amongst four riotous students not much more than forty miles away in Leipzig, he was giving him only a busman's holiday.

The "Auerbachs Keller" scene is of interest to us as evidence that Goethe must have consulted Pfitzer's chapbook before November, 1775, as he here freely and skilfully combines two different anec-dotes from it, which are missing in the abridgment of the "Christ-licher Meynender," with a motif familiar to him from an early seventeenth-century fresco in Auerbach's Cellar showing Faust riding on a huge barrel. This use of Pfitzer is presumptive evidence against the frequently maintained theory that the scene was written as early as 1767 or 1768.[9] It has already been seen that the argu-ments against its having been written as late as 1774 or 1775, especially so far as they turn on the issue of supposed immaturity, are inconclusive.[10] Effective though the scene is, it will hardly bear comparison with the great drinking scenes in Shakespeare's *Henry IV* and *Twelfth Night* which clearly had some share in inspiring it. The chief change Goethe made in it in 1788–1789, apart from re-writing it in Knittel and Madrigal verse throughout, was to transfer all the magical activities to Mephisto from Faust, who, in the final version, only twice opens his mouth, the first time to say: "Seid uns gegrüsst, ihr Herrn!" (Greetings to you, gentlemen!), the second to say: "Ich hätte Lust, nun abzufahren" (I should like to go away now). In fact, he is bored by the whole proceedings and might just as well not be there at all.

The original version of "Auerbachs Keller" is the only evidence of any weight that anybody has ever been able to produce for the widely accepted view that Goethe initially intended only to drama-tize his primitive sources, without making his Faust a very different character from the worker of cheap magical wonders found in them. The scene is, however, alike in its earlier and in its final form, nothing more than a farcical episode, irrelevant to the more serious purport of the drama, and as such Goethe's most substantial concession to the spirit of his sources, according to which it was *de rigueur* that Faust should be seen engaged in such magical horse-play as conjuring wine from table-edges or tricking people into almost cutting one another's noses off. It is fully conceivable that he should, for the sake of variety, fulness and entertainment, have made this concession at any point of time right up to the eve of his departure to Weimar in 1775, just as it was only natural that he should on more careful consideration decide in 1788–1789 that such pranks were too much out of keeping with his idea of Faust's character and that the only way to save the scene at all was—in defiance of tradition—to transfer them to Mephisto. The passage added in the final version to motivate Mephisto's conducting Faust to Auerbach's Cellar at all, namely in order that he may see "wie leicht sich's leben lässt" (how easily life can be taken), carries no conviction and is hardly meant to carry any. This adventure can form no part of Mephisto's real plans with Faust and is best disregarded in a serious interpretation of the drama in its totality. Goethe must have had this scene particularly in mind, when he denied to Eckermann on May 6, 1827 that there is any "Idee, die dem Ganzen und *jeder einzelnen Szene im besonderen* zugrunde liege" (any idea underlying the whole of Faust and *each individual scene in particular*), and also when he wrote sardonically thirty years earlier in the "Vorspiel auf dem Theater": "Besonders aber lasst genug geschehn! / ... Wer vieles bringt, wird manchem etwas bringen." It was one of the most extraordinary of Coleridge's aberrations that he singled out "Auerbachs Keller" as "one of the best, perhaps the very best" scene in the whole of *Faust I.*

The deleted two-couplet fourth scene of the *Urfaust*, "Landstrasse," has already been dealt with.[11] It may be noted here, however, that Hermann Schneider is not the only critic who unwarrantedly reads the most momentous meanings into it. Minor, for example, sees in the stage direction, "Rechts auf dem Hügel ein altes Schloss, in der Ferne ein Bauernhüttchen" (To the right on the hill an old castle, in the distance a cottage),[12] an anticipation of the Philemon and Baucis theme at the end of Part Two, which, so far as we know, was not written before 1830. That theme may indeed have been present before Goethe's mind when he wrote the *Urfaust*, but it is highly improbable that the stage direction in "Landstrasse" has anything to do with it.

We come back to the view already expressed above that the Mephisto-Student and "Auerbachs Keller" scenes and perhaps also "Landstrasse" were probably written about 1774 or 1775 to help towards filling the "great gap" and to counterbalance the Gretchen tragedy.

7. The Gretchen Tragedy

WHEN GOETHE, during the years 1829–1832, again and again insisted that the plan of *Faust* as it was then completed tallied substantially with his earliest conception of some sixty years before, he was, of course, thinking almost exclusively of the second part, which at that time entirely engrossed his attention. Goethe's statements about *Faust* often contradict one another, but this particular, much repeated one is nowhere contradicted by him and is to be regarded as reliable. It can be taken for certain, at least, that Faust's visit to the Emperor's court and his union with Helen of Troy were parts of Goethe's earliest *Faust* plans, as he brooded over them probably from about winter 1770–1771 onward in Strasburg. Amongst all the heterogeneous and often far too trivial material in the old Faust books, these were the two themes that most lent themselves to impressive poetic and dramatic treatment. This was recognized by Marlowe, whose example was followed in all the German popular stage-plays and puppet-plays, only with the modification that, in order to avoid *lèse-majesté*, Faust was commonly shown as visiting the court of the Duke of Parma, instead of that of the German Emperor. It is difficult to see how the youthful Goethe, in forming his first conception for a Faust drama, could have missed these two promising themes, and one can well believe that he even at that early stage devised the general outlines of the way in which he was eventually to treat them so many decades later. It can also be regarded as certain—though many critics deny it—that Goethe had from the outset some vision of Faust's later fortunes, after the encounter with Helen of Troy, particularly of

the mode and circumstances of his death and of the utlimate destiny of his soul. He must have seen the Faust drama before him
as a *whole,* before he could write any *part* of it—whether the whole
he saw before him in 1771 was radically different from what he
actually did complete in 1831 or not, is another question. "Hat
man sich im Ganzen vergriffen, so ist alle Mühe verloren" (If one
has made a mistake about the whole, all one's labour is in vain),
he said to Eckermann on September 18, 1823.

It has already been argued above that the Gretchen tragedy cannot have formed any part of Goethe's original Faust plan, still less
have been, as so many would have us believe, his point of departure
for treating the Faust theme at all.[1] Roethe's view is to be rejected
that Goethe "mit ihr [der Gretchentragödie] begann" (began his
Faust with the Gretchen tragedy),[2] as is also that of Hefele: "Die
Faustidee . . . ist doch erst durch das Gretchenerlebnis für Goethe
wahr und wirklich geworden" (The idea of Faust only became true
and real for Goethe through the Gretchen experience),[3] and that
of Krogmann: "In ihr [der Gretchentragödie] haben wir keine
überwuchernde Nebenhandlung, sondern vielmehr die Haupthand-
lung zu erblicken. Nicht der 'Nur-Faust' steht am Anfang der
Faustdichtung, sondern vielmehr die 'Nur-Gretchentragödie' . . ."
(In the Gretchen tragedy we should see not a subplot which has
got out of hand, but rather the main plot. Not "Faust alone" stands
at the beginning of the composition of *Faust,* but rather "the
Gretchen tragedy alone").[4] It has been shown that none of the
incessantly repeated, amplified and so widely accepted arguments
for these views, from the use of prose and verse, from comparative
crassness or subtlety of diction and sentiment, from parallelisms of
phrasing, from supposed contradictions in thought, characterization
or conduct of the plot, or from what is known of Susanna Margarethe Brandt's trial and execution—none of these arguments,
singly or collectively, can really invalidate the commonsense view
that the opening monologue with the invocation of the Erdgeist
must at least have been drafted and was pretty certainly also fully
worked out, much in the form in which we now know it, before the
first scene of the Gretchen tragedy, whichever scene that may have
been, was written or even thought of. The Gretchen tragedy is
substantially a production of the years 1773–1774, and there are

no sound grounds for believing that it was begun long before winter 1772–1773 at the earliest or that very much remained to be added to it, except the Valentin scene, in 1775. There is no hint at all in the entire opening scene that anything like the Gretchen tragedy is to follow, such as Goethe would have been psychologically bound and indeed aesthetically almost obliged to give, if at the time of his writing it the Gretchen tragedy had already been almost completed or even only contemplated. The only appropriate form of introductory Invocation scene to the Gretchen tragedy as such would have been the sort of thing that is found in the poetically appalling libretto produced by Barbier and Carré for Gounod's *Faust*, where Faust invokes not the Erdgeist, but Satan and then, when in response to this invocation, Mephisto appears, comes straight to the point with the words:

> Ein Wunsch mich beseelt, der alles vereint.
> So höre: die Jugend!
> O gib junges Blut, gib Wonne und Glück,
> O gib neuen Mut und Kraft mir zurück!
> *O gib süsse Lieb', Süss-Mägdeleins Kuss,*
> *Und wonniger Trieb vereint uns zur Lust!**

Gounod's librettists understood very little of great poetry or of Goethe, but they did at least understand the necessary implications of the Gretchen tragedy, so far as Faust's character is concerned. It is on such lines as theirs that Goethe would have been bound to write his introductory Invocation scene, if the Gretchen tragedy had really been his point of departure. We can be infinitely thankful for it that it was not, that Goethe's Faust says no word about love or happiness, or even about the desire for rejuvenation, in the opening scene. But somehow, once Goethe had embarked on the Gretchen tragedy, a certain continuity of identity had to be established between the proud invoker of the Erdgeist, with his superhuman, infinite aspirations, and the lover of Gretchen. It was, strictly speaking, an insoluble problem, but Goethe was all along

---

* One wish inspires me, which unites all others. / Listen then: it is youth! / O give me youthful blood, give me joy and happiness. / Give back to me fresh courage and strength! / *O give me sweet love, the kiss of a sweet young girl, / And may voluptuous desire bring us together in delight!*

fully conscious of its magnitude, and, so far as it was soluble at all, he ultimately did solve it, though it took him nearly thirty years and some skilful use of legerdemain to do it.

Everything that can be said about the discrepancy between the Gretchen tragedy and the essential spirit and idea of the Faust legend is true, whatever allowances may be made for the legitimate refashioning of that legend by a great poet in accordance with his peculiar genius. But there are one or two points to be considered on the other side. One is, that it has always proved difficult to find adequate employment for characters temporarily endowed by unlawful means with superhuman and supernatural powers. Marlowe's *Dr. Faustus* is a striking example of this. The opening, up to Faustus's pact with Mephistophilis, and the conclusion, with his death and damnation, are magnificent, but of all that lies between only the encounter with Helen of Troy maintains itself at the same level, the rest being chiefly poor buffoonery. Still more is this the case with the German puppet-plays, nor does one find anything more satisfactory in the chapbooks. Only Faust's abortive fits of repentance and struggles to free himself from the devil can really make a strong impression on the reader, not his magical enterprises as such. It would not matter so much that magic in practice disappoints the magician himself, if it did not tend to disappoint all but the most naive readers and spectators as well. In our own days this standing problem of the Faust theme has been circumvented in the subtlest ways by Paul Valéry and Thomas Mann, who draw into the orbit of magic the ultimate questions of metaphysics, ethics, psychology, and creative genius. Without some such boosting up it is hardly possible for more sophisticated modern man to make anything out of Faust's magical powers, and it is here then that there is particular licence and scope for free invention. It is to be supposed that Lessing felt this when he grappled with the Faust theme, and we shall see how much Goethe had to manipulate, modernize, enrich and deepen the two great motifs he was able to take over from his sources, the visit to the Emperor's court and the encounter with Helen of Troy, in order to make what he did out of them in his second part. Much of this remoulding of the old tradition had, we can well believe, already been carried out in his imagination in the very early stages of his preoccupation with

Faust, but Helen of Troy, however much endowed with new symbolical undertones, was still remote from him then, and when the
impulse stirred within him to introduce into his *Faust* the theme
of love more in the sense in which it was of immediate importance
to him in those years, it is intelligible enough that he should have
thought it might be risked. That it was a risky thing to undertake
he did, however, quite certainly realise.

If Goethe had been concerned in the first place simply to relieve
his pent-up feelings by treating the theme of infanticide, as it had
been painfully brought home to him by the fate of Susanna Brandt
at the moment when he was troubled in conscience on Friederike
Brion's account, the least likely decision for him to have come to
would have been to make a Faust drama out of it. For such a step
was bound to be prejudicial not only to the Faust theme, but also
to the theme of seduction and infanticide itself. There would be
no point in treating that theme at all, unless everything essential
to it is represented as coming about in a perfectly natural and
human way, out of purely natural and human motives, impulses,
passions and fears. It must at every point be psychologically convincing, and that means that the supernatural and superhuman,
the very essence of the Faust legend, can at most play a peripheral
and strictly speaking unnecessary part in it. And this is exactly
what we find in Goethe's Gretchen Tragedy. That he has achieved
this is a stupendous *tour de force* and testifies to the maturity of
his intuitive and also of his quite conscious and deliberate artistic
powers in the years 1773–1774. He might so easily have done what
Gounod's librettists presumably thought he should have done, or
at least themselves saw fitter to do, namely represented the jewels
procured by Mephisto for Gretchen as having some special, magical
love-charm attached to them, and made the Evil Spirit who besets
her in the Cathedral scene Mephisto himself, telling her she is
damned and must go to hell. In Goethe's own text there is no indication of anything like this in either case. The jewels appeal only
to Gretchen's natural vanity, the "böser Geist" that haunts her is
only her own troubled conscience, her love and her crime are the
outcome of human nature and of the given situation, in which
mysterious, infernal agencies play no essential part. Even Faust's
desire for her and his later desertion of her are the spontaneous

outcome of his own nature, in spite of his having drunk the witch's potion. "Magic" here only lets loose and intensifies the natural and human; it does not counteract it with alien forces. The supernatural itself appears as a part of nature, the superhuman and also the subhuman as a part of humanity.

The obvious form in which to treat the Gretchen theme would have been the domestic tragedy, as Lessing had introduced it into German literature in 1755 with his *Miss Sara Sampson* and as so many contemporaries were practising it, notably Goethe himself in his *Clavigo* of 1774 and in his *Stella* of 1775, and his fellow Storm and Stress writers Lenz, Klinger, and Wagner in their most important dramatic works. It was in the form of a domestic tragedy that Heinrich Leopold Wagner actually did treat the Gretchen theme in his *Kindermörderin* ("The Infanticide") of 1776. This grim, naturalistic, and—in spite of certain crudities—deeply moving drama, the only really satisfactory Storm and Stress drama outside the works of the youthful Goethe and Schiller, is regularly looked upon far less favourably than it deserves, because posterity has never been able to see in it anything more than a shameless plagiary of Goethe's Gretchen tragedy. Goethe himself is responsible for this view of it, which he expresses with considerable bitterness in Book XIV of *Dichtung und Wahrheit*. The infanticide theme was very much in the air in those days, but Goethe seems to have been the first in the field with it, and in all probability Wagner did derive the idea of his drama from the little he knew of the Gretchen tragedy. He can at most have heard a few fragments of it read by Goethe, and even about that we cannot be certain. All Goethe himself says on the subject is: "So *erzählte* ich ihm, wie andern, meine Absicht mit *Faust*, besonders die Katastrophe von Gretchen" (So I *told him*, as I did others too, about my intentions with *Faust*, especially about the catastrophe with Gretchen).[5] This can only have been in autumn, 1774. How near the Gretchen tragedy then was to completion we do not know. Goethe's statement, for what it is worth, that he told Wagner at that time how he *intended* to treat the catastrophe of Gretchen certainly does not support the commonly accepted view that the scenes "Trüber Tag. Feld" and "Kerker" had already been written well over two years earlier. Actually Wagner's *Kindermörderin* has so little in common with the Gretchen tragedy that it is not easy to see why Goethe should have been so annoyed about it. There is a *Frau Marthe* in both works indeed, but they are two entirely different types of character, and play entirely different rôles in the plot. In both works sleeping draughts are administered to the heroine's mother, but in Wagner's by Evchen's seducer, in order that he may have the opportunity to overcome by force Evchen's otherwise unassailable virtue, in Goethe's by Gretchen herself, in order that she may be able to surrender herself freely to Faust's love. The most striking resemblance is in the following dialogue between Wagner's Evchen and her seducer, Lieutenant von Gröningseck, immediately after he has violated her:

> *von Grön.*: Ums Himmelswillen, so komm doch zu dir!—du bist ja nicht die erste—
> *Evchen*: Die du zu Fall gebracht hast?—bin ich's nicht— nicht die erste? o sag' mir's noch *einmal*.
> *von Grön.*: Nicht die erste, sag' ich, die Frau wurde, eh' sie getraut war.—Von dem jetzigen Augenblick an bist du die Meinige! . . .*

This is regarded as a plagiary of Mephisto's cynical words to Faust in "Trüber Tag. Feld": "Sie ist die erste nicht."[6] But that phrase was much in the air in those days. Goethe found it in the 1725 Faust chapbook and used it in the original version of *Götz von Berlichingen* and also, with special reference to the case of a deceived girl, in *Clavigo*, which was published shortly before his conversations with Wagner of autumn, 1774, and certainly also influenced Wagner—his villainous Lieutenant von Hasenpoth, who is far more guilty of Evchen's disaster than the seducer von Gröningseck, clearly owes much to the sinister Carlos in that play. However high we may assess Wagner's debt to Goethe's Gretchen tragedy, of which he can have had at most only an imperfect knowledge, he has made of the theme something distinctively his own and something also, in its own way, highly valuable—the one great

---

* *von Grön.*: For Heaven's sake pull yourself together!—it is not as though you were the first— / *Evchen*: —that you have seduced?—Am I not—not the first? O say it *once* more. / *von Grön.*: Not the first, I say, who has become a wife, before she was married. From this moment you are mine!

consistently naturalistic drama of German eighteenth-century literature. Of course Goethe's Gretchen Tragedy has nothing to fear
from the comparison with Wagner's *Kindermörderin,* though it
is surprising that Goethe himself should apparently not have felt
quite confident about that. But neither need Wagner's *Kindermörderin* fear comparison with Goethe's Gretchen tragedy. The
two works treat the same theme indeed, but treat it in two entirely
different ways, each of them justifiable and admirable, Wagner's
way being the natural, obvious one, Goethe's highly exceptional
and strange, because he was faced with the additional problem of
fitting the theme into the larger framework of a drama of magic,
of pacts with the devil, of the supernatural and the superhuman.
In any case, Wagner's *Kindermörderin* comes nowhere near to
being a plagiary of the Gretchen tragedy in the sense in which, for
example, Goethe's own *Hermann und Dorothea* is a plagiary of
Voss's *Luise,* down to the very form, tone, manner, milieu, humour,
sentiment, and characterization. With reference to Byron, Goethe
said on this whole question of plagiarization: "Gehört nicht alles,
was die Vor- und Mitwelt geleistet, dem Dichter von Rechts wegen
an? Warum soll er sich scheuen, Blumen zu nehmen, wo er sie
findet? Nur durch Aneignung fremder Schätze entsteht ein Grosses.
Hab ich nicht auch im Mephistophiles den Hiob und ein Shake-
spearelied mir angeeignet?" (Has not the poet a right to everything achieved by his predecessors and contemporaries? Why
should he scruple to pluck flowers where he finds them? It is only
by the appropriation of borrowed plumes that great work comes
into existence. Did I not myself pillage the book of Job and a song
of Shakespeare's for my Mephisto?)[7] It is not easy to see why
Wagner should be denied the privilege Goethe here claims for
himself and Byron. Actually Wagner's drama is of particular
interest to us for the light it throws by contrast on Goethe's unique
achievement in the Gretchen tragedy.

In writing the Gretchen tragedy, Goethe was faced with a twofold problem. On the one hand he had, because this was a Faust
drama, to bring specifically magical, diabolical and supernatural
elements into it, but he had to do it in such a way that they should
not interfere with the natural unfolding of a genuinely human
relationship, as they do in Gounod's libretto. On the other hand,

what was inherently naturalistic about the theme and clamoured to be represented in a naturalistic manner, as in Wagner's *Kindermörderin*, had to be reduced to the barest minimum, as it would otherwise have been totally incompatible with the specifically magical, Faustian character of the dramatic framework. In fact Goethe had here to find his way along a narrow rocky ridge with steep precipices on each side. He had to combine the fantastic and the naturalistic in a sustained synthesis, and in such a way that neither of these two opposed elements should at any point assert itself with its true force or in its true character at the expense of the other. He could not afford to let the fantastic luxuriate in accordance with its own immanent laws at the expense of vivid, poignant, immediate human reality; nor could he afford to let the naturalistic consolidate itself to massive starkness, in accordance with its immanent laws, at the expense of the magical, dreamlike and visionary. One of the chief means by which he prevented the fantastic from running away with him was by subduing it with a certain irony. One of the chief means by which he prevented the naturalistic from running away with him was by subduing it with a veil of transfiguring poetic beauty. Out of these so cramping negative conditions, however, he produced something triumphantly positive, and the somnambulistic ease and spontaneity with which he avoided all the pitfalls to right and left in this perilous venture should not deceive us into believing that his alert critical faculties did not have also to play a considerable part in it. That is not the sort of thing that anybody achieves without knowing what he is about.

It might have proved more difficult than it did for Goethe to provide some scope for Mephisto and magic in the Gretchen tragedy, if he had based his work on the orthodox conception of evil and sin, according to which the devil is concerned to corrupt what he knows and admits to have been originally good and perfect. For Goethe's Mephisto—and this applies not only to the Gretchen tragedy, but to the Faust drama in its totality—the creation is intrinsically imperfect and "bad," and his concern is only to demonstrate that it is so, not first to make it so. He regards the world, and particularly man, as God's great mistake; this is his genuine conviction, in which, if in nothing else, he is sincere, and he only wants to prove that he is right on this point. He bears mankind no real malice, but he is anxious to pull God down a peg or two, and that he can only do by showing in drastic, catastrophic examples what troubles, absurdities, and guilt man lands himself in through cherishing lofty, spiritual aspirations his physical nature cannot live up to. "Evil" is for Mephisto not something peculiarly his own, which he wants to insinuate from without into a world originally free of it; it is something he finds inherent in the world, particularly in human nature, and for which he even disowns any personal responsibility; the blame for it lies ultimately with God, who has not made a better job of creation. Mephisto is in his own eyes not himself the "power of evil," but simply one who has seen through the fraud, the spuriousness of what passes for good. So far as he is "the accuser," it is not "our brethren," but God himself whom he accuses. He feels himself as honest and God as somehow cheating. Goethe does not indeed formulate this conception of the devil in so many words until 1797 in the "Prolog im Himmel" and 1800 in the first "Studierzimmer" (Study) scene, but it is implied already throughout the *Urfaust*. Mephisto does not aim at making an evildoer out of Faust, but only at demonstrating that all his lofty spiritual aspirations amount to nothing, so that at the end he can demand of him: "Wer wars, der sie [Gretchen] ins Verderben stürzte? Ich oder du?" (Who was it that ruined Gretchen? I or you?) ("Trüber Tag. Feld"). Throughout he meticulously avoids doing any violence to Faust's own nature, will and inclinations, anything that might fairly entitle Faust to disclaim the responsibilities for his actions. If this Mephisto had had to play the part of the Serpent in Eden, he would have warned Adam and Eve against the dangers of the forbidden fruit, and then sat back with pleasure, confidently expecting them in spite of, or even because of, his warnings, to eat it of their own accord. All he asks is that things should be allowed to take what he conceives to be their natural course, and even as a tempter he confines himself to gently encouraging this natural course of things. He is, so to speak, a white-collar devil, who believes that all the really dirty work of his profession does itself or has perhaps even been clandestinely taken care of in advance by the Lord. This is all part of the humorous view he takes of his own devilship.

This conception of the devil was helpful to Goethe when he

faced the problem of adapting the theme of the seduced and in-
fanticidal girl of the humbler classes to the requirements of the
Faust legend and to the atmosphere of the Faustian world. He had
to provide opportunities within it for the activities of Mephisto,
for the employment of magic and for some display of Faust's own
specifically titanic mental powers—this last a well-nigh impossible
task, which he nevertheless tackled with remarkable resourceful-
ness. It has again and again been pointed out that supernatural
and superhuman powers are not required to seduce a simple, ignorant girl; that this is for ever being done without them. Goethe
knew this too from his personal experience. At the age of eighteen
he had written to Behrisch: "Aber ohne zu schwören, ich unter-
stehe mich schon, ein Mädchen zu verf—wie Teufel soll ichs
nennen?" (Without swearing, I would trust myself to sed—— a
girl—how the devil shall I put it?)[8] How much personal experience
of this kind he had and how far he went, particularly in the case
of Friederike Brion, we do not know and do not need to know.
But he had certainly had enough experience, coupled with his own
powers of observation and anticipatory imagination, to know all
about it. He makes Faust himself declare explicitly at the very
beginning of the Gretchen tragedy:

> Hätt ich nur sieben Stunden Ruh,
> Braucht keinen Teufel nicht dazu,
> So ein Geschöpfchen zu verführen.*

Yet for Goethe's purposes what could have been done by perfectly
ordinary human and natural means has here to be done, or at least
to appear to be done, by magical means, not because there is any
real need for them, but only because this is a Faust drama. Sump-
tuous gifts of jewelry are provided through Mephisto's agency,
where much humbler gifts would presumably have answered just
as well. Mephisto is given the role of a go-between—a diabolical
rôle, suitable enough for him, but one that is regularly played by
ordinary human beings; and in playing it he not only exhibits his
diabolical character, but also makes use of his supernatural knowl-

---

* If I only had seven hours' peace, / I should not need any devil / To seduce
such a little creature.

edge and powers. The one thing he is not allowed to do, however, is actually to tempt Gretchen, for the insolent suggestion that if it is too early for her to have a husband, she should accept a lover, is not to be regarded as a serious or effectual venture in temptation. The real business of tempting her is left to Faust himself; anything else would run counter alike to the plans of Mephisto and to those of Goethe. Still less is Mephisto allowed to provide Faust with a love-potion to administer to Gretchen: that would have been fatal to Goethe's design that the love between the two should be spontaneous and natural. Instead we must suppose—though there is no word in the text about it—that it is Mephisto who provides the insidious sleeping-draught that kills Gretchen's mother. It is the sort of thing that might easily have happened only by accident, but Mephisto makes sure that it does indeed happen. Similarly he provokes the quarrel between Faust and Valentin and paralyses Valentin's arm at the critical moment. But the actual slaying of Valentin is a deed for which Faust must bear the full responsibility.

To give scope for the display of Faust's Promethean mental powers within the Gretchen tragedy was more difficult, for his love was to reduce him from the level of the superman to that of the ordinary man, and Gretchen could not possibly have fallen in love with Faust *qua* Faust, could never have understood or had any relationship to those qualities in him that make him Faust. She never from beginning to end has any idea of who or what he really is, except in the very last moment when she turns away from him appalled with the words: "Mir grauts vor dir, Heinrich" (You fill me with horror, Henry). She sees in him the handsome nobleman, the "herzlich guten Mann" (man with such a good heart), and cannot understand why he should not be a believing Christian like herself. There is no indication that she even knows his real name is Faust, and the name by which she calls him, "Heinrich," is presumably only an assumed one, though it is always quite unwarrantedly taken for granted that Goethe meant this to be regarded as Faust's real Christian name, instead of the traditional "Johannes." The Faustian elements in him are all in abeyance. Yet Goethe felt the necessity of letting some glimmering of the Faust of the opening monologue become perceptible once at least within the relationship between the two, and this he brilliantly contrived in the "Catechism" scene. It is idle to speculate, as so many do, whether it is a conversation with Friederike Brion or with Lotte Buff that Goethe is here reproducing, and it is undiscerning to dismiss Faust's famous profession of faith which culminates in the words: "Gefühl ist alles!" (Feeling is everything!) with Hermann Schneider as mere "verblasenen Pantheismus" and "Verlegenheitsausdruck" (diluted pantheism [and] expression of embarrassment).[9] It is as much of the specifically Faustian as could be expected to persist in the given, cramping situation. Only twice does Faust appear alone during the entire Gretchen tragedy in the *Urfaust* text, and when we see him then in the mode of expression most characteristic of his solitary, self-centred nature, in the monologue directly after his first sight of Gretchen, and then contemplating her bedroom, erotic longings and sentiments have so completely changed him from what he was in the great opening scene that he speaks for us as well as for himself, when he says: "Armselger Faust, ich kenne dich nicht mehr" (Wretched Faust, I can no longer recognize you). It must have been chiefly to remedy this that Goethe in 1788 added in *Faust, ein Fragment* the impressive blank verse monologue of "Wald und Höhle," where Faust, immediately after the seduction of Gretchen, appears once more for a moment with something of his true superhuman stature and in an environment more appropriate to his Faustian destiny. For the rest we see Faust throughout the Gretchen tragedy either in the company of Gretchen or, far more often, in that of Mephisto. It is only in the presence of Mephisto and in protest against him that the daemonic, elemental nature of Faust manifests itself genuinely and undilutedly, and this occurs but twice, and on each occasion it is not Faust's love for Gretchen as such that finds expression, but his horrified recognition of the inevitable destructive consequences of that love. The first is in his long speech—later transferred to "Wald und Höhle" but originally part of the still fragmentary "Valentin" scene (the seventeenth)—in which he denounces himself as "der Flüchtling, Unbehauste, / Der Unmensch ohne Zweck und Ruh" (the fugitive, the homeless one, / The monster without purpose or repose), and sees no outcome of the situation but that Gretchen and he should perish together—though it appears that soon after he leaves her to perish alone. The other occasion is in "Trüber Tag. Feld," particularly in the passages often referred to above and later expanded to the opening monologue of "Wald and Höhle," where he apostrophizes the "great, glorious, infinite Spirit" and inveighs against Mephisto. It is indeed only an ineffectual, self-dramatizing despair that is expressed in both passages, but it is not the less genuinely Faustian for that. Self-dramatizing despair is one of the most characteristic manifestations of Faust's titanism—there is much of it in the opening monologue. The true Faust is daemonically great and passionate and full of energy, but he is not what is called "strong-minded." He is on the heroic scale, but he is not a hero, except in the sense of being the hero of Goethe's drama.

One of Goethe's most important devices for bringing the supernatural into the Gretchen tragedy without detriment to its essentially human and natural character was the "Walpurgisnacht" scene, of which there will be more to say later. It is not indeed strictly speaking a part of the Gretchen tragedy proper, but only a highly important interlude within it, and was not actually written till after 1797. It is commonly assumed that it did not belong to Goethe's early Faust plan, but it certainly already belonged to his plan in 1788, as Mephisto in the "Hexenküche" scene written that year says to the Witch:

> Und kann ich dir was zu Gefallen tun,
> So darfst du mirs nur auf Walpurgis sagen.*

For one who believes, in opposition to prevailing opinion, that Goethe in 1788–1789 had no thoughts of materially altering his original Faust plan—this is a question which will be dealt with in due course—it will seem highly probable that, if he contemplated some kind of "Walpurgisnacht" scene then, he must also have contemplated it in the years 1772–1775, when the *Urfaust* was written. He must certainly have contemplated something to stand immediately before the scene "Trüber Tag. Feld," where the "Walpurgisnacht" scene now stands, as otherwise Faust's words to Mephisto at the beginning of "Trüber Tag. Feld" would be unin-

---

* And if there is anything I can do for you, / You need only tell me at the Walpurgis festival.

telligible: "Und du wiegst mich indess in abgeschmackten Freuden ein, verbirgst mir ihren [Gretchens] wachsenden Jammer und lässest sie hülflos verderben" (And meanwhile you lull me to inertness with inane pleasures, concealing from me her misery and allowing her to perish without help). In the final text the "abgeschmackte Freuden" (inane pleasures), or "abgeschmackte Zerstreuungen" (inane amusements)—as they there become—can only refer to the "Walpurgisnacht," which they fit very well; there is no reason to suppose the phrase was intended to apply to anything else when Goethe first wrote it. One of his chief inspirations for the "Walpurgisnacht" scene, J. F. Löwen's poem of that title, was known to him, as we have seen when he was only sixteen years old.[10] There is furthermore in a later deleted passage in the *Urfaust* version of the "Auerbachs Keller" scene a Breughelesque allusion to the scene of the Walpurgis Night revelries, Brocken mountain, which may well have been intended by Goethe to prepare the reader for the uncanny, Breughelesque goings-on there. Siebel says: "Wetter und Tod! Grüss mein Liebchen—Eine Hammelmauspastete mit gestopften dürren Eichenblättern *vom Blocksberg,* durch einen geschundenen Hasen mit dem Hahnenkopf überschickt, und keinen Gruss von der Nachtigall" (Thunder and death! A greeting to my sweetheart!—Let a pasty of crickets stuffed with oak-leaves *from the Brocken* be conveyed to her by a flayed hare, with the head of a cock, and no greeting from the nightingale!). In the passage substituted for this one in 1788–1789, the allusion to the Walpurgis night celebrations is brought out still more clearly:

> Ein alter Bock, wenn er vom Blocksberg kehrt,
> Mag im Galopp noch gute Nacht ihr meckern!*

Everything suggests that it was Goethe's intention from the start to display the "abgeschmackte Freuden," with which Mephisto tries to lull Faust into forgetfulness of Gretchen's plight, in the form of a Walpurgis Night scene. Such a scene would admittedly, if it had been written between 1772 and 1775, have differed from

---

* May an old billy-goat returning from the Brocken / Bleat Good-night to her as he gallops past.

what Goethe ultimately made of it after 1797. But it is quite possible that the scene as we know it embodies splinters of the Storm and Stress years.

In the last three scenes of the Gretchen tragedy supernatural motifs are also introduced—with Mephisto's magical black horses, which are to make the rescue of Gretchen possible; with the covey of witches dancing around the place of execution, whom Faust and Mephisto pass on their weird, Lenore-like ride; and with the spell by which Mephisto deprives the jailer of his senses. But none of this penetrates to Gretchen herself, or even ultimately to Faust. She sees in Mephisto what she has all along intuitively apprehended and shrunk from in him, the evil one, with whom she will have nothing to do, not even for the saving of her life.

Not only, however, has Goethe adapted the fantastic world of Faust to the Gretchen theme, which in itself called for purely realistic treatment in the form of a domestic tragedy, by keeping the superhuman and supernatural within close limits. He has also, in a less obvious, but even more important way, adapted the Gretchen theme to the world of Faust. This he has achieved by quite deliberately making the entire action of the Gretchen tragedy fragmentary, episodic, and incoherent, and omitting from it some of the most important personages and events. Anybody reading only this one play of Goethe's and judging it by normal standards of the drama, classical or Shakespearean, would be bound to conclude that Goethe simply had no notion of how to write a play and would not believe that he had before 1770 shown himself a master of dramatic construction in *Die Laune des Verliebten* and *Die Mitschuldigen*. The effect of all this is to give the Gretchen tragedy in its totality a certain fairy-tale-like, dream-like character, to remove it from reality, to approximate it to the "nebulous dream-world" of Faust. There is progressively less continuity of action and background from scene to scene. The characters, especially Gretchen, bring only as much of their environment along with them as a tin soldier has ground beneath his feet to stand on. The scenes are all extremely short, and the longest is one in which Faust himself does not appear at all and Gretchen has very little to say, the main interest being concentrated on Frau Marthe and Mephisto; it is of very little importance for the main action. The

"Garten" scene is constructed in the naivest—or apparently naivest
—stylized way. Three times Faust and Gretchen cross the stage,
followed by Mephisto and Frau Marthe, and from appearance to
appearance their intimacy increases very rapidly, Gretchen's dif-
fidence giving way first to artless prattle about her family
and her way of life, then to the ingenuous device for throwing
herself at Faust's head by chanting "Er liebt mich," "Er liebt mich
nicht" (He loves me, he loves me not), as she pulls out one by one
the petals of a daisy-like flower. Gretchen's mother, who is so
immensely important for the action, never appears on the stage,
and her brother only appears just in time to get himself killed.
We see Faust and Gretchen together but twice[11] between their
first meeting outside the Cathedral, when they only exchange four
brief lines of dialogue, and the "Kerker" scene. Their entire conversation on those two occasions amounts to less than 150 lines,
and in his later revisions Goethe saw no necessity to amplify this.
That is to say, considerably less space is devoted to showing the
progress of their love than to the opening monologue, to Mephisto's
conversation with the Student, or to the "Auerbachs Keller" scene.
Minor points, which could well have been omitted altogether, like
the handing over of the first set of jewels to the priest and Faust's
scruples over swearing to Schwerdtlein's death, are amply developed
in a leisurely manner, and such important events as the death of
Gretchen's mother, the birth and killing of her child, her flight,
arrest, and trial, are only referred to in brief and uninformative
phrases long after the event. An immense amount is left to the
reader's imagination. There is no indication how often Faust and
Gretchen have met between the first Garden scene and the Catechism scene, or of how often they come together as lovers, and
there is much wrangling on this latter point amongst the critics.
Some find it intolerable that the two should have lived in "a vulgar
liaison" with one another, to employ the phrase of Calvin Thomas,
who finds evidence that at least the elderly Goethe thought of
Gretchen as having "sinned but once" in the lines at the very end
of the Second Part, where the saints interceding for her forgiveness
describe her as "diese gute Seele, / Die sich *einmal nur* vergessen"
(this good soul who *only once* forgot herself).[12] This "einmal
nur," to which Albert Daur in particular attaches immense im-

portance,[13] can, however, in accordance with normal German usage, hardly have any such specifically numerical significance. The way in which Valentin speaks, especially in the later additions, about the scandal and gossip, and about Frau Marthe's activities as a coupler, together with various other circumstances, suggests a relationship that has continued for some time. It is remarkable that Valentin in his indictment never refers to the death of the mother. The entire later fate of Gretchen between her fall and the birth of her child is indicated in the *Urfaust* only by the three brief scenes—"Am Brunnen (At the Well), "Zwinger" (Barbican), and "Dom" (Cathedral)—which show her becoming estranged progressively from her old companions, from herself, and from God; and these three scenes contain only the vaguest indications of the course of outward events and no single reference to Faust, no statements or questions about what has become of him, no desire even that he should return—an omission which Gounod's librettists, of course, felt it necessary to repair. The Requiem in the "Dom" scene is expressly stated to be for Gretchen's mother, which creates insuperable chronological problems; it is then, in Part I, transferred to Valentin which, far from solving these problems, only creates new ones. Altogether, it is impossible to construct anything like a consistent chronological scheme for the Gretchen tragedy, and the later additions, after 1797, make it more impossible than ever: Valentin is killed two days before Walpurgis night, Gretchen is executed immediately after it. All this is quite deliberate and was clearly intended by Goethe from the outset. The order of the scenes is interchangeable: "Wald und Höhle" at first (in the *Fragment* of 1790) followed upon the actual seduction of Gretchen, but then in 1808 was made to precede it. The "Dom" scene appears in different positions in each of the three texts. All these things would be grave defects, if the play were meant to be on naturalistic or even only on realistic lines, and sometimes they are indeed regarded as defects, for example by Coleridge, who censured *Faust I* as having "neither causation nor progression." But Goethe has here carefully gone out of his way to avoid the naturalistic and realistic, and was bound to do so, if he did not want the Gretchen theme to ruin his Faust drama completely. Wagner, in his in its own way admirable treatment of the same theme, amply evokes and consistently maintains a specific social milieu, clearly and coherently setting before us a complex pattern of human relationships; even Gounod's libretto tawdrily and mawkishly does something of the same kind, showing us Valentin going out to the wars with his comrades and consigning Gretchen to the care of the faithful, generous-hearted Siebel, Faust's rival for her love. Goethe gives us instead a series of vivid, but brief, fragmentary, and disjointed, glimpses, which fade out at once into the surrounding mist and still partake in some measure of its obscurity and confusion.

It is remarkable that even the most important point in the Gretchen tragedy, Faust's desertion of Gretchen, is only implied and nowhere directly presented or even mentioned. Some critics, especially those who think Faust should be regarded as an ideal, exemplary superman, have even tried to make out a case for his never having in the strict sense of the word deserted her at all. Thus H. Schneider speaks of Goethe's having devised "eine neue geschickte Motivierung dafür, dass er [Faust] Gretchen verlassen hat. Es geschah nicht aus Leichtherzigkeit, er musste . . . Faust hat einen Mord auf dem Gewissen" (a skilful new motivation for Faust's desertion of Gretchen. It did not happen out of fickleness, but because he had to . . . He has a murder on his conscience).[14] The killing of Valentin is, of course, the immediate occasion of Faust's forsaking of Gretchen, but it can hardly be called the motive for it. One of the reasons why Mephisto provokes the situation in which Faust kills Valentin is presumably in order that it may be made extremely difficult and dangerous for him to show his face in Gretchen's town again. But this would not help Mephisto at all in his ultimate designs if Faust did not very soon after this enforced separation from Gretchen become indifferent to her and forget her, as Mephisto had confidently expected him to do. Mephisto can indeed plead that the murder of Valentin has created obstacles against which even his supernatural powers are unavailing: "rächende Geister" (avenging spirits) hover over the grave of Faust's victim and Faust himself has been outlawed as a murderer. But if Faust really cared enough or gave the matter any thought, there are all sorts of ways in which these obstacles could be circumvented. He could, for example, have commanded Mephis-

to to convey Gretchen before or after the birth of her child to some
place where she could have been united with him or at least been
taken care of. Such commands Mephisto could not have refused
to obey, as appears in "Trüber Tag. Feld," when Faust insists on
the rescue of Gretchen being attempted. But it does not so much
as occur to Faust to ask Mephisto to keep him informed about
Gretchen's fate, simply because he has lost all interest in her and
gives no thought to the kind of trouble she may be in through him.
He goes on forgetting her thus, we must suppose, for many weeks
and months; she no longer appeals to his pity, to his conscience, or
even to his lust. Only on the eve of her execution does he remember
her. Mephisto's hopes that he might not remember her until after
the execution are indeed disappointed, but only just. The circumstances under which he is reminded of her are not indicated in the
Urfaust; but after 1797, in the "Walpurgisnacht" scene, Goethe
did something about this: in the middle of his obscene revellings
with the witches he sees a mysterious female figure with a red
mark round her neck, indicating that the head is severed, and
recognizes her as Gretchen. It is likely that this corresponds in
essentials to Goethe's pre-1775 plan. We must suppose that this
vision leads Faust to ask Mephisto what has happened to Gretchen,
and that Mephisto, after trying for a time unsuccessfully to put
him off, is at last obliged to discover the truth to him. There is
just time for him to undertake to rescue Gretchen: that is a defeat
for Mephisto. But Gretchen rightly refuses to be rescued when
she realises that it must be through Mephisto's agency, and elects
to die on the scaffold instead, expiating her sins and committing
herself to the justice and the mercy of God. The sight of Mephisto
reawakens her long-dormant moral sense in the eleventh hour—
another defeat for Mephisto, in spite of his endeavour to brazen
it out with his declaration: "Sie is gerichtet!" (Judgment has been
passed on her!). But everything could have been averted if Faust
had remembered her earlier, before the killing of her child. The
responsibility for her fate lies entirely with Faust. He has preferred
the "abgeschmackte Freuden" offered to him by Mephisto to the
thought of Gretchen. He has tired of her and been glad to have
got rid of her. Mephisto, on whom he would thrust the blame,
would never have been able to "lull him into inertness" with these

"inane pleasures," if his love for Gretchen had been genuinely considerate and constant. The single night of Walpurgis in *Faust I* represents symbolically months of nonchalant drifting around and of crude erotic adventures, during which Faust's conscience has remained entirely dormant. All this is nowhere explicitly stated, but it is quite unambiguously implied, already in the *Urfaust*. Yet there are critics who can misinterpret Goethe's eloquent silences here and find extenuations for Faust's unextenuable callousness, as H. Schneider does and as Agnes Bartscherer also does, when she writes: "Wohl ist Faust selber schuldig . . . aber gewollt hat er den unseligen Ausgang seiner Leidenschaft nicht" (Faust is indeed himself guilty but he had not intended his passion to have such a fatal outcome).[15] Of course he had not actively intended it, but he had had no thoughts about preventing it, until it was too late. The point of his last moment remembrance of Gretchen and of his abortive attempt to rescue her is quite lost, if we do not recognize that he is no more or less of a responsible agent in all his previous ruthlessness and indifference which have reduced her to her plight than in these redeeming gestures. Karl Wolff says very discerningly of the opening of the "Walpurgisnacht" scene: "Und kein Gedanke an die Verlassene oder an den begangenen Mord stört die ausgezeichnete Laune, die ihn schon bei der Brocken-Besteigung erfüllt" (And no thought of the deserted Gretchen or of the murder he has just committed impairs the excellent spirits that fill him as he ascends the Brocken).[16] It is strange to see a justification for Faust's leaving Gretchen to get on as best she can, in the circumstance that he unfortunately happens just to have killed her brother. That might at least have been a good opportunity to carry out his heroic resolve to perish together with her; but instead he thinks only of saving his own skin.

The technique of stylization, fragmentariness, incoherency, omissions, laconic hints, and eloquent silences, by which Goethe strove to assimilate the Gretchen theme to the world of Faust and to prevent Gretchen from imperilling the ideal unity of the mystery play, proved unavailing. Once Gretchen appears, and whenever she appears, she concentrates all the limelight upon herself and Faust loses in stature. She brings her own world with her, and the kind of interest that belongs to that world. It was therefore an

immense problem for Goethe to work his way back from the
Gretchen tragedy to the Faust proper of the opening monologue
and forward to the Faust proper of the projected episodes at the
Emperor's court and with Helen of Troy. Ultimately he could
only manage this by contriving two radical breaches in the continuity of Faust's personality, the "Hexenküche" scene of 1788,
where the rejuvenating potion largely expunges what he has hitherto
been and makes virtually a new character out of him, and the opening scene of Part II, *Anmutige Gegend* ("Pleasant Region") of 1825,
where Ariel and his Elves eradicate from his mind the memory of
all he has been through with Gretchen. Through these two scenes
Faust, the lover of Gretchen, is so to speak bracketed out from
Faust, the Magus. Faust sets out on his adventure in the second
part from much the same point as where he had stood immediately
after the pact with Mephisto, almost as though there had been no
Gretchen tragedy. To such extreme measures was Goethe reduced
in his struggle to integrate the Gretchen theme into his Faust
drama.

That the specifically, diabolically supernatural powers and activities of Mephisto are only of secondary importance for what happens
to Gretchen, and that he nowhere directly and effectually "tempts"
her does not mean that he plays no essential rôle in the Gretchen
tragedy, still less, as is so vociferously asserted by the majority of
critics, that Faust's meeting with her and the love between the two
are not intended by him and chiefly arouse annoyance and apprehension in him as obstacles to his plans for Faust's degradation.
In the "Hexenküche" scene of 1788, which was specially designed
amongst other things to link up the disjointed sections of the
drama that were already in existence or definitely planned, Mephisto says to Faust, with reference to the vision of a beautiful nude
woman which has just appeared to him—certainly not without
Mephisto's instrumentality—in the magic mirror:

> Für diesmal sieh dich immer satt;
> Ich weiss dir so ein Schätzchen auszuspüren . . . *

---

* For the present gaze your fill; / I shall be able to ferret out such a sweetheart as that for you.

He repeats this promise at the end of the scene, when Faust, having drunk the rejuvenating potion, desires to gaze in the magic mirror once more:

> Nein! Nein! Du sollst das Muster aller Frauen
> Nun bald leibhaftig vor dir sehn.†

He then mutters aside:

> Du siehst mit diesem Trank im Leibe,
> Bald Helenen in jedem Weibe.‡

Immediately upon these words follows Faust's first meeting with Gretchen as she leaves the church. The natural interpretation of all this is that Gretchen is the "Schätzchen" whom Mephisto has promised to Faust and that Goethe is at the same time offering a kind of explanation for presenting us with Gretchen as Faust's beloved instead of Helen whom, in view of the Faust legend and tradition, we have a right to expect: the woman Faust had seen in the magic mirror *before* drinking the rejuvenating potion was indeed Helen, the type of beautiful woman *par excellence*, but the potion was also a powerful aphrodisiac, and under its influence he at once falls in love with the first attractive girl he runs into, Gretchen, who is not only the sweetheart promised to him by Mephisto, but also a kind of grotesquely inappropriate substitute for the woman he really should have loved, Helen. Thus the Helen of Troy episode, from the beginning a part of Goethe's plan, is here foreshadowed and brought into a certain nebulous relationship with the so very different Gretchen tragedy which has taken precedence of it.

The validity of this natural interpretation is, however, widely denied, as is that of the equally natural interpretation of the correspondences between the Invocation scene and "Trüber Tag. Feld," and even sometimes of that between Mephisto's reference to the coming Walpurgis festival in the "Hexenküche" scene and

---

† No! No! You shall very soon see the model of all women / Before your eyes in the flesh.

‡ With that drink in your body / You will soon take any woman for Helen of Troy.

Goethe's own "Walpurgisnacht."[17] Far too many of the interpreters
of *Faust* are like a person who, finding a clean right hand glove in
one street and a muddy left hand one of exactly the same size and
make in the next street, should insist that they must have been
lost by two entirely different people, each of whom had only one
arm. The evidence chiefly appealed to as refuting the natural
interpretation in the present case is Mephisto's declaration immediately after Faust's first meeting with Gretchen: "Über die
hab ich keine Gewalt" (Over her I have no power).[18] Thus Karl
Wolff wrote in 1949:

> Dass Faust für Gretchen in Liebe entbrennt, ist nicht
> Teufelswerk. Es geht dabei ganz natürlich zu. Auch ist
> Gretchen keineswegs das "Schätzchen," das Mephistopheles
> aufzuspüren versprochen hat (und von dem später nie mehr
> die Rede ist). Dass er an dieser Begegnung keinen Anteil hat,
> geht schon daraus hervor, dass er auf Fausts Befehl: "Hör',
> du musst mir die Dirne schaffen," erst fragen muss: "Nun,
> welche?" Er hätte auch keine verkehrtere Wahl treffen, kein
> für seine Pläne weniger geeignetes Werkzeug finden können
> als dieses Mädchen, von dem er selbst sogleich sagen muss:
> "Über die hab' ich keine Gewalt."*[19]

Most of this is taken over almost verbatim from what Kuno Fischer
had written on the question in 1877 in his *Faust-Kommentar*. It
has been said again and again by many critics, amongst whom
Scherer and Rickert are of particular interest to us. The latter wrote
in 1932: "Dass Fausts Wahl gerade auf Gretchen fällt, scheint
ihm [Mephisto] nicht zu passen. Das Mädchen ist fromm und
unschuldig und insofern als Werkzeug für den Teufel wenig
geeignet" (That Faust's choice should fall on Gretchen of all

---

* That Faust falls in love with Gretchen is not the work of the devil. It all
happens quite naturally. Gretchen is also not the "sweetheart" whom Mephisto
has promised to ferret out for Faust (and of whom there is never any further
mention). That he has no share in this encounter emerges from the fact that,
when Faust commands him: "Listen, you must procure that wench for me," he
first has to ask: "Well then, which one?" He could also not have made a more
inept choice, could not have found a less suitable tool for his designs than this
girl, of whom he must at once himself say: "Over her I have no power."

girls seems not to please Mephisto. The girl is pious and innocent and therefore little fitted to serve as an instrument for the devil).[20] Scherer wrote more emphatically in 1884: "An Gretchen will Mephisto nicht heran: er empfindet den Zauber der Heiligkeit und seine Ohnmacht gegenüber der Unschuld und Einfalt des Herzens. Aber er *muss* als gehorsamer Diener; und alsbald zeigt sich Faust selbst geheiligt, indem er Gretchens Zimmer betritt und ihn die reine Lebensluft des guten Kindes umweht" (Mephisto does not like to venture on Gretchen; he feels the magic of her saintliness and is conscious of his own powerlessness against her innocence and simplicity of heart. But as Faust's obedient servant he *has to* try it; and immediately Faust himself appears sanctified, when he enters Gretchen's room and the pure air of the good child's life is wafted around him).[21] Many other critics could be quoted to the same effect; but this is enough for our purposes.

The issue here involved is delicate and complex and also of central importance for a true understanding of the Gretchen Tragedy. Everything turns here upon the evaluation of the love of the sexes that underlies the work. It is generally assumed that such love is in Goethe's eyes the most sacred of phenomena—and so indeed it is: he calls it himself in the dedicatory verses to *Werther*, "der heiligste von unsern Trieben" (the holiest of our impulses). But he also designates it in the same verses the source of "die grimme Pein" (bitter suffering). Max Morris is speaking more or less in the spirit of Goethe himself when he says: "Faust . . . liebt und wird geliebt. Er erlebt das höchste Wunder unserer Seele" (Faust loves and is loved. He experiences the highest miracle of our soul).[22] However, that highest miracle is also for Goethe a dubious, insidious, problematic, and ambiguous miracle. Few writers have exalted woman and the love of the sexes so fervently and idealistically as Goethe does, for whom "the Eternal Feminine" is the supreme religious mystery. He could, however, also on occasion with equal conviction speak surprisingly scornfully, bitterly, cynically, and even grossly about women and sex. This was one of the fundamental polarities of Goethe's existence, and like all such polarities, it can only be properly understood when *both* poles are always kept in mind. The many critics like Kuno Fischer, Scherer, Witkowski, Rickert, and Karl Wolff, who see in the relationship

between Faust and Gretchen only idealized love, labour under a
similar limitation to that which Faust ironically envies in Wagner:

> Du bist dir nur des einen Triebs bewusst;
> O lerne nie den andern kennen! ("Vor dem Tor")*

The idea that the "Heiligkeit" of Gretchen and of what she feels
for Faust and he for her should have any validity in Mephisto's
eyes, or that he should see in it any threat to his scheme for Faust's
degradation, betrays an abysmal misunderstanding of what Goethe
is here getting at. Mephisto explicitly formulates his plan with
Faust in a monologue added in the 1788–1789 stage of Goethe's
work on the drama, in what ultimately became the second "Studierzimmer" scene:

> Den schlepp' ich durch das wilde Leben,
> Durch *flache Unbedeutenheit* . . .†

This is no new idea that only occurred to Goethe in 1788. It only
puts into so many words what he had represented Mephisto as doing
in the *Urfaust*. These words are, however, sometimes appealed to,
for example in the new Hamburg Edition of Goethe's works, as
evidence that the encounter with Gretchen cannot possibly have
been a part of Mephisto's scheme, but rather threatens to overthrow
it completely. Instead of "flache Unbedeutenheit" Faust is here
experiencing the "holiest" of human possibilities, the "highest
miracle of our soul," and he is even being "sanctified" by it. He
is falling in love, genuinely in love with a girl who through her
sweetness, purity, and piety is deserving of his love. Must not this
alarm and exasperate Mephisto? So the critics argue. But it takes
something very different from this to alarm or exasperate Mephisto.
It is indeed just what he wants. In his cynical eyes all the noble
and tender feelings which Gretchen inspires in Faust are nothing
but "flache Unbedeutenheit," and—a still more important point—
he is not completely mistaken in this estimate of them. He knows
all about "love" and has seen through it, as he has seen through

---

* You are conscious only of the one impulse; / O may you never learn to
know the other.

† I will drag him through the turmoil of life, / *Through insipid triviality.*

all the other idealistic aspirations of humanity. It is what he calls "allerlei Brimborium" (all sorts of humbug). He is confident that the kind of tender, romantic love that Faust feels for Gretchen will degrade him far more effectively and profoundly than any gross liaison with an abandoned woman could do, just because his whole being and not only his physical appetites will be involved in it. It delights him to see Faust forming highminded resolutions and indulging in ethereal sentiments that he will never be able to live up to. And in all his calculations he proves right up to the eleventh hour when Faust after all remembers Gretchen and at least attempts to save her and when Gretchen's own conscience reawakens—the all-important peripeteia of the Gretchen tragedy, which takes place, however, at a level inaccessible and incomprehensible to Mephisto.

Gretchen is quite certainly the "Schätzchen" whom Mephisto has promised to Faust. He has carefully picked her out and thrown Faust into her path, and he could not, from his own point of view, have made a better choice. That she is pure, innocent and religious makes Faust's guilt in ruining her all the greater and is no obstacle to her seduction, once Faust has Mephisto's master mind in this field to give him a little assistance. Gretchen is eminently seducible. Goethe had written as early as April 8, 1769 to Friederike Oeser: "Dass jedes junge, unschuldige Herz, unbesonnen, leichtgläubig, und deswegen leicht zu verführen ist, das liegt in der Natur der Unschuld. Läugnen Sie mir das!" (That any young, innocent heart is naive, credulous and therefore easily seduced lies in the very nature of innocence. Deny that if you can). The same conception underlies what he was to say many years later about Ophelia through the mouth of Wilhelm Meister:

> Ihr ganzes Wesen schwebt in reifer, süsser Sinnlichkeit . . .
> Ihre Einbildungskraft ist angesteckt, ihre stille Bescheidenheit
> atmet eine liebevolle Begierde, und sollte die bequeme Göttin
> Gelegenheit das Bäumchen schütteln, so würde die Frucht
> zugleich herabfallen.*23

---

* Her whole nature is poised in ripe and sweet sensuality. Her imagination is infected, her quiet modesty breathes a tender desire, and if the obliging goddess Opportunity should shake the tree, the fruit would at once fall.

And again, on the subject of Ophelia's improper songs:

> Wissen wir doch gleich zu Anfange des Stücks, womit das Gemüt des guten Kinds beschäftigt ist. Stille lebte sie vor sich hin, aber kaum verbag sie ihre Sehnsucht, ihrer Wünsche. Heimlich klangen die Töne der Lüsternheit in ihrer Seele, und wie oft mag sie versucht haben, gleich einer unvorsichtigen Wärterin, ihre Sinnlichkeit zur Ruhe zu singen mit Liedchen, die sie nur mehr wach halten mussten!†[24]

There is something of Ophelia in Goethe's Gretchen. The song that she sings to herself, "Der König von Thule," is indeed very much more respectable than Ophelia's songs, but—that is the point of it and therein Goethe's artistic sense of fitness even in his Storm and Stress years again signally manifests itself—it is still, with its glorification of a king's love for his mistress, not exactly the kind of song that Gretchen would sing, if she were so extremely devout as many of the commentators take her to be. Actually Gretchen is to begin with only religious in the sense and degree in which the average respectable girl of the community she belongs to is so, though admittedly this largely conventional devoutness takes on a specially endearing character from the gentleness and natural goodness of her disposition. Only as she drifts further and further into trouble and disaster does her religious sense progressively deepen to the final intense realization voiced in the cry: "Gericht Gottes, komm über mich! dein bin ich; rette mich!" (Judgment of God, descend upon me, I am Thine! Save me!)

It is here assumed that Gretchen's innocence at the time when she first meets Faust is something entirely different from that total ignorance of the "facts of life" explicitly ascribed to her by at least one critic, Ronald Gray, and perhaps tacitly ascribed to her by quite a number of others. Gray writes: "True love . . . in the crude physical sense . . . would take Gretchen completely by surprise—

---

† We know, however, from the beginning of the play what the mind of the good child was occupied with. She lived quietly, taking things as they came, but she scarcely concealed from herself her longings, her wishes. The strains of voluptousness sounded secretly within her soul and how often may she have tried, like an imprudent nurse, to lull her sensuality to sleep with songs which were bound only to keep it all the wider awake.

she has no notion, until the play is almost over, of what it means."[25]
Is there really any evidence to support this surely somewhat un-
usual view of the way in which and the degree to which Gretchen
is innocent? She is hardly to be conceived of as less than seventeen
years old, and at that age no normal girl either of the sixteenth or
of the eighteenth century, and belonging to Gretchen's social
milieu, could possibly have remained ignorant of the facts of life;
Faust himself by implication sets the age-limit to such ignorance
appreciably lower with his: "Ist über vierzehn Jahr doch alt" (After
all, she is over fourteen years old). We have Gretchen's own word
for it that before her first meeting with Faust she had often vilified
fallen girls in much the same terms as Lieschen with her: "Sie
füttert zwei jetzt, wenn sie isst und trinkt" (She feeds two now,
when she eats and drinks), and her: "War ein Gekos und ein
Geschleck; / Ja da ist dann das Blümchen weg" (There was a fine
lot of billing and cooing; and then it is all over with virginity).
Through the way in which she refers to the birth of her sister and
still more through her words: "Mein Schoss, Gott! drängt / Sich
nach ihm hin" (My womb, God! yearns towards him),[26] Gretchen
shows that she is quite well aware of the "crude, physical" aspects
of sex. She quite certainly understands what Faust means with his
phrase "Brust an Brust und Seel an Seele drängen" (To press breast
to breast and soul to soul), and fully realises what she is letting herself in for when she says:

> Ich habe schon so viel für dich getan,
> Dass mir zu tun fast nichts mehr übrig bleibt.*

Against this sufficiently massive evidence the very much later written, totally uninspired and curiously inept and vague description
of Gretchen in "Bergschluchten" as "diese gute Seele, . . . die
nicht ahnte, dass sie fehle" (this good soul who had no idea that
she was doing anything wrong), carries no weight at all. There
was no need for Goethe to be more explicit than he is in the
Urfaust, or to use the language of Günther Grass, in a century
which was immensely fascinated by the theme of female innocence

---

* I have already done so much for you that there is hardly anything left for
me to do.

seduced or threatened with seduction, and for which that theme
would have lost its point and its attraction, if the girl in question had been ignorant of what was involved. Such ignorance
radically changes the situation and the kind of interest it awakens;
it was not till the later nineteenth century that this kind of ignorance, with the situation and interest arising from it, came to play
a considerable part in literature, with Wedekind's *Frühlings Erwachen* ("Springtime Awakening") of 1891 as a particularly striking example. Richardson's Clarissa, Rousseau's Julie, Lessing's
Emilia Galotti, and the heroines of Lenz are none of them sexually
ignorant, nor do they make any pretence of being so; and the same
is true still of the female characters of Jane Austen, the Brontë
sisters, and George Eliot. How Goethe thought on such questions
is shown sufficiently by Wilhelm Meister's remarks on Ophelia
quoted above.

It is absurd to maintain, as so many do, that Gretchen is without
any little weaknesses. It does flatter her vanity to be taken for a
"Fräulein" by Faust and even by Mephisto. She does dream of the
great world of lords and ladies and wish that she could somehow
belong to it. Her head *is* turned by the jewels smuggled into her
press by Faust and Mephisto. There is nothing reprehensible in all
this; it is perfectly natural and charming, and would be harmless
if Faust had not crossed her path. But it does make the term
"Heiligkeit" (saintliness), which Scherer applies to her, excessive
and inappropriate. Nor is she just the "child of nature," which
many other critics represent her to be. If she were, her pregnancy
and the birth of her infant would not shatter her as they do. She
is far less a child of nature than Egmont's Clärchen is. She is the
product of centuries of Christian tradition and of a Christian upbringing, and also of a rigid social order from which she could never
dissociate, still less emancipate herself. She has none of the strength
or courage that might have enabled her to cope with the situation in which she finds herself; if she had, she would become an
entirely different person and lose the greater part of her charm,
which lies in her very weakness and vulnerability. Another integral
and still more problematic feature of her charm and lovability is
her limited intelligence. Kuno Fischer says that she is "das holdeste
Geschöpf der Welt" (the dearest creature in the world), and so

she is indeed, so long as one looks at her reverently and *sub specie aeternitatis*. But that, of course, is not the way in which Mephisto can be expected to look at her. Seen as he sees her, *sub specie temporalitatis*, she is—we need not hesitate to apply to her a term which Goethe himself applies to nature—a goose, such a charming little goose as Friederike Brion may have been. As such she delights Faust to begin with by her artless prattle, but in the long run she must get on his nerves, and in the Catechism scene she is already beginning to do so. The qualities that particularly attract Faust to her are those that must in the long run inevitably make him tire of her and want to get away from her. All this Mephisto sees and takes into his calculations. What he does not see is that beyond all these limitations of Gretchen there is something in her and in the feelings between her and Faust which unites them eternally, in spite of the total disparity of their intellects and natures.

How then are we to account for Mephisto's own declaration that he "has no power over Gretchen"? It is spoken disingenuously, to tease Faust and to intensify his impatience. It is an utterance of Mephisto the mocker and liar, and is not for a moment to be taken at its face value as revealing his real views about Gretchen, although it ultimately turns out to be true in a sense he could never have had in mind. Similarly his profession of ignorance as to what "Dirne" (wench) Faust is speaking about is transparently a mere pretence. He shows in the following instant that he is very exactly informed about Gretchen and all the circumstances of her life, and must therefore have been previously taking a great interest in her. Goethe would have shaken his head over those who believe that the meeting between Faust and Gretchen is disagreeable to Mephisto. In his "Maskenzug" of 1818 he makes Mephisto point to Faust and Gretchen together with the words:

> Ihr seht den Ritter, den Baron
> Mit einem schönen Kinde schon.
> Und *so gefällt es meinem Sinn,*
> Der Zauberin und der Nachbarin.*

---

* You see here the knight, the baron / With a pretty child. / *And that is just what I like to see,* / As do also the witch and the neighbour.

If Mephisto really acknowledged any limits at all to his powers where human nature is concerned, he would not be the devil.

What applies to Gretchen applies also to Faust's love for her, which is certainly badly misinterpreted by Daur, for instance, when he maintains that in it Faust "finds God": "In den Wissenschaften und in magischer Schau fand er ihn (Gott) nicht, aber dann in der Liebe" (In the sciences and in magic vision Faust did not find God, but then he did find him in love).[27] The critics are fond of bringing in here a distinction similar to that between white and black magic with which they seek to clarify but really only further obscure the problem of the Erdgeist. They distinguish between love and lust, or between spiritual and merely physical love, and assume that it causes Mephisto great chagrin to find Faust experiencing genuine, spiritual love where he had intended him to feel nothing but mere physical love or lust. But for Mephisto this distinction has no validity, and so far as he goes he is substantially right in Goethe's own eyes on this issue. The whole point of the Gretchen tragedy lies in its being impossible to make any such hard and fast distinction. Faust loves Gretchen genuinely and "spiritually," but that does not prevent him from tiring of her and ruining her; and, she being what she is, if there were anything on her side to prevent him from ruining her, it would mean that she did not love him at all. That the soul is ultimately at the mercy of the body is a central article of Mephisto's creed and therefore he sees nothing to be alarmed at in the soul-love of the two. He knows perfectly well what it is bound to lead to. He has only to see to it that the catastrophe, which is in any case inevitable, should take on the most unmitigatedly drastic external form and so demonstrate how right he has been in his estimate of the situation. Those who think that "seduction" is too crude a word to be applied to what Faust does to Gretchen have themselves too crude a notion of seduction, which is by no means always a simple, cold-blooded process. There is a representative type of seducer who is by no means heartless and unscrupulous, but rather an incorrigible sentimentalist; he is as genuinely in love with his victim, as anxious not to do her any harm, as sorry for her after the event, as Faust is. The true point of Mephisto's share in the Gretchen tragedy is well formulated by Thomas Mann when he says: "Dies ist in Wahrheit sein ewiges

Bestreben: das Höchste im Menschen, das mit seinem Niedrigsten verquickt ist, von diesem verschlingen zu lassen" (This is indeed his eternal pursuit: to cause what is highest in man to be swallowed up by what is basest in him, with which it is indissolubly amalgamated).[28]

Interpreted thus, as a revelation of the intrinsic, ineluctable, daemonic ambivalence of the erotic, and not as a perfect, edifying love-idyll, which only goes wrong through diabolical machinations impinging upon it from without, the Gretchen tragedy stands after all in a certain cogent relationship to the opening monologue. For Faust receives here, in the form of directest personal experience, yet another possible, and in its own way valid, answer to his basic question, "Was die Welt im Innersten zusammenhält"—namely, the mystery of ruthless, ungainsayable concupiscence. This is in a line with that "unendliche Ausdruck von Geilheit im Verbiegen und Verschmiegen der ganzen Natur, Anbiegen und Anschmiegen," which Goethe takes cognizance of in his jottings for *Hanswursts Hochzeit*.[29] He had thoughts after 1797, if not earlier, of working out this idea very forcibly and amply in the "Walpurgisnacht" scene, where Satan himself (as distinct from Mephisto) was to have appeared in person and unveiled lust as the ultimate secret "des ewigen Lebens, der tiefsten Natur" (of eternal life and deepest nature):

> Und wenn auch die Böcke
> Noch stinkiger wären,
> So kann doch die Ziege
> Des Bocks nicht entbehren.*

This plan was, however, not carried out and we know of it only from the paralipomena. It is remarkable that the name of Gretchen, variously distorted, occurs three times in the long and very obscene Dramatis Personae of *Hanswursts Hochzeit* of summer, 1775, which is, with its unbridled priapism, one of Goethe's valid professions of faith. It is likely that the Gretchen tragedy was already substantially completed before that date, since Goethe would otherwise hardly thus have dragged the name of his heroine

---

* And even if the he-goats stank worse than they do, the she-goat would still not be able to get on without the he-goat.

through the mire, as he does also that of Werther and, by implication, that of Lotte, of whom we read:

> Sie schwaumelt oben in höhern Sphären,
> Lässt sich unten mit Marks der Erde nähren.†

The same kind of reaction against the extreme idealization of love
appears again and again in Goethe's work and life, most notably in
his turning away from Frau von Stein to Christiane Vulpius and in
the lubricious *Römische Elegien* and *Venezianische Epigramme*.
There is much of Mephisto as well as of Faust in Goethe, and the
sensualists have as much right as the idealists to claim him as one
of their own; that is something Schiller was always painfully conscious of. It is absurd to claim, as is constantly claimed, that
Goethe's sensuality is different in kind from and infinitely nobler
than that of other people. He would have been the first to deny it.
Peculiar to Goethe is not his sensuality as such, which he shares
with the rest of mankind, but only what he makes out of it.

Characteristic of academic criticism's unwillingness to face the
full implications of the Gretchen tragedy is Burger's curious theory
that Goethe originally conceived of it in his Storm and Stress years
on purely idyllic and idealistic lines and only much later, under
the influence of his pagan, erotic experiences and development of
the Italian journey, superimposed upon it a more earthly and sensual character:

> Die Gretchengeschichte als Musterbeispiel sinnlichen Ge-
> nusses—jedermann empfindet ohne weiteres, sollte man mein-
> en, wie übel damit das wahre Gesicht dieser rührend schönen
> Liebesdichtung entstellt wird. Das konnte auf keinen Fall
> schon in der ursprünglichen Konzeption für die Verbindung
> von Faust- und Gretchenmotiv gelegen haben . . . Wie aber
> war es möglich, dass Goethe sein Gedicht nachträglich derart
> vergewaltigte? / Er war selbst ein anderer geworden, und dem-
> entsprechend verwandelte sich auch Faust.*30

---

† Above she soars in higher spheres, / But below she allows herself to be
nourished by the marrow of earth.

* The Gretchen story as a typical example of sensual enjoyment—everybody,
(it is to be supposed), at once feels how badly the true countenance of this

Burger's chief reason for refusing to admit that the "Walpurgis-nacht" scene can have been contemplated before 1797 is that, through it and the "Hexenküche" scene, "die Entweihung des köstlichen Juwels unter Goethes, ja unter allen deutschen Liebes-geschichten" (the desecration of the most precious jewel amongst Goethe's, indeed amongst all German love stories)[31] is accom-plished. But this is all quite untenable. The twofold character of the Gretchen story as a touching love idyll and as a "Musterbeispiel sinnlichen Genusses," which so much disconcerts Burger, is inherent in it already in the *Urfaust*, independently of the "Hexenküche" and the "Walpurgisnacht," and therein lies its point: that these two contradictory phenomena are inseparably united, are at bottom identical with one another. "Sinnlichkeit, Tod der Liebe" (Sensual-ity, death of love), he wrote to Lavater in 1774.[32] But equally emphatically and far more often he proclaims in the same years that sensuality is also the *life* of love. That was the paradoxical dualism which he had all along to contend with and which he bodies forth again and again in his work, above all in the Gretchen tragedy. It corresponds exactly to the dualism in his view of nature now as "so hold und gut" (so dear and good), now as a wieder-käuendes Ungeheuer" (regorging monster).

The abuses and dangers of the biographical approach to Faust here employed by Burger appear in yet extremer form in Roethe, who maintains that Goethe's conception of the three chief per-sonages in the Gretchen tragedy underwent far-reaching changes during the four or so years within which the *Urfaust* was produced. He writes:

> In den Anfängen des *Faust* [i.e. in the prose scenes, "Trüber
> Tag. Feld" and "Kerker," which according to Roethe were
> written first] lag die Schuld an Friederike noch schwer auf
> ihm [Goethe] . . . Die Heldin dieser Prosatragödie hat noch
> nichts vom Lottentypus . . . Das Naive, das Hausmütterliche,

---

touchingly beautiful love drama is thereby disfigured. That can under no cir-cumstances have belonged to the original conception of the relationship be-tween the Faust and Gretchen motifs. But how was it possible for Goethe subsequently to deface his work in such a way? / He himself had become an-other, and Faust was transformed correspondingly.

das Genrehafte des späteren Gretchen fehlt hier noch ganz.
Mephisto ist nur böser Teufel von zähnefletschender Freude
an Niedertracht und Zerstörung, noch ganz ohne . . . über-
legene Weltklugheit . . . Im Übrigen ist die Gestalt [Fausts]
noch etwas dünn . . . Er ist noch ganz unfertig. Vom Faustischen keine Spur; auch das Universitäts- und Gelehrtenwe-
sen fehlt in der Ausführung völlig, wenn es auch im Plan von
vornherein gesteckt haben muss.*[33]

Now the real explanation of why the three personages do not in the
final scenes of the Gretchen tragedy display those qualities Roethe
singles out as distinguishing their fully developed characters is not
that we have before us here an earlier, as yet immature, specimen
of Goethe's psychological skill, but that they are all three in situations that allow no scope for the unfolding of such qualities. How
can Gretchen still appear naively domestic and genre-like when
she has just killed her child and is on the point of being beheaded
for it? How can Mephisto indulge in his usual airy, urbane, and
entertaining banter when his plans have at last come to fruition
and he no longer has any occasion to mask his diabolical nature
with caustic geniality? How can Faust mount his Faustian high
horse or parade his professorial mentality when he stands face to
face with what he has brought down upon Gretchen? All three are
still exactly the same persons as they had been in the preceding
scenes of the Gretchen tragedy; we should admire the discernment
and skill with which Goethe has shown each reacting characteristically to the changed external circumstances. There is the same
necessary and organic relationship between the last scenes of the
Gretchen tragedy and the earlier ones as there is between a morning
hangover and the conviviality of the evening before. One is still

* In the beginnings of Faust Goethe's guilt regarding Friederike still heavily
oppressed him. The heroine of this prose tragedy has still nothing of the Lotte
type. The naive, domestic, genre-like quality of the later Gretchen is still quite
missing here. Mephisto is only the wicked devil, gloating with bared teeth
over baseness and destruction, still quite without superior worldly wisdom.
Moreover the figure of Faust is still somewhat meagre. He is still unfinished.
There is no trace of the specifically Faustian; the characteristics of the university and scholar type are still completely missing, though they must have
belonged to Goethe's plan from the start.

the same person only in reverse, as it were, and reduced to one's skeletal self. It would have been a monstrous artistic defect, if the characters did *not* appear in the totally different circumstances with just those differences which such critics as Roethe treat as inconsistencies to be accounted for only by great changes in Goethe's own powers, plans, experiences, interests, and outlook. Nothing could be a more satisfactory unity than the Gretchen tragedy, if one sees it as what it is and was clearly intended to be: as the phantasmagoric presentation of the progress from delightful illusions to the grimmest disillusionment, from an entranced, Icarian soaring above the ordinary limits of humanity to the horrifying realization of those limits. The scene "Dom," characteristically dismissed by Scherer as a primitive earlier production that was meant to be replaced by the maturer "Zwinger" scene, in fact shows the decisive turning-point in the process by which Gretchen gradually loses the bloom and foliage of her naively domestic and genre-like existence. All the hypotheses and speculations of Scherer, Seuffert, Schuchardt, Roethe, Burger, and others about the supposed contradictions in the Gretchen tragedy fail to take into account its essentially paradoxical and dialectical character. The supreme test of a great dramatist is his power to show his personages passing from one state of mind to another very different, perhaps exactly opposite one, and because Goethe has achieved this in the Gretchen tragedy, his work is looked upon by many as an inconsistent agglomeration of "splinters" dictated not by any sustained artistic vision and purpose, but only by his own kaleidoscopically varying private moods, views, and experiences over the years and decades.

One very important way in which Goethe has integrated the Gretchen tragedy into the actual Faust theme still remains to be considered. Although the memory of Gretchen is eliminated from Faust's mind by Ariel and his Elves at the beginning of the second part, and from that moment to his death only one poignant but dim and inexact recollection of her visits him (at the opening of the fourth act), she does appear again and plays a decisive part in the epilogue in the other world ("Bergschluchten") as "Una Poenitentium, sonst Gretchen genannt" (one of the penitent women—otherwise known as Gretchen). It is in large part through her intercession that Faust's soul is ultimately saved, and the mystery drama concludes with his celestial reunion with her as the embodiment of the redemptive "Ewig-Weibliches" (Eternal Feminine). The passage in question was certainly not written until after 1799 and perhaps not till after 1825, and it is almost universally assumed that it belongs only to a late plan of Goethe's and that he envisaged nothing corresponding to it in the years when the *Urfaust* was conceived and written. In fact the great majority of critics agree that according to Goethe's original intentions Faust was meant to be damned, and that his salvation can only have been a late afterthought. Minor would date this supposed radical change of plan about 1784 or 1786 and attributes it to the influence of Lessing's projects for a Faust drama, which were made publicly known in those years. In Lessing's Faust plan everything was to have turned upon Faust's "unauslöschlichen Durst nach Wissenschaften und Kenntnis," through which the devil confidently hopes to destroy him "sicherer . . . als bei jeder andern Leidenschaft" (unappeasable thirst after science and knowledge, through which the devil confidently hopes to destroy him, more certainly than through any other passion), but of which an angel at the end was to declare: "Die Gottheit hat dem Menschen nicht den edelsten der Triebe gegeben, um ihn ewig unglücklich zu machen" (God has not bestowed the noblest of impulses upon man to make him eternally unhappy). The devil was to triumph over Faust only in a dream, while the real Faust was to be saved. It is assumed that only Lessing was capable of thus revolutionizing the Faust legend, and that Goethe must therefore have been modelling himself on him in this matter. Hertz would date Goethe's decision to save Faust after all about winter, 1787–1788 and attributes it to the classical sense of harmony and perfection the poet acquired during the Italian journey. The most commonly accepted view is that Goethe first thought of making Faust's salvation possible about 1797, when the plan for the whole drama is known to have undergone considerable changes. What is seldom duly taken into consideration here is that, by introducing the Gretchen theme into the Faust legend, Goethe had, at the earliest stage of his work on *Faust* necessarily raised the issue of whether Gretchen is supposed to be saved or lost, and that this was bound to have certain implications, one way or the other, for the ultimate fate of Faust's own soul. If in the *Urfaust* Gretchen is damned, then obviously Faust is damned too; but if she is saved—and hardly anybody doubts that she is—the Storm and Stress Goethe may have considered the possibility of Faust's ultimately participating in some way in her salvation. He has at least indicated some kind of link between the destinies of Gretchen's and Faust's souls by putting into Mephisto's mouth at the end of the "Kerker" scene the words "Sie ist gerichtet!" (Judgment has been passed upon her!) which recall and are meant to recall the words addressed to Faust by a mysterious voice off stage at the end of the puppet-plays: *"Judicatus es!"* Of course Mephisto himself is not qualified to pass such a judgment even on Faust, still less on Gretchen, over whom he certainly *now* has no power, and it is clear that by her refusal to escape through his agency she has obtained the divine mercy. Goethe brought this out more clearly in the final version of the "Kerker" scene, as it was produced in 1798, by making a "Stimme von oben" (Voice from above) contradict Mephisto's declaration with the words "Ist gerettet!" (She is saved!) But that involved no change of plan. It has even been suggested that when Mephisto disappears with Faust at the end of the "Kerker" scene he is, in the *Urfaust*, to be thought of as dragging him to hell and that therewith the entire drama is over. Burger writes in 1942 on this question:

—so besitzt das Ganze [the *Urfaust*] doch so weit eine innere Geschlossenheit, dass es nicht unbedingt nach einer Fortsetzung verlangt . . . Für Goethe hat sich Fausts Schicksal am Ende der Gretchentragödie ebenso erfüllt wie einst am Ende des Puppenspiels . . . Sehr fein überträgt Goethe den Urteilsspruch von Faust auf Gretchen, denn ihm kommt es ja nicht darauf an, dass Faust zur Hölle fährt, sondern dass er und wir mit ihm seine Schuld zu fühlen bekommen. Einzig die "Höllenfahrt der Selbsterkenntnis" ist wesentlich . . . Nicht bloss die Gretchen-, sondern auch die Fausttragödie ist hier zu Ende. Faust ist vernichtet.*[34]

* The *Urfaust* is then as a totality so far rounded off within itself that it does not absolutely call for any continuation. For Goethe, Faust's destiny has

Against this view Hermann Schneider protested seven years later:

> Nur die wunderlichste Verkennung dieser Zusammen-
> hänge konnte mit Margaretens Ende auch des Helden Schick-
> sal besiegelt wähnen. Ihre Begnadigung durch Gott . . . solle,
> so meinte man, Fausts Verdammung in sich schliessen. /
> Faust . . . ist nicht reif zum Tode noch zur Hölle, und das
> Drama von ihm nicht zur Katastrophe. Fausts . . . Verhalten
> und Vergehen gegenüber Gretchen konnte und durfte ihn
> nicht in die Hölle bringen, dazu war Faust doch noch zu sehr
> Magier, und Goethe selbst zu sehr Faust. / Noch weniger aber
> als einen schlimmen Lebensausgang seines Faust kann Goethe
> in diesem Stadium der Dichtung schon Möglichkeit und Art
> seiner Erlösung erwogen haben.*[35]

This view that Goethe himself had up till after 1775 still not made
up his mind whether Faust should be damned or saved was also
expressed by Burdach in 1932 and by Beutler in 1940.

A formidable array of arguments has been advanced to prove that
Goethe's original intention was that Faust should be damned, ever
since A. W. Schlegel maintained it in reviewing *Faust, ein Fragment* immediately after its appearance in 1790. In addition to
Burger, Minor (1901), Köster (1902), Roethe (1920), Petsch
(1926), and Hertz (1930) may be named as having, amongst

---

fulfilled itself at the end of the Gretchen tragedy, just as it had done previously
in the puppet-plays. Very subtly Goethe transfers the sentence of judgment
from Faust to Gretchen, for what matters to him is not that Faust should
actually go to hell, but that he and we with him should be made to feel his
guilt. Only the "passage to hell of self-knowledge" is essential. Not only the
tragedy of Gretchen, but also that of Faust is here terminated. Faust is an-
nihilated.

* Only the most curious misapprehension of these relationships could lead
to the view that with the death of Gretchen the fate of the hero was also
sealed. Her forgiveness by God, it has been thought, is supposed to involve
Faust's damnation. / Faust is not yet ripe for death or hell, nor is his drama
ripe yet for its catastrophe. Faust's behaviour towards and offence against
Gretchen could not and should not bring him into hell; Faust was too much a
magician and Goethe himself was too much Faust for that. But even less than
a bad end for his Faust can Goethe at this stage in the work already have
contemplated the possibility or means of his salvation.

others, declared themselves for this view during our own century. Some, like Schlegel, find their evidence for Faust's damnation within Goethe's actual text, as it was before the addition of the "Prolog im Himmel." This is one of the many arguments utilized by Roethe:

> Ich bin überzeugt, [he writes], wäre nie etwas Anderes von Goethes Faust zutage getreten [als der Urfaust], niemand würde zweifeln, dass dieser Faust genau so zur Hölle fahren sollte wie die Faust der übrigen Stürmer und Dränger[36] . . . Die Rettung Fausts aus den Klauen des Teufels ist nicht vorbereitet. Sollte das Drama je mit der Kerkerszene schliessen, so war Faust dem Teufel verfallen.†[37]

But particularly it is argued that the sheer weight and authority of the existing Faust tradition were too strong for it to be thinkable that Goethe could as early as 1772–1775 have made himself independent of it, as (without his then knowing about it) Lessing had done and as the otherwise undistinguished Austrian writer Paul Weidmann did in 1775. For the Enlightenment optimist Lessing there was, Roethe says, "an inner necessity" to save Faust from damnation, but: "Diese innere Notwendigkeit bestand für den Frankfurter Goethe nicht" (This inner necessity did not exist for the Frankfort Goethe),[38] with his tragic outlook on life. Virtually all serious Storm and Stress dramas and novels end tragically, particularly when they treat the Faust theme; and Goethe here is no exception, declares Roethe: "So zeugt der Sturm und Drang . . . geschlossen für Fausts tragischen Untergang; die Rettung müsste für Goethe erst erwiesen werden, und dafür gibt der Urfaust keinen greifbaren Anhalt" (So Storm and Stress bears witness solidly for Faust's tragic downfall; it would need first to be specially demonstrated that Goethe thought of saving him, and that is some-

† I am convinced that if nothing more of Goethe's *Faust* had become known [than the *Urfaust*], nobody would doubt that this Faust was intended to go to hell, just like the Fausts of the other Storm and Stress writers. Nothing has been done to prepare the way for Faust's deliverance from the claws of the devil. If the drama was ever meant to terminate with the Dungeon scene, then Faust was the devil's prey.

thing for which the *Urfaust* contains no palpable evidence).[39] A further argument, advanced by Köster, is that none of those to whom Goethe talked about his Faust plans during the Storm and Stress years record a word "von einem aussergewöhnlichen Ausgang des Dramas" (about any out of the way conclusion),[40] as they would have been bound to do, if Faust's salvation had formed part of those plans. But above all Roethe and others rely on the analogy of the poem *Schwager Kronos* ("Coachman Kronos") of October 10, 1774, in which Goethe pictures himself as being, at the end of his life, triumphantly driven through

> der Hölle nächtliches Tor.
> Töne, Schwager, dein Horn,
> Rassle den schallenden Trab,
> Dass der Orkus vernehme: ein Fürst kommt,
> Drunten von ihren Sitzen
> Sich die Gewaltigen lüften.*

If Goethe could at this time thus glory in the idea of going to hell himself, the critics ask, what is more probable than that he should have designed a similar ending for the career of his hero Faust—a damnation indeed, but a triumphal damnation?

One more argument for the damnation of Goethe's original Faust must be mentioned here for the sake of completeness. Hertz is worried by a monologue of Mephisto's, not written, we can be reasonably certain, before 1788–1789, which ends with the lines:

> Und hätt' er [Faust] sich auch nicht dem Teufel übergeben,
> Er müsste doch zugrundegehn!†

"Wie man diesen Monolog auch auffassen mag," writes Hertz, "immer setzt er voraus, dass der Dichter damals, als er ihn schrieb, seinen Helden scheitern lassen wollte" (However one understands this monologue, it still presupposes that the poet, when he wrote

---

* Hell's sombre gateway. / Blow your horn, coachman, / Rattle ahead in resounding trot, / That Orcus may perceive: a monarch comes, / That the mighty ones below / May raise themselves from their seats.

† And even if he had not abandoned himself to the devil, / He would still be bound to end in ruin.

it, intended to make his hero suffer shipwreck).[41] This greatly worries Hertz, whose chief contention is that Goethe arrived just about spring, 1788, at the decision that Faust must be saved. The only solution Hertz finds for this problem which he has created for himself is that Mephisto's monologue must be "ein Überbleibsel . . . eines bei der Abfassung des ersten Teils bereits verworfenen früheren Plans, das bei der endgültigen Formgebung hätte gestrichen werden müssen . . ." (a survival from an earlier, rejected plan, which ought to have been deleted when the completed first part was given its final form).[42] He assumes that it must have been written either before the Italian journey or, more probably, shortly after it, between Goethe's return to Weimar in summer, 1788, and the publication of *Faust, ein Fragment* in 1790, when the discouraged Goethe had abandoned the "neuen römischen Plan" and made up his mind "kurz und gut die Jugenddichtung im alten Sinne zu Ende zu führen" (to finish the work of his youth as best he could in the old sense).[43] Actually Mephisto's monologue proves nothing at all about Goethe's intentions. Mephisto is constitutionally incapable of understanding why or how *anybody* escapes damnation, and goes on persuading himself that even Gretchen is damned, when she is most clearly saved. He is not a competent authority on such questions or on Goethe's own intentions with regard to them.

As representatives of the minority who believe that Faust's salvation belonged to Goethe's original plan Schelling may be named from the early years 1790–1808, between the publication of *Faust, ein Fragment* and *Faust I*, and Sarauw (1917), Burdach (1923), and Grumach (1953) from our own century. Schelling, unlike Schlegel, found that the intrinsic character of the actual early text pointed to an optimistic *dénouement*: "Aber die heitere Anlage des Ganzen schon im ersten Wurf, die Wahrheit des missleiteten Bestrebens, die Echtheit des Verlangens nach dem höchsten Leben lässt schon erwarten, dass der Widerstreit sich in einer höheren Instanz *lösen* werde, und Faust in höhere Sphären erhoben vollendet werde" (The cheerful character of the whole, even in the first outline, the truth of Faust's misguided striving, the genuineness of his longing for the supreme light, lead us to expect that the conflict will be *resolved* in a higher court of appeal and that Faust will be elevated to higher spheres and there achieve perfection).[44] Similarly Sarauw finds evidence that "das Programm der Rastlosigkeit," through which Faust is redeemed, "gewiss zu den ältesten Teilen der Faustkonzeption . . . gehörte" (the programme of restlessness certainly belonged to the oldest parts of the conception of *Faust*).[45] Burdach wrote in 1923: "An einen tragischen Ausgang in dem Sinne, dass Mephisto triumphierte, kann ich trotz allem, was in den letzten Jahren dafür geltend gemacht worden ist, . . . auch für den Urfaust nicht glauben" (In spite of all the arguments that have been advanced for it during recent years, I cannot believe that even the *Urfaust* was meant to terminate tragically in the sense that Mephisto would have triumphed).[46] Grumach's eccentric dating of the "Prolog im Himmel" in the year 1769 of course makes the salvation of Faust an integral part of Goethe's original plan. It has also been variously pointed out that one of the later rejected devices for presenting Faust's salvation, known to us only from the Paralipomena of the 1797–1801 stage, according to which he should have undergone a kind of celestial legal trial involving God the Father, Christ as judge, the Virgin Mary as advocate, and Mephisto as appellant, must have been partly inspired by the curious old "Jacobi Ayreri historischer Processus juris, in welchem Luzifer über Christum, darum, dass dieser ihm die Hölle zerstöret, eingenommen, die Gefangenen daraus erlöset usw . . . habe, beschweret" (Historical *processus juris* of Jacob Ayrer [1611], in which Lucifer indicts Christ for having laid waste his hell, captured it, and set the prisoners free from it, etc.), a work on which Goethe made some notes as early as 1770 in his commonplace book or *Ephemerides*.

A point which used not to be sufficiently taken into consideration in the discussion of these questions but has since been variously brought out, particularly well by Burdach, is that in great literature a triumphant ending does not necessarily mean the same thing as a happy ending, nor a tragic ending the same thing as a total defeat. Although Goethe's Storm and Stress heroes—Götz, Werther, and Egmont—all come externally to a tragic ending, inwardly they triumph and die with a certain sense of fulfilment. This distinction is still more important in the case of Faust, whose destiny is, in view of the intrinsic nature and idea of his legend, not finally decided until *after* his death. That is binding even for a writer who has the most unorthodox, vague, or negative private beliefs about the after-life. The real issue involved here can only be whether Faust's soul is damned or saved, not whether the story of his earthly life does or does not "end happily." Even when Faust's soul is ultimately saved, at the end of Part II, his earthly existence has, as we shall see, ended tragically, and Goethe attached great importance to the work being regarded as "eine Tragödie"; this appears from his expressly designating it as such in the title. We very well can and indeed must assume that he from the outset thus conceived of his *Faust* as a tragedy and that he never from beginning to end really wavered in that view of it. But that still leaves the possibility open that, just as Götz, Werther, and Egmont triumph inwardly in spite of their tragic end, so also Faust may very well have been conceived of from the beginning as being "saved," in spite of the tragic end appointed for him. In any case, it is simply not true that all Storm and Stress heroes are "dem Untergang geweiht" (foredoomed to perish tragically), as Roethe asserts. Klinger's *Simsone Grisaldo* is not, as Roethe would have us believe, the only notable exception. The three most representative dramas of Goethe's fellow Storm and Stress poets, Lenz's *Hofmeister* and *Die Soldaten* and Klinger's *Sturm und Drang*, all have comparatively happy endings, and so has Goethe's *Stella*; it is also quite uncertain that his fragmentary *Prometheus* was meant to conclude tragically. Though there was certainly a reaction amongst the Storm and Stress writers against the facile optimism of the Enlightenment, and with it a strong recrudescence of the tragic sense, they were none of them—least of all the youthful Goethe—decisively pessimistic in their outlook on existence.

Köster's argument that, if Goethe had originally planned to treat the conclusion of *Faust* in an out of the way manner, something of it would have been recorded by the various friends to whom he talked about the work, presupposes that Goethe kept nothing to himself on those occasions. That is, however, a quite untenable hypothesis. He was, even in those early years, decidedly uncommunicative about his work, so far as it was still only in the em-

bryonic stage, especially about *Faust,* and it was a law of his creative genius that he had to be so. Until he had almost completed
a production he never did more than drop cryptic hints about it,
and *Faust* is the last of his works with regard to which he is likely
to have made an exception. What he told people about chiefly was
the Gretchen tragedy, so far as that was already almost completed,
not the rest of *Faust.* There is no reason to suppose that he ever
betrayed any of his real poetic secrets in such conversations.

The most powerful argument of those who believe that Faust
was originally intended to be damned, the analogy of *Schwager
Kronos,* reposes, as Burdach pointed out in 1932, upon a fallacy.
What Goethe glories in in that poem is not really the thought of
"going to hell" in the usual sense of the word, that is to say "being
damned," but simply that of dying with an unbroken spirit. The
word "Hölle" (Hell) was quite often used in those days for the
realm of death in general, without any reference to the specifically
Christian idea of damnation, as it still is in the phrase in the creed:
"He descended into Hell." There are good Old Testament precedents for this usage, and Burdach points out that the concluding
lines of *Schwager Kronos* closely reproduce the ninth verse in the
fourteenth chapter of *Isaiah*:

> Hell from beneath is moved for thee to meet thee at thy
> coming; it stirreth up the dead for thee, even all the chief ones
> of the earth; it hath raised up from their thrones all the kings
> of the nations.

The Authorized Version gives as an alternative rendering for
"Hell" (*Sheol*) here, "the grave." Goethe had dabbled in Hebrew
and was in his own ways enough of a biblical scholar to know
about these things.

It is not true that no "innere Notwendigkeit" existed for the
youthful Goethe to avert Faust's damnation. On the contrary, there
was for him an "inner necessity" to do just this, which was quite
as strong as that animating Lessing, if not stronger. On partly
pantheistic, partly Pelagian grounds he revolted against the idea
of damnation altogether and was unwilling to admit that even the
most depraved sinner could be damned for ever. His most striking

expression of this view is to be found in the *Brief des Pastors zu* —— *an den neuen Pastor zu* —— ("Letter of the Pastor of —— to the new Pastor of ——"), written about autumn, 1772— that is to say, about the time when we must suppose him seriously to have begun work on Faust. A humane, enlightened, but simple-minded, old country pastor, modelled on Rousseau's *Vicaire savoyard*, here declares: "man wird ja nicht verdammet, weil man sündigt" (one is not damned for having sinned), and "dass wir nicht Ursache haben, an jemands Seligkeit zu verzweifeln" (that we have no reason to despair of any person's salvation). He professes his belief in Origines' doctrine of apokatastasis (*Wiederbringung*). The man who wrote this is hardly likely two years later to have revelled in the thought of himself being ultimately damned. However strained Goethe's relationship to Christianity already was, there was still very much in it, particularly in its conceptions of the after-life and of the salvation of the soul, that—at least symbolically—still had, and was aways to retain, great significance for him. Traces of the ideas expressed by the benevolent pastor occur elsewhere in Goethe's writings of the Storm and Stress years, particularly in *Werther*. Can we suppose that he would, with such convictions, have taken over undemurringly the intransigent idea of damnation that he found in the Faust chapbooks and puppet-plays? The notion that his mind was not yet mature, independent, or audacious enough to think of modifying the traditional Faust legend in this respect at so early a date as 1772 is completely unfounded. From the *Rede zum Schäkespears Tag* of October, 1771, onward there is no mental boldness that he cannot be credited with. Everything we know about his development from winter, 1770–1771, onward suggests that one of his first and chief concerns in resolving to write a Faust drama of his own must have been to devise some satisfactory means for Faust's salvation. He needed no Lessing or anybody else to put *that* idea into his head. It is unthinkable that he should in beginning work on *Faust* have been indifferent to the central issue of Faust's damnation or salvation, on which everything else depends, or that he should have been content to defer making up his mind about it till some later date. Particularly the common notion that he should have allowed it to depend upon his own as yet unforeseeable ultimate development quite leaves out of account the way in which, to the mind of a poet, not only the immediate, personal experiences of the moment and year in which he is actually writing are present, but also, through his imaginative powers, the widest range of human possibilities. The more genuine a poet he is, the more will his imagination tend to visualize only a whole, or parts only as parts of a postulated whole, not just as chippings that belong nowhere in particular. One can even say that it would have been impossible for Goethe to write a single line of *Faust*, if he had not all along had some definite idea about whether his hero was to be damned or saved in the end. He certainly did not graft the Gretchen theme on the Faust legend without considering whether it might not be brought into relationship with the all-important issue of the final destiny of Faust's soul.

There is, in the "Kerker" scene of the *Urfaust* (and also of Part I), a brief phrase, so inconspicuous that it can easily be overlooked and indeed usually has been overlooked, but which much worries Roethe, Burger, and H. Schneider in their exertions to demonstrate that Goethe cannot possibly have contemplated Faust's salvation in the Storm and Stress years. Amongst the disjointed utterances which fall from Gretchen's lips in her distraction and despair are the words: "Wir sehn uns wieder" (We shall see one another again), which Minor in 1901 interprets as meaning that "sie Faust auf das Wiedersehen im Jenseits verweist" (she tells Faust that they will meet again in the other world).[47] Enders, however, in 1905, rejects this interpretation as "spoiling the effect" (Minors Interpretation zerstört die Wirkung),[48] and explains the phrase as meaning only that Gretchen and Faust will see one another again at her execution. Roethe grudgingly admits that a reference to the other world here is "wohl nicht . . . ausgeschlossen" (perhaps not out of the question), but if that is what is indeed meant by it, he finds it "undeutlich" (unclear) or "mindestens zweideutig" (at least ambiguous), and he concludes: "Aber für des Dichters Absicht würde das dann auch nichts beweisen, wenn jene Deutung gesicherter wäre" (If that interpretation were more reliable than it is, it would still prove nothing about the poet's intention).[49] Burger and H. Schneider similarly argue against the interpretation of Gretchen's words, which Schneider calls "seltsam" (strange), as indicating any intention of Goethe's part to reunite her with Faust in the other world, and even Beutler, who inclines towards this interpretation, says that they are "zunächst nicht viel mehr als eine verlorene Andeutung. . . . Und mehr konnte Goethe 'ja auch garnicht geben, da ihm das Ende und seine Ausführung noch recht im Unklaren lagen" (to begin with not much more than a forlorn hint. And more than that Goethe could indeed not possibly give, since he was still quite unclear about the end of *Faust* and how it was to be worked out).[50]

Now there is nothing "strange," "unclear," or "ambiguous" about Gretchen's words: "Wir sehn uns wieder."[51] They quite certainly refer only to a reunion in the other world, not to anything so macabre and in such impossible taste as a rendezvous at the execution, which Faust can hardly be supposed to attend. The theme of such otherworldly reunion of lovers runs through the literature of the eighteenth century in Germany, England, and France, reaching its peak in the 1770's, and is found at several other points in Goethe's Storm and Stress writings. The phrase, "Wir sehn uns wieder," is used in the same otherworldly sense by Goethe in *Götz von Berlichingen* (1771–1773), *Werther* (1774) and *Stella* (1775), and came to enjoy a considerable vogue; it was employed seven times by Klinger in his *Sturm and Drang* (1776), served as title to Karl Christian Engel's treatise on reunion after death of 1780, and appears in 1798 in Hölderlin's *Hyperion*, in 1801 in Tiedge's *Urania*, and—turned to ridicule—in 1851 in Heine's *Romanzero*. Although it was certainly not till after 1797, and perhaps not till after 1825, that Goethe actually wrote the passage in which Gretchen and Faust are reunited in the other world, her words, "Wir sehn uns wieder," in the "Kerker" scene of the *Urfaust* forcibly suggest that that reunion was planned as early as 1772–1775, and those years, in which he evoked the otherworldly reunion of Werther and Lotte, of Clavigo and Marie, of Ferdinand and Cäzilie, are a particularly likely time for him to have thought of similarly reuniting Faust and Gretchen. But if so, Faust's salvation, which is at once the condition and the result of his reunion with Gretchen in

Heaven, must also have been planned in those early years, that is to say from the outset. Goethe was very likely thinking of Faust's salvation and his celestial reunion with Gretchen, amongst other things, when he said again and again during the last two or three years of his life that the second part of *Faust* was only the realization of his "älteste Konzeption."

We are not without some reasonably reliable indications of the way in which Goethe originally intended to show Gretchen playing a decisive part in Faust's salvation. Our point of departure for understanding this somewhat complicated matter must be the final scene of *Egmont*, written in 1787 in Rome, where the hero, immediately before his execution, is strengthened and assured of the efficacy of his sacrifice by a vision of his dead beloved, Clärchen, transfigured into the Goddess of Freedom. Hertz, in his *Zu Goethes römischem Faustplan*,[52] demonstrates that Goethe was here making use of a motif he had already considered employing in 1773 and 1774 in a projected sequel to his miniature drama *Künstlers Erdewallen*: the dead beloved of the artist was to have appeared before him, transfigured into the goddess Venus Urania, and pronounced his apotheosis. Hertz brings these facts into relationship with a letter written on May 23, 1788, in Milan on the way back from Rome to Weimar, in which Goethe enigmatically declares, "dass ich meine grösste Spekulation darauf richte: ein Madonnenbild zu malen, das noch bei meinen Lebzeiten in Rom Wunder tun soll" (that I direct my greatest speculation to painting a picture of the Madonna that shall work miracles in Rome during my lifetime). Hertz argues, rightly enough in all likelihood, that this can only refer to *Faust*, which we know much occupied Goethe's mind at this time, and finds evidence in it for his having during his last weeks in Rome formed an entirely new plan for completing the drama, according to which Faust should, instead of being damned, as was originally intended, have seen at the moment of his death a vision of Gretchen transfigured into a Madonna, with her babe in her arms, and pronouncing a favourable judgment upon him; just as Goethe had written to Frau von Stein on October 7, 1776: "Sie kommen mir eine Zeither vor wie Madonna, die gen Himmel fährt" (For some time now you have appeared to me like the Madonna ascending into Heaven), and as he was in 1809 to evoke the picture of Ottilie in the *Wahlver-wandtschaften* as the Virgin Mary with the infant Jesus in her arms. Hertz's theory is extremely tenuous and unconvincing, but from the material he has amassed it does emerge that Goethe must at one time have thought of representing Gretchen trans-figured into a Madonna, and that is probably what is referred to in the cryptic declaration of May 23, 1788. That declaration is not only cryptic, but also playful and ironical: such a transformation of the infanticide Gretchen into a Madonna might well be ex-pected to give a tremendous shock to all good Roman Catholics and so to "work miracles"—that is to say, cause a great stir—in Goethe's lifetime. The concluding scene of *Faust II*, in which Faust's salvation is pronounced by the Madonna in her capacity as *Mater gloriosa* at the intercession of the penitent Gretchen, must be regarded as a characteristic later modification of this all too audacious and provocative original plan, which would deeply have offended the religious sensibilities of many. That plan cannot, however, first have originated in Rome in 1788. It must be much older than that and belong to the phase when the *Urfaust* was written. The evidence for this is hidden in the last place where one would think of searching for it, in *Hanswursts Hochzeit* of 1775, and it is not surprising that Hertz overlooked it. There, amongst the numerous unquotably Rabelaisian *Dramatis Personae*, we find "Margretlin, madre di tuti [sic] i santi." This "Margretlin" is un-questionably Faust's Gretchen, who is once within the text of the *Urfaust* alluded to as "Margretlein" by Mephisto. When Goethe made ribald fun of *Werther* and of his own poetic genius and fame in *Hanswursts Hochzeit*, even Gretchen was not sacred to him; she appears in the *Dramatis Personae* also as "Musgretgen" and is paired off, again as "Margretlin," with the obscene "Piphan." Her identification here with the "Mother of all the Saints," that is to say with the Virgin Mary, can only mean that Goethe already at this early stage planned to transfigure her into a Madonna. Her own prayer to the *Mater dolorosa* in the scene "Zwinger" must have been meant in some way to foreshadow this transfiguration, as it in the final text similarly foreshadows her celestial reunion with

Faust through the mercy of the *Mater gloriosa*. That prayer begins
and ends with the verses:

> Ach neige,
> Du Schmerzenreiche,
> Dein Antlitz ab zu meiner Not!*

In the scene "Bergschluchten," Gretchen repeats these verses, with
appropriate modifications, at the moment of Faust's reunion with
her, in a prayer to the *Mater gloriosa*:

> Neige, neige,
> Du Ohnegleiche,
> Du Strahlenreiche,
> Dein Antlitz gnädig meinem Glück!*

Late though this scene was written, it evidently still preserves much
of what must have belonged to Goethe's plan from the first inception of the Gretchen tragedy, namely, that Gretchen should not
only herself be saved, but should also be instrumental in bringing
about Faust's salvation, and that in this her devotion to and
affinity with the Virgin Mary should play a decisive part.

In this connexion it is important that Gretchen is not, as has
already been pointed out, simply a "child of nature," but also in a
still greater degree the product of a Christian upbringing and
milieu and of centuries of Christian tradition. It might at first
surprise us that Goethe should have gone out of his way, as he
has done, to make of Gretchen a girl whose soul is indissolubly
bound by those Christian doctrines and beliefs for which he himself, as we know, had so little use—especially in the Catholic form
here involved. He has thereby made things appreciably more difficult for himself, and the question arises: what necessity can have
compelled him to do it or what advantages he promised himself
from it? It would have been much easier for him and, one might
suppose, also very much more in keeping with his own disposition
and outlook, to keep the whole question of religion well in the

---

* Ah, bend down / Thou who aboundest in sorrows, / Thy countenance in
grace to my distress!

* Bend, bend, / Thou incomparable one, / Thou who aboundest in radiancy, / Thy countenance in grace to my happiness!

background, as he does in the case of Clärchen and her relationship
to Egmont, although otherwise religious issues necessarily play so
important a part in *Egmont*. But with Gretchen the case is quite
different. Goethe has so conceived of her and presented her that
the Catholic Christianity in which she has been brought up is for
her the only true religion, the only thinkable interpretation of
existence, and must in the long run mean more to her even than
her love for Faust. She must be saved by it and in accordance with
it, if she is to be saved at all; and so she is saved. That means that
she cannot have or acquire any standard by which her love for
Faust and her surrender to him can ultimately be judged as anything but sinful. Her blood can and indeed does move on other
lines, but her mind cannot. Goethe indicates that she all along
secretly cherishes the quite absurd hope that Faust may in the
end marry her. This emerges in "Am Brunnen" (At the Well),
where she says of the "flinker Jung" (lively youth) who has seduced
and deserted the unfortunate Bärbelchen: "Er nimmt sie gewiss zu
seiner Frau" (He will certainly make her his wife), and again in
her delirious words to Faust in the "Kerker" scene, when she
imagines that the coming day is to be her wedding day, instead of
the day of her execution: "Der letzte Tag! Der Hochzeittag!—Sag's
niemand, dass du die Nacht vorher bei Gretchen warst. —Mein
Kränzchen!" (The last day!—The wedding day!—Don't tell anybody that you were with Gretchen the night before. —My maiden-
head!) She can never have a good conscience about her love for
Faust; she can at most temporarily drug or forget her conscience.
This view is unacceptable to most critics, who insist that there is
nothing about this love and surrender of hers that Gretchen need
be ashamed of, that they are just natural, beautiful, and admirable,
as they indeed are by almost any standards except those to which
she is ineluctably committed. It is usual to see her most valid
utterance on this point in the words:

> Und bin nun selbst der Sünde bloss!
> Doch! —alles, was mich dazu trieb,
> Gott! war so gut! ach, war so lieb!*

---

* And now I myself am at the mercy of sin. / Yet, everything that drove me
to it / God! was so good! ah, was so sweet!

But this touching plea of extenuating circumstances, which does not amount to anything like a profession of faith in the principle of free love, is not Gretchen's last or most valid word on the question. That last word is, "Mir graut's vor dir, Heinrich!" (You fill me with horror, Henry!) By her own religious and moral standards, which she can sometimes forget, but from which she can never even desire to emancipate herself, she is a sinner, and it is only through her acknowledgment of this that she is saved.

Goethe does not, for the purposes of his Faust drama, dissociate himself from Gretchen's religious attitude, as one might expect him to do, in view of his so frequently and forcibly expressed hostility to Christian orthodoxy. On the contrary, it is one of the fundamental postulates on which everything in the Faust drama depends. Of course everything is done to gain and maintain our sympathy for Gretchen throughout, to make us feel the immense difference between her love and crude sensuality, between her offences and deliberate, criminal depravity; also we are made to feel indignant with the harshness of society towards her and to those in her plight, whether it be represented by the spitefulness of Lieschen, the fury of Valentin, Mephisto's sneering comment: "Sie ist die erste nicht!" or the hints that fall about her flight, trial, and execution. But we miss the point of the Gretchen tragedy if we dwell exclusively on these aspects of it, seeing in her only a pure, innocent victim and siding with her against her own Christian conscience. All these redeeming aspects, all these extenuating circumstances, which can easily make us think of Gretchen not just as more sinned against than sinning, but rather as only sinned against, without herself really sinning at all, do but poignantly reinforce the essential point that, in spite of them, her sacrifice of her life—for that is what it amounts to, once the possibility of escape has been opened to her—is not unnecessary, not merely a waste, or a miscarriage of justice, or an example of the brutality of rank and file humanity, but something that *has* to be, that is demanded by the innermost laws and needs of her own nature. The validity of that sacrifice, which not only procures Gretchen's own salvation, but also contributes essentially to Faust's salvation, depends upon its being made by one who feels and rightly feels herself to be not innocent, but a sinner. Gretchen has in this respect a good deal in common with her so much subtler and more sophisticated younger sister, Ottilie in the *Wahlverwandtschaften* ("Elective Affinities") of 1809. Goethe mentioned the two together in a conversation with Rühle von Lilienstern shortly after the publication of this latter work: "Ich heidnisch? Nun ich habe doch Gretchen hinrichten und Ottilie verhungern lassen; ist das den Leuten nicht christlich genug? Was wollen sie noch Christlicheres?" (I a pagan? Now, I have caused Gretchen to be beheaded and Ottilie to starve herself to death; isn't that Christian enough to satisfy people? What do they want more Christian than that?) There is indeed something remarkably Christian or at least quasi-Christian about what Goethe has made out of Gretchen: not so much indeed about his tentative earlier plan for transfiguring her into the Virgin Mary, or about his finally providing her, in the "Bergschluchten" scene, with a spectacular symbolical setting of what was to him only the "mythology" of Catholicism, but about the ethics of her repentance and her expiatory sacrifice.

We are here confronted with yet another of the fundamental dualisms of Goethe's mind, life, and work. On the one hand and in the first place he was an extreme modern individualist with a belief in the exceptional rights and privileges of genius, which he often, though not always, thought of as being through its peculiar inner mission exempt from the moral law and so beyond good and evil. In so far he was, as he himself put it in his letter to Lavater of July 29, 1782, "ein dezidierter Nichtchrist" (emphatically non-Christian). On the other hand, however, he could not and did not reject Christianity completely; so far at least as modern Europe is concerned he regarded it, with certain far-reaching qualifications, as the right and indispensable religion for the ordinary man and for woman at all levels, especially the highest level. That is to say, he would have considered a world, in which everybody was spiritually as emancipated as he himself was, undesirable, intolerable, and indeed impossible. He also by no means felt himself all the time as an exceptional individual of genius, beyond good and evil; he was conscious of having much of the ordinary human being in his nature, of living a great part of his own life at the common human level and of being in so far subject to and in need of what he understood by Christianity—that is to say, of an austere moral

code with otherworldly sanctions, counterbalanced by some idea
of infinite divine love and mercy. In this sense he could say: "Das
Christentum ist so tief in der menschlichen Natur und ihrer
Bedürftigkeit begründet, dass auch in dieser Beziehung mit Recht
zu sagen ist: Des Herrn Wort bleibet ewiglich" (Christianity is so
deeply rooted in human nature and its penury that in this respect
too it may rightly be said: "The word of the Lord endureth for
ever").[53] That was the "Christentum zu seinem Privatgebrauch"
(Christianity for his own private use) which he speaks of himself
(in *Dichtung und Wahrheit,* Book XV) as having devised about
1771, after his breach with pietistic orthodoxy, and which accompanied him in varying forms throughout the rest of his life, finding
characteristic expression in his earlier period in the *Ewige Jude*
and in his later period in the section of *Wilhelm Meisters Wander-
jahre* ("Wilhelm Meister's Years of Travel") entitled: *Die päda-
gogische Provinz* ("The Pedagogical Province"). What chiefly distinguishes this private, esoteric Christianity of Goethe's from
traditional Christian orthodoxy, apart from its undogmatic, subjective, predominantly figurative and therefore somewhat vague
character, is that the conceptions of original sin, of the nothingness
of the merely human and earthly, of the fear of God, and of the
dangers of eternal perdition are almost entirely missing from it.
Nevertheless it does embody much more of distinctively Christian
tenets and values than Goethe is usually thought to have accepted.
One of the chief reasons why this is not as a rule perceived is the
tendency to mutual accommodation or synthesis between Goethe's
amoral individualism of genius and his esoteric Christianity. This
very often goes so far that what is specifically individualistic and
amoral on the one hand, what is specifically Christian on the other,
tends to be attenuated or obscured beyond recognition, and only a
harmonious humanism, most clearly exemplified by *Iphigenie,* remains, which contrives to be individualistic, without falling foul
of social and moral obligations, and works out its own salvation
from inside, without any need for the "grace from above." But this
kind of humanistic synthesis is unstable, and it is not in the light
of it that Goethe can be comprehended in his totality or that all his
works can be adequately interpreted. He himself dismissed *Iphigenie* impatiently in 1802 as "verteufelt human" (devilishly hu-

mane). Least of all can *Faust* be interpreted in terms of the kind of humanistic synthesis embodied in *Iphigenie*. It was planned and begun before that humanism had become possible for Goethe and was continued and completed when that humanism had grown suspect for him.

Not that no synthesis between amoral individualism and esoteric Christianity is aimed at in *Faust*. It most decidedly is aimed at, but in a very much more uncompromising, complex, and dialectical form than in any other of Goethe's works, except possibly the *Wahlverwandtschaften*. In *Faust* the two opposed principles confront one another in undiluted intensity, the one represented, of course, by Faust himself, the other chiefly by Gretchen, and no mild, conciliatory humanism mediates between them. Each in its own way is defeated and triumphs, and it is only on the other-worldly plane that the conflict between them can at last be resolved. There the quasi-Christian principle merges into the Eternal Feminine, in accordance with Goethe's well-known declaration that he could only conceive of the ideal under a feminine form, the role which was originally to have been played by God the Father and Christ being assigned now solely to a far from orthodoxly envisaged Virgin Mary as *Mater gloriosa* who in her turn delegates it to Gretchen. H. A. Korff calls the amoral individualism of genius embodied in Faust "das Ewig-Männliche" (the Eternal Masculine), a coinage which felicitously brings out the character of the dualism upon which the *Faust* drama turns.

There will be more to be said on these questions later. For the moment it is enough to note that the Eternal Masculine is not completely submerged in the Eternal Feminine and that Faust is not saved by Gretchen's intercession alone, though that is one of the indispensable conditions of his salvation. What is really involved here is the will to a transcendental synthesis between the amoral self-assertion of genius and what Goethe understood by Christianity. Faust criticism has all along tended to be one endless, often acrimonious debate on the question, whether Goethe intends to glorify or to denounce the Faustian superman, to justify or to condemn his self-centredness and ruthlessness, to represent Faust as being saved *because of* what he is or *in spite of* what he is. It is assumed that one or the other of these two views must be the right

one, and each has its violent partisans. But whichever side is
chosen in this debate, one is faced with serious difficulties. Extreme believers in the Faustian superman as an ideal and exemplary
type sometimes deplore the epilogue in the other world with its
final hymn in praise of the Eternal Feminine, as an irrelevant and
regrettable afterthought with which Goethe has spoilt the true
point of the work, made unworthy concessions to conventional
morality, and patched on to his great tragedy a spurious, invalid
happy ending that is better ignored. Extreme believers in Faust as
a warning example against the delusions and dangers of amoral
Titanism, on the other hand, resolutely withhold all admiration
and sympathy from him, even in those frequent cases where Goethe
most clearly intends us to admire him and sympathize with him.
The paradoxical view is here proposed that *Faust* is in equal measure
a glorification *and* a denunciation of the superman, that his self-
centredness and ruthlessness are in equal measure justified and
condemned, that Faust is saved *both* because of what he is and in
spite of what he is. The work is in this respect ambivalent and is
meant to be so, as *Werther, Tasso,* and the *Wahlverwandtschaften*
are ambivalent, and as Goethe himself felt human existence and
his own ego to be ambivalent. Nor is this ambivalence to be accounted for by changes in plan due to the changes Goethe himself
underwent in the course of his long life, to his first having un-
reservedly admired the Faustian type and completely identified
himself with it, and then later having come to disapprove of it and
dissociate himself from it. To some extent this did indeed happen,
but not to such an extent that it produced any radical change in
the purport of the work. The *Faust* drama was as ambivalent in
its first origins as it is at the later and latest stages, and always with
the same kind of ambivalence. This appears already in the *Urfaust,*
when the hero is brought face to face with what seemed to Goethe
purest and most universally valid in Christianity, as it is represented
by Gretchen and her expiatory sacrifice. The question was ultimately, whether a superman living beyond good and evil and never
to the last fulfilling any of those conditions which, according to the
Christianity devised by Goethe for his own private use, are binding
for the rest of mankind, could yet find favour in the eyes of God
and be saved; and if so, how. This question and the answer to it,

although they were not fully worked out and explicitly formulated until many years later, in the "Prolog im Himmel" and "Bergschluchten," are already adumbrated in the *Urfaust*, and it is above all through them that the Gretchen tragedy is organically linked up with the Faust theme proper. During the years when the *Urfaust* was written Goethe was deeply concerned with exceptional possibilities of salvation for those who cannot or will not take the Christian way. This appears in the fictitious letter of the country pastor of 1772, and also in Werther's words: "Sagt nicht der Sohn Gottes: dass die um ihn sein würden, die ihm der Vater gegeben hat. Wenn ich ihm nun nicht gegeben bin! Wenn mich nun der Vater für sich behalten will, wie mir mein Herz sagt!" (Does not the Son of God himself say that those shall be with him whom the Father has given to him? Suppose I have not been given to him? Suppose the Father desires to keep me for himself, as my heart tells me?) That is one of the ways in which Goethe must have thought also of Faust at that time, as one of those whom the Father desired to keep for himself, and who are, therefore, unlike the ordinary run of mankind, exempt from the laws of Christianity. There will be more to be said about this when we discuss the often maintained contention that Faust is intended to be a kind of modern Everyman, representative of the human race in its totality.

8. *Faust, ein Fragment,*

1788-1790

THE ATTEMPTS of some scholars to demonstrate through parallelisms that Goethe made certain additions to Faust during his first eleven years in Weimar (1775–1786) are unconvincing and can here be disregarded; at most he can have jotted down an occasional, now quite unidentifiable, odd "splinter." He continued to give readings from the *Urfaust* manuscript sporadically down to 1780, but his work on it had come to a standstill; and in summer 1786, shortly before his departure for Italy, in making proposals for the first authorized edition of his collected works, he resigned himself to the idea of publishing it as a fragment. He took the manuscript to Rome with him, along with many others, so that he could prepare it for the press there, and feeling his poetic powers renewed, wrote to Herzog Carl August on December 16, 1786, that he had after all some hopes of completing both it and *Tasso*: "Da ich mir vornahm meine Fragmente drucken zu lassen, hielt ich mich für tot, wie froh will ich sein, wenn ich mich durch Vollendung des Angefangenen wieder als lebendig legitimieren kann!" (When I decided to publish my fragments, I regarded myself as dead; how glad I shall be, if I can, by completing what was begun, prove that I am alive again!) He wanted, however, first of all to deal with his numerous other fragmentary works, and it was not till February, 1788, a few weeks before his departure from Rome, that he at last settled down to *Faust,* feeling towards it, as he said, "eine sonderbare Neigung und neuerdings wunderbare Aussichten und Hoffnungen" (a special inclination and also recently strange prospects and hopes).[1] He had sanguinely thought that he might be able to finish it in three or four months, but found this an impossible task, especially as *Tasso* was also making exacting claims on him. His chief concern was, of course, to fill up the great gap between the opening scene and the Gretchen Tragedy, incorporating Mephisto's dialogue with the student and "Auerbachs Keller" in the process. That meant above all introducing Mephisto into the action and dealing with the pact between him and Faust. This is indicated in a letter of January 10, 1788, which is of additional interest because in it he makes fun of the still current notion that he could only write effectually as a poet about things he had just before experienced personally at first hand: "—so muss ich mich im Laufe dieses Jahres in eine Prinzessin verlieben, um den *Tasso*, ich muss mich dem Teufel ergeben, um den *Faust* schreiben zu können, ob ich mir gleich zu Beidem wenig Lust fühle" (I must in the course of this year fall in love with a princess, in order to be able to write *Tasso*, and abandon myself to the devil, in order to be able to write *Faust*, although I feel little inclination to do either).

Thanks chiefly to Hertz it is widely assumed that Goethe worked out an entirely new plan for *Faust* in Rome in February and March, 1788. Hertz makes great use here of the autobiographical method of interpretation: "Wir sind gewohnt, in den verschiedenen Entwicklungsstufen der Faustgestalt zu erblicken Abbild und Ausdruck der jeweiligen Stufe der geistigen Gestalt ihres Schöpfers. Darum sind wir befugt, auch dem römischen Faustplan diese autobiographische Funktion zuzuschreiben" (We are in the habit of seeing in the different stages of development of the Faust figure a reproduction and expression of the corresponding stages in the spiritual development of his creator. Therefore we are entitled to assign this autobiographical function also to the Roman Faust plan).[2] That is to say, we must, according to Hertz, postulate that the "seelische Wandlung des Dichters in Rom" (change undergone by the poet's soul in Rome)[3] mirrored itself in his plan for *Faust* of February, 1788, and that change was in the direction of classicism, which leaves out of account that Goethe's classical development as such had begun nearly ten years before he went to Italy. Hertz therefore assumes that it must have been Goethe's purpose to impose a classical tone, form, and purport on the fragmentary works of his Storm and Stress years in attempting to complete them in 1787 and 1788, which would, of course, have meant totally changing their original, decidedly unclassical character. Hertz finds evidence for this in the fifth act of *Egmont*, written in 1787, designating it as the "klassische Wendung, die er dem Drama in Rom gab" (classical turn which he gave to the drama in Rome).[4] We know, however, from Goethe's letters of the time, that his great concern was to complete *Egmont* as far as possible in a manner consistent with that in which he had begun it twelve years previously, and not to allow his subsequent classical development to hinder him in that undertaking. Therein he was unsuccessful, producing instead a hardly satisfactory fifth act, which, while quite failing to recapture the Shakespearean manner of the earlier acts, is also not in the least classical either in intention or in achievement. In any case, the conception of a play beginning Shakespeareanly and ending classically is a monstrosity that Goethe can never have entertained; a work is either classical in its totality or it is not classical at all. Another piece of evidence appealed to by Hertz is Goethe's statement in a letter of February 6, 1787 to P. C. Kayser: "Ich hoffe man soll künftig meinen Sachen das Ultramontane [that is, the southerly, classical character] ansehen" (I hope that in future the ultra-montane element will be observable in the things I write). He can here only be thinking of the works he hopes to produce in the near future, but Hertz applies his words to *Egmont* and more particularly to *Faust*: "Die im Sturm und Drang der Jugend hingeworfenen Szenen sollten also jetzt mehr oder weniger umgeformt zu Bausteinen klassischer Werke werden" (It was intended then that the scenes dashed off in the Storm and Stress of youth should be more or less refashioned into bricks for the constructing of classical works).[5] It is on these very dubious assumptions that Hertz bases his hypothesis of the "neuen römischen Plan, der im Gegensatze zum *Urfaust* zur Lossprechung des Helden führte" (new Roman plan, which in contradistinction to the *Urfaust*, led to the absolution of the hero).[6] He takes it for granted that what Goethe planned in Rome in 1788 was not merely the completion, but also the "Umgestaltung" (refashioning) of the *Urfaust*;[7] and that this refashioning, which never went beyond the initial plan, was to have been on emphatically classical lines. Since Hertz's contention is so widely accepted without any further scrutiny, simply on his authority, it is not superfluous to see what Goethe himself has to say on these questions in his already twice-quoted letter to Herder of March 1, 1788,[8] which is the *only* piece of direct evidence we have about his Roman plan. Of special interest are those passages that Hertz nowhere quotes or refers to in his detailed exposition. Goethe writes:

> Zuerst ward der Plan zu *Faust* gemacht, und ich hoffe, diese Operation soll mir geglückt sein. Natürlich ist es ein ander Ding, das Stück jetzt oder vor fünfzehn Jahren auszuschreiben; ich denke, es soll nichts dabei verlieren, besonders da ich jetzt glaube, den Faden wiedergefunden zu haben. Auch was den Ton des Ganzen betrifft, bin ich getröstet; ich habe schon eine neue Szene ausgeführt, und wenn ich das Papier räuchere, so dächt' ich, sollte sie mir niemand aus den alten herausfinden. Da ich durch die lange Ruhe und Abgeschiedenheit [that is, of his sojourn in Italy] ganz auf das Niveau meiner eigenen Existenz zurückgebracht bin, so ist es merkwürdig, wie sehr ich mir gleiche und wie wenig mein Inneres durch Jahre und Begebenheiten gelitten hat.*

Then, after having described the original Faust manuscript,[9] he goes on:

> —so dass ich, wie ich damals in eine frühere Welt mich mit Sinnen und Ahnen versetzte, mich jetzt in eine selbstgelebte Vorzeit wieder versetzen muss.†

---

* First of all the plan for Faust was made, and I hope that I have been successful in this operation. It is a different thing, of course, to complete the play now from what it would have been fifteen years ago; I think nothing will be lost in the process, especially as I believe I have now found the thread again. So far as the tone of the whole work is concerned I also feel reassured; I have already written one scene, and if I were to smoke the paper, I don't think anybody would be able to distinguish it from the old ones. Now that I have been completely restored to the level of my own existence by the long quiet and seclusion, it is remarkable how much I resemble myself and how little my inner life has suffered through the passage of years and events.

† As I had in those days to transport myself back imaginatively and intuitively into an earlier world, so now I must transport myself back to a bygone epoch of my own life.

There is not a word in all this to suggest that the "plan" Goethe here speaks of was a "new" one, still less that he aimed at refashioning *Faust* on classical lines, in conformity with his more recent developments. On the contrary, he was only anxious to "find the old thread," to recapture the old tone, and to transport himself back in his imagination to the state of mind in which he had been about 1773. It was as clear to Goethe in 1788 as it was when he wrote "Zueignung" and the "Vorspiel auf dem Theater" in 1797 that the only way for him to complete *Faust* was to shelve his more recently acquired classical standards and ideals for the time being. A great artist is never so attached to one particular aesthetic principle, doctrine, or school that he is not prepared and sometimes even compelled to sacrifice it in exceptional circumstances, and *Faust* was for the classical Goethe such an exceptional case. The plan he worked out in February, 1788, with some inevitable modifications due to lapses of memory and the passage of time, was substantially still the original plan of the years 1770–1775 which, we can be certain, had never been systematically committed to paper. His problem now was to reconstruct that plan with the help of his memory from the *Urfaust* manuscript and all the existing "splinters." This is shown by such phrases as: "ich glaube, den Faden wiedergefunden zu haben." It worries Hertz greatly that *Faust, ein Fragment* of 1790 shows no appreciable differences in character and purport from the *Urfaust*, except in the opening monologue of "Wald und Höhle." He can only account for this by the further hypothesis that Goethe abandoned the "new Roman plan" for "refashioning" *Faust* almost as soon as he had formed it, and went back to the original plan of the Frankfort years. The real explanation is that there never was any such radically new Roman plan. Hertz's theories could be ignored if they had not so much confused the issue of what happened in summer, 1797, when Goethe's *Faust* demonstrably did undergo certain important modifications and amplifications; there is an unfortunate tendency to antedate some of those changes by nine years, as though they had been part of the supposed new Roman plan.

Goethe seems to have gone on working sporadically at *Faust* after his return to Weimar in June, 1788, although his mind was chiefly taken up with the very different and extremely exacting task of completing *Tasso*. But on July 5, 1789, he wrote to Herzog Carl August that he had after all decided "Faust . . . als Fragment [zu] geben aus mehr als einer Ursache" (for more than one reason to publish *Faust* as a fragment). As such it appeared in the following year. The great gap with its two essential motifs, the first appearance of Mephisto and the pact, still remained unfilled. "Auerbachs Keller" was rewritten in Knittel verse throughout, with Mephisto playing the part originally assigned to Faust, and with various other changes. The language was toned down and the prosody was made smoother at many points. Everything in the *Urfaust* after the "Dom" scene was suppressed, except for two fragments incorporated in the new scene, "Wald und Höhle," one of them the appeal to the "grosser herrlicher Geist" from "Trüber Tag. Feld," which was now expanded into the great blank verse monologue: "Erhabner Geist . . . ," the other Faust's famous indictment of himself as "Der Unmensch ohne Zweck und Ruh" (The monster without purpose or repose) from the fragmentary "Valentin" scene. One hundred and three lines of dialogue between Faust and Mephisto and seventeen lines of monologue for Mephisto were supplied to precede and follow the Student scene, which was retrenched at some points, amplified at others and generally revised to give it a maturer character and make it cover all four Faculties, instead of Arts and Medicine alone. But this new dialogue still begins after the first appearance of Mephisto and after the conclusion of the pact between him and Faust, on which all-important motifs there is still no light thrown. The only other addition to the *Faust* text at this stage that remains to be mentioned is "Hexenküche," written, like "Wald und Höhle," in Rome in early spring, 1788. As the text of the *Fragment* breaks off abruptly at the end of the "Dom" scene, not only the ultimate fate of Faust, but also that of Gretchen, is left uncertain.

The new fragmentary scene between Faust and Mephisto, incorporating the latter's conversation with the Student, presents various problems. It was eventually, in the 1808 text of *Faust I. Teil*, to become the concluding half of the second "Studierzimmer" scene, through the addition of 240 preceding lines, written presumably in 1800, in the course of which the pact between Faust and Mephisto was at last actually worked out and presented. In the 1790 text it follows immediately upon the departure of Wagner, and its fragmentary nature is emphasized by its beginning in the middle of a sentence and half way through a quatrain—that is to say, with two verses that obviously should be preceded by two others to rhyme with them:

> Und was der ganzen Menschheit *zugeteilt ist,*
> Will ich in meinem innern Selbst *geniessen—**

These missing rhymes are supplied in the 1788 text:

> Mein Busen, der vom Wissensdrang *geheilt ist,*
> Soll keinen Schmerzen künftig sich *verschliessen.*†

Now it is inherently improbable that Goethe began his work on this dialogue in 1788 or 1789 not only halfway through a speech, but also halfway through a sentence and even halfway through a quatrain. It is far likelier that the preceding lines of this speech, or at least the two with the missing rhyme words, were written in 1788–1789, at the same time as the rest, and that Goethe withheld them in preparing the text of *Faust, ein Fragment* for the press. One can see what motive he might have had for doing this: it was to be brought home to the reader that he was here being plunged *in medias res*, that this was only the continuation of a conversation, the commencement of which was still missing and had to be imagined. There could be no more effective means of preventing the reader from jumping to the mistaken conclusion that what he had before him here was meant to be a complete scene than thus to withhold from him the rhymes which he would otherwise have had a right to expect. But if the first half of this speech of Faust's was at this date (1788–1789) already in existence and was only suppressed for editorial reasons—as it probably was—then it is theoretically possible that Goethe may at the same time have been withholding a good deal more, and many critics, amongst them Sarauw, have argued on these grounds that the still missing, all-important part of the dialogue in which the actual pact between

---

* And what is parcelled out to all mankind / I am resolved to enjoy within my inmost self.

† My bosom, cured now of the urge for knowledge / Shall henceforth shut itself off from no suffering.

Faust and Mephisto is concluded was really written as early as 1788–1789 and not, as all the other evidence so forcibly suggests, after 1797. There are, however, strong objections to this view. Whereas it is easy to see what motives Goethe could have had for suppressing the first half of Faust's speech with the missing rhyme words, it is impossible to find any reasonable motives that could have induced him to withhold the actual concluding of the pact between Faust and Mephisto, if it had really been in existence when *Faust, ein Fragment* was prepared for the press. There are, it will be seen, good grounds for supposing that the idea on which that pact is based in *Faust I. Teil* cannot have occurred to Goethe before 1797. In 1788–1789 he still adhered to the original idea of having Mephisto given to Faust as a companion by the Erdgeist; that is shown by the opening monologue of the new scene, "Wald und Höhle," written at that stage. So long as that was his plan, the pact must have been envisaged in a different form from that found in *Faust I. Teil,* one of the essential postulates of which is that the idea of Mephisto's being sent to Faust by the Erdgeist has been abandoned. Furthermore the connexion between the two sections of the second "Studierzimmer" scene is only a loose one and shows certain contradictions, which were not such as to worry Goethe himself, but do worry many of his commentators, and which could hardly have arisen, if the pact passage had been written in 1788–1789, together with what was published in *Faust, ein Fragment.* The most noteworthy of these contradictions or apparent contradictions will concern us when we discuss Faust's pact with Mephisto. It turns on the question, whether Mephisto plans to bring about Faust's destruction by satisfying his desires or by keeping him eternally dissatisfied. The section of the second "Studierzimmer" scene published in *Faust, ein Fragment* does, however, contain—and that was certainly important to Goethe—a more definite indication than is to be found in the *Urfaust* that some kind of pact has been concluded between Faust and Mephisto. That is the point of those verses in the latter's monologue which are, as has been seen,[10] so curiously misinterpreted by Hertz:

> Und hätt' *er sich auch nicht dem Teufel übergeben,*
> Er müsste doch zugrunde gehn!

This suggests that Goethe originally contemplated, and up to 1789 still did contemplate, a far more unconditional type of pact than what he ultimately presents us with in *Faust I. Teil*; for in that pact Faust by no means "abandons himself to the devil." Up to 1789 Goethe had evidently still not found any satisfactory solution to the problem of the pact.

The most important points about the "Hexenküche" scene—the way in which it mediates between Faust the Magus and Faust the lover of Gretchen through the aphrodisiac rejuvenating potion, pre-pares us for the "Walpurgisnacht" and leads up to the Gretchen tragedy, tenuously linking it with the Helen of Troy theme—have already been dealt with.[11] In its totality it is not one of the most successful scenes of *Faust*. It affords plenty of theatrical spectacle and magical hocus-pocus, such as the Faust theme demands, but Goethe has elected not to treat these as a source of terror, wonder, or any other serious interest. Instead he indulges his humour, and that humour only shows itself at its best in the utterances of Mephisto, not in those of the Witch herself and her familiar spirits, the two cats. In order to lead up to the rejuvenation process in the Witch's Kitchen, Goethe emphasizes the difference between Faust as Magus and as lover of Gretchen by putting into his mouth, in the dialogue at the end of the new half-scene, where he and Me-phisto get ready for their journey first into the "kleine Welt" (little world) of Gretchen and then into the "grosse Welt" (great world) of the imperial court, the far from felicitous words:

> Allein bei meinem langen Bart
> Fehlt mir die leichte Lebensart.
> Es wird mir der Versuch nicht glücken;
> Ich wusste nie mich in die Welt zu schicken.
> Vor andern fühl' ich mich so klein;
> Ich werde stets verlegen sein.*

It is not with this pusillanimous confession that the Magus who had invoked the Erdgeist should have abdicated. In reading the

---

* But with this long beard of mine / I have no easy manners. / I shall not succeed in the attempt; / I never did know how to adapt myself to the ways of the world. / Confronted with other people I feel so small: / I shall always be embarrassed.

Urfaust alone one pays no particular attention to the question of the hero's age, but this addition obliges us to visualize him in the opening scene as an old man. This is reinforced at the beginning of the "Hexenküche" scene itself, when Faust says that he needs to be rejuvenated by "dreissig Jahre" (thirty years). In the opening monologue, on the other hand, it appears that it is only "an die zehen Jahre" (about ten years) since he was himself a student. This contradiction itself would not trouble us, if only Goethe had avoided making Faust—of all people—speak so much out of character, almost as though he were subject to an all too human inferiority complex.

The chief problem raised by "Wald und Höhle" is that of the opening monologue. On the one hand it is only an expansion of the old apostrophe to the "grosser herrlicher Geist" from "Trüber Tag. Feld," and as such confirms us in the view that Goethe originally intended Mephisto to be sent to Faust by the Erdgeist and that he had still not given up that intention in 1790. On the other hand, however, it is surprising to find him using here the blank verse of the classical *Iphigenie* and *Tasso*. That is best to be accounted for by the assumption that he thought almost any kind of verse admissible under certain circumstances in a work on principle as heterogeneous as *Faust*. Certainly it cannot mean, as Hertz would have us believe, that Goethe aimed at anything so impossible as giving the *Faust* drama a classical character. But the first twenty-three verses of the monologue amplify the original phrase: "Grosser herrlicher Geist, . . . der du mein Herz kennst und meine Seele," on strange lines:

> Gabst mir die herrliche Natur zum Königreich,
> Kraft, sie zu fühlen, zu geniessen. Nicht
> Kalt staunenden Besuch erlaubst du nur,
> Vergönnest mir, in ihre tiefe Brust,
> Wie in den Busen eines Freunds, zu schauen.*

There follows a long rhapsody on his communion with nature (curiously Wordsworthian in character), and then Faust goes on

---

* You gave me glorious nature for my kingdom, / Power to enjoy and feel her. Not alone / A coldly wondering visit you allow me, / But grant me leave to gaze in her deep breast / As in the breast of one who is my friend.

to say that the "erhabner Geist" has also revealed to him the mysterious wonders of his own breast and "Der Vorwelt silberne Gestalten" (the silvery forms of the primaeval world), which "lindern der Betrachtung strenge Lust" (tranquillize the austere joy of his contemplation). All this raises many problems and has occasioned much speculation and controversy. There are many who regard the monologue up to this point simply as an expression of Goethe's own pantheistic devotion to nature and more particularly of what the Italian journey had meant to him, and therefore as really having nothing to do with Faust and being quite inappropriately put into his mouth. Others are unwilling to admit that Goethe could thus have interpolated an irrelevant personal "confession" into *Faust*; but in their exertions to prove it relevant, they feel that some special explanation is needed for the discrepancy between what Faust here says of the "erhabner Geist" and the humiliating defeat that he had undergone from the Erdgeist in the opening scene. Some suggest—and there is much to be said for his view—that Goethe intended the Erdgeist to manifest itself again, this time more favourably and graciously. Another reasonable suggestion is that Faust is speaking here not of any concrete, particular manifestations of the Erdgeist in visible form, but just of his own communings with nature, which he interprets symbolically as favours bestowed upon him by that Spirit. Another suggestion is that his invocation of the Erdgeist has with the passage of time transfigured itself in his memory, losing all its painful, alarming, and humiliating aspects, and so appearing to him now only as something elevating and glorious. Hans Jaeger proposes the curious theory that the great gift that Faust is here conscious of having received from the Erdgeist "can only be Gretchen's love,"[12] everything being "given to man by the Earth Spirit, the executor of the Divine Will."[13] Some, particularly Rickert, think the monologue so irreconcilable with the character of the Erdgeist and with Faust's experiences of it that the "erhabner Geist" here addressed must be some other quite different spirit, probably that of the Makrokosmus. If the great gap after Wagner's departure had been filled in the way in which Goethe still contemplated filling it when the "Erhabner Geist" monologue was written, we should presumably not be so much in the dark here as we are. We can only resign ourselves to our ignorance. The suggestion is made here that, while the "Erhabner Geist" addressed in "Wald und Höhle" quite certainly must be the Erdgeist, Goethe seems either deliberately or more likely inadvertently to have obscured the original distinction between that Spirit and the Sign of the Makrokosmus. It has already been noted that in his later years he often treated the Erdgeist as identical with the Weltgeist, and he seems to be doing this already to a considerable extent in the "Wald und Höhle" monologue: the sublime Spirit there addressed is the spirit of "austere contemplation"; it has taken on the idealistic character of the Makrokosmus and no longer stands for blind, ruthless activity. This makes it difficult to see how or why it could have given Mephisto to Faust as a companion. In discussing "Paralipomenon I" in the following chapter, we shall find further evidence for this view that Goethe had himself become confused in his own mythology.

In the 1790 text, "Wald und Höhle" was placed between "Am Brunnen" and "Zwinger," that is to say *after* the seduction of Gretchen has been fully accomplished. In that position it must be interpreted as meaning that Faust has fled into the country with the resolve to leave Gretchen in peace for the future and in the hope that the harm he has done her may still not be irreparable, but that Mephisto successfully tempts him back to her with the exquisite lines which show that for all his cynicism and coldheartedness he still has in his own way a strong aesthetic appreciation of Gretchen's charm and of her love:

> Sie steht am Fenster, sieht die Wolken ziehn
> Über die alte Stadtmauer hin.
> Wenn ich ein Vöglein wär'! so geht ihr Gesang
> Tage lang, halbe Nächte lang.
> Einmal ist sie munter, meist betrübt,
> Einmal recht ausgeweint,
> Dann wieder ruhig, wie's scheint,
> Und immer verliebt.*[14]

---

* She stands at the window, watching the clouds drift by / Over the old city wall. / Would I were a bird! So goes her song, / All day long, half the night long. / Sometimes she is cheerful, more often distressed, / Sometimes worn out with weeping, / Then again tranquil, so it seems, / And always in love. /

Faust's outburst at the end of the scene, "Was muss geschehn, mag's gleich geschehn!" (Let what must happen, happen at once), can then only refer, as it does in the *Urfaust*, to the inevitable tragic ending of the already tragic situation. The position to which Goethe transferred the scene in *Faust I. Teil* is more satisfactory: immediately after the two "Garten" scenes, in which Gretchen declares her love, but before "Gretchen am Spinnrade" (Gretchen at the Spinning Wheel) and the "Katechismus" scene—that is to say, *before* her actual seduction. Faust's flight into the country, Mephisto's description of Gretchen longing for his return, and Faust's talk of "what must happen," all seem better motivated at this point of time, when it still appears not too late for the catastrophe to be averted—although we soon learn that Gretchen's "Ruh' ist hin" (her peace is gone) and that she will never find it again. In the "Spinnrad" scene, where this declaration is made, Goethe, it is to be noted, toned down her original words: "Mein Schoss, Gott! drängt sich nach ihm hin" (My womb, God, yearns towards him), to "Mein Busen drängt sich nach ihm hin" (My bosom yearns towards him). This concession to decorum implies, of course, no change in the conception of Gretchen's character.

One of Mephisto's jibes at Faust in "Wald und Höhle" has given rise to much speculation; it is this:

> Und wär' ich nicht, so wärst du schon
> Von diesem Erdball abspaziert.†

It has been suggested that Goethe at this stage planned a scene in which Faust should have been prevented from committing suicide by Mephisto, that possibly being Mephisto's first appearance, just as Faust is, in one of the additions made after 1797, prevented from committing suicide by the Easter bells. Such a scene may conceivably have been projected. But there is another, likelier interpretation of Mephisto's words: he may only be saying that Faust with his fantastic idealistic aspirations was in danger of losing contact with earthly reality altogether, and that he, Mephisto, has cured him of such visionary extravagances and brought him back to earth and its pleasures.

† And if it were not for me, you would by now / Have wandered right off this earthly globe.

Some of the higher critics have argued that the "Wald und Höhle" scene was meant in its original form to stand before the beginning of the Gretchen tragedy and to refer not to her at all, but to some other woman or to the image Faust had seen in the magic mirror in the "Hexenküche." These arguments are based above all on the lines near the end of Faust's blank verse monologue:

> Er facht in meiner Brust ein wildes Feuer
> Nach jenem *schönen Bild* geschäftig an.*

But this phrase *"schönes Bild"* was in the language of Goethe and his contemporaries regularly used to designate a beautiful woman of flesh and blood whom the speaker loves, and there are no grounds for thinking that it was ever meant to apply here to anything or anybody but Gretchen. Max Morris constructs an elaborate hypothesis on the basis of the two succeeding verses, which conclude Faust's monologue:

> So tauml' ich von Begierde zu Genuss,
> Und im Genuss verschmacht' ich nach Begierde.†

Morris, herein a good Victorian, finds these words too fraught with sensuality to have been originally meant to apply to the relationship between Faust and Gretchen: "Bei Gretchen "taumelt" Faust nicht von Begierde zu Genuss und nie hören wir, dass Faust in Gretchens Armen im Genuss schon nach Begierde schmachtete, also Überdruss empfände" (With Gretchen, Faust does not "reel" from desire to enjoyment, and we never hear of his languishing in Gretchen's arms in enjoyment for desire—that is to say, of his feeling satiety).[15] But that Faust does indeed feel "Überdruss" in respect of Gretchen is just what we must postulate, if we are to account for his desertion of her and his long forgetfulness of her; and in these very lines, which originally stood *after* the actual seduction, we are informed that he does so. Rather than admit this, Morris postulates that Goethe planned about 1788 some never-written scene or scenes in which Faust would have been shown

---

* He fans within my breast industriously / A stormy passion for that *lovely image.*

† Thus I reel from desire to enjoyment, / And languish in enjoyment for desire.

indulging in gross sexual adventures of the most depraved kind, between his rejuvenation in the "Hexenküche" and his first meeting with Gretchen:

> Es sind nur die beiden Schlusszeilen des Monologs *Wald und Höhle*, auf die sich dieser Nachweis von Goethes italienischer Intention stützt, aber sie sprechen ganz eindeutig . . . Als sie gedichtet wurden, wiesen sie eben nicht, wie jetzt, auf Gretchen hin, sondern auf dieses Zwischenstadium niederen Sinnengenusses. . . . Also der Monolog *Wald und Höhle* . . . gehört ursprünglich überhaupt nicht in die Gretchentragödie . . . Aus Ekel und Überdruss reinigt sich Faust in der Einsamkeit und jetzt erst lässt Mephisto Gretchen folgen als eine feinere Lockspeise, da die alte, grobe nicht mehr verfängt.*

Similar considerations lead Sarauw to maintain that "Wald und Höhle" was originally meant to stand immediately before "Nacht. Offen Feld" and "Kerker," in place of "Trüber Tag. Feld," and refers to the erotic depravities later evoked in the "Walpurgisnacht."[16] Once the true, ambivalent character of the relationship between Faust and Gretchen is properly grasped, every shadow of justification for such random hypotheses vanishes.

The most important point that emerges from a careful and sober examination of *Faust, ein Fragment* is that Goethe in the years 1788–1790 still contemplated no radical change in his original Faust plan, particularly not in the all-important question of Mephisto's being sent to Faust by the Erdgeist.

---

* It is only on the final lines of the monologue *Forest and Cave* that this demonstration of Goethe's Italian plan is based, but their evidence is unequivocal. When they were written they did not—that is the point—apply to Gretchen, as they do now, but to that intermediate phase of base sensual indulgence. Therefore the monologue *Forest and Cave* did not originally belong to the Gretchen Tragedy at all. Faust is purifying himself from disgust and satiety in solitude, and only now does Mephisto resort to Gretchen as a more delicate bait, when the old, gross one no longer takes effect.

9. The Completion of FAUST I. Teil, 1797-1808

FAUST, EIN FRAGMENT was at first given a cold reception when it was published in 1790. Readers were estranged by the "ballad-monger" tone ("Bänkelsängerton") of it, by its apparent utter formlessness and incoherency and often also by what seemed to them immoral and pessimistic in it. But before long the more discriminating began to see it in a better light and even to feel enthusiastic about it. What most impressed readers in the years 1790 to 1808 was the Erdgeist, which gave rise to considerable speculation and imitation. But Tieck's comment was: "Man begreift nicht, was einem Menschen, dem der Erdgeist erscheinen ist, der elende Mephistopheles soll, und dann ein beschränktes junges Mädchen wie Gretchen" (One does not understand what a man to whom the Spirit of Earth has appeared can find in the wretched Mephisto and then in a young girl with such limitations as Gretchen).[1] This expectation and curiosity aroused by the Erdgeist was, as we shall see, to remain unsatisfied. The Gretchen story failed to make the impression that it was later to make because Goethe had still withheld the three final scenes with the tragic conclusion.

In particular Schiller was impressed by *Faust, ein Fragment*. Only three months after the beginning of his friendship with Goethe he wrote to him asking him to let him see "die Bruchstücke von Ihrem *Faust*, die noch nicht gedruckt sind" (the fragments of your

Faust which have not yet appeared in print).[2] Goethe replied that
he could not face opening "das Paket, das ihn gefangen hält" (the
packet that holds him prisoner).[3] But about the end of June, 1795,
he outlined the entire plan of *Faust* as he then envisaged it in a
conversation with Schiller, a thing he is not known to have done
on any other occasion. Our only information about this is in a
letter written to Schiller by Wilhelm von Humboldt on July 17,
1795: "Für die ausführliche Nachricht von Goethens *Faust* meinen
herzlichen Dank. Der Plan ist ungeheuer, schade nur, dass er eben
darum wohl nur Plan bleiben wird" (My hearty thanks for the
detailed account of Goethe's *Faust*. The plan is tremendous; the
only pity is that for that very reason it is likely to remain a mere
plan). Schiller's letter to Humboldt here acknowledged is unfortunately not preserved. That is one of the major losses of literary annals. It must have contained the answers to many of the
problems about which the critics have been wrangling so virulently
and inconclusively ever since. What does at least emerge from
Humboldt's words is that Goethe must at this time have outlined
to Schiller a whole series of further adventures, which Faust was
to undergo *after* the end of the Gretchen tragedy, corresponding
probably in a general way to what we actually do find in *Faust II*
of 1825–1831; that "ungeheuerer Plan" must still have been in
substance the one that Goethe had brooded over about 1770–1772.

In his so-called *Annalen*, compiled between 1819 and 1825,
Goethe records that he attempted in 1796 to make something out
of *Faust* which might be suitable for practical production on the
Weimar stage, but "was ich auch tat, ich entfernte ihn mehr vom
Theater, als dass ich ihn herangebracht hätte" (whatever I did, I
made it remoter from the theatre, instead of nearer to it). This
is not, however, borne out by the actual diaries of 1796, or by
Goethe's correspondence with Schiller of the same year, in which
it would have been bound to leave some traces, if it had really
happened. It would appear that Goethe was here simply mixing
up his dates a little and assigning to 1796 what really belongs to
1797 and the following years. It can at most be supposed that he
was in summer, 1796, stimulated to meditate on his *Faust* plan
once more by Schink's *Fausts Bund mit der Hölle* of that year,
which he attacked as prosaic in one of his *Xenien*, but from which

he was to take over a few minor motifs, as Pniower demonstrates.[4] The view that Goethe wrote his "Vorspiel auf dem Theater" about 1795–1796 is untenable.[5]

On June 22, 1797 Goethe wrote to Schiller: "—so habe ich mich entschlossen, an meinen *Faust* zu gehen und ihn, wo nicht zu vollenden, doch wenigstens um ein gutes Teil weiter zu bringen" (I have decided to do some work on my *Faust* and, if not to complete it, at least to make some substantial progress with it). Two or three days before this he must have opened the packet of *Faust* manuscripts once more. We must suppose this packet to have contained, in the first place, the *Urfaust*, as it is known to us from the Göchhausen transcript; then a printed copy of *Faust, ein Fragment*, then a considerable number of the most heterogeneous "splinters" of varying length, but hardly with any complete or almost complete scenes amongst them; then probably certain very rough drafts covering long stretches of the action in a sketchy manner. His first step was to get all this material sorted out and, as he wrote to Schiller, "so die Ausführung des Plans, der eigentlich nur eine Idee ist, näher [vorzubereiten]. Nun habe ich eben diese Idee und deren Darstellung wieder vorgenommen und bin mit mir selbst ziemlich einig" (thus to prepare more in detail the execution of the plan, which is really only an idea. And just now I have been tackling this idea and the presentation of it once more, and have more or less made up my mind about it). In this connexion it is to be remembered that he had written over nine years before, on March 1, 1788 in Rome: "Zuerst ward der Plan zu *Faust* gemacht."[6] That "plan" must have been an outline of the whole action of the play, *written down on paper* and included amongst the masses of material in the packet which he was now trying to reduce to order. But it seems to him at this juncture "eigentlich nur eine Idee"—that is to say, too sketchy and summary; what he understands now by a "Plan" is something much more detailed and precise, in fact a systematic scheme, divided up into sections, scene by scene, without any gaps. Nothing is to be left to the chance inspiration of the moment.

That the working out of such a comprehensive scheme was not a simple task that could be completed at the first attempt emerges from the way in which Goethe again and again comes back to it during the succeeding two weeks. On June 23, he noted down in his diary: "Ausführlicheres Schema zum _Faust_" (A more detailed scheme for _Faust_). On June 24, he wrote to Schiller: "Ich werde nur vorerst die grossen erfundenen und halb bearbeiteten Massen zu enden und mit dem, was gedruckt ist, zusammen zu stellen suchen, und das so lange treiben, bis sich der Kreis selbst erschöpft" (To begin with I shall only try to complete the large sections which have been invented and partly worked out and to combine them with what has already appeared in print, and go on doing that until the circle rounds itself off). On July 1, he writes:

> Meinen _Faust_ habe ich, in Absicht auf Schema und Über-sicht, in der Geschwindigkeit recht vorgeschoben, doch hat die deutliche Baukunst die Luftphantome bald wieder ver-scheucht. Es käme jetzt nur auf einen ruhigen Monat an, so sollte das Werk zu mannigfacher Verwunderung und Entset-zen, wie eine grosse Schwammfamilie, aus der Erde wachsen . . . Ich lasse jetzt das Gedruckte wieder abschreiben und zwar in seine Teile getrennt, da denn das Neue desto besser mit dem Alten zusammenwachsen kann.*

About this time, however, the archaeologist Hirt, whom Goethe had known in Rome, turned up in Weimar and distracted Goethe's attention from _Faust_. On July 5, he wrote to Schiller: "_Faust_ ist die Zeit zurückgelegt worden, die nordischen Phantome sind durch die südlichen Reminiszenzen zurückgedrängt worden, doch habe ich das Ganze als Schema und Übersicht sehr umständlich durch-geführt" (_Faust_ has meanwhile been put on one side; the Nordic phantoms have for the time being been crowded out by reminis-cences of the south, but I have worked out the scheme and outline of the whole drama very circumstantially). As there is a gap at this point in Goethe's diaries we do not know whether he resumed

* I have in a short time made considerable progress with my _Faust_, so far as the scheme and overall plan are concerned, but this precise architecture has soon scared away the airy phantoms. All that is needed is a month without dis-tractions, then the work would shoot up out of the earth like a family of fungi, bewildering and shocking quite a lot of people. I am now having the printed text copied out in separate sections, as it will then be all the easier for the new to grow together with the old.

work on *Faust* during the three and a half weeks between the writing of this letter and his departure for Switzerland on July 30, 1797. It is quite likely that he did so. During that journey, however, and on his return to Weimar, his mind was chiefly occupied with other things, and it was not till April 9, 1798 that he settled down seriously to *Faust* again. Meanwhile the laborious task of transcribing all the existing material on separate sheets and filing it in accordance with the new detailed scenario was entrusted to his amanuensis, Geist.

It would not be necessary to give this circumstantial account, were it not for a startling hypothesis advanced in 1953 by Ernst Grumach, one of the principal editors of the new "Akademie" edition of Goethe's work—a hypothesis which is already beginning to be widely accepted and which, if it is correct, completely overthrows our hitherto most firmly established assumptions regarding the development of the *Faust* drama. What is here involved is the date of composition of the all-important "Prolog im Himmel," on which the entire structure of the final text of *Faust* depends. In the Chronology of Goethe's works given by Eckermann and Riemer in 1836–1837—the reliability of which is indeed not always above suspicion—this "Prolog im Himmel" is stated to have been written in 1797, which would mean in the six weeks between the middle of June and the end of July, since those are the only ones of that year in which Goethe worked on *Faust*. For insufficient reasons it has more commonly been assigned to the year 1800, but it was almost universally accepted that neither the conception nor the actual writing of it could be dated *earlier* than 1797. Grumach insists, however, on the strength of his re-examination of a long since known odd sheet of manuscript bearing on one side a transcript of the last twenty-one lines of the "Prolog im Himmel" in Geist's handwriting, and certainly not to be dated later than April, 1798, that the "Grundmotive" (fundamental motifs) of the "Prolog" and probably also a good part of the actual execution belong to Goethe's supposed pre-Strasburg "ältesten Faustplan" of the years 1769–1770. There is no need to go into the extremely intricate details of Grumach's argumentation here. It is enough to notice that it stands or falls by his postulate that the "ausführlicheres Schema zum *Faust*," drafted by Goethe on June 23, 1797, was exactly the same as that with which he was working in April, 1798, and that we have "nicht den geringsten Grund . . . anzunehmen, . . . dass das Schema vom 23. 6. 97 nachträglich erweitert wurde" (not the faintest reason for supposing that the scheme of 23.6.97 was subsequently amplified).[7] Actually we have the strongest reasons for supposing that the scheme of June 23rd was still only provisional and had to be variously amplified in the succeeding week or two, particularly in order to make room for the new conceptions arrived at and partly worked out in those very days. For Goethe was not only engaged in going over and classifying his old *Faust* material in those days, in order to devise a clear plan for the whole. He was also producing new material, certainly the dedicatory poem "Zueignung," written, as his diary testifies, on June 24th, a day *after* the drafting of the first provisional "ausführlicheres Schema," and on strong circumstantial evidence also the first drafts of the "Vorspiel auf dem Theater" and of the "Prolog im Himmel," which is what chiefly concerns us here. All that Grumach's investigations really prove is that the "Prolog im Himmel" was pretty certainly written before July 5, 1797, and quite certainly before May, 1798. That in itself is a very valuable result. But it is not the result Grumach wanted to arrive at and that he would compel us to accept. On the contrary, he says:

> Der Prolog muss jedenfalls ebenso wie der Epilog schon konzipiert gewesen sein, als Goethe seinen Faustplan am 23. Juni 1797 schematisierte. Wer dieser Folgerung ausweichen will, der müsste beweisen, dass der Prolog und d.h. die tragende Idee des Ganzen, in den wenigen Tagen zwischen der Öffnung des Pakets und dem Brief vom 22. Juni 1797 bzw. dem Schema vom 23. Juni konzipiert wurde.*[8]

The flaw in this argumentation is, once more, that it refuses to allow for the possibility that the "ausführlicheres Schema" of June

---

* The Prologue, like the Epilogue, must at all events already have been drafted, when Goethe made the scheme for his *Faust* plan on June 23, 1797. He who would evade this conclusion would have to prove that the Prologue, and that is to say the underlying idea of the whole work, was drafted during the few days between the opening of the packet and letter of June 22 or the scheme of June 23.

23, 1797 may not have been final. Once that possibility is faced, it becomes clear that the "Prolog im Himmel" may very well have been written between June 23, and July 5, 1797, and that is in the opinion of the present writer just the time when it *must* have been written—not later and quite certainly not earlier. Alone on stylistic grounds it is unthinkable that the last twenty-one lines of the "Prolog im Himmel" should have been produced before Goethe went to Strasburg.

An important document that throws light on these problems is the *Faust* synopsis known as "Paralipomenon 1." This used to be dated some time after July, 1799, because it was thought that the concluding phrase: "Epilog im Chaos auf dem Weg zur Hölle" (Epilogue in Chaos on the Way to Hell), must have been inspired by Milton's *Paradise Lost*, which Goethe is known to have looked at in that month. This is a quite inconclusive argument, since, as Burdach points out, Goethe had already in one of his earliest poems, *Poetische Gedanken über die Höllenfahrt Jesu Christi* ("Poetical Thoughts on Jesus Christ's Descent into Hell"), written when he was only sixteen years old, located Hell in Chaos:

> Sie lag entfernt von allem Lichte,
> Erfüllt von Qual im Chaos hier.*

Quite untenable is Scheithauer's assumption that this phrase "Epilog in Chaos auf dem Weg zur Hölle" in "Paralipomenon 1" implies that Faust was to be damned;[9] it implies rather that Faust's soul was to be rescued in the eleventh hour at the very threshold of Hell, which is what we actually do find in the scene "Grablegung" (Interment) at the end of *Faust II. Teil*. "Paralipomenon 1" is quite certainly to be dated in June, 1797. It must have been one of the first jottings Goethe made after deciding to resume work on Faust, in his exertions to devise a satisfactory plan for the whole drama. It is too sketchy to be identified with the "ausführlicheres Schema" of June 23; but it *must* have been written earlier than the scheme finally worked out by July 5th, since it is clearly a *first* attempt to reduce *Faust*—so far as it had actually been written, drafted, or planned by 1797—to a concentrated metaphysical pat-

---

* It lay remote from all light, / Filled with torment, here in Chaos.

tern by means of pregnant, in part Schilleresque (or even Kantian) and for us sometimes cryptic, key words. The sections about which no immediate problems arose are dismissed very succinctly; thus the purport of the entire Gretchen tragedy is summed up in the few words: "Lebens-Genuss der Person von aussen gesehn (I. Teil) in der Dumpfheit Leidenschaft" (Enjoyment of life personally [1st Part] in the passion of blind instinct). The still unwritten Helen of Troy tragedy is envisaged as the complementary opposite of this: "Genuss mit Bewusstsein. Schönheit" (Enjoyment with consciousness. Beauty). The visit to the Emperor's Court—also at this point hardly more than outlined—is summed up as "Taten-Genuss nach aussen" (Enjoyment of activity externally), contrasted with which is the final stage of Faust's earthly career: "Schöpfungs-Genuss von innen" (Enjoyment of creation from within). This mysterious phrase probably adumbrates something similar to the blinded Faust's vision immediately before his death of a thriving community established through his own exertions, as it stands in the final text of Act V of *Faust II*. Wagner and the Student are brought into polarized relationship to one another through the formulae: "Helles, kaltes wissenschaftliches Streben" (Clear, cool, scientific striving) and "Dumpfes, warmes wissenschaftliches Streben" (Unconscious, warm, scientific striving). The "Auerbachs Keller" scene is passed over, and there is nothing corresponding to the scenes which were eventually to fill the great gap in the *Urfaust* and *Faust, ein Fragment*. The development of Faust is seen as running through three ascending stages: "Lebens / Taten / Wesen" (Life / Activity / Essence), of which the two first correspond clearly to Gretchen and the Imperial Court, while the last must correspond to the enigmatic "Schöpfungs-Genuss von innen." Helen of Troy's position in this threefold development is evidently still not decided, except in so far as she, of course, comes *after* Gretchen. The point on which Goethe dwells most in this document is the "Makrokosmus" and "Erdgeist" scene; it is here that he evidently feels his chief problem to lie. The relevant passage runs: "Ideales Streben nach Einwirken und Einfühlen in die ganze Natur. Erscheinen des Geists als Welt- und Tatengenius. Streit zwischen Form und Formlosen [sic]. Vorzug dem formlosen Gehalt vor der leeren Form. Gehalt bringt die Form mit, Form ist nie ohne Gehalt.

Diese Widersprüche, statt sie zu vereinigen, disparater zu machen"
(Ideal striving to enter into union with the whole of nature both
actively and receptively [through feeling]. Appearance of the Spirit
as genius of the world and activity. Conflict between form and the
formless. Preference given to content without form over empty
form. Content brings its form with it. There can be no form without content. These contradictions, instead of being unified, should
be made more disparate). The usually accepted interpretation of
the five phrases from "Streit zwischen Form und Formlosen"
onward is that propounded by Max Morris in his *Goethe-Studien*
of 1898, according to which they refer to the Wagner scene and
indicate a never-carried-out intention on Goethe's part: "Wagner
zu erhöhen" (to raise Wagner) and make him appear as "ein
gleichberechtigter Gegner" (an equipollent adversary) to Faust in
their dispute over rhetoric. But it is out of the question that Goethe
should ever thus have thought of "raising" Wagner, who is from
first to last only very much of a minor figure; no problems arose
about him, and Goethe could be thankful that nothing needed
to be done about that particular scene. Wagner's significance is
exhausted in his inferiority and fatuousness; he is in "Paralipomenon 1" contrasted with the Student as the embodiment of "helles,
kaltes wissenschaftliches Streben," and there was nothing more
than that to be said about him on this occasion. The five phrases
can only apply to the distinction between the Sign of the Makrokosmus, as "Form," with which Faust enters into union through
"Einfühlen," or contemplatively, but from which he turns away
again, feeling it to be "leer," and the Erdgeist, with which, as "dem
Formlosen," he enters into communion through "Einwirken," or
actively, giving the preference to it because of its fulness, its
"Gehalt," its palpable reality. That was the distinction originally
intended between the two symbols when they were first devised,
but it no longer commended itself altogether to Goethe who had,
in his high classical phase and under the influence of Schiller, come
to value "form" a good deal more highly than he had done in his
Storm and Stress years and, consequently, also to find the rigid
distinction between "content" and "form" far too crude. In fact,
the present tendency of his mind was to unite the principles of
form and content, of contemplation and action, of idealism and

realism in a higher synthesis, which would have been fatal, however, to the purposes of the opening scene of Faust, where the hero
was to be faced with an ineluctable choice between these two principles, as symbolized by the Sign of the Makrokosmus and the
Erdgeist. Goethe has to drill it into himself that, whatever his own
personal views on the matter may be, the contrasts in question
should be "made more disparate," instead of being "unified." In
any case those contrasts had, as we have already seen, from the
beginning not been as sharp and clearly recognizable as they should
have been; and now Goethe tends inadvertently to obscure them
still further—as, for example, when he designates the Erdgeist not
only as the "Tatengenius," but also as the "Weltgenius," which
approximates it far too much to the Makrokosmus. Goethe's ultimate solution of this problem was to leave the opening scene exactly as it stood and to provide a new symbolical framework for
the entire drama of Faust. The working out of that new symbolical framework was one of the principal achievements of the summer weeks of 1797; it underlies the detailed scheme which Goethe
then produced. "Paralipomenon 1" must have been written when
Goethe was still struggling with the problems that found their
solutions in that detailed scheme—that is to say, before July 5,
1797—while on terminological and other grounds it is highly improbable that it was written earlier than the opening of the Faust
packet about June 20 of the same year. What we have here then
is his synopsis of Faust, so far as it existed on paper or in his head,
immediately before the working out of the great comprehensive
scheme. But this synopsis, "Paralipomenon 1," begins with Faust's
opening monologue: "Ideales Streben nach Einwirken und Einfühlen in die ganze Natur." It provides indeed for a certain as
yet unwritten "Epilog im Chaos auf dem Weg zur Hölle," but
it does *not* provide for any "Prolog im Himmel." If any part of the
"Prolog im Himmel" had already been in existence or had only
been an element in Goethe's older plans, it would have been bound
to be mentioned in "Paralipomenon 1." The absence of anything
like an allusion to it in that paralipomenon is therefore strong evidence that it indeed was, as it has always been assumed to be, a
new idea of summer, 1797, and that it cannot have been written

before June 22nd of that year. In fact, Eckermann and Riemer were absolutely correct in their dating of the "Prolog."

There is further evidence for the "Prolog im Himmel" probably having been written about this time. In his letter of June 27, 1797, to Schiller (the words are not quoted by Grumach), Goethe wrote: "Ich werde sorgen, dass die Teile anmutig und unterhaltend sind und etwas denken lassen; bei dem Ganzen, das immer ein Fragment bleiben wird, mag mir die neue Theorie des epischen Gedichts zustatten kommen" (I shall see to it that the parts are agreeable and entertaining and give the reader something to think about; so far as the whole, which will always remain a fragment, is concerned, the new theory of the epic poem may come in useful to me). The explanations usually given of this passage are unconvincing. Gräf thinks it refers to Schiller's declaration in a letter of April 21, 1797, "dass die Selbständigkeit seiner Teile einen Hauptcharakter des epischen Gedichts ausmacht" (that the independence of its parts is a chief characteristic of the epic poem). But Goethe says that the new theories of the epic poem that he and Schiller had been working out together during the preceding months is going to be helpful to him not with the "parts" of *Faust*, but "with the whole." It is more probable that Goethe is thinking here of what he had himself written about "das Gesetz der Retardation" (the law of retardation) in the epic poem, in his reply to the letter of Schiller's quoted by Gräf: "dass man von einem guten Gedicht den Ausgang wissen könne, ja wissen müsse. . . . Dadurch erhält die Neugierde gar keinen Anteil an einem solchen Werke und sein Zweck kann . . . in jedem Punkte seiner Bewegung liegen" (that one can and indeed should know the ending of a good poem in advance. Thereby inquisitiveness has no share in such a work, and its purport can lie in every point of its movement). (April 22, 1797) He gives as an example the *Odyssey*, in which we are from the outset and again and again assured by the poet, "dass die Sache einen glücklichen Ausgang haben werde" (that the story will end happily). Now this is just what Goethe himself did for his *Faust*, conferring upon it a pseudo-epical rather than a purely dramatic character, in terms of the definitions here given, when he decided to write the "Prolog im

Himmel" and show from the outset that God himself was on
Faust's side and that therefore, whatever happened, "the story
would end happily." This did not indeed prevent people from still
being uncertain and inquisitive about the ending throughout the
twenty-four years between the publication of *Faust I. Teil* and
Faust II. Teil, although it should have—and Goethe loved to keep
them guessing on the point. If the "Prolog im Himmel" was, as
is here maintained, in the process of being written on June 27,
1797, one can see what Goethe was getting at when he wrote to
Schiller on that day that the "neue Theorie des epischen Gedichts"
was proving useful to him with the *Faust* poem in its totality.

In spite then of Grumach's great authority and prestige we shall
regard ourselves as entitled to reject his theory that the "Prolog
im Himmel" was planned and partly written in 1769–1770, just
as we have already rejected his views that the entire *Faust* is unintelligible except in the light of Welling's *Opus mago-cabbalisticum*
and that the Erdgeist is not really a terrestrial Spirit at all, but one
of Welling's Spirits of the Air, and the "basest of all Spirits." We
adhere to the old view repeatedly endorsed by Goethe himself that
the "Prolog im Himmel" is based directly upon the first chapter
of the Book of Job, in which Satan presents himself before the
Lord, and maintain that Grumach must be more familiar with
Welling than with the Bible, in order to be able to assert that
such phrases as "herrlich wie am ersten Tag" (glorious as on the
first day), or such conceptions as that of the serpent's being cursed
"auf dem Bauche zu gehen und Erde zu fressen" (to go on its
belly and eat dust), have anything specifically theosophical or
cabbalistic about them. Goethe would have been a poor poet, if
he had (as Grumach believes) produced a work, the "ganze Zusam-
menhang" of which is "erst auf dem Hintergrund der Wellingschen
Theosophie voll verständlich" (of which the entire connection is
only fully intelligible against the background of Welling's theos-
ophy).[10] The whole point of the "Prolog im Himmel" is that
Goethe in 1797 at last decided to base his *Faust* no longer on those
private adaptations of obscure theosophico-occult concepts on
which it had hitherto reposed, and to make use instead of the universally known supernatural system of the Bible and Christian

tradition, with its God-Father, its Archangels, its Heaven and its Satan.

In doing this Goethe was in a considerable measure reinstating the specifically Christian postulates of the Faust legend which he had previously not indeed altogether eliminated, but reduced to a bare minimum. This does not mean that he had, as Wehnert and others have suggested, become any more of a Christian during the 1790's than he had been when he wrote the *Urfaust*. He is indeed here found employing Christian theological and cosmological terms, concepts and images, but not as a believer would employ them. They are for him little more than a convenient piece of mythological machinery, into which he can read his own anything but traditional or orthodox meanings, and he treats them throughout ironically. His motive for putting his *Faust* on a quasi-Christian, biblical instead of a pansophical, occultist basis in 1797 is not religious or philosophical, but aesthetic. It was a question of definiteness and intelligibility. In adopting the biblical framework suggested to him by the Book of Job for the "Prolog im Himmel" Goethe was swayed by the same considerations as in adopting the Catholic framework for the closely related epilogue, "Bergschluchten," of which he said: "dass ich bei so übersinnlichen, kaum zu ahnenden Dingen, mich sehr leicht im Vagen hätte verlieren können, wenn ich nicht meinen poetischen Intentionen durch die scharf umrissenen christlich-kirchlichen Figuren und Vorstellungen eine wohltätig beschränkende Form und Festigkeit gegeben hätte" (In dealing with such supersensual, hardly apprehensible things I could easily have lost myself in vagueness, if I had not given my poetic intentions a beneficially confined form and definiteness through the sharply outlined figures and conceptions of the Christian church).[11]

The great change in the plan of *Faust* in 1797 was, in fact, fundamentally only a formal change, a replacing of the originally contemplated complex of symbols and myths with another more lucid, palpable and familiar one, of a private mythology derived largely from the cabbalists with the universally known "mythology" of Christian tradition. It did not involve, beyond this, any radical change in the essential purport of the play or in the conception of Faust's nature and destiny. In that respect, there is no reason for believing that Goethe ever fundamentally changed his mind throughout the sixty years or so of his work on *Faust*. He was concerned from first to last with one and the same particular and extreme manifestation of that "geheimen Punkt . . . , in dem das Eigentümliche unsres Ichs, die prätendierte Freiheit unsres Willens mit dem notwendigen Gang des Ganzen zusammenstösst" (mysterious point where our individuality, the supposed freedom of our will, comes into conflict with the necessary course of the whole).[12] The radical modification of the plan of the drama through the introduction of the mythological machinery derived from the Book of Job was only designed to bring out the original conception more clearly, to solve the problem formulated in "Paralipomenon 1": "Diese Widersprüche, statt sie zu vereinigen, disparater zu machen." That is to say, the dialectic of other-worldly idealism ("Form without content") and this-worldly realism ("Content without form") was to be expressed in more definite and familiar symbols. The other-worldly, ideal sphere, only fleetingly and not sufficiently emphatically presented within the play itself in the Makrokosmus passage, was now to be shadowed forth independently in the "Prolog im Himmel."

This contrast between the idealistic and realistic principles is the theme of the hymn of the Three Archangels with which the "Prolog" opens. The opening stanza, sung by Raphael, gives such a harmonious vision of existence at the cosmic level as Faust has in contemplating the Sign of the Makrokosmus:

> Die Sonne tönt nach alter Weise
> In Brudersphären Wettgesang,
> Und ihre vorgeschriebne Reise
> Vollendet sie mit Donnergang.*

With this is contrasted in the stanzas of Gabriel and Michael the unstable, feverish, incalculable turmoil of existence at the terrestrial level, corresponding to the restless, ruthless activity of the

---

* The sun resounds in ancient wise / In chorus of fraternal spheres, / Completing its pre-ordained journey / With a report of thunder.

Erdgeist, an imposing but also alarming spectacle, in which "Stürme brausen um die Wette" (storms rage for all they are worth) and in which the solemn roll of thunder, at the celestial level only a grand final chord in the music of the spheres, is accompanied by a blazing trail of destruction. But the Archangels, without being able to understand these less reassuring manifestations of the divine power, proclaim their faith in its wisdom and in the order and serenity which, in spite of appearances, must secretly be operative here too, as in the rest of creation. Already here Goethe introduces that symbolism of light and darkness of which he is to make such extensive use in the 1797–1801 stage of his work on *Faust*. On earth, as opposed to the celestial spheres, "Paradieseshelle" (paradisal brightness) alternates with "tiefe, schauervolle Nacht" (deep, horrifying night).

Then Mephisto appears as the Spirit of Negation, without any sense of reverence, and gives *his* comments on earth, that is to say above all on human existence. He has none of the Archangels' confidence in the hidden wisdom of God. He dwells on the discrepancy between man's spiritual aspirations and his physical limitations, telling the Lord that he has badly bungled the creation of earth and humanity. When the Lord points to Faust, just as the God of the Bible does to Job, using of him the same word: "Mein Knecht" (My servant), Mephisto replies that Faust is a particularly good example of that disharmony between the spiritual and the physical which makes man so pitiable and contemptible a creature:

> Vom Himmel fordert er die schönsten Sterne
> Und von der Erde jede höchste Lust—
> Und alle Näh' und alle Ferne
> Befriedigt nicht die tiefbewegte Brust.*

On this basis Goethe's hitherto insoluble problem of bringing Mephisto together with Faust was at last solved. The old, intrac-

---

* From Heaven he demands the most beautiful stars / And from earth every supreme pleasure— / And all that is near and all that is remote / Fails to satisfy his deeply agitated breast.

table idea of having him in some way "given" to Faust by the Erdgeist was abandoned, and instead he was shown as being sent to him *by God himself*. Mephisto, the cynic, who had derided the lofty sentiments even of the angels and refused to take seriously the lofty aspirations of man in general, is particularly contemptuous of the lofty aspirations of this Faust, whom the Lord has singled out as his "Knecht," and declares that, if he is only given a fair chance, he will soon make it appear that there is nothing in them. It is at this point that Goethe introduces the ingenious idea of Mephisto's wager with God, which was to give to his *Faust* the kind of unity he thought appropriate to it. His point of departure was Satan's words to God in the Bible: "But put forth thy hand now, and touch all that he hath, and he will curse thee to thy face." Luther interpolates here freely in his translation the words: "was gilts?" which mean "what is the betting?" and it has been plausibly suggested that this little licence of Luther's put the idea into Goethe's head of making Faust's soul the subject of a wager between Mephisto and the Lord, as he does by putting into Mephisto's mouth the decisive words:

> Was wettet Ihr? Den sollt Ihr noch verlieren!
> Wenn Ihr mir die Erlaubnis gebt,
> Ihn meine Strasse sacht zu führen!*

There were two advantages for Goethe in this. It was calculated to bring a certain element of suspense into the entire drama, though indeed only of factitious suspense, since it was evident enough that God could never lose a wager or even really enter into a wager with the devil: it is only Mephisto who regards it as a genuine wager. The other, more important advantage was that it provided, with the highest biblical precedent, a situation in which God could plausibly be represented as himself more or less commissioning Mephisto to go to Faust and try out his diabolical arts upon him. It appears from what follows that it may well have been part of the Lord's plan with Faust to send Mephisto to him,

---

* What do you bet? You shall yet lose him! / If you give me permission / To conduct him gently along my path.

whether Mephisto had challenged him with the wager or not, for he says:

> Des Menschen Tätigkeit kann allzuleicht erschlaffen,
> Er liebt sich bald die unbedingte Ruh';
> Drum geb ich gern ihm den Gesellen zu,
> Der reizt und wirkt und muss als Teufel schaffen.†

The initiative here is far less with Mephisto than he imagines; he is only a pawn in the Lord's hands.

Through this change of plan the Erdgeist was, as has often been pointed out, deprived of the central function it had originally been intended to fulfil, and made superfluous. Some have wondered why Goethe did not for the sake of consistency eliminate the Erdgeist scene altogether. If there had not been other considerations that were more important to him than mere consistency, this is indeed what he would have felt obliged to do. But he was not going to sacrifice the best part of the *Urfaust* just for consistency's sake, or even to tinker about with it, and so he allowed it to remain as a kind of erratic block, unrelated to what had now become the supernatural structure underlying and framing the multifarious action of the play. One can think of various ways in which he could have smoothed out this inconsistency. He could have introduced somewhere a word or two indicating a relationship or even identity between the Erdgeist and the Herr of the "Prolog"— and in this connexion it is interesting to note that in the well-known Gründgens film of *Faust* the Erdgeist is acted by the same player as the Lord, recognizably showing the same features. On the other hand Goethe could—though it would have been a barbarous thing to do—have brought in some indication that the apparition of the Erdgeist was really only a phantasm engendered by Mephisto, or Mephisto himself in one of his many disguises. Or he could have brought in something to suggest that, although Mephisto is really sent to Faust by the Lord, Faust himself has

---

† Man's activity can all too easily relax; / He soon grows fond of absolute repose; / Therefore I like to give him the companion / Who goads him on and keeps him in a ferment and has to perform the function of the devil.

some definite though mistaken grounds for imagining that he has been sent to him by the Erdgeist. Goethe cannot have failed to see the discrepancy here, and it is inconceivable that he did not at least think of one or the other of these three possibilities for eliminating it. But he was satisfied with bringing in one further allusion to the Erdgeist in the new passage written after 1797 to follow immediately upon the Wagner scene and two in the Pact scene, where Faust refers to "des hohen Geistes Kraft" (the power of the lofty Spirit) and says: "Der grosse Geist hat mich verschmäht" (The great Spirit has spurned me). For the rest, he allowed the Erdgeist simply to disappear out of the play, without any explanation of what it really is or of what relationship it is supposed to stand in to the Lord or to Mephisto, thus providing a problem about which generations of scholars and critics have gone on disputing endlessly. We must assume that Goethe did this not inadvertently and quite deliberately, finding such a discrepancy entirely in keeping with the intentionally nebulous and fantastic character of the drama.

In its opening passages the "Prolog im Himmel" is concerned with the problem of "theodicy." This problem could only sporadically, indirectly, or perfunctorily be raised and discussed in pre-Enlightenment days, when the omnipotence, wisdom, justice, and love of God were sacrosanct tenets, but during the last two hundred years or so it has come to be in one way or another a central theme of all weightier literature. It is a question of the pros and cons of optimism and pessimism, of whether or not life is in spite of everything worth living and has any satisfactory meaning. The favourite German formulation for this is whether we should "say Yes" or "say No" to life—"das Leben bejahen oder verneinen." In the "Prolog," however, this theme is soon narrowed down to the more particular issue, upon which everything else in the drama is made to turn, namely the trustworthiness and self-sufficiency of human nature, especially in its most aspiring, turbulent, and insatiable manifestations, as represented by the outstanding Promethean individual, by the man of genius, by such a man as Faust. What is above all to be noted is the way in which Goethe, in his treatment of this theme, inconspicuously substitutes for the uncompromising ethical and theological postulates of his im-

mediate sources—the Book of Job and the original Faust legend—
a set of totally different, very much less definite and highly ambivalent modern postulates of his own. There is no word or thought
here of "sin" or "sinfulness," least of all of anything in the nature
of "original sin." The old concept of the fall of man is replaced
here by the modern, evolutionary concept of the rise of man. Anything that might seem disconcerting about such a man as Faust is
to be accounted for simply by the fact that he has not yet reached
the highest stage of his destined development; he is as near to perfection as can reasonably be expected of him at his present transitional stage and as God himself desires and intends him to be,
and it would be wrong at this point to expect or demand any more
of him:

> Wenn er mich jetzt auch nur verworren dient,
> So werd ich ihn bald in die Klarheit führen.*

"Verworrenheit" may be seen here as corresponding to what the
Erdgeist stands for, "Klarheit" to what the Makrokosmus stands
for. In other words, what may be called an "idealistic" attitude is
by no means to be rejected altogether, but the necessary condition
for entering upon it properly and without crippling self-depriva-
tion is that one should first of all have fully exploited the possibilities of "realism" with its firsthand experience of everything
through all the senses. This is completely in keeping with Goethe's
own development. It is the process that Wilhelm Meister is represented as going through in his apprenticeship and which is there
summed up in the aphorism: "Der Mensch ist nicht eher glücklich,
als bis sein unbedingtes Streben *sich selbst* seine Begrenzung
bestimmt" (Man is not happy until his unconditional striving
imposes *its own* limits upon itself).[13] It is the process that Faust
goes through when he first loves Gretchen "in der Dumpfheit
Leidenschaft" and then Helena "mit Bewusstsein," as the embodiment of ideal "Schönheit." It is also in keeping with the mentality
of the youthful Storm and Stress Goethe, who again and again
made it clear that he regarded his unbridled voracity for every
kind of excitement in those years only as a transitional stage, upon

---

* Although he now only serves me confusedly, / I will soon lead him to
clarity.

which a move towards self-discipline and order must follow. This essential idea of the "Prolog im Himmel" is clearly enough anticipated as early as 1772 in the essay "Von Deutscher Baukunst": "Wenn dann . . . du gestrebt und gelitten genug hast, und genug genossen, und satt bist irdischer Schönheit, und wert bist auszuruhen in dem Arme der Göttin, . . . [dann] nimm ihn auf, himmlische Schönheit, du Mittlerin zwischen Göttern und Menschen . . ." (When you have then striven and suffered enough and enjoyed enough and are sated with earthly beauty and are worthy to repose in the arm of the goddess, then receive him, celestial Beauty, you mediatrix between the gods and men). What is here put into the mouth of the Lord in the "Prolog im Himmel" is then not any new idea of the 1790's, by which the underlying purport of the Faust drama was essentially modified. It is as old as the *Urfaust* itself. Only now it is brought out more clearly than through the enigmatic symbolism of Faust's choice between Makrokosmus and Erdgeist. Goethe has here acted on his resolution of "Paralipomenon 1": "diese Widersprüche disparater zu machen."

The only quality to which any positive value is attached in the Book of Job is unquestioning submission and resignation to the will of God. Similarly in the original Faust legend humility, meekness, contrition and renunciation of all self-will are taken for granted as the only possible true values, the rejection of which brings about Faust's damnation. Goethe reverses this. The hypothetical, ironical Lord of his "Prolog" attaches no importance at all to any of these qualities, which are not so much as touched upon here, not even by Mephisto. Instead, the qualities to which this God apparently alone assigns any worth are "Streben" (striving) and "Tätigkeit" (activity)—long since favourite words of Goethe and his age and destined from now onward to serve as keywords for Faust's character and destiny. The Lord's chief concern is that man's activity should not relax. Thereby the old issue of good and evil is ruled out as irrelevant or only of secondary importance. All those qualities of unbounded, aspiring, and defiant individualism which had made the traditional Faust so very displeasing in the eyes of the traditional God make him—as manifestations of "activity"—particularly pleasing in the eyes of this new God of the "Prolog im Himmel," and lead to his singling out Faust as his special favourite, his

"Knecht." That is what he wants Faust to be like. That such unconditional activity is bound to have disastrous effects he readily admits: "Es irrt der Mensch, solang er strebt" (Man errs, so long as he strives). But that does not matter. In his eyes it is far better that such a man as Faust should act harmfully than that he should not act at all. What does matter is human greatness: this counts for even more in the eyes of God than it does in those of men. Unlike the God of the New Testament, this God of Goethe's is very much a "respecter of persons." As Kommerell neatly formulates it, "es ergibt sich, dass Faust, indem er nichts von Gott wissen will, diesem am besten gefällt" (It turns out that Faust, by refusing to have anything to do with God, pleases God best).[14]

Here, as so often elsewhere in Faust and throughout his writings, Goethe seems to commit himself irretrievably to a position beyond good and evil. But however much he relativizes good and evil, Goethe always draws the line at rejecting them altogether. And so even here a kind of synthesis is aimed at between the divergent claims of the ethical law and the unconditional self-assertion of the superman. This is found in the much-quoted words of the Lord to Mephisto:

> Nun gut, es sei dir überlassen!
> Zieh diesen Geist von seinem Urquell ab
> Und führ ihn, kannst du ihn erfassen,
> Auf deinem Wege mit herab;
> Und steh beschämt, wenn du bekennen musst:
> Ein guter Mensch in seinem dunklen Drange
> Ist sich des rechten Weges wohl bewusst.*

The sense in which Faust is to be regarded as "ein guter Mensch" has been much debated. That he is not one in the trite sense of the words Goethe himself would scarcely have denied. The whole point about Faust is that he has far too many important things to do and experiences to go through to be able to bother about being good or trying to be good. What seems to be implied is rather that,

---

* Very well then, let it be left in your hands. / Lure this spirit away from its original source / And conduct it, if you can get a hold upon it, / Along your downward path: / And be reduced to shame, when you have to confess / That a good man in his obscure impulse / Is still aware of the right path.

in addition to everything else and in spite of everything else, he still somehow just preserves a rudimentary moral sense. It looks as though he might perhaps even be able to work out his own salvation through his own powers, but this is left open. These are only hints which are not followed up till the very end of *Faust II*. Goethe does not lay all his cards on the table at once.

There is one little problem about the "Prolog im Himmel" which has caused a good deal of trouble. When the Lord gives Mephisto permission to try his arts on Faust, "solang er auf der Erde lebt" (so long as he is living on earth), Mephisto replies:

> Da dank ich Euch; denn mit den Toten
> Hab ich mich niemals gern befangen.
> Am meisten lieb ich mir die vollen, frischen Wangen.
> Für einen Leichnam bin ich nicht zu Haus;
> Mir geht es wie die Katze mit der Maus.†

From this it has often been deduced that Mephisto, quite unlike the devil of tradition, is not in the least concerned with the fate of Faust's soul after death—in fact, that every notion of anything corresponding even symbolically to hell and damnation is here ruled out. Thus Scherer says: "im Prolog . . . gibt es keine Hölle" (in the Prologue there is no hell)[15]—and even Staiger is inclined to agree with him.[16] If this were so, it would constitute a serious contradiction in the Faust drama, in which a symbolical reality of some kind or other is again and again ascribed to hell and damnation: alike in the parts written before 1775—for instance, "Du, Hölle, wolltest dieses Opfer haben!" (Thou, hell, didst demand this sacrifice); in those written between 1797 and 1801—"Vom Himmel durch die Welt zur Hölle" (From Heaven through the world to hell); and in the final act of *Part II*, not written till after 1824—"Der greuliche Höllenrachen tut sich links auf" (The horrifying jaws of hell open on the left). It is difficult to see how any drama of Faust can be written at all, unless some kind of at least

---

† Thank you for that; for I have never liked / Occupying myself with the dead. / What I like best is full, fresh cheeks. / For a corpse I am not at home; / I feel like the cat does with the mouse.

symbolical validity is assigned to the ideas of hell and damnation. The problem here is, however, only an apparent one and arises, like so many others, from the critics insisting on taking the poet's words more literally than they are meant to be taken. In fact, this is yet another case to which Goethe's words of 1827 apply: "Überall sollen wir es mit dem Pinselstriche eines Malers oder dem Worte eines Dichters nicht so genau und kleinlich nehmen" (We ought not everywhere to take the brush-stroke of a painter or the word of a poet so literally or pedantically).[17] Goethe assumed, and had every right to assume, that the traditional ideas of the devil and hell and damnation were too firmly fixed in the minds of all ingenuous readers to be shaken by this playful sally of Mephisto's— for it is just a playful sally and nothing more than that. It could be taken for granted that the devil would not be the devil at all if the ultimate object he pursued were not the damnation of souls with everything that implies. This is assumed by the Lord and by Mephisto here when the latter says of Faust: "Den sollt Ihr noch verlieren!" The only way in which God can *lose* a soul is when that soul is damned; "damnation" and "perdition" are synonymous— both meaning "loss." No particular weight or significance attaches to the Lord's words: "solang er auf der Erde lebt," which are there chiefly because they rhyme with the really important: "Es irrt der Mensch, solang er strebt." That is the standing arrangement between God and the devil in these matters in any case: the Lord cannot concede anything less or anything more to Mephisto than that he should be allowed to tempt Faust so long as he lives. Mephisto cannot demand anything more, nor anything less. If Goethe had wanted to suggest here a system utterly opposed to all traditional conceptions, he would have had to indicate it very much more explicitly and consistently than anybody can represent him as having done in this passage. However ironically Goethe treats the supernatural ideas of Christianity, however much he plays fast and loose with their original spiritual significance, he still preserves all their external features intact. It is only with living human beings that Mephisto can play the game of cat and mouse in which he glories; once they are dead, their souls are either in Heaven or Purgatory and beyond his reach, or in hell, where that particular

game can no longer be played with them. It is in this sense that
Mephisto's words are understood by Paul Valéry, whose *Mon Faust*
is a kind of whimsical and arbitrary commentary on Goethe's *Faust*.
Valéry's Méphistophèles says: "Que ferais-je d'un mort? Un défunt
est pour moi une chose finie" (What can I do with a corpse? When
a man is dead, the affair is settled, so far as I am concerned). This
point is important because the Higher Critics have tried to demonstrate one of their beloved contradictions between the "Prolog im
Himmel" and the rest of *Faust*, especially the Pact scene, which is
in reality most closely co-ordinated with it.

There is one other phrase in the "Prolog" which calls for comment. In giving Mephisto permission to do his utmost with Faust
the Lord says to him, as has been seen: "Zieh diesen Geist von
seinem Urquell ab." The "original source" (*Urquell*) of Faust's
spirit, as of the human spirit in general, can, of course, only be
the higher, celestial world represented by the Archangels and by the
Lord himself, in accordance with Goethe's own declaration quoted
above: "Der Mensch, wie sehr ihn auch die Erde anzieht . . . , fühlt
. . . tief und klar in sich, . . . dass er ein Bürger jenes geistigen Reiches
sei."[18] To be "lured away from one's original source" is, then, to
lose the consciousness of one's heavenly provenance and to feel
oneself only as belonging to this earth. Faust, who has hitherto
been torn between desires for "die schönsten Sterne *vom Himmel*"
and for "jede höchste Lust *von der Erde*," is henceforward to be
devoted to earthly pleasures only and to forget the stars of Heaven.
The usual interpretation is that the Lord is here challenging
Mephisto to lure Faust's spirit away from its celestial origins, as
to an undertaking that he will find impossible and the achieving
of which would amount to the winning of his wager. It is here
suggested, however, that these words should be understood not as
a part of the Lord's challenge to Mephisto, but as a part of the
general permission he gives him to do his worst. Mephisto may lure
Faust away from his celestial origins; the Lord will not prevent
him from doing that, will not intervene with his protecting providence, or do anything specially to remind Faust of the divine side
of his nature. Even then, when Faust has been reduced to the
purely earthly, realistic level, when God has withdrawn his guiding

hand from him, Mephisto will find in him a last insuperable residue of decency, of sense for what is right. It fits in with this interpretation that we are in the opening scenes of *Faust I. Teil* shown the actual process by which Faust is gradually lured away from his celestial origins—the first stage in that process being his turning towards the Erdgeist, the last stage being the interruption of his translation of the Bible by Mephisto in poodle form. From that moment onward the higher, celestial side of his nature is in abeyance. With the words: "Zieh diesen Geist von seinem Urquell ab," the Lord is in fact giving Mephisto *carte blanche* and promising not to thwart his designs. This is important for the question whether Faust's love for Gretchen is a part of Mephisto's plan or runs counter to it. If it is the unambiguously divine and holy experience that so many critics make it out to be, then the Lord has broken his bargain to leave matters entirely in Mephisto's hands and let him conduct Faust gently along his own downward path. It is not the Lord, but Mephisto, who brings Faust together with Gretchen.

It is worth noting that the popular German Faust stage-plays and puppet-plays usually began with a "Prologue in Hell," in which Satan, Lucifer, or "Pluto" sends Mephistophiles to tempt Faust, a motif regularly taken over in eighteenth-century literary adaptations of the Faust story—for example, by Lessing and by Schink. This traditional "Prologue in Hell" may well have had some share in suggesting to Goethe the idea of his own "Prolog im Himmel," though, of course, nothing like so important or direct a share as the Book of Job.

The "Prolog im Himmel" closes with the endearingly irreverent words spoken by Mephisto when he is left alone after the Lord and the Angels have vanished:

> Von Zeit zu Zeit seh ich den Alten gern
> Und hüte mich, mit ihm zu brechen.
> Es ist gar hübsch von einem grossen Herrn,
> So menschlich mit dem Teufel selbst zu sprechen.*

---

* From time to time I like to see the old fellow / And take care not to break off relations with him completely. / It is awfully nice of such a great gentleman / To talk so humanly even with the devil.

We are hereby prepared for the descent to the earthly, human plane, which is the essential plane of the drama's action.

The "Prolog im Himmel" is preceded by the poem "Zueignung," which is known with certainty to have been written on June 24, 1797, and by the "Vorspiel auf dem Theater," which was in all probability written within the same summer weeks. There is little to be added here to what has already been said about these two productions in the chapter on the "Chronology and Unity of Goethe's Faust."[19] They are less integral to the plan of the drama than the "Prolog" and deal chiefly with the tension between Goethe as he had been when the *Urfaust* was written and as he was about 1797, between his earlier Shakespearean, Storm and Stress outlook on poetry and his subsequent classical ideals. Grumach's theory that the detailed scheme for *Faust* was completed by June 23, 1797 at the latest and underwent no subsequent amplifications, compels him to assume that Goethe first planned some kind of dedicatory poem in cold blood and only a day or two later set about writing it—a very unnatural assumption.[20] "Zueignung" is one of Goethe's finest poems and bears all the marks of being an unforeseen, spontaneous lyrical effusion, produced on the spur of the moment, and whatever detailed scheme Goethe may have arrived at by June 23rd must have needed to be amplified to accommodate it. We know, however, that the scheme, as it was in the end worked out, certainly by April 9, 1798, and probably by July 5, 1797, provided with its thirty headings for a certain symmetry between the beginning and the end, with an "Epilog im Himmel" to correspond to the "Prolog im Himmel," a farewell speech addressed to the audience by one of the actors under the title "Abkündigung" to correspond to the "Vorspiel auf dem Theater" and a valedictory poem ("Abschied") in *ottava rima* stanzas to correspond to "Zueignung." This valedictory poem was actually written and "Abkündigung" was drafted, at some unspecifiable point of time between summer, 1797 and spring, 1801; Goethe eventually decided to suppress them both, but they are preserved amongst his Faust Paralipomena. (Quotations from them will be found above in Chapter 2.)[21] The place of the projected "Epilog im Himmel" was taken by "Bergschluchten," which is not explicitly designated as an "epilogue" and is enacted not in "Heaven" proper, but in a nebulous transitional domain between Earth and Heaven, and also in other respects presents fewer close parallels to the "Prolog" than Goethe presumably at first contemplated. Grumach's theory that Goethe in April, 1800, decided to substitute for the previously projected "Epilog im Himmel" an "Epilog im Chaos auf dem Weg zur Hölle," reposes on Max Morris's untenable dating of "Paralipomenon 1" in that month and can be ignored.[22]

It is usually and quite rightly assumed that Schiller influenced Goethe a good deal in the work he did on *Faust* between 1797 and 1801. In informing Schiller on June 22, 1797 of his intention to take *Faust* up again, Goethe indeed openly asked him for suggestions and advice: "Nun wünschte ich aber, dass Sie die Güte hätten, die Sache einmal, in schlafloser Nacht, durchzudenken, mir die Forderungen, die Sie an das Ganze machen würden, vorzulegen und so mir meine eignen Träume, als ein wahrer Prophet, zu erzählen und zu deuten" (Now I wish you would have the kindness to think the matter over some time when you cannot sleep at night and set before me the demands that you would make upon the work in its totality, thus narrating and interpreting my own dreams to me, like a true prophet).

On July 11 Schiller came to Weimar for a week and undoubtedly Goethe and he talked a good deal about *Faust* together on that occasion—possibly in detail. But by then Goethe had already worked out his exact scheme and written not only "Zueignung," but also—it may be assumed on the grounds here advanced—the "Vorspiel" and "Prolog." During those decisive weeks he and Schiller communicated with one another only by letters, all of which are known to us. There is nothing in those letters on points of detail, and what they contain on questions of general principle does not indicate that Schiller directly influenced or even tried to influence Goethe's procedure at this juncture. His most important utterances occur in his letter of June 23rd in which he singles out the conflict of "das Göttliche und Physische im Menschen" (the divine and the physical in man) as the problem on which everything turns in *Faust* and goes on: "Kurz, die Anfoderungen an den *Faust* sind zugleich philosophisch und poetisch, und Sie mögen sich

wenden, wie Sie wollen, so wird Ihnen die Natur des Gegenstandes
eine philosophische Behandlung auflegen, und die Einbildungs-
kraft wird sich zum Dienst einer Vernunftidee bequemen müssen"
(In short, the demands made upon the *Faust* drama are both
philosophical and poetic, and however you may try to get round it,
the nature of the theme will force a philosophical treatment on
you, and your imagination will have to submit to serving an intellectual idea). Schiller had not forgotten how ill Goethe had
taken it less than a year previously, when he had too readily offered
him suggestions and advice about the completion of *Wilhelm
Meisters Lehrjahre,* and he was evidently here playing for safety.
He knew quite well that what he was here saying about the philosophical implications of the Faust theme would not be new or
displeasing to Goethe, although the general principle involved was
one on which it was almost a point of honour for them to differ
and engage in friendly disputes. Indeed he went on: "Aber ich
sage Ihnen damit schwerlich etwas Neues, denn Sie haben diese
Foderung in dem, was bereits da ist, schon in hohem Grade zu
befriedigen angefangen" (But what I am saying is hardly anything
new to you, for you have in what is already written begun to satisfy
this demand in a high degree). *Faust I. Teil* is not at bottom any
more "philosophical" than the *Urfaust* had been; it only brings
out the metaphysical implications of the *Urfaust* more amply and
lucidly. That may, however, be ascribed in good part to Schiller's
influence. In their references to *Faust* in their further letters up
to July 5, 1797, the two poets both stick to generalizations and keep
on saying how much they are in agreement with one another.
Schiller comes nearest to saying something definite when he speaks
on June 26, of the "grosse Schwierigkeit, zwischen dem Spass und
dem Ernst glücklich durchzukommen" (great difficulty of steering
one's way successfully between humour and seriousness) in *Faust*
and continues:"Der Teufel behält durch seinen Realism vor dem
Verstand, und der Faust vor dem Herzen Recht. Zuweilen aber
scheinen sie ihre Rollen zu tauschen und der Teufel nimmt die
Vernunft gegen den Faust in Schutz. / Eine Schwierigkeit finde ich
auch darin, dass der Teufel durch seinen Charakter, der realistisch
ist, seine Existenz, die idealistisch ist, aufhebt" (The Devil is
through his realism in the right for the understanding, Faust is in

the right for the heart. But sometimes they seem to exchange rôles and the Devil takes the side of reason [idealism] against Faust. I also find it a difficulty that the Devil, through his character, which is realistic, cancels out his existence, which is imaginary). Schiller's indirect influence on *Faust* at this stage was very great. This was the time when Goethe's mind was most strongly dominated by Schiller's ideas, his thought most strongly permeated with Schilleresque categories. But there is no evidence that Schiller exercised any decisive direct influence on the Faust scheme of summer, 1797, and it seems quite certain that he had no share in inspiring the "Prolog im Himmel," which is what matters most. We must suppose that Goethe quite spontaneously hit upon the idea of adapting the opening chapter of the Book of Job to the purposes of his *Faust* in June, 1797, and that that discovery, more than anything else, made it possible for him to resume the work and complete Part I.

On May 5, 1798 Goethe wrote to Schiller: "Meinen *Faust* habe ich um ein Gutes weiter gebracht. Das alte, noch vorrätige, höchst konfuse Manuskript ist abgeschrieben und die Teile sind in abgesonderten Lagen, nach den Nummern eines ausführlichen Schemas hintereinandergelegt. Nun kann ich jeden Augenblick der Stimmung nutzen, um einzelne Teile weiter auszuführen und das Ganze früher oder später zusammenzustellen" (I have made good progress with my *Faust*. The old extremely confused manuscript, which is still in existence, has been copied out and the sections have been arranged in separate files according to the numbers of a detailed scheme. Now I can make use of every moment when I am in the right mood for it, to work out the individual sections and sooner or later to put the whole together). How far the "ausführliches Schema" which he here speaks of is identical with that arrived at by July 5, 1797 is uncertain. He had taken *Faust* up again on April 8, 1798, and continued to work at it intermittently till April, 1801. During those three years he not only almost completed *Faust I. Teil* as we know it, but also wrote (in 1800) the opening scene of the Helena episode and an early, no longer extant version of the final scene or scenes of *Part II*. After April, 1801, his interest flagged, probably as a result of the serious illness he had recently gone through. In June, 1805, he decided to publish *Part I* by itself,

and in March and April, 1806, he was busy revising it and preparing
it for the press. In those weeks he at last completed the "Valentin"
scene, rounded off the "Walpurgisnacht" and very lightly revised
"Trüber Tag.   Feld," keeping it, however, in prose. This is the
only real work on Faust that he is known to have done between
spring, 1801, and February, 1825. The text then established was still
defective: the highly important "Disputation" scene was still missing and so also was the part of the "Walpurgisnacht" scene in
which Faust was to have beheld Satan on the summit of the
Brocken. The loose, deliberately incoherent construction of *Faust*
prevents us from missing these episodes, of which we only know
from the paralipomena. The manuscript of *Faust I. Teil* was
handed over to the publisher Cotta in May, 1806, but owing to the
disturbances occasioned by the battle of Jena (October 14, 1806)
and Napoleon's occupation of Germany it did not appear till
spring, 1808. It soon created a great sensation, not only in Germany,
but all over Europe. Goethe, who had hitherto been known above
all as the author of *Werther*, now came to be known as the author
of *Faust*.

Once Goethe had in the "Prolog im Himmel" found his new
and more satisfactory solution for the problem of explaining how
the devil, without ever being actually invoked by Faust, nevertheless comes to him, the filling out of the "grosse Lücke" presented
only minor difficulties. The opening scene was continued with a
further monologue in which Faust, immediately after Wagner's
departure, is reduced to such despair through his failure with the
Erdgeist that he decides to commit suicide and is only at the last
moment deterred from doing so by the sound of the first Easter
bells. It is possible to interpret this as the last occasion on which the
Lord intervenes to guide Faust's destiny, before giving Mephisto
permission to "lure him away from his original source." At this
point Goethe puts into Faust's mouth some words which can
hardly be regarded as felicitous:

> Zu jenen Sphären wag ich nicht zu streben,
> Woher die holde Nachricht tönt.*

* I dare not strive towards those spheres / Whence the gracious tidings
sound.

It is surely incongruous that the audacious superman, Faust, whose striving otherwise knows no limits, should, as he himself puts it, not dare to strive towards that which his despised inferiors, the most ordinary people, all strive after, and which in any case, as he must know, can only be striven after with entirely different qualities from "daring." It is difficult to see any other explanation for this incongruity (which worries extremely few of the commentators) than that it must have been due to a moment of carelessness on Goethe's part. More to the point is Faust's explicit declaration here that he no longer believes in Christian teaching, as he had done in his youth: "Die Botschaft hör ich wohl, allein mir fehlt der Glaube" (I hear the message, indeed, but I have no faith). Even this turns out, however, to be the expression rather of one of his fluctuating moods than of an irrevocable intellectual decision: before he finally engages himself to Mephisto he is to experience something in the nature of a renewal of Christian belief. But the effect that the Easter bells have on him is very different from that which they are intrinsically intended to have on mankind. Instead of arousing in him the sense of being a citizen of another, higher world, they revive and strengthen his attachment to this world. "Die Träne quillt, die Erde hat mich wieder" (My tears flow, earth has me once more).

Upon this follows the "Spaziergang vor dem Tor," which is on insufficient grounds supposed by some to have been written at least in part before 1775. It is throughout in language and spirit— though, of course, not in form—completely characteristic of the classical Goethe of the later 1790's. From the confined atmosphere of the Gothic study in which Faust had appeared always alone or with one sole companion, and to which we must soon return again for a long stretch, we are here, a welcome contrast and relief, transported into the open air, to the countryside before the walls of Wittenberg. After the introspective broodings of an exceptional individual, isolated by his strange powers, aspirations, visions, and despair, we are given a broad panorama of everyday human life, as represented by such timeless types as the three apprentices, the two servant-girls, the two students, the older citizens, the beggar, the middle-class girls, the soldier, the old fortune-telling crone, and

the peasants—all of them enjoying in festive mood the first sun-
shine of spring on Easter day. We are prepared here too for the
"kleine Welt" (little world) to which Gretchen belongs. This is
the only scene from beginning to end of both parts of *Faust* in
which the human average, the stable continuity of life is presented
as such. The clarity, mellowness, warmth, and kindly irony with
which this world of blessed ordinariness is here evoked remind
one again and again of that most un-Faustian of all Goethe's major
works, *Hermann und Dorothea,* which he completed shortly before
deciding to resume work on *Faust* in June, 1797.

Into this throng of simple, straightforward people Faust enters,
accompanied by Wagner. After all the violent extremes through
which he had passed during the previous night he is now temporarily in a serener state of mind, attuned to the Easter gaiety around
him. Characteristically he gives to this Easter gaiety a secular,
pagan, this-worldly interpretation:

> Jeder sonnt sich heute so gern.
> Sie feiern die Auferstehung des Herrn,
> Denn sie sind selber auferstanden . . .
> Aus der Kirchen ehrwürdiger Nacht
> Sind sie alle ans Licht gebracht.*

But his aspiring spirit is roused again by the spectacle of the
setting sun; he wishes he could fly and follow it on its westward
course. This gives Goethe the opportunity to introduce that almost
too explicit formula, which is so much quoted, and which links
up directly with Mephisto's contemptuous description of Faust's
dualistic nature in the "Prolog im Himmel":

> *Zwei Seelen wohnen, ach! in meiner Brust,*
> Die eine will sich von der andern trennen:
> Die eine hält in derber Liebeslust

---

* Everybody likes to sun himself to-day; / They are celebrating the Resur-
rection of the Lord, / For they themselves are resurrected . . . / Out of the
venerable night of the churches / They have all been brought out into the
light.

>Sich an die Welt mit klammernden Organen;
>Die andre hebt gewaltsam sich vom Dust
>Zu den Gefilden hoher Ahnen.†

In speaking thus of his supramundane ancestry Faust is almost for the last time expressing a sense of that "Urquell" of which the Lord had spoken in the "Prolog" and from which Mephisto is to lure him away. The time is coming when he will try to live only from his earthly soul, which "clings to the world in gross, sensual desire." But now, in the upsurging of the divine side of his nature, Faust goes on to invoke whatever spirits there may be hovering between earth and heaven:

>O gibt es Geister in der Luft,
>Die zwischen Erd' und Himmel herrschend weben,
>So steiget nieder aus dem goldnen Duft
>Und führt mich weg zu neuem, buntem Leben!*

This is in no sense at all a magical incantation; it is really nothing more than a poetic outburst of intense feeling; but it is the signal, the pretext for that mischievous Spirit, Mephisto, who happens at that moment to be hovering between Heaven and earth, to put in his appearance. He does this in the guise of a black poodle which seems uncanny to Faust, but perfectly normal to Wagner. Goethe links up here with his old plan in the *Urfaust* that Mephisto should appear to him in "Hundsgestalt" (form of a dog) ("Trüber Tag. Feld"), though none of the other points envisaged in that early scene are here reproduced.[23] While the scene very likely incorporates various earlier "splinters," there is no reason for supposing that this final part or any other part of it was actually written before 1798.

---

† *Two souls, alas, reside within my breast;* / The one wishes to detach itself from the other: / The one clings to the world in gross, sensual desire / With prehensile organs; / The other raises itself vehemently from the dust / To the domains of its lofty forebears.

* O if there are Spirits in the air / Who hover exercising power between Heaven and earth, / Descend from the golden haze / And conduct me to a new, many-coloured life!

Satisfied that there is after all nothing abnormal about this stray poodle, Faust takes it home with him, and we see him in the next scene ("Studierzimmer I") back in his room in a serene and almost devout frame of mind, embarking on the task of translating St. John's Gospel into German. The sense of his celestial ancestry, of his "Urquell" is still strong in him and manifests itself in a quasi-Christian form. He feels his heart moved by "die Menschen-liebe" (the love of mankind) and even by "die Liebe Gottes" (the love of God):

> Vernunft fängt wieder an zu sprechen,
> Und Hoffnung wieder an zu blühn,
> Man sehnt sich des Lebens Bächen,
> Ach! nach des Lebens Quelle hin.†

This is something very much more temperate and spiritual than his wild clamouring for the breasts of nature as the "Quellen alles Lebens" in the opening monologue; he seems here to be almost ready to accept the Christian answer to the question: "was die Welt im Innersten zusammenhält." But again and again he is disturbed in these sage meditations by the rushing about and growling of the poodle: Mephisto is attempting to lure him away from his original source. When he feels his old restlessness and discontent coming over him again, Faust fights against them:

> Doch dieser Mangel lässt sich ersetzen,
> Wir lernen das Überirdische schätzen,
> Wir sehnen uns nach Offenbarung,
> Die nirgends würd'ger und schöner brennt
> Als in dem Neuen Testament.*

With his characteristic, ingrained realism he boggles, however, at the opening verse of St. John's Gospel and decides to render it: "In the beginning was the *Deed*" ("Im Anfang war die *Tat*")

---

† Reason begins to speak again, / Hope to blossom again; / One longs for the streams of life, / Alas! for the source of life.

* But there is a remedy for this shortcoming; / We learn to appreciate the supramundane. / We long for revelation, / Which nowhere shines with more dignity or beauty / Than in the New Testament.

instead of: "In the beginning was the *Word*," thereby reinforcing his former decision in favour of the Erdgeist, which corresponds to "the Deed" as against the Sign of the Makrokosmus, which corresponds to "the Word." At this point he has to stop because the barking and howling of the poodle become quite intolerable— whether because Faust is falsifying the Bible or because he is reading it at all, is left uncertain and need not much concern us.

The rest of the scene is sheer grotesque comedy and spectacle, indulged in for its own sake, and contains only one passage—but that a very important one—which has any bearing on the deeper significance of the play. No scene in the whole of *Faust,* except "Auerbachs Keller," owes so much to the old chapbooks and works on magic as this one does. Goethe was concerned to bring in at this point as much as he could of the old apparatus and atmosphere of magic and mysterious apparitions traditionally associated with the Faust legend, while contriving everything in such a way that Faust should still not actually invoke the devil, as his prototype had done. Whereas in the opening monologue magic had been reinterpreted symbolically in terms of Goethe's own modern pantheism, it is here presented ironically. The poodle goes through all sorts of transformations and antics. Faust tries exorcising it, first of all on the assumption that it is a spirit of one of the four elements, which involves the possibility of its being perhaps an "earth spirit" in the old, conventional, folklore sense of the word, very different from the great Erdgeist of the opening monologue, a kind of "Kobold" (hobgoblin) or "Incubus." When all this fails it is clear to Faust that the poodle can only conceal a "Geist der Hölle" (a spirit of hell), and he conjures it accordingly with a crucifix and with a threat of the sacred name of the Trinity. This is the nearest Goethe's Faust ever comes to invoking the devil, and it is not substantially different from what a devout priest might be supposed to perform in his capacity as an exorcist. It has a startling effect. The poodle swells to the size of an elephant and than turns into a vapour. We are prepared for something terrible, something unspeakable, but Mephisto steps jauntily out of the vapour in the guise of a strolling student with the mocking words: "Wozu der Lärm? was steht dem Herrn zu Diensten?" (What is all the fuss

about? What can I do for the gentleman?) This is an excellent
example of humour as Kant defines it: "die plötzliche Verwandlung
einer gespannten Erwartung in nichts" (The sudden transformation of a high-pitched expectation into nothing). We realise
that Mephisto has appeared very much less because of Faust's
incantations and the power they have over him than because the
Lord has in any case sent him, and that he has entered into the
spirit of this magical hocus-pocus in good part ironically: the laws
of magic require of him indeed that he should go through all these
performances, but he does not take those laws any more seriously
than he takes the rest of existence.

The scene becomes more earnest for a moment, when Mephisto,
in reply to Faust's questions, gives the famous definitions of himself
as:

> "Ein Teil von jener Kraft,
> Die stets das Böse will und stets das Gute schafft—"*

and as: "der Geist, der stets verneint" (the Spirit that always
denies). These declarations are to be seen and understood in the
light of Goethe's lifelong will to see "evil" (in all the various
senses given to that word) as something at bottom after all not so
very alarming, as something that can be reduced to manageable
proportions and about which we therefore need not be anything
like so worried as Christianity or the kind of austere idealism
represented by Kant and Schiller maintains that we should be.[24] As
early as 1771 Goethe had written in his *Rede zum Schäkespeares
Tag*: "Das, was wir bös nenne, ist nur die andere Seite vom Guten
...." The same idea underlies Mephisto's definition of himself here.
For purposes of clarity Goethe has assigned to him in these words
a deeper insight into his positive cosmic function than it is strictly
appropriate for him to have. Mephisto then goes on to explain
in terms of the symbolism of Light and Darkness introduced in the
"Prolog im Himmel" that the "Kraft" of which he is a "Teil" is
"die Finsternis" (Darkness), "die Mutter Nacht" (the Mother
Night), the primaeval chaos. He regards it as his special mission to

---

* A part of that power / Which always desires evil and always brings about
good.

demonstrate that all creation is a miserable mistake and "wert, dass es zugrunde geht" (deserves to perish). This makes of him the Spirit of Negation, of pessimism, of nihilism, or, as Faust contemptuously puts it: "des Chaos wunderlicher Sohn" (the strange son of Chaos). In expounding all this, however, Mephisto never ceases to be the mocker who makes fun not only of everybody and everything else, God included, but also of himself. This is in keeping with that attitude of Goethe's which Scherer not infelicitously sums up in the words: "Das Böse ist nur lächerlich, es ist nicht gefährlich" (Evil is merely ridiculous, not dangerous).[25]

It would have been the obvious thing for Goethe, once he had thus succeeded in bringing Mephisto and Faust face to face, to proceed immediately to the concluding of the pact between them. For reasons that we can recognise he did not, however, do this. Faust had been shown here in too serene and confident a frame of mind, and given too much the ascendancy over Mephisto, for the purposes of the pact as Goethe envisaged it. The scene was therefore terminated in the ironical, almost burlesque tone which had hitherto predominated in it, with more magical hocus-pocus in the course of which Mephisto is shown as held captive by a mystical pentagram and making his escape with the help of his ministering spirits and a rat, resolved to postpone further attempts on Faust till circumstances are less disadvantageous for him. He has, however, at least succeeded in putting the idea of a pact with the devil into Faust's head. Taking a hint probably from the question asked by the Faust of the 1725 chapbook: "Ob die Teufel auch eine Ordnung und Regiment wie weltliche Fürsten unter sich haben" (whether the devils have an order and government amongst themselves like earthly princes), Goethe has devised a fantastic situation in which Faust can plausibly say to Mephisto:

> Die Hölle selbst hat ihre Rechte?
> Das find ich gut, da liesse sich ein Pakt,
> Und sicher wohl, mit euch, ihr Herren, schliessen?*

It was evidently important to Goethe that the first suggestion of

* Has even hell its rules and regulations? / I find that good! Then it would be possible / To conclude a pact with you gentry, and a reliable one too?

a pact should thus be made by Faust himself, not by Mephisto.
All Mephisto does now, however, is to assure Faust in a general
way that he can be relied upon to keep any bargain he may make
with him and to insist that all further discussion of the question
shall be deferred to some later occasion.

Only one scene remains to be dealt with of those with which
the great gap in the *Urfaust* and *Faust, ein Fragment* was filled,
the actual Pact scene, "Studierzimmer II," from the point of view
of the underlying idea and inner structure of the play the most
important of them all. It is not really a complete scene, but only
the first half of a scene, the other half being constituted by the
fragmentary scene constructed by Goethe in 1788 or 1789 around
the old isolated dialogue between Mephisto and the Student. It
has already been pointed out[26] that that fragmentary scene began
half way through a quatrain, and various arguments were advanced
against those critics who find evidence in this for the entire Pact
scene, or at least the passage embodying the actual pact, having
also been written in 1788 or 1789 and then suppressed for some
reason when the text of the *Fragment* was prepared for the press.
The issue involved here is, whether the Pact scene was written
before or after the "Prolog im Himmel" and, still more important,
whether these two scenes are consistent with one another or not.

Almost the only points that the pact between Goethe's Faust
and Mephisto has in common with the corresponding pact in the
Faust legend is that Faust signs it with his blood (a theatrical
flourish with no deeper significance), and that Mephisto's object
is to gain possession of Faust's soul after his death. The first thing
to note about it is that it is not really a pact at all, but a wager
offered by Faust and accepted by Mephisto, whereby an element
of uncertainty and dramatic suspense is introduced, as by the
wager between Mephisto and the Lord in the "Prolog im Himmel."
These two wagers, although not another word is heard of either of
them until the very end of *Faust II. Teil*, hold the entire farraginous
work together and constitute in conjunction with one another such
unity as it has. Those critics, however, who maintain on quite
insufficient grounds that Mephisto in the "Prolog im Himmel"
disavows or renounces all interest in the fate of Faust's soul after
his death,[27] find an irreconcilable contradiction between these two

wagers—a contradiction only to be accounted for by Goethe's having written one of the relevant passages (probably that in the Pact scene) so much earlier than the other, that during the interval his original plan was forgotten or changed. This view is to be most energetically rejected. The two wagers are quite clearly geared to one another and are as consistent with one another as Goethe himself, who knew what he was getting at, saw any necessity for making them, and in *both* it is a question of whether Faust's soul is to belong after his death to Mephisto or to the Lord. One of the two wagers must have arisen out of and been suggested by the other, and it is far more probable that the Pact scene was written some time after 1797, with the "Prolog im Himmel" as point of departure, than that it was written as early as 1788 or 1789. If we do not postulate that the two wagers, whatever difficulties may arise about them, *must* be reconcilable with one another, there is something wrong with our own minds and we have no right to pronounce any judgments on *Faust*.[28]

Not only has Goethe substituted a wager for the traditional hard-and-fast pact between Faust and Mephisto: he has also, as in his manipulation of the Book of Job in the "Prolog im Himmel," completely eliminated the clear-cut, uncompromising religious and ethical issues of the original Faust legend and put in their place something so impalpable and ambivalent that one is tempted to find it merely vague and almost meaningless. In the old legend Faust had solemnly undertaken to forswear God and the heavenly hosts, to be the enemy of all men, especially the clergy, to abjure church-going and matrimony, and, in some versions, never to cut his hair or his nails. It had been a question here of his relationship to what exists objectively outside himself and independently of himself, particularly to God and his fellow men. In his radical subjectivization of the Faust theme Goethe has, as we shall see, made everything turn solely upon Faust's relationship to *himself*, and so far as any religious or ethical principles are implied, they remain very shadowy, and the only thing one can say of them with certainly is that they are fundamentally different from those underlying the original legend.

The never-written "Disputation" scene was probably intended to stand between the first and second "Studierzimmer" scenes.

In this Mephisto, still in the guise of a strolling student, would
have been shown engaged with Faust in a formal academic debate
on the relative merits of first-hand experience and intuitive vision
or imagination; and it is surprising to find that in this debate, which
would have turned upon virtually the same issue of action and
contemplation as the opening monologue, Faust was to have
spoken as the champion not of experience, as one would have
expected, but of intuitive vision, symbolized by the "schaffende
Spiegel" (the creative mirror). That is to say, his higher, idealistic
soul was still, or once more, to have been in the ascendancy, as in
"Studierzimmer I." What matters to us, however, is that at the
beginning of the Pact scene, "Studierzimmer II," the situation
between Faust and Mephisto appears to be the exact reverse of that
in "Studierzimmer I." It had to be so for Goethe's purposes, and
that is presumably the chief reason why he gives us two distinct
"Studierzimmer" scenes separated from one another by an unspecified interval of time, instead of attempting to develop the pact
directly out of the first encounter of the two participants. This
time it is Faust who is the pessimist, sceptic, cynic, and nihilist.
He is once more in a mood of blackest depression and disillusionment, for which no explanation is given beyond the disappointment
caused him by Mephisto's escape. Scherer characteristically sees in
this "ein Fehler des Dramas, so wie es uns vorliegt" (a flaw in the
drama, as it stands).[29] It would perhaps have been more definitely
motivated, if the "Disputation" scene had ever been written. But
it is in any case quite in keeping with the extreme lability of
Faust's nature. In this despair Faust pronounces his famous curse
upon existence in all its aspects—spiritual and material alike—and
renounces all lofty spiritual aspirations. Mephisto, on the other
hand, who turns up this time in the guise of a dashing young
nobleman, becomes the defender of "die schöne Welt" (the beautiful world) and praises the joys and pleasures of life. The two have,
however, only apparently changed roles. Just as the resolute, realistic
this-worldliness that had made Faust choose the Erdgeist and
enabled him to invoke it had been sharply distinguished from
crass materialism by the lofty, infinite, and—in a certain sense,
after all—"idealistic" aspiration, "all Erden Weh und all ihr Glück
zu tragen," underlying it, so also here the very despairing nihilism

he feels and so violently expresses is such as can only be felt by a lofty soul whose high-soaring fervour is never really to be extinguished. That is something that Mephisto, whose nihilism is quite crude and undifferentiated and whose real estimate of the beauty of the world and the joys of life (which he here pretends to praise) is quite cynical, cannot believe in or understand. It is enough for him that Faust renounces all his lofty aspirations and appears ready to devote himself solely to material and sensual pleasures. He undertakes to satisfy Faust with such pleasures, and now everything turns upon the insatiability of Faust's nature, as in the "Prolog im Himmel." Faust says:

> Werd' ich beruhigt je mich auf ein Faulbett legen,
> So sei es gleich um mich getan!
> Kannst du mich schmeichelnd je belügen,
> Dass ich mir selbst gefallen mag,
> Kannst du mich mit Genuss betrügen:
> Das sei für mich der letzte Tag!
> Die Wette biet ich!*

Mephisto eagerly accepts this wager, which Faust reinforces with the words:

> Werd' ich zum Augenblicke sagen:
> Verweile doch! du bist so schön!
> Dann magst du mich in Fesseln schlagen,
> Dann will ich gern zugrunde gehn!
> Dann mag die Totenglocke schallen,
> Dann bist du deines Dienstes frei,
> Die Uhr mag stehn, der Zeiger fallen,
> Es sei die Zeit für mich vorbei!†

---

* If ever I lie down on a couch of indolence, / May it at once be all over with me! / If you can ever flatter me with your lies / Into being satisfied with myself, / If you can deceive me with pleasure, / Then may that be the last day for me! / This wager I offer!

† If I say to the passing moment: / Stay! You are so beautiful! / Then you may cast me into fetters, / Then I will gladly perish! / Then may the passing-bell toll, / Then you shall be free of your service, / Let the clock stop, its pointer fall, / Let time for me be at an end!

This passage is particularly important for the structure of the play because the time is to come, at the end of Part II, when Faust does address to the passing moment the words: "Verweile doch, du bist so schön!" Another phrase employed here by Faust in the same connexion constitutes a structural link with the "Prolog im Himmel"; he says to Mephisto:

> Wie ich beharre, bin ich Knecht,
> Ob dein, was frag ich, oder wessen.†

Faust himself, if he must be "Knecht" at all, would as soon be Mephisto's servant as anybody's; the thought of servitude of any kind is abhorrent to him. But we know from the "Prolog im Himmel" that he is all along, without himself realizing it, *God's* servant; the Lord refers to him as "mein Knecht." A dim apprehension of this visits him at this moment, when he fleetingly considers the possibility of his becoming or being the servant not of the devil, but of "another."

Goethe had set himself the difficult task of making Faust stake his soul to the devil in words that should at the same time testify to the infinite loftiness and superiority of his nature. The much-quoted speeches before us, in which Goethe solved this problem, answer the purpose for which they are intended extremely well. But to take them out of their context and see in them Goethe's own personal profession of faith, as if often done, is to overtax them. There is something inflated, theatrical, blustering and even immature about them, which only the particular context can justify. Taken literally and uncritically they appear to postulate that the one central problem of all humanity is something that has never been a real problem for any human being and certainly never can be a problem for Faust, namely the danger of too much and too permanent happiness; and in the process all the concrete, urgent problems that actually do beset mankind are shelved. When one probes deeper for some more satisfactory meaning in them, a wide range of possibilities is opened, from the respectable and innocuous to the ruthless and daemonic. An interpretation in the latter sense is obviously the only one appropriate to the given situation and to the

† If I stand still, I am a servant, / Whether yours or another's, what do I care?

character of Faust. What emerges then is that it is absolutely irrelevant for Faust's salvation or damnation whether the experiences and activities in which he indulges are in the accepted sense good or evil, whether they produce beneficial or harmful consequences for others or for himself, so long as he never "stands still." Least of all is there any objection to his devoting himself exclusively to sensual and material pleasures, as he now proposes to do. All that counts is that he should never be contented with anything, that he should always continue to be active and to strive; for so long as he continues to do that, his real goal will be nothing particular or finite, but the universal and infinite. No matter what their immediate objects and consequences may be, activity and striving as such are highest values for their own sakes. This is the modern doctrine of what has since been dubbed "divine discontent," presented here in a cryptical but extreme form and almost for the first time. The categorical imperative here postulated is no longer Kant's: "Handle so, dass die Maxime deines Willens jederzeit zugleich als Prinzip einer allgemeinen Gesetzgebung gelten könne" (Act in such a way that the maxim of your will could always at the same time serve as the principle for a universal legislation), but: "Act at all costs, whatever comes of it." There is only one deadly sin: to be contented, to be inactive. It is the gospel of extreme individualism, and taken by itself once more implies a position beyond good and evil. But though it is presented at this point by itself, quite unqualified, in the larger context of the Faust drama it turns out to be subject to certain important qualifications. Faust can only pronounce it and commit himself to it because he is now cut off from his "Urquell." Goethe's *Faust* is at once a justification and a criticism, a glorification and an indictment of such extreme individualistic amoralism.

One of the problems that arise with regard to this principle of unconditional striving is whether it applies to all mankind. It certainly does not apply to Gretchen, the essence and law of whose being is contentment, and who perishes when Faust, "der Unmensch ohne Zweck und Ruh," undermines this blessed contentment of hers. It does not apply to women at all; it does not apply to the world of ordinary humanity shown in the "Spaziergang vor dem Tor." In fact, it only applies to the great exceptions, to such a superman as Faust, and even to him it does not ultimately apply without reservation. It is just enough to avert his damnation, but not to procure his salvation, for which something further is required: "Die Liebe von oben" (the love from above).

Max Morris, Niejahr, Spiess, and others have tried to demonstrate with minutest philological evidence, and with the most varied results that there are traces of Goethe's having about 1788, or perhaps even as early as 1774, negligently superimposed upon an original plan, according to which Mephisto should have been merely Faust's "servant" ("Dienstverhältnis"), a later plan, according to which he was to have been merely his "companion" ("freier Bund")—or *vice versa*. This is supposed to have occasioned all sorts of "insoluble contradictions." The fact would appear to be that Goethe from the outset wished to leave this issue open. Mephisto is never so exclusively Faust's servant that he is not also his companion, and never so exclusively his companion that he is not also his servant. Neither a quite unambiguous "Dienstverhältnis" nor a quite unambiguous "freier Bund" would have answered Goethe's purposes: the latter would have been incompatible with Faust's tragic destiny, the former, by implying that he had actually sold his soul to the devil ("Seelenverschreibung"), would have been incompatible with Goethe's conception of Faust's character. Goethe here deliberately pursues a policy of buoyant, elusive ambiguity, which culminates in the pact, as it was finally worked out after 1797. This intentional nebulousness of Goethe's has even led some critics, amongst them Grutzmacher, Wollf, and Daur, to maintain the quite impossible thesis that the pact, as we now have it, turns solely upon the duration of Faust's earthly life and that his "Seelenheil" (the salvation of his soul) is not at stake in it. It is true that Faust, in offering his wager to Mephisto, does not explicitly refer to his "Seelenheil"; that is in keeping with his declaration immediately before: "Das Drüben kann mich wenig kümmern" (I can't worry much about the other world). But he still has in mind Mephisto's condition that he should, in return for Mephisto's services in this world, give him his services in the other world. Nothing has been said or done to abrogate that condition. "*In diesem Sinne* kannst du's wagen" (In that sense you can risk it), Mephisto had said, and that is just what Faust does when he offers the wager.

One of the most bewildering points in the structure of the

drama is that Mephisto so eagerly accepts the terms of the wager offered to him by Faust. The contradiction often pointed out between his here undertaking to lull Faust into inactivity and the Lord's declaration that it is the devil's function to goad man into activity is indeed more apparent than real. There is no need to suppose that Mephisto himself concurs in or even properly understands what the Lord says about his function in the "Prolog." He is as unlikely to see eye to eye with the Lord in this matter as in any other matter, and may well fulfil the function assigned to him by the Lord unknowingly and in spite of himself, with totally different objects of his own in view, as one, "der stets das Böse will" (in this case inactivity), but "stets das Gute schafft" (in this case activity). But that he, with his penetrating and malicious sense of the inadequacy of any earthly pleasures to satisfy man's craving for happiness, should undertake to make Faust contented really does present a serious problem. Nobody knows better than he how little permanency or contentment is to be found in sensual pleasures and how impossible it is really to satisfy such a man as Faust. The first thing he had said about him was:

> Und alle Näh' und alle Ferne
> Befriedigt nicht die tiefbewegte Brust.*

It would, of course, be a great triumph for Mephisto to reduce Faust to glutted sensual torpor, but he must know how impossible that would be, nor does it look as though he had any real intention of attempting it. Immediately after the conclusion of the pact, in a soliloquy that belongs indeed to the second half of the scene and was therefore written over ten years earlier, he likens Faust to a bird caught with birdlime:

> Er soll mir zappeln, starren, kleben,
> Und seiner Unersättlichkeit
> Soll Speis' und Trank vor gier'gen Lippen schweben;
> Er wird Erquickung sich umsonst erflehn . . .†

* All that is near and all that is remote / Fails to satisfy his deeply agitated breast.

† He shall wriggle, stiffen and stick, / And food and drink shall dangle before / The greedy lips of his insatiability; / In vain shall he beg for refreshment.

Herein the "Higher Critics" see one of those "irreconcilable contradictions" which interest them more than anything else in
Goethe's *Faust*. But the programme that Mephisto here formulates
is that which he consistently pursues throughout the rest of the
drama. Instead of trying to satisfy Faust, as he had undertaken
to do in accepting the wager, he always goes out of the way to
keep him unsatisfied, to throw cold water on all his hopes, desires,
and fine sentiments, and to contrive disastrous outcomes for all
his ventures, thereby indeed goading him on to further ceaseless
activity and striving, as the Lord had intended. More than once
he could, if he wished, fairly claim that Faust has "lain down upon
a couch of indolence" and, without actually saying so, desired that
the passing moment might stay because it is so beautiful; but
Mephisto lets these opportunities to declare that he has won his
bet pass by, and deflates Faust's temporary cheerfulness and contentment with a sardonic jeer, plunging him back in his old
turbulence, as though that were after all the best means of procuring his damnation. Mephisto's undertaking to satisfy Faust is
in fact inconsistent not only with his later monologue in the same
scene, but also with the entire rest of the drama. We can, of
course, explain this discrepancy with the favourite hypothesis of
the "Higher Critics" that Goethe has here simply muddled up two
different plans. But there may be some other, more satisfying explanation than this.

We can assume, although Goethe gives no explicit declaration
on the point, that what attracts Mephisto in the wager offered to
him by Faust is not so much its actual terms, as the renouncement
of all higher, ideal aspirations which it seems to imply. Something
that Faust says shortly afterwards is calculated to confirm him in
this view. The passage in question is of special interest because
it also seems to link up with the words of the Erdgeist: "Du
gleichst dem Geist, den du begreifst, nicht mir," and it may well
go back to the earlier stages when Mephisto was still thought of as
being sent to Faust by that Spirit. Faust says:

> Ich habe mich zu hoch gebläht.
> In deinen Rang gehör ich nur,
> Der grosse Geist hat mich verschmäht,

Vor mir verschliesst sich die Natur.
Des Denkens Faden ist zerrissen,
Mir ekelt lange vor allem Wissen.
Lass in den Tiefen der Sinnlichkeit
Uns glühende Leidenschaften stillen!*

That is enough for Mephisto. He does not take the particular conditions of the pact or wager seriously; the only thing that matters in his eyes is that Faust has committed himself to him *on any terms*. Ignoring those conditions, he sets about procuring Faust's damnation by the good, old-fashioned, and well-tried method of involving him in guilt, crime, and sin—just like any other normal devil; not by the strange, paradoxical method of trying to make him so contented that he might feel inclined to say to the passing moment: "Verweile doch, du bist so schön!" In spite of the infinite labour and thought bestowed by Goethe on finding a new, a nobler basis for the relationship of his Faust to Mephisto, that relationship turns out, once it has been established, substantially similar to that of the original legend, much as though this new Faust had after all deliberately invoked the devil by black magic and concluded the old type of pact with him. That is how Goethe wanted it to be. Only, all along there is in Faust still an ineradicable, redeeming striving after the universal in the particular, after the infinite in the finite and therefore also after something spiritual and ideal in the sensual and material. This finds expression most explicitly in his speech of which only the second half appeared in the fragmentary text of 1790, the first half being supplied in the text of *Faust I. Teil*:

Du hörest ja, von Freud' ist nicht die Rede.
Dem Taumel weih ich mich, dem schmerzlichsten Genuss,
Verliebtem Hass, erquickendem Verdruss.
Mein Busen, der vom Wissensdrang geheilt ist,
Soll keinen Schmerzen künftig sich verschliessen,

* I inflated myself too high. / I belong only to your rank; / The great Spirit has spurned me, / Nature locks herself up against me, / The thread of thought is broken, / I have long been disgusted by all knowledge. / Let us appease glowing passions / In the depths of sensuality!

Und was der ganzen Menschheit zugeteilt ist,
Will ich in meinem innern Selbst geniessen,
Mit meinem Geist das Höchst' und Tiefste greifen,
Ihr Wohl und Weh auf meinen Busen häufen,
Und so mein eigen Selbst zu ihrem Selbst erweitern,
Und, wie sie selbst, am End' auch ich zerscheitern.*

This is simply a renewal of the aspiration, "all Erden Weh und all ihr Glück zu tragen," with which Faust had summoned the Erdgeist. No special significance attaches to the circumstance that he had not then specifically referred to "mankind," as he here does. It is sometimes argued that Faust has here advanced spiritually from an anti-humanistic love of nature to a humanistic love for his fellow men, but the sufferings and happiness of earth spoken of on the former occasion already included and were indeed in the first place made up of the sufferings and happiness of mankind.

Mephisto professes that he can understand this will of Faust's to universality, and he does understand it just enough to be able to ridicule it as the impossible, highflown fantasy of a poet. He drills it into him that neither he nor any other human being can ever really transcend the limits of his own personal identity: "Du bleibst doch immer, was du bist" (You will still always remain what you are). But Mephisto sees in Faust's will to universality solely an egoistic desire for endless self-enjoyment and self-aggrandisement, thereby missing the most important element which is also present in it, the element of love. For there is, in however imperfect a form, something of genuine love for mankind in Faust's desire to expand his self to their selves, mingled with his unbridled greed for fulness of experience. This, however, Mephisto cannot understand and fails to take into account, because of that

* But don't you hear, it is not a question of pleasure? / I dedicate myself to delirium, to the most painful enjoyment, / To loving hatred, to refreshing distress. / My bosom, cured now of the urge for knowledge, / Shall henceforth shut itself off from no suffering, / And what is parcelled out to all mankind / I am resolved to enjoy within my inmost self, / To grasp with my spirit what is highest and lowest, / To heap their happiness and sorrow upon my breast, / And so to expand my own self to their self / And like them in the end to perish, I too.

limitation which makes him the devil and which Gretchen un-
erringly recognizes:

> Es steht ihm an der Stirn' geschrieben,
> Dass er nicht mag eine Seele lieben.†

Without this love for humanity, which can and does manifest itself
in humbler and less spectacular ways and amongst quite ordinary
people, all Faust's aspirations towards the infinite would remain
something ambiguous and hardly suffice to avert his damnation.

There is little to add to what has already been said in the chapter
on the Gretchen tragedy[30] about the "Walpurgisnacht" scene, also
a production of the 1797–1806 stage of Goethe's work on *Faust*,
though it was fairly certainly planned well before 1775. It begins
admirably with the presentation of Faust and Mephisto ascending
the Brocken on foot after dark; Faust, quite untroubled by any
thoughts of Gretchen, is enjoying the exercise and the wildness of
the weather and the landscape, Mephisto characteristically is hating
the one and insensitive to the other. We have here some of
Goethe's finest nature poetry. But when the witches, warlocks, and
other grotesque beings appear, they do not evoke anything like
sufficiently the insane, exhilarated uncanniness, the sense of high-
spirited, obscene depravity that they are meant to evoke. One of
the reasons for this is that Goethe here employs chiefly those
comic quatrains he could improvise so easily—far too easily. His
humour, excellent at its best, displays itself here much of the time
at its second best. He makes much use of out of the way lore about
witchcraft and superstitions and also of a curious old seventeenth-
century engraving of the Witches' Sabbath by Michael Heer. At
the same time he introduces many satirical allusions to contemporary politics, literary feuds, and writers, particularly to the old
diehard champion of the Enlightenment, Friedrich Nicolai (1733–
1811), who is brought in under the Rabelaisian name "Prokto-
phantasmist." Even if we knew nothing of the projected but never
executed epiphany of Satan, we should feel that the scene is working
up to a supreme infernal crescendo that fails to come, and which
would have served as a far more appropriate contrasting setting

---

† It stands written on his brow / That he cannot love any soul.

for the apparition of Gretchen than Faust's dance with the charming young witch does. Instead of the unveiling of the mystery of evil which we had a right to expect, all we are given is the red mouse that jumps out of the mouth of that young witch; it is indeed a case of: *Parturiunt montes, nascitur ridiculus mus.* But what is more to be deplored than Goethe's failure to write the Satan scene is his introduction of the so-called *Walpurgisnachtstraum oder Oberons und Titanias goldne Hochzeit* ("Walpurgis Night Dream or the Golden Wedding of Oberon and Titania"). This inferior piece of satire on contemporary literary and intellectual trends was written shortly before Goethe resumed work on *Faust* in June, 1797, as a belated offshoot of the quarrels occasioned by his and Schiller's polemical *Xenienalmanach* of the previous autumn. It has really nothing to do with *Faust*, and Goethe only superficially adapted it to serve as an "Intermezzo" to the "Walpurgisnacht," because Schiller was unwilling to print it in his *Musenalmanach.* The notion that Faust should submissively listen to that sort of thing just after his conscience has been awakened by the vision of Gretchen is intolerable.

Enders censures the apparition of Gretchen in the "Walpurgisnacht" scene on the following grounds: "*Vor* der Szene *Trüber Tag* dürfte man nach dem *Urfaust* keinerlei Andeutung der letzten Katastrophe erhalten . . . Faust erfährt ja allzu deutlich das Schicksal Gretchens im Voraus" (*Before* the scene "Dull Day. Field" we should, according to the *Urfaust*, not receive any hint of the final catastrophe. Faust learns too clearly in advance about Gretchen's fate).[31] There is no justification for this criticism, which might apply at most to Goethe's later rejected original drafts for the passage in question, not to the final text. The true point of the "Walpurgisnacht" scene would be quite lost without the apparition of Gretchen. That apparition really arises from within Faust's own mind. If he had to wait for Mephisto to raise the topic of Gretchen's fate, he would have to wait too long. The Gretchen apparition is one of the best conceived and best executed dramatic crises in the whole of *Faust*.

In conclusion, the following synopsis of Goethe's work on *Faust* between 1797 and 1806 may be given:

(a) "Zueignung," "Vorspiel auf dem Theater," and "Prolog im Himmel"—all written in the last half of June, and the first days of July, 1797.

(b) A detailed plan for the entire drama with thirty headings, worked out with considerable hesitation and difficulty during the same summer weeks of 1797 and possibly not brought into final form till April, 1798; "Paralipomenon 1" is to be regarded as one of the first drafts for this plan.

(c) The two scenes and two half scenes (comprising together 1,095 lines), which fill the gap remaining in *Faust, ein Fragment* between Faust's conversation with Wagner and his conversation with Mephisto. This was the most substantial and important addition of the years 1798–1801 and, while it certainly incorporates some far older "splinters" and ideas, is to be regarded as essentially a new conception of these years, with its basis in the "Prolog im Himmel." "Studierzimmer I" can be exactly dated in April, 1800, as Goethe wrote to Schiller on the sixteenth of that month: "Der Teufel, den ich beschwöre, gebärdet sich sehr wunderlich" (The devil whom I am conjuring up is behaving himself very queerly).

(d) The completion, pretty certainly in close conformity with Goethe's early conception, of the "Valentin" scene; Goethe was engaged on this task in 1800, but did not finish it till March 1806.

(e) The "Walpurgisnacht," written partly at least in November, 1800, but partly also in April, 1806.

(f) The recasting, in May, 1798, of the old prose "Kerker" scene in verse, "um die unmittelbare Wirkung des ungeheuren Stoffs zu dämpfen!" (to tone down the immediate effect of the fearful theme).[32]

(g) The opening scene of the Helen of Troy episode for the Second Part, (215 lines in all) written about September,

1800, and incorporated in the final version twenty-five years later.

(h) Various other drafts and fragments for the Second Part, some of them later utilized, others not, above all a version of the last scenes showing Faust's salvation, which must have differed much in various points of detail from the final version of 1825 and 1830, but probably already contained some of the most important passages in that final version. Likeliest date for this: 1800–1801.[33]

(i) The suppressed valedictory stanzas ("Abschied") and a draft for "Abkündigung."[34] These are as likely to have been written in summer, 1797, as at any later date.

This synopsis postulates that the "Prolog im Himmel" was a new conception that Goethe arrived at in summer, 1797, and which alone made it possible for him to resume work on *Faust*, providing him with a solution of the problems that had so long baffled him. Here and here alone, in the course of the sixty years from 1771 to 1831, a radical change is to be recognized in his Faust plans, and even that was a change only in the symbolical economy, not in the essential purport of the drama. That essential purport was inevitably enriched and deepened with the passing of the decades; it grew like a tree, adding ring after ring to its girth; it took on new colouring, absorbed into itself new interests, mirrored new experiences and new insights as Goethe advanced from youth to middle age, and from middle age to old age, so that the second Part reads almost as though it were the work of an entirely different poet from the first. But the original conception was such that its essentials never required to be radically altered. It turned upon something central in Goethe's nature and outlook that remained constant through all his developments from the early 1770's onward, upon the question whether there is some special way of salvation for the Promethean superman beyond good and evil.

10. A Glimpse
of FAUST II. Teil
and the Problem
of
Faust's Salvation

IT IS HIGHLY improbable that Goethe thought of dividing his *Faust* into two distinct parts before 1797. The earliest documentary evidence known to us of his having formed such an intention is in *Paralipomenon I*, which we have dated in late June of that year. It is to be supposed that this division into two parts was already provided for in the "ausführliches Schema" of those summer weeks. Goethe was most likely swayed here in the first place by purely practical considerations. He must have felt that to complete the entire drama was too vast an undertaking for him to embark on with any hope of accomplishing it in the foreseeable future, and therefore he must have decided to concentrate his energies for the time being on the more limited and manageable task of supplying all that was missing up to the end of the Gretchen tragedy. If once he could in that way at least produce a publishable first part, the remainder could for the moment be left to look after itself.

It is moreover unlikely that Goethe foresaw in the years 1797–1801 that the second part would prove so entirely different in character

from the first as it actually did, or that it would swell to considerably
more than one and a half times the other's bulk. Quite a lot has
long since been known from the paralipomena about Goethe's
1797 plan for *Faust II*, but not till 1943 was it clearly and virtually
for the first time pointed out that he in the long run more or less
consistently jettisoned most of the factors in that plan which
would have made the second part substantially a straightforward
continuation of the first, so far as dramatic emphasis and the conception of Faust's character are concerned. To recognize this was
one of the many contributions to Goethe scholarship made by
Wilhelm Emrich, who, however, in maintaining his legitimate
enough paradoxical thesis that "Faust II nicht als 'Fortsetzung'
des I. Teils zu betrachten ist" (Faust II is not to be regarded as a
continuation of the first part[1]), does not altogether escape the danger of often insisting too one-sidedly and dogmatically on his new
discoveries and criteria. It is indeed remarkable that, until Emrich
came along, nobody had attached much importance to Goethe's
own frequent declarations during his last years about the difference
between the two parts of Faust, a particularly striking example of
which is what he wrote to Stapfer on April 4, 1827: "Cette seconde
partie . . . ne peut en aucune façon se rattacher à la première partie"
(This second part can in no respect link up with the first part).
Emrich appeals to such utterances of Goethe's as this and also to
other, more cogent evidence, in support of his contention that the
second part is only apparently concerned with Faust's destiny or
even with his personality, as the first part had been. To him, it
should really be understood as a complex symbolical presentation
of the ambivalent, often daemonic forces and phenomena underlying all existence, in their dialectical relationship to one another,
Faust's own role being reduced to that of a detached onlooker.
Emrich insists on the "Herrschaft solcher . . . Grundsymbole über
äussere Handlung, Personencharakter, Idee usw., welche mehr oder
weniger nur der Zeit oder einer zufälligen Wirklichkeit verschrieben
sind" (The predominance of such fundamental symbols over the
external action, the character of the personages, the idea etc.,
which are in a greater or lesser degree merely determined by the
times or by a fortuitous reality).[2] This symbolical panorama of the
forces determining all the particular phenomena of nature, history,

and art is, according to Emrich, presented with "einer Absolutheit, ... vor der der dumpfe Wahrheitsdrang des Faust I wie ein schwerer Albdruck in Goethes Gedächtnis versinkt" (an absoluteness before which the groping after truth of *Faust I* vanishes like an oppressive nightmare from Goethe's memory).[3] It is therefore a mistake, in reading *Faust II*, to assume that the characters or the dramatic action as such really matter: "Jedes starre Festhalten am dramatischen 'Charakter', an durchlaufenden Personenbestimmungen ... erscheint ... nichtig angesichts der Gewalt dieses Ursprungsproblems" (All rigid insistence on dramatic "character," on the permanent identity of the personages, appears futile by comparison with the might of this problem of origins).[4] One most weighty consequence arises from all this: "Faust kommt nicht mehr in Versuchung" (Faust no longer comes into temptation).[5] Again and again Emrich insists that the question of guilt, of "Schuld," in any traditional senses of the word, while it had been all-important in *Faust I*, has become completely irrelevant in *Faust II*.

These revolutionary views of Emrich's, though one might demur at some of his extremer formulations, are in the main indubitably sound, so far as the first four acts of *Faust II* are concerned. In those acts, on which Emrich has done work of the highest value, but which can only be considered very summarily in the present study, Goethe certainly did largely use the Faust theme as a pretext for setting forth symbolically and mythologically the interplay of the "Urkräfte" and "Urphänomene" of existence, as they presented themselves to his imagination in his final years. The difference between the two parts of *Faust* is, however, in this respect, not quite so absolute as Emrich makes it out to be. For even in the *Urfaust*, and in *Faust I* as a whole, Goethe had been concerned to present not only dramatic characters and actions, but also a symbolical vision of primal forces and phenomena, most obviously in the Erdgeist scene; only in the Gretchen Tragedy is this symbolical intention largely lost sight of. It lay in the very nature of the Faust theme that such a writer as Goethe should from the outset and all along envisage it not only dramatically, but also symbolically. The specifically dramatic and symbolical modes of treatment and interpretation are by no means incompatible with one another, and ideally it must have been Goethe's object to unite these two principles harmoniously without sacrificing one to the other. It can be questioned, whether even in the first four acts of *Faust II* he has really sacrificed the dramatic to the symbolical so completely as Emrich believes him to have done. In Act V the dramatic certainly comes into its rights again, after it had long been comparatively in abeyance, so that Kommerell can, in words quoted with much disapproval by Emrich,[6] single out the first half of that act as "eigentliches Drama" (genuine drama), and Heller can similarly write: "There is more consistent drama in the brief sequence of scenes than emerges from the bewildering totality of the poem."[7] This fifth act, with which we shall be chiefly concerned here, constitutes the termination not only of *Faust II*, but also of *Faust I*, linking together the two parts, for all their formal, stylistic and other disparities, and establishing at last a satisfactory equilibrium between the dramatic principle, which had asserted itself so onesidedly in the Gretchen Tragedy, and the symbolical principle, which had asserted itself so one-sidedly in the first four acts of Part II.

When Goethe decided in 1805 to publish *Faust I* alone, without more than perfunctorily completing it, he had lost hope of ever being able to finish the entire work. But certain sections of the second part had, as we have seen, already been written by 1801, most notably the beginning of the Helena episode and an early version of the conclusion, and the scheme for the whole of it had been worked out since July, 1797, in some detail, probably on the lines of his earliest conception. Goethe thought of publishing these existing fragments with a synopsis of the whole plan, to make them intelligible. He actually dictated such a synopsis on December 16, 1816, for inclusion in Book XVIII of *Dichtung und Wahrheit*, but then suppressed it.

The death on April 19, 1824 at Missolonghi of Byron, the only contemporary poet in whom he was prepared to recognize something like an equal, a worthy disciple, and a kindred spirit, made a deep impression on Goethe and stimulated him to resume serious work on *Faust* in the following February. He modified the plan of the Helena episode in various ways, particularly in order to link it up with the death of Byron, who was to be represented under the figure of Euphorion, the son of Faust and Helena. Between March

14, and April 5, 1825, he made a start on this Helena episode, and about the same time he wrote the opening scene of the first act and revised and completed the final scenes, producing, so far as one can make out, "Mitternacht" (Midnight), "Grosser Vorhof" (Great Forecourt), and either "Grablegung" (Interment) more or less as it now stands, followed by a shorter predecessor of "Bergschluchten" (Mountain Gorges), or an earlier version of "Grablegung" incorporating towards the end some of the most important passages that now stand in "Bergschluchten" and so having a finality not found in "Grablegung" as we knew it. The conclusion, as Goethe worked it out in these weeks, must at least in his own eyes have had a satisfying finality about it; this emerges from his declaration in a letter of 24 May, 1827, to Zelter that the "völliger Schluss" (absolute end) of *Faust* was "schon längst fertig" (long since completed). On February 11, 1826, he resumed work on the Helena episode, completing it in the summer of the same year. It was published in April, 1827, under the title *Helena/ classischromantische Phantasmagorie. Zwischenspiel zu Faust* ("Helen: A Classico-Romantic Phantasmagoria: Interlude to Faust").

From summer, 1827 to summer, 1831, the completion of *Faust II* was Goethe's "Hauptgeschäft" (principal task). Unlike the first part, it was to be divided into five acts, with "Helena" as the third act. It was also to be less fragmentary and subjective, and everything was to be found "auf einer höhern und edlern Stufe" (on a higher and nobler plane).[8] Once more it was a matter of filling up gaps— the gap from the opening scene to the beginning of "Helena," and the gap from the end of "Helena" to the middle of the fifth act. The first two acts were completed in about three and a half years, by the end of 1830, the first 1,424 lines of Act I being published in 1828. In December, 1830, Goethe was no longer satisfied with the "völliger Schluss," as it had been established in March, 1825, and set about revising and amplifying it. It must have been at this time that "Bergschluchten" was produced in the form now known to us. How much of this scene was not actually written till December, 1830, it is impossible to decide; but reasons will be given for the view that some of the most important passages in it must have been in existence probably since 1800 or 1801 and quite certainly since 1825. On January 4, 1831, Goethe wrote to Zelter: "Der fünfte

[Akt] bis zum Ende des Endes steht auch schon auf dem Papier."
This refers, however, only to the last four scenes. The three first
scenes, in which the Philemon and Baucis episode is presented,
were still missing; in April, 1831, he interrupted his work on the
fourth act to write these scenes.

The last part to be completed was the fourth act, chiefly
the work of summer, 1831. On this occasion Goethe said to
Eckermann: "Mein ferneres Leben kann ich nunmehr als ein
reines Geschenk ansehen, und es ist jetzt im Grunde ganz einerlei,
ob und was ich noch etwa tue" (What remains of my life I can
now regard as a pure gift, and at bottom it does not in the least
matter whether I still do anything or what I do). Some time in
August or early September, 1831, possibly on his eighty-second
birthday, August 28, 1831, he sealed up the manuscript with instructions that it should not be opened till after his death, giving
as one of his chief reasons, "damit ich nicht etwa hier und da
weiter auszuführen in Versuchung käme" (in case I might be
tempted to amplify it at one point or the other. [Dec. 1, 1831, to
Humboldt]). But the temptation to occupy himself with *Faust*
once more was too great for him, and on January 8, 1832, he opened
the sealed packet to read from it to his daughter-in-law Ottilie,
making various minor alterations in it during the succeeding three
weeks and one important addition to the final scenes on January
24, less than two months before his death.

From 1825 onward he insisted again and again with regard to
each separate act of *Faust II* and with regard to it as a whole that
it was worked out substantially in accordance with his earliest conception. There is one noteworthy formula, which he uses for the
first time in writing to Heinrich Meyer on July 20, 1831, and then
again and again with slight variations in other letters during the
succeeding months: "Ich wusste schon lange her, *was*, ja sogar *wie*
ich's wollte, und trug es als ein inneres Märchen seit so vielen Jahren
mit mir herum, führte nur aber die einzelnen Stellen aus, die mich
von Zeit zu Zeit näher anmuteten" (I have long since known *what* I
wanted and even *how* I wanted it to be, and carried it about with
me as an inner fairy tale for so many years, but only worked out
those single sections that from time to time more specially appealed
to me).[9]

This is misleading, in so far as it does not take into account the long interval from 1801 to 1825 in which we can be certain that Goethe did not add a word to *Faust II*, but the phrase "ein inneres Märchen" is reliable and revealing, and that inner fairy tale must, according to his repeated statements during the last years of his life, have originated about 1771. Another illuminating phrase about *Faust II* in these late letters is: "diese ernst gemeinten Scherze" (these seriously intended jokes [Nov. 24, 1831]), which recurs in the form "diese sehr ernsten Scherze" (these very serious jokes) in the immensely important letter to Humboldt of March 17, 1832. He repeatedly insisted on the enigmatic, esoteric, "incommensurable" character of the drama, which will present posterity with insoluble problems of interpretation, speaking tantalizingly "von allem dem, was da hineingeheimnisset ist" (all the secrets that have been smuggled into it [July 26, 1828, to Zelter]).

Faust II presents indeed endless highly complex problems that could only be treated adequately at great length in a separate publication. Ada M. Klett, in her valuable *Der Streit um Faust II seit 1901 (Mit kommentierter Bibliographie von 512 Titeln)* ("The Quarrel about Faust II since 1901, with an annotated bibliography of 512 titles") of 1939, shows how sharply divided critical opinions are on virtually every aspect of the drama. We must be satisfied with a brief summary of the essential points arising from the main body of the work before going on to consider in more detail the final scenes, which are of the greatest importance for a proper understanding of the first part.

To begin with Faust is seen lying in a state of coma in an "Anmutige Gegend" (Pleasant Region), to which he has presumably been conveyed by Mephisto after collapsing at his parting with Gretchen in the Dungeon. He is "ermüdet, unruhig, schlafsuchend" (exhausted, restless, and seeking sleep), but does not utter a word. Some critics make a great deal of the terrible remorse with which he is afflicted on Gretchen's account, but that is something Goethe has deliberately avoided showing us. It is one of the laws of Faust's titanic nature that he should be incapable of repentance in the ordinary sense of the word. This raised a serious problem for Goethe. A Faust haunted with a troubled conscience for the rest of his life on Gretchen's account would no longer have been a genuine Faust at all; he would have been too much of an ordinary human being, incapable of undergoing the specifically Faustian destiny. On the other hand a Faust who could simply by an act of his own mind and will brush Gretchen on one side would have appeared too much of a mere callous brute. Goethe's solution of this problem was to cause Ariel and his elves to lull Faust to sleep and expunge from his mind all memories of the horrors he has just been through and of the guilt he has incurred. He awakens to a new existence with a virtually new identity, refreshed and eager for new experiences, but no longer for experiences of an immediate, sensual kind. He will henceforth approach existence with a certain intellectual and aesthetic detachment. His new watchword is: "Am farbigen Abglanz haben wir das Leben" (We have life in its colourful reflection). In this we can recognize something in the nature of a victory of the principle represented by the Makrokosmus over that represented by the Erdgeist: Faust has advanced to a higher stage. Mephisto brings him to the court of the Kaiser Maximilian, where, after various adventures that turn chiefly on the introduction of a system of paper currency, he is asked to raise up the spirits of Helen of Troy and Paris. Mephisto, unable to perform this himself, sends Faust to the mysterious "Mütter" (Mothers)—mythological entities of Goethe's own invention who have won great popularity in the vocabulary of German intellectuals and are regularly, on the strength of their name alone, assumed to stand for the primeval, still undifferentiated, vitalistic principle of all things. But Goethe himself conceived of them as representing almost the opposite of this: namely, the guardians of all particular *forms* in which the vital principle variously manifests itself in the course of its endless metamorphoses:

> Gestaltung, Umgestaltung,
> Des ewigen Sinnes ewige Unterhaltung.
> Umschwebt von Bildern aller Kreatur;
> Sie sehn dich nicht, denn Schemen sehn sie nur.*

---

* Formation, transformation, / The eternal meaning's eternal entertainment. / Surrounded by the images of all creatures: / They will not see you, for they see only phantoms.

Faust brings back from these "Mothers" the phantoms of Paris and Helena, and presents them at the Kaiser's court. But, enamoured of Helena's beauty, he seizes hold of her, the magical apparitions vanish with an explosion and Faust sinks to the floor unconscious. At this point the first act ends.

Mephisto conveys the still unconscious Faust back to his old study. Through the aid of Homunculus, an artificial manikin just produced by Wagner in a retort (with the clandestine co-operation of Mephisto), the discovery is made that Faust's whole heart is still fixed on Helena and that he must be transported to Greece, if he is to survive. Mephisto conveys the sleeping Faust on his magic cloak to Thessaly where, on the anniversary of the battle of Pharsalus, which was decisive for the fate of the ancient world, the Classical Walpurgis Night is about to begin. He takes with him as guide the retort containing the Homunculus, who is eager to enter upon real existence and hopes to find the best way to attain this amongst the phantoms of ancient Greece. The "Klassische Walpurgisnacht" is one of the most stupendous and original achievements of Goethe's imagination and excels in richness and effectiveness the Nordic "Walpurgisnacht" of the first part. He brings together all the minor spirits and monsters of ancient Greek demonology in a riotous phantasmagoria full of cryptic allusions to questions that interest him—particularly, to the rival geological schools of the Neptunists and Vulcanists and to the struggle between Romanticism and Classicism. The three visitants from the north part company: Mephisto seeks congenial spirits amongst the most macabre monsters of Greek myth, and is constantly at a disadvantage until he at last contrives to come to terms with the hideous, witchlike Graeae (Phorkyaden) and to borrow the form of one of them—a necessary part of his scheme for bringing Faust and Helena together. The Homunculus, after various inquiries about the best means of achieving real existence, shatters his retort against the prow of a vessel bearing Galatea over the waves, and in thus perishing must be supposed to enter into the intensest stream of life, on the principle of "Stirb und werde" (Dying and Becoming), and to unite the Neptunian and the Volcanic, the Classical and the Romantic in a higher synthesis. The key phrases in the great chorus of Sea-nymphs, which terminates the "Klassische Walpurgisnacht" and with it the second act of *Faust II*, are: "So herrsche denn Eros, der alles begonnen!" (So may Eros prevail, who has begun all things!) and: "Heil dem Wasser! Heil dem Feuer!" (Hail to water! Hail to fire!). Meanwhile Faust has recovered consciousness and finds himself amongst the nymphs and swans of whom he has all this time been dreaming—a reproduction of the circumstances of the begetting of Helena by Zeus in the form of a swan upon the bathing Leda. The centaur Chiron brings Faust together with the sibyl Manto, who, with the much-quoted words: "Den lieb' ich, der Unmögliches begehrt" (I love him who desires the impossible), shows him the way down to Hades, so that he may intercede with Proserpina to allow Helena to return to the upper world, as Orpheus had interceded with her for the restoration to life of Eurydice. This is the point to which everything works up in the "Klassische Walpurgisnacht." Goethe himself said of it in a conversation with Eckermann on January 15, 1827:

> Und dann, bedenken Sie nur, was alles in jener tollen Nacht zur Sprache kommt! Fausts Rede an die Proserpina, um diese zu bewegen, dass sie die Helena herausgibt, was muss das nicht für eine Rede sein, da die Proserpina selbst zu Tränen davon gerührt wird! Dies ist alles nicht leicht zu machen und hängt sehr viel vom Glück ab, ja fast von der Stimmung und Kraft des Augenblicks.*

This great speech, which was originally to have been made not by Faust, but by Manto, was never written. Some critics have found subtle philosophical reasons for its absence, but the true explanation is probably that the hoped-for moment of inspiration never came.

In the third act Mephisto has so contrived things that the resurrected Helena, unaware of ever having been dead but also not

---

* And then consider all the different things that must be dealt with in that crazy night! Faust's speech to Proserpina, with which he moves her to surrender Helena—what a speech that must be, since Proserpina herself is touched to tears by it! All that is not easily done and depends very much on luck, nay almost entirely on the power and mood of the moment.

quite sure that she is really alive, believes herself to be returning to the palace of Menelaus after the destruction of Troy, but finds preparations made for her to be sacrificed. A hideous housekeeper, Phorkyas (who eventually turns out to be Mephisto in the borrowed form of one of the Graeae), after warning Helena of this danger, suggests a possible means of escaping it. Certain strange warriors from the north have under their brave leader established themselves in the mountains near the source of the Eurotas, where they have built a castle, which, from Phorkyas' description of the way in which it differs from Greek architectural forms, must be Gothic. Phorkyas undertakes to transport Helena to this castle and put her under the protection of its overlord. This offer is accepted and Helena finds herself with her attendants inside the courtyard of the Gothic castle, the overlord of which, of course, is Faust in the guise of a medieval knight. Ancient Greece and medieval Germany —the classical and the romantic principles are brought face to face. Helena accepts Faust's love, the two live together in Arcadian happiness and a son, Euphorion (representing Byron), is born to them. But in his reckless violence Euphorion refuses to be confined by the limits of this dream-world, attempts to fly, and perishes. This puts an end to the shadowy existence of Helena in the upper world; she bids Faust farewell, cries: "Persephoneia, nimm den Knaben auf und mich!" (Persephone, receive the boy and me!), and her bodily form vanishes. But urged by Phorkyas–Mephisto, Faust retains her robe in his hand—a symbol for the antique ideal of beauty as it survives in the art and culture of all later ages. Before they dissolve into the elements Helena's attendants sing a dirge for Euphorion, which is really Goethe's elegy on Byron.

This Helena episode is one of Goethe's finest and subtlest achievements. To give it a genuinely Hellenic character he in 1800 adapted the iambic trimeter of Greek tragedy to the German language—a prosodic *tour-de-force*. Much of the effect of the act depends on this beautiful but difficult metre, of which only a faint idea can be given in translation:

> Admired much and much reprehended, Helena,
> I come from sea-board, where we landed even now,
> Still drunk and dizzy with the waves' impetuous

Pulsation, which from Phrygian plains have borne us here
On high-reared shoulders, favoured by Poseidon's aid
And power of Eurus, back to these ancestral gulfs.*

On her encounter with the Germanic world, Helena is taught by
Faust to speak in rhyme. In Helena herself Goethe has remarkably
succeeded in bringing together in a convincing figure, with a
strangely transparent reality, the demi-goddess and the incorrigible,
wilful, timid, slightly vicious wanton, the phantom from the underworld and the woman of flesh and blood, ideal beauty and distinct
personality, the statuesque and moving tenderness. There is no
doubt that in his love for Helena, Faust is supposed to experience
that lofty, idealistic apprehension of pure beauty which is only
possible at a high level of aesthetic culture and awareness, entail-
ing in a considerable degree the renunciation of direct sensual
appetite and enjoyment, in keeping with his new watchword: "Am
farbigen Abglanz haben wir das Leben," and in keeping also with
the doctrine of Weimarian classicism. This is the "Genuss mit
Bewusstsein—Schönheit" that is contrasted in *Paralipomenon I*
with "Genuss . . . in der Dumpfheit Leidenschaft." It is a spiritual,
even an intellectual, experience of some austerity. Various critics
have objected to this interpretation as too frigid and bloodless,
pointing out that the senses and passions are very much involved
in the relationship between Faust and Helena and that, if they
were not, the birth of Euphorion could hardly be accounted for.
This is all true enough. Goethe did not want simply to produce an
allegory illustrating Schiller's *Briefe über die ästhetische Erziehung
des Menschen* ("Letters on the Aesthetic Education of Man"). But
the very passionate and sensuous reality with which he has invested
the love of Faust and Helena has a rarified, dreamlike, and slightly
ironical quality: it is real with another reality than that of everyday human existence; it has itself been aestheticized, and the
whole remains a dream within a dream.

---

* Bewundert viel und viel gescholten, Helena, / Vom Strande komm' ich,
wo wir erst gelandet sind, / Noch immer trunken von des Gewoges regsamem /
Geschaukel, das vom phrygischen Blachgefild uns her / Auf sträubig-hohem
Rücken, durch Poseidons Gunst / Und Euros' Kraft, in vaterländische Buchten
trug.

Other critics, notably Böhm, who are out above all to demolish
the belief that Faust is meant to have anything admirable or exemplary about him, search in the Helena episode for evidence on
which he can be convicted of ruthlessness or immorality, applying
standards that are here certainly irrelevant. The stratagems by
which Faust gets Helena into his power, the undeserved accusa-
tions and threats to which the sentinel Lynkeus is exposed, the
speed and high-handedness with which Faust takes possession of
Helena's heart, and the ease with which she allows herself to be
overcome—all this belongs to the fantastic, half-ironical stylization
that characterizes the entire act; and it should be received in the
spirit in which it was conceived, not in the spirit of a court of
law—just as the birth of Euphorion does not conform to humdrum
physiological processes. The Helena episode, like the "Klassische
Walpurgisnacht," has next to no bearing one way or the other on
the central issues of the "Prolog im Himmel," the two wagers and
Faust's salvation; and one should not try to construct here con-
nexions that do not exist and are not meant to exist. Actually Faust
does here, at least aesthetically, "lie down upon a couch of indolence." When he and Helena say between them:

> Nun schaut der Geist nicht vorwärts, nicht zurück,
> Die Gegenwart allein ist unser Glück*

they are virtually addressing to the "Augenblick" the forbidden
words: "Verweile doch, du bist so schön." But Mephisto, instead
of claiming that he has won the wager, as he well might do, himself undergoes a remarkable change and temporarily becomes—this
point is particularly well brought out by Karl Wollf—humane and
almost noble-minded. This is the one great adventure in which
Faust incurs no real guilt and in which his specifically Faustian striving and amoral turbulence are in abeyance. In this episode alone
Goethe effectually carries out one of the points in his programme
which was very important to him—namely, that Faust should
steadily advance to higher planes of existence. That intention is
clearly enough adumbrated in *Paralipomenon I*; and we also find

---

* Now the mind looks neither forwards nor backwards, / The present alone
is our happiness.

Goethe speaking to Eckermann, on May 6, 1827, of Faust as "ein aus schweren Verirrungen immerfort zum Besseren aufstrebender Mensch" (a man forever striving upwards from grave aberrations to what is better), and again, on June 6, 1831, also to Eckermann, of Faust's "immer höhere und reinere Tätigkeit bis ans Ende" (ever higher and purer activity up to the end). We shall see how difficult it is to interpret the fourth and fifth acts in this sense, but the third can and should be so interpreted.

This means, however, that we are meant to see in the love between Faust and Helena something higher than in that between him and Gretchen. That is not easily accepted. But Goethe asserts it very definitely in an unpublished review of spring, 1827, where he designates Faust's love to Helena as, "ein Verhältnis, das in freierer Kunst-Region hervortritt und auf höhere Ansichten hindeutet als jenes frühere [zu Gretchen], das in dem Wust missverstandener Wissenschaft, bürgerlicher Beschränktheit, sittlicher Verwirrung, abergläubischen Wahns zugrunde ging und nur durch einen Hauch von oben, der sich zu dem natürlichen Gefühl des Guten und Rechten gesellte, für die Ewigkeit gerettet werden konnte" (a relationship emerging in a freer domain of art and pointing to loftier views than that earlier one, which came to grief in the chaos of misunderstood learning, middle-class narrowmindedness, moral disorder and superstitious delusions, and could only be saved for eternity by a breath from above, in conjunction with the natural feeling for what is good and right).[10] This is an extremely valuable indication of how the Gretchen Tragedy should be interpreted, but we are still inclined to protest that, after all, the love between Faust and Gretchen is genuine love in a sense in which that between him and Helena is not, that the former has a human warmth and immediacy which the latter lacks. It is, however, just this comparative distance and detachment that makes the love between Faust and Helena the "higher" of the two. Whether that makes it in every respect the "better" is another question, which Goethe does not leave unanswered.

At the opening of the fourth act Faust is shown transported to the summit of a high mountain by Helena's robe, which has turned into a cloud and now floats away to the east, assuming for a time the form of Helena herself, but leaving behind a faint wisp of vapour that, before it vanishes in the ether, also assumes a female form. The monologue in which Faust describes these apparitions is important for the understanding of the whole work. The first half presents no difficulties. Helena is here a symbol for the transfiguring power of idealistic art, which confers permanent value and beauty on what is imperfect and transitory, "und spiegelt blendend flücht'ger Tage grossen Sinn" (and dazzlingly reflects the noble significance of fleeting days). But what of the other apparition? The passage runs:

Doch mir umschwebt ein zarter lichter Nebelstreif
Noch Brust und Stirn, erheiternd, kühl und schmeichelhaft.
Nun steigt es leicht und zaudernd hoch und höher auf,
Fügt sich zusammen.—Täuscht mich ein entzückend Bild,
Als jugenderstes, längstentbehrtes höchstes Gut?
Des tiefsten Herzens frühste Schätze quellen auf:
Aurorens Liebe, leichten Schwung bezeichnet's mir,
Den schnellempfundnen, ersten, kaum verstandnen Blick,
Der, festgehalten, überglänzte jeden Schatz.
Wie Seelenschönheit steigert sich die holde Form,
Löst sich nicht auf, erhebt sich in den Äther hin
Und zieht das Beste meines Innern mit sich fort.*

This passage is nearly always—and rightly—interpreted as applying to Gretchen, although there is no direct reference to her in it and the circumstances seem all to point rather to somebody else, to a girl about whom we otherwise hear nothing, loved by Faust in his early youth, in the dawn, the "Aurora" of his development. But Faust's real youth is non-existent for the purposes of the drama. We only know of the artificial youth conferred upon him by the

---

* But a bright ethereal wisp of vapour / Still hovers about my breast and brow, enlivening, cool and captivating. / Now, lightly and hesitantly, it ascends higher and higher, / Solidifying. Is it a delusion, that I see before me an enchanting image, / The long-missed highest good of my first youth? / My deepest heart's most early treasures rise to view. / It manifests to me Aurora's lightly soaring love, / The first look, swiftly felt but scarcely understood, / Which if I could have held it fast, would have outshone every other treasure. / The gracious form is transfigured into beauty of the soul, / It does not dissolve, but mounts up into the ether, / Bearing along with it what is best in my inmost being.

Witch's potion. We must suppose that in Faust's memory, from which the actual, painful circumstances of his encounter with Gretchen have all been eliminated by Ariel and his elves, one last dim recollection of her remains, and that under the influence of the present vision, which is indeed an apotheosis of Gretchen, he imagines his love for her as it might have been and should have been. And thus transfigured, it appears after all as equal in value to his love for Helena, or rather still higher in value. Helena stands for ideal beauty, beauty as apprehended by the mind, and her validity is for this life, on whose fleeting days she confers a noble significance. Her cloud recedes laterally and remains visible in the east as an enhancing, elevating radiancy to supplement the earthly horizon. It is only so long as we exist within the limits of earthly realities that we need and can employ the idealistic and idealizing principle. Gretchen, on the other hand, stands for "Seelenschönheit," which is different in kind from ideal beauty—aesthetically and philosophically less, but ethically and religiously far more. She recedes from Faust not horizontally, but vertically, into the celestial regions, into the other world, taking with her "das Beste seines Innern"; and her form does not dissolve, as does that of Helena: it persists with an eternal validity. This clearly foreshadows the Epilogue, "Bergschluchten," in which Faust is to rejoin Gretchen in the other world, saved largely through her love and her intercession. It is possible that something is preserved here of those earlier plans in which Gretchen was to have appeared before Faust in the form of the Virgin Mary. The standard by which Faust's love relationship to Helena is "higher" than his love relationship to Gretchen is then not an absolute standard. For all her limitations, Gretchen herself is, with her "Seelenschönheit," something more than the lovely phantom Helena. But Faust fails disastrously in his love for Gretchen, as he does not fail in his love for the daemonic Helena. The latter terminates tragically not because of any shortcoming on his part, but because the violence and recklessness, which have been temporarily arrested in his own nature, break out again in the nature of his son, Euphorion. And that tragical ending is as remote from immediate flesh and blood reality as the idyllic happiness preceding it had been. Compared with the Gretchen Tragedy, it is hardly a tragedy at all; it moves us quite differently and very much more gently. If Faust had been able to hold his love for Gretchen fast, it would have "outshone every other treasure"; but then he would not have been Faust. Just because he is a "specialist" in the impossible and superhuman, he is not equal to the demands of the possible and human. That is the price genius has to pay for its pre-eminence.

Mephisto now rejoins Faust, who sets out on further adventures. Helena is completely banished from his mind, as Gretchen had been. He never recalls her, expresses no regrets for her loss, and seems to have learnt nothing of what might have been learnt from his encounter with her. This appears to be a law of his being, and the exertions of many critics to demonstrate that he grows in wisdom, virtue, or spiritual stature from one adventure to another are unavailing. They seem indeed sometimes to have Goethe on their side in this matter, but they have Faust himself against them all the time—Faust who says immediately before his death:

> Ich bin nur durch die Welt gerannt;
> Ein jed' Gelüst ergriff ich bei den Haaren,
> Was nicht genügte, liess ich fahren,
> Was mir entwischte, liess ich ziehn.
> Ich habe nur begehrt und nur vollbracht
> Und abermals gewünscht und so mit Macht
> Mein Leben durchgestürmt . . .*

The only kind of progress he almost contemptuously gives himself credit for is that, whereas his striving had at first been "gross und mächtig" (grand and forceful), he has now, in his old age, become "weise und bedächtig" (wise and circumspect). This does not in its context indicate anything of the mellow wisdom of old age, and is certainly not meant to do so. Of such wisdom Faust to the last shows no trace.

Faust's new and penultimate goal is suggested to him by the

---

* I have only rushed through the world; / I seized hold of whatever I desired; / What did not suffice I let go again, / What eluded me I relinquished. / I have only desired and achieved / And then wished again for something else, and so with violence / Stormed through my life.

sight of the eternally, fruitlessly surging tides of the ocean, which exasperate and challenge him:

> Was zur Verzweiflung mich beängstigen könnte!
> Zwecklose Kraft unbändiger Elemente!*

With this he is declaring war upon just those forces in the external world which correspond most closely to his own turbulent, untamable soul. His object is to reclaim land from coastal areas by building dams to keep back the tides, and to establish on this land a flourishing human community, of which he will be the ruler. According to the somewhat arbitrary scale of values postulated by Goethe for the purposes of the Faust drama this aim must be estimated as "higher" than that represented by Helena—just as that represented by Helena must be estimated as "higher" than that represented by Gretchen. A case could be made out for reversing this scale of values, which is not necessarily Goethe's own. Faust's striving after land-reclamation and monarchical power stands higher than his previous ventures by his own standards, because it involves, as they did not, "activity"; it is only at this point that he, the great champion of "the deed," at last himself really becomes active. One sees at once another sense in which it could rank highest: as a piece of useful service to mankind, as a tempering of Faust's arrogant egoism with the feeling of human brotherhood, as the idealistic and altruistic will to establish a perfect human community dominated by justice, liberty, and happiness. That is how it frequently is interpreted. But such considerations play no part at all in the formation of Faust's plan or in his way of carrying it out. He sums up his aspirations in the pregnant phrase: "Herrschaft gewinn' ich, Eigentum!" (I shall attain dominion and property). He is in fact animated by the genuine superman's "will to power," and is more interested in triumphing over the elements than in the character of the kingdom he will establish. Mephisto procures for him the desired opportunity. On their visit to the Kaiser's court they had found him in great financial difficulties and had helped him with the proposal that he should issue unlimited quantities of paper

---

* What could alarm me to the point of despair / Is the aimless strength of tameless elements.

money, with the treasures buried in the imperial territories as backing. After initial success this scheme has worked out catastrophically. A revolution has broken out to establish another Emperor, the "Gegenkaiser." Faust offers the true Kaiser his support, and with the aid of Mephisto's arts defeats the Gegenkaiser. The means that Mephisto uses and for which Faust must be held responsible are decidedly brutal and unchivalrous. He lets loose on the enemy the "drei Gewaltigen" (the Three Mighty Ones), grotesque and barbarous monsters, named "Raufebold," "Habebald," and "Haltefest," and produces a magical flood at the critical moment. As a reward for his services Faust is given a strip of coast that he desires, with the right to any land adjoining it that he may be able to reclaim from the sea.

By the time the fifth act begins, whole decades must be supposed to have elapsed, as Faust is now, according to Goethe's own statement, recorded by Eckermann, just a hundred years old. His land-reclamation schemes have been carried through with great success. He is ruler over an extensive territory. But this has not been achieved by natural means. It is really the work of Mephisto with his uncanny assistants, and "Menschenopfer mussten bluten" (Human sacrifices have had to bleed) for it. We learn nothing of the community Faust has established or of its government, except that it is prosperous. But everything suggests that he is more of a ruthless despot than a model ruler. He still makes use of the services of Mephisto, although according to the draft outline for the second part of December, 1816, Goethe must at one time have intended that he should by now have dismissed him—an extremely important motif, of which, however, only an indirect hint is preserved in the final version, immediately before Faust's death. One of Mephisto's chief employments is the captaining of the new kingdom's mercantile fleet, in which he is assisted by the Drei Gewaltigen. He makes this an occasion for piracy, with Faust's knowledge and for his enrichment, and without his remonstrating against it. Faust can, however, take no satisfaction in the fulfilment of his plans or in the "dominion and property" he has acquired, because there is at the edge of his territory, on a piece of high ground that used to be the coast, a little cottage inhabited by the humble and devout old couple, Philemon and Baucis, with a chapel adjoining it. He covets

this insignificant piece of land and loathes the sound of the bells
from the chapel—an indication of the change his soul has undergone since the hour when the Easter bells had moved him to tears.
In his embitterment he cries:

> Verdammtes Läuten! Allzuschändlich
> Verwundet's, wie ein tückischer Schuss;
> Vor Augen ist mein Reich unendlich,
> Im Rücken neckt mich der Verdruss,
> Erinnert mich durch neidische Laute:
> Mein Hochbesitz, er ist nicht rein,
> Der Lindenraum, die braune Baute,
> Das morsche Kirchlein ist nicht mein.*

Faust has offered Philemon and Baucis another place to live in
the new territory, in exchange for their property, but they prefer
to stay where they are. He is now, as he says, "weary of being just,"
and in an impatient moment he gives Mephisto the order: "So
geht und schafft sie mir zur Seite!" (Go and get rid of them for
me!) Mephisto does this with the help of the Drei Gewaltigen, and
in the process the old couple and a guest in their cottage are killed.
This event is presented by the device of "Teichoskopie" through
the mouth of the watchman Lynkeus, who—a superb stroke of
dramatic irony—immediately before has been chanting from his
tower a great Paean on the goodness and beauty of all existence,
one of Goethe's finest pieces of lyrical writing, beginning:

> Zum Sehen geboren,
> Zum Schauen bestellt,
> Dem Turme geschworen,
> Gefällt mir die Welt—†

---

* Damnable bells! All too ignominiously / They wound me like a treacherous
shot; / Before my eyes my dominion is infinite, / But at my back vexation
plagues me, / Reminding me with envious sound / That my great possessions
are not complete, / That the limetree plot, the brown cottage / And the little
crumbling church are not mine.

† Born to see, / Called upon to behold, / I am pledged to the watch-tower /
And the world delights me.

and concluding:

> Ihr glücklichen Augen,
> Was je ihr gesehn,
> Es sei wie es wolle,
> Es war doch so schön!‡

Faust disowns all responsibility for the barbarous liquidation of the aged couple, crying to Mephisto and his henchmen:

> Dem unbesonnenen wilden Streich
> Ihm fluch' ich: teilt es unter euch!§

This is the only definite example we are given of the spirit and manner in which Faust exercises his monarchical authority. It must be regarded as representative, and it hardly shows him in a creditable light, especially because it is not only brutal, but also betrays a streak of mean and petty envy, which accords ill with the heroic stature of the superman and which we should not expect of Faust as we have hitherto seen him. It looks as though Goethe had gone out of his way to show us Faust at this last stage of his career falling very low—lower even than in his desertion of Gretchen. The remarkable point is, however, that very many critics, especially during the period 1870–1930, refused to accept this obvious conclusion and insisted that Faust's treatment of Philemon and Baucis cannot be representative of his activities as colonizer and monarch, but must be an exception to which no great importance attaches, or which is not really so bad as all that. They confute what Goethe here actually does tell us about Faust's ruthlessness with what they think he might and should have told us about all the benefits he has conferred upon his fellow men by his land-reclamation and his wise governorship. Some have even tried to justify his treatment of the old couple as a regrettable but necessary sacrifice of "das Recht des Einzelnen" to "grösseren Zwecken" and to the "Wohl des

---

‡ O fortunate eyes, / Whatever you have seen, / Be it what it may, / Was in spite of everything so beautiful.

§ My curse upon the wild, rash exploit! / Share the guilt of it amongst yourselves.

Ganzen" (the rights of the individual [to] larger issues and for the good of the whole).[11] Emrich writes of it: "Im Grunde ist dies keine Schuld, sondern ... ein Schicksal des Weltlaufs, das unlösbar mit allem Herrschen und Arbeiten verknüpft ist" (At bottom this is not guilt, but a fate arising from the course of the world and bound up with all ruling and working).[12] Various postulates, arguments, preconceived ideas and motives are responsible for such interpretations, which have only been effectively discredited during the last thirty years or so; and still they linger on in modified forms. There are, to begin with, Goethe's already quoted words about Faust's "immer höhere und reinere Tätigkeit bis ans Ende," which are certainly, like the Lord's description of Faust as "ein guter Mensch," to be understood not literally but paradoxically, and which perhaps also betray a certain fluctuation and inconsistency in Goethe's conceptions and intentions. By no manipulation of the text can what Faust does to Philemon and Baucis be interpreted as either a "high" or a "pure" activity. There is too the not unchallengeable assumption that Faust is set before us as a magnificent, heroic, exemplary figure whom we must unconditionally admire, and that therefore nothing—not even this last exploit of his —should lower him in our eyes. The real guilt lies not with Faust, but with Mephisto, who has carried out his orders in a way in which they were not intended. That is indeed the excuse with which Faust tries to exculpate himself. It is a moot point, how far a ruler is responsible for the results of his commands, especially when he employs such agents as Mephisto and the Drei Gewaltigen, and how far Mephisto may have understood the orders given to him better than Faust himself is willing to admit after the event. But even if Philemon and Baucis, instead of being killed, had only been forcibly ejected from their property and settled elsewhere, it would still have remained a despotic, unjust act; that Faust can palliate such an act as "grossmütige Schonung" (magnanimous forbearance) is particularly revolting. But as a result largely of the influence of Nietzsche there has since the 1890's been a tendency to think of genuine greatness and superiority as manifesting themselves chiefly or even solely in acts of cruelty and injustice—a tendency with which Goethe would certainly have been quite out of sympathy, although he played a considerable part in paving the way for it. By this standard Faust's treatment of Philemon and Baucis is just something that proves him to be a really great man, a superman. Closely connected with this mentality, but not identical with it, was the practice which began to prevail about 1870 of acclaiming Faust as the great personification of pan-Germanism and of seeing his colonizing activities in terms of Germany's world-mission: from this point of view the Philemon and Baucis episode seemed a mere bagatelle, the sort of blood-and-iron expansionist policy that is justified by the paramount interests of the nation. Not only the patriots of the Hohenzollern era interpreted *Faust* in this way; the National Socialists also read their ideology into it. These last two trends have been searchingly analysed and attacked by Böhm and Hans Schwerte. But apart from all the extraneous, preconceived ideas that have led to the sinister aspects of Faust's cult of worldly power being denied, belittled, condoned, or even glorified, there is something in Goethe's actual text which complicates the issue and seems to lend some colour to such interpretations. That is Faust's final monologue, which will be considered when the time comes.

The assault on Philemon and Baucis is the beginning of the end for Faust. In the following scene, "Mitternacht" (Midnight), smoke from the burning ruins of their cottage drifts towards Faust's palace and solidifies into the forms of four mysterious "graue Weiber" (Grey Women), allegorical figures, precursors of their brother, "Death," who give their names as "Mangel," "Schuld," "Sorge," and "Not" (Want, Guilt, Care, and Distress). The only one of them who can penetrate into the palace is Sorge; the others have to withdraw. That Schuld cannot enter is felt to be an almost insoluble difficulty by many commentators, in view of the great guilt Faust has just incurred through his treatment of Philemon and Baucis; and it is sometimes maintained that the word "Schuld" should therefore be understood here not as "guilt," but in its other possible sense: "Debt," "financial embarrassment," which would make it almost identical with "Mangel." But it is highly improbable that Goethe should employ the word, as Staiger points out, in a "trivialeren Sinn" (more trivial sense) in such a context.[13] Staiger argues, however, that no causal relationship can be intended between the Philemon and Baucis episode and Faust's struggle with "Sorge," which follows immediately upon it. We have here, according to Staiger, merely a "juxtaposition" of two scenes written at different times and based upon conceptions that really have nothing to do with one another:[14] if they had anything to do with one another, Schuld would not have had to turn back; she, instead of Sorge, would have been the chief adversary against whom Faust has to contend in his last moments. There are few critics from whom one differs more reluctantly than from Staiger; but this is a case in which we must part company with him. The point of Schuld having to withdraw is not that Faust is free from guilt—he most certainly is not—but that he refuses to *admit* his guilt, that he is incapable of seeing and feeling himself as guilty, or, in other words, that he is incapable of repentance. We see this when he disclaims responsibility for the fate of Philemon and Baucis, thrusting all the blame on Mephisto and the Drei Gewaltigen. We saw it much earlier, in "Trüber Tag. Feld," when he similarly thrust the blame for Gretchen's fate on anything and anybody but himself. He is here the embodiment of Goethe's aphorism: "Der Handelnde ist immer gewissenlos." That Schuld cannot penetrate into Faust's palace means that he is immune to the sense of guilt. But he is not immune to care, to Sorge. Where other men—where ordinary humanity would feel pangs of conscience, Faust, the superman, feels only anxiety, deep uneasiness, "Sorge." Care is the most rudimentary form of conscience, which even a Faust cannot escape. It is the same care of which he had spoken so vehemently in the continuation of the first scene of *Faust I*, written after 1797:

> Die Sorge nistet gleich im tiefen Herzen,
> Dort wirket sie geheime Schmerzen,
> Unruhig wiegt sie sich und störet Lust und Ruh;
> Sie deckt sich stets mit neuen Masken zu . . .*

It is the same care of which Goethe speaks again and again outside *Faust*, notably in the already quoted draft for *Dichtung und*

---

* Care builds its nest deep down in the heart, / Engendering secret pains there, / Tossing restlessly to and fro and marring joy and peace; / It is forever concealing itself behind new masks.

Wahrheit: "Tat steht mit Reue, Handeln mit Sorge in immer währendem Bezug." Goethe has at this point put a great deal of himself into Faust. As a rule, he deliberately and more or less successfully staved off the feeling of repentance, and also rejected it theoretically on psychological grounds as a particularly morbid form of self-torment and self-destruction. This was one of his chief quarrels with Christianity. One of his late epigrammatic quatrains runs:

> Nichts taugt Ungeduld,
> Noch weniger Reue;
> Jene vermehrt die Schuld,
> Diese schafft neue.*

He inveighs against the danger "von einem zu zarten Gewissen" (of a too tender conscience).[15] But Sorge still remains, and cannot be thus exorcized, and ultimately it is necessary and right that this should be so. For above all, it is through the experience of care that we are reminded of and then brought back within those "Grenzen der Menschheit" (limits of humanity), which no one— not even a Faust—can flout or attempt to flout with impunity. Care is therefore by no means an unmitigated evil. Burdach is right when, in opposition to many other critics, he says of Sorge that she is "nicht etwa ein dienstbarer Geist des Mephisto und nicht etwa von ihm gerufen" (by no means a ministering spirit of Mephisto's and has by no means come at his summons).[16] Care has a positive ethical and metaphysical significance and function; on this point too one can appeal to Burdach: "Die antike Ethik . . . hat . . . die *cura* [die Horaz *atra* et *vitiosa* nennt,] gefeiert als Quelle des Guten im Menschen" (The ethics of the ancients honoured Care [which Horace calls "black" and "depraved"] as a source of the good in humanity).[17] Particularly is this true for Faust. If he were not still subject to care, he would be just a maniac or a criminal. That is the point of his last great struggle, when care is personified as one of the Grey Women. The scene is usually interpreted as though he triumphed completely over Sorge and

---

* Impatience is worth nothing, / Repentance is worth even less; / The former magnifies the guilt, / The latter creates new guilt.

therein once more manifested his invulnerable, superhuman greatness. He defies her indeed with the words:

> Doch deine Macht, o Sorge, schleichend gross,
> Ich werde sie nicht anerkennen.†

He re-asserts his Faustian nature in the great speech already cited
above (p. 329), "Ich bin nur durch die Welt gerannt," which,
simply because of the position in which it stands, is impossibly
interpreted by Daur as "ein Siegesfahrtgesang" (a triumphal hymn),
as evidence that Faust is "jetzt auf *neuer* Bahn" (on a new path),[18]
although he is here really for the last time striving to maintain
himself on his old path, and even as Goethe's own "moralisches
Bekenntnis" (moral profession of faith). But it is not with such
vaunting that Sorge can be silenced. Far more important than all
this grandiloquent defiance is the inner revolution that begins for
Faust with the entry of care. It is not a religious conversion, of
course. That is something Faust would be incapable of. Staiger's
comment is right enough, so far as it goes: "Gewissen, Reue,
Schuldbewusstsein, dies alles fällt gänzlich ausser Betracht. Die
Sorge spricht, nichts als die Sorge" (Conscience, repentance, the
sense of guilt, all this is ruled out. Care speaks, nothing but care).[19]
But what Faust experiences when care thus assails him is the
nearest that he, with his titanic nature, can come to a religious
conversion, to a renunciation of what had hitherto been the guiding
principles of his existence:

> Noch hab' ich mich ins Freie nicht gekämpft.
> Könnt' ich Magie von meinem Pfad entfernen,
> Die Zaubersprüche ganz und gar verlernen,
> Stünd' ich, Natur, vor dir ein Mann allein,
> Da wär's die Mühe wert, ein Mensch zu sein.*

---

† But your insidiously great might, O Care, / I will not recognize.

* I have still not fought my way out into the open. / If only I could expel
magic from my path, / If only I could completely forget the words of enchant-
ment / And stand before you, Nature, simply as a man. / Then it would be
worth while to be a human being.

Burdach comments on this passage as follows:

> Welchen geistigen, welchen menschlichen Fortschritt hat
> denn das lange strebende Bemühen zu einem höheren Dasein
> an der Seite Mephistos errungen? War Faust nicht dem Ideal,
> als freier, ganzer Mensch der Natur gegenüber [zu stehen],
> nach seinem eigenen Geständnis am Anfang der im Faust-
> drama dargestellten Lebensbahn viel näher als jetzt, da er
> von hinnen geht? Man muss diese Frage meines Erachtens
> mit einem tapferen Ja beantworten. Und diese Antwort ist
> durchaus im Sinne Goethes.†20

Faust regrets the great curse upon all life which had prepared the
way for his agreement with Mephisto. When he feels tempted to
overcome Sorge by magical instead of simply human means, he
resists it: "Nimm dich in Acht und sprich kein Zauberwort" (Be
cautious not to utter any magical words). In renouncing magic he
is above all renouncing his superhuman pretensions. It is at this
point that he must be regarded as dismissing Mephisto, though
it is strange that Goethe does not bring out this extremely important
motif more explicitly, and that there is indeed no real winding-up
of the relationship between the two, such as the structure of the
drama seems to demand. Faust's victory over Sorge is also only
half a victory: before she departs, she breathes on him and blinds
him. His spirit is indeed still unbroken; even blindness cannot
break it:

> Die Nacht scheint tiefer tief hereinzudringen,
> Allein im Innern leuchtet helles Licht.*

---

† What spiritual, what human advance has the long, arduous striving after
a higher existence at Mephisto's side achieved? Was not Faust, as he himself
confesses, nearer to the ideal of standing as a free and whole man before nature
at the beginning of the career presented in the *Faust* drama than he is now, at
the point of death? This question should in my opinion be answered with an
unintimidated "Yes." And this answer is quite in keeping with Goethe's intention.

* Night seems to penetrate deeper and deeper; / But within bright light
shines.

Faust's last moments are illuminated only by this ambiguous inner light, which on the one hand reveals a supreme vision to him, but on the other hand leaves him subject to the most dismal of delusions. He gives orders for the immediate commencement of a great piece of work that shall crown all his land-reclamation schemes.

The next scene, "Grosser Vorhof des Palasts" (Great Forecourt of the Palace) shows Mephisto leading in the "Lemures" (certain ghoulish, grotesque spirits), who begin at his instructions to dig Faust's grave, singing as they do so a German adaptation of the gravediggers' song from *Hamlet*. The blinded Faust, groping his way out of the palace, hears them digging and believes that they are his own workmen carrying out the orders he has given. He cries: "Wie das Geklirr der Spaten mich ergetzt!" (How the clinking of the spades delights me!) He has no thought or word of lamentation for his own plight; everything else is forgotten in his joy at the thought of the future community for which he is preparing a living space, and he evokes a vision of the future in ecstatic words, which were perhaps not given their final form till a few weeks before Goethe's death.[21] It is not a matter this time of winning land from the sea, but of draining an extensive swamp at the edge of a mountain range, which with its pestilential exhalations makes all the land so far reclaimed unsafe to live in. If that swamp is drained, Faust will have opened up space for millions. The decisive passage runs:

> Ja! diesem Sinne bin ich ganz ergeben,
> Das ist der Weisheit letzter Schluss:
> Nur der verdient sich Freiheit wie das Leben,
> Der täglich sie erobern muss.
> Und so verbringt, umrungen von Gefahr,
> Hier Kindheit, Mann und Greis sein tüchtig Jahr.
> Solch ein Gewimmel möcht' ich sehn,
> Auf freiem Grund mit freiem Volke stehn.
> Zum Augenblicke dürft' ich sagen:
> Verweile doch, du bist so schön!
> Es kann die Spur von meinen Erdentagen
> Nicht in Äonen untergehn.—

Im Vorgefühl von solchem hohen Glück
Geniess' ich jetzt den höchsten Augenblick.*

Immediately after speaking these last words Faust sinks down dead and the Lemures seize upon his body in readiness to bury it.

This is one of the key passages in the whole of *Faust*. It is here that the peripeteia of the entire drama, which had begun with the incursion of Sorge, comes to its culmination. The terrible irony of Faust's thus rejoicing in his last moment at the digging of his own grave, as though it were the commencement of his greatest undertaking, of which not a single stroke will ever be accomplished, is obvious. In so far his end is tragic and the entire work vindicates its right to be called a tragedy. This tragic aspect is intensified by an aside in which Mephisto discloses that even what Faust has already achieved with his land-reclamation will only outlast him a short time: It is all only the work of magic, without any genuine and abiding reality in it:

Du bist doch nur für uns bemüht
Mit deinen Dämmen, deinen Buhnen;
Denn du bereitest schon Neptunen,
Dem Wasserteufel, grossen Schmaus.
In jeder Art seid ihr verloren;—
Die Elemente sind mit uns verschworen,
Und auf Vernichtung läuft's hinaus.†

In addition to everything else, Faust has, in his extravagant halluci-

---

* Yes! to this aim I am entirely devoted; / That is wisdom's last conclusion; / He alone earns freedom and life / Who has to fight for them every day. / And so, beset by dangers on all sides, / Childhood, manhood, and old age will spend their vigorous year. / Such a throng as that I would like to see, / To stand on free territory with a free people. / Then I might say to the passing moment: / Remain! You are so beautiful! / The trace of my earthly days / Cannot perish in aeons.— / In anticipation of so lofty a happiness / I now enjoy my highest moment.

† It is only for us that you are toiling / With your dams and dykes; / You are already preparing a great feast / For Neptune, the water-devil. / Whatever comes, you are lost— / The elements are in league with us / And the upshot of it is destruction.

nation, at the last moment spoken the fatal words and lost his wager. At least Mephisto claims and can very plausibly claim that he has done so. Of course Faust has not asked the passing moment to stay in a spirit of complacent, sensual sluggishness, such as he had envisaged when the wager was offered, but rather in the very opposite spirit. No specific conditions had been laid down, however, about the spirit in which the words were to be pronounced. Faust has also only declared that he *might* beg the passing moment to remain, *if* he could "stand on free territory with a free people." It is interesting to note that this was one of Goethe's last-minute changes in the text; originally he had put into Faust's mouth the words: "Zum Augenblicke *darf* ich sagen . . ." "I *may*," not "I might." But such niceties do not disturb Mephisto. He is confident that he has won his wager, and there is pity as well as contempt in his comment:

> Ihn sättigt keine Lust, ihm gnügt kein Glück,
> So buhlt er fort nach wechselnden Gestalten;
> Den letzten, schlechten, leeren Augenblick,
> Der Arme wünscht ihn festzuhalten.*

The concluding words of Faust's wager-speech, "Die Uhr mag stehn, der Zeiger fallen,/ Es sei die Zeit für mich vorbei" (Let the clock stop, its pointer fall,/ Let time be for me at an end), are now echoed by Mephisto and the Lemures; and Mephisto also blasphemously brings in Christ's last words on the cross: "Es ist vollbracht" (It is finished)—a kind of flippancy at the expense of Christianity which Goethe indulged in regularly throughout the greater part of his life.

But this, like all Goethe's tragic endings, is neither unmitigatedly tragic nor a real ending. Even if nothing more were to follow (and actually there are still two long scenes to come), we should feel that Faust after all dies triumphantly and at least deserves to be delivered from Mephisto. Not only is his spirit unbroken to the last; his final vision, however deplorable a delusion it may be out-

---

* No pleasure satisfies him, no happiness suffices him, / So he goes on running after ever-changing forms; / The last miserable, empty moment / Is the one that the poor wretch desires to hold fast.

wardly and by realistic standards, has indisputably the highest claims to inward validity by idealistic standards. It hardly matters that none of those great hopes and aspirations which console and elevate Faust at the moment of his death will ever be fulfilled. What does matter is that he has them at all, that he dies with a profession of faith in a worthy and noble ideal.

But this final vision of Faust's has often been misinterpreted, and that is something for which Goethe himself is in a considerable measure responsible. At first sight it looks as though what we have before us here were merely a more explicit and emphatic restatement of the original programme with which Faust set out upon his schemes of land-reclamation. It is indeed still a matter of establishing a human community where there had never been one before, by engineering and colonization. Some find it a poor, lame, utilitarian conclusion that Faust, after having invoked the Erdgeist, consorted with the devil and loved Gretchen and Helena, should become a mere engineer, a mere modern technologist. But such criticisms take too literally what are after all in the first place symbols for the relationships between human civilization and the elemental forces of nature and for the relationship between such an exceptional individual as Faust and the rest of mankind. We may not like these symbols, but they are the ones Goethe chose to use, and we can only accept them. The point is that Faust's dying vision, humanly and ethically considered, embodies a magnanimous, altruistic programme motivated by high ideals and a sense of the brotherhood of man, and that as such it shows Faust in the most favourable light. It is easy to assume—and very commonly has been assumed—that these high-minded, selfless, idealistic motives are nothing new at this point, but had animated Faust from the outset and all along in his activities as land-reclaimer, colonizer and ruler, and are only now for the first time explicitly formulated. The entire final phase of Faust's career was thus interpreted in terms of the noble sentiments of his dying speech, not in terms of his treatment of Philemon and Baucis, which, it was felt, could be brushed aside as unrepresentative, or even excused, condoned, justified, or glorified. If this view is correct, the revolution in Faust's soul when he renounces magic under the influence of "Sorge" must be very much more limited in scope and importance than we have here represented it to be. In fact, it would then be difficult to see what need there was for him to undergo any spiritual revolution at all: he had already reached the pinnacle of his perfection, and there was no new lesson left for him to learn, no new insight for him to attain, before he should be ripe for death. His renunciation of magic would then have to be seen as a last, crowning gesture of super-human self-assertion, not as a kind of abdication of the superman in him: having made himself independent of everything else, he was now going to make himself independent even of magic and Mephisto too.

There are, however, clear enough indications that Goethe conceived of Faust's final vision as going far beyond and largely abrogating his previous attitude and activities. We should see here not so much persistence in the course hitherto pursued as a fundamental change of direction, a decisive contrast. There may well be some symbolical significance in the fact that Faust is here no longer concerned with gaining new land from the sea, but with draining an old pestilential swamp that has been causing disease in his new territory throughout all the preceding decades, without anything so far having been done about it: no triumph over the hostile elements without is of any value, unless the more insidious dangers within are also overcome. But this juxtaposition of two entirely different forms of land-reclamation may, as Hohlfeld[22] and Staiger[23] suggest, be only fortuitous, the result of a fluctuation in Goethe's plans, and without any symbolical meaning. A less uncertain point, and one fairly often recognized, is that Faust is now bent on dispensing with Mephisto's magical aid and insists on carrying out this latest plan with human labour only; admittedly he is still enough the old Faust to have no scruples about employing forced labour, if occasion arises. But what is most important is that he is above all concerned with the well-being and happiness of the human beings who will live on the reclaimed land and with their *freedom*, and that he feels himself one with them and desires to share their lives with them. That is something of which there had been no trace in his original land-reclamation schemes, when he had said: "Herrschaft gewinn' ich, Eigentum," and had for the rest been animated chiefly by the will to struggle with the elements and subdue them. It implies a renunciation of the ruthlessness with which he had treated Philemon and Baucis. One should not read into the often quoted verse: "Auf freiem Grund mit freiem Volke stehn," too much either of nationalism, with which Goethe sympathized little, or of democratic ideals, with which he sympathized even less. Nor is the particular form of "der Weisheit letzter Schluss": "Nur der verdient sich Freiheit wie das Leben, der täglich sie erobern muss," of such great moment as all that; one can see in it a broadening out of the Faustian doctrine of "Streben" to embrace the ordinary man. What really counts most is the sense of human solidarity and brotherhood. Faust had indeed set out with it, when he entered into the simple gaiety of the Easter holiday-makers and resolved "to enjoy within his inmost self what is parcelled out to all mankind," but he had become completely alienated from it in his morose, solitary, self-centred existence as superman, magician, and companion of Mephisto. Here, at least inwardly, he stands before Nature "ein Mann allein" once more and feels that it is "der Mühe wert, ein Mensch zu sein." He has gone through something in the nature of a "change of heart" in the eleventh hour. This and this alone must be the mysterious "Schöpfungsgenuss von Innen" (enjoyment of creation from within) spoken of in *Paralipomenon I*, which can be equated with that "Klarheit" (clarity) the Lord had promised to conduct Faust to in the "Prolog im Himmel." Faust experiences it only for a brief moment—immediately before his death, when his relationship to the outer world has been destroyed by blindness; but he himself acclaims it as his "höchsten Augenblick."

Amongst the many critics who interpret these decisive scenes embodying the peripeteia of *Faust II* on lines diametrically opposed to those here adopted, Emrich calls for particular notice. He summarily denies "dass . . . es im 5. Akt um einen Eintritt ins Gemeinschaftlichethische geht" (that in the fifth act it is a matter of entering into the field of social ethics).[24] He speaks of Faust's "schrittweisen Sieg über Sorge, Magie und Tod *unter Eliminierung der ethisch-sozialen Schuldfrage, um die es grundsätzlich gar nicht ging*" (Faust's gradual victory over care, magic, and death, to the exclusion of the ethical and social question, which was, on principle, not in the least involved).[25] Goethe has here, he maintains, eliminated "das Schuldproblem im üblichen Sinne" (the problem of guilt in the ordinary sense of the word).[26] Faust is "nicht schuldig im Sinne einer einmaligen Verfehlung, sondern eines totalen Naturschicksals" (not guilty in the sense of any particular moral offence, but only in that of a total natural destiny),[27] which means that he is not really "schuldig" at all, not even in his treatment of Philemon and Baucis. One could at most speak in his case of a highly metaphysical, impalpable guilt, which has nothing to do with what is usually understood by that word, namely the guilt of a "blinde Vermischung des Gewünschten mit dem Vorhandenen" (a blind confusing of what is desired with what actually exists).[28] According to Emrich everything turns here not upon ethical issues, as in *Faust I*, but solely upon the "Kampf zwischen immanenter und transzendental-zeitloser Tat" (the struggle between immanent and transcendental, timeless activity).[29] That is to say, what really worries Goethe about activity is not, as has here been argued, that it inevitably leads to guilt and "bankruptcy," but that it cannot in the empirical world make itself "ewig" (eternal): "Um die Dauer der Tat, nicht um ihre ethische Sicherung scheint es also Goethe primär zu gehen. Daher scheint das Schuldproblem einer anderen, überaus komplizierten Dialektik der Tat zu weichen" (Goethe seems then to be primarily concerned with the duration of the deed, not with its ethical sanction. Therefore the problem of guilt seems to yield place to another, highly complex dialectic of the deed).[30] The possibility that Goethe may have envisaged any other principle, higher than or at least equipollent to that of sheer activity as such, is not considered. Faust's dying monologue is to be understood not as indicating any change of heart, but simply as a metaphysical "Sprung aus der Zeit" (a leap out of time),[31] as the greatest of all his deeds, in which the active principle within him— far from submitting itself to any limits—at last succeeds in expressing itself no longer just empirically and relatively, but absolutely. Thus the principle of activity is seen by Emrich as remaining without any qualifications, triumphant to the very end: "Schuld und Erlösung scheinen beide aus Fausts Tätigkeit zu entspringen" (Guilt and salvation seem both alike to arise out of Faust's activity).[32] This means that for Emrich even the "Love from above" and the "Eternal Feminine" are subsumed under, indeed explicitly identified with, the one supreme, all-embracing, and solely valid

concept of the "deed"—a questionable obliteration of the fundamental polarity on which the entire *Faust* drama reposes. Emrich's
purely symbolical method of interpretation, which produces such
admirable results when applied to the first four acts of *Faust II*,
proves inadequate and even treacherous in face of the fifth act
with its dramatic and ethical tensions.

What happens at the end of *Faust II* is similar to what had
happened at the end of *Faust I*. Here too the Lord's prophecy is
fulfilled that Mephisto will find: "Ein guter Mensch in seinem
dunkeln Drange/ Ist sich des rechten Weges wohl bewusst." If
Faust had died only an hour or two earlier (immediately after the
episode of Philemon and Baucis, and before the visitation of Sorge
had made him abjure magic and find his way back, at least inwardly, to the limits and fellowship of humanity, thus enabling
him to experience "Schöpfungsgenuss von Innen"), his soul would
have fallen into the hands of Mephisto far more irrevocably than it
can do through his technically losing the wager and speaking the
fateful words about the passing moment. The radical difference
between the despotic way in which he has pursued his colonizing
policy hitherto, and the humane way in which he resolves to pursue
it in the future that never comes for him, is all-important. The
"height" of Faust's last moment would be far less significant, if he
had needed to take only one or two steps from an already elevated
position to reach it, instead of having to rise almost instantaneously
and in an unhoped-for way from the depths of callousness and
arrogance to which he had sunk in his treatment of Philemon and
Baucis. But Goethe has not brought out this distinction anything
like so clearly as one might have expected him to do and as it might
have seemed judicious for him to do—just as he has not brought
out the similarly important distinction between the Sign of the
Makrokosmus and the Erdgeist as clearly as might seem desirable.
The result is that both these distinctions, upon which so much
depends, have more often than not been overlooked or only imperfectly recognized. Hermann Türck can even argue that in renouncing magic Faust sinks to the level of a mere philistine,[33]
while Böhm sees in Faust's dying vision a mere "Flucht in die
Phantasie" (an escape into the imagination),[34] which shows him
to be incorrigible and undeserving of salvation to the last.

Goethe's failure here—if it is to be called a failure—is quite characteristic of his genius. He was, unlike Schiller, no friend of hard
and fast definitions or irreconcilable antitheses—not even where he
needed them and had deliberately decided to use them. He inclined
rather towards the nuance, to imperceptible transitions, to fine
shadings. He loved the organic, in which the great polarities supplement one another harmoniously. We have seen already how he had
to bring it home to himself that such "Widersprüche, statt sie zu
vereinigen, disparater zu machen [sind]."[35] But it went against the
grain for him to formulate what he was getting at so directly and
unambiguously that even the most literal-minded pedant could not
fail to understand him, and when he occasionally yielded to the
necessity of attempting it, the result was too often bald and almost
trite—almost like a copy-book maxim, as in the phrase: "Zwei
Seelen wohnen, ach! in meiner Brust." He far preferred to operate
with gentle, half-concealed hints, with eloquent silences, or with
laconic understatements. As it is, *Faust II* would reveal even less
than it does of what Goethe intended, if he had not on January 24,
1832, made certain alterations and additions to it, "in Rücksicht
grösserer Ausführung der Hauptmotive, die ich, um fertig zu
werden, allzu lakonisch behandelt habe" (with a view to working
out in more detail the principal motifs, which I had treated all too
laconically in my desire to get it finished).[36]

It is now possible to understand better why many critics regret
that Goethe did not terminate his drama with Faust's death, and
deprecate the two succeeding scenes ("Grablegung" and "Bergschluchten," which present Faust's salvation)—especially "Bergschluchten," as an inorganically patched-on happy ending detri-
mental to the austerity and sublimity of the tragedy. In particular
there is a common tendency either to dismiss "Bergschluchten" as
an unfortunate afterthought of Goethe's very latest years, or to
interpret it in a purely subjective, symbolical sense, without admitting that it implies any real belief in the supernatural order which
it seems to postulate, or even in the immortality of the soul. Thus
Korff writes: "Nur sofern die metaphysischen Szenen eine blosse
Gefühlsgegebenheit des Helden zu einer gleichnishaft gemeinten
Vorstellungswelt entfalten, schaut die grosse Dichtung scheinbar
ins Metaphysische hinein. Ihr scheinbar weiterer Horizont ist nach

seinem *wahren* Sinne auch der Horizont des Helden" (Only in so far as the metaphysical scenes unfold a purely objective emotional experience of the hero to a figuratively intended world of ideas does the great work apparently gaze out into the metaphysical. Its apparently wider horizon is in its *real* meaning also the horizon of the hero).[37] But while it is quite certain that Goethe did not believe in an orthodox sense in the specifically Christian concepts he here uses, he did, in spite of the irony and flippancy he indulges in, take them a good deal more seriously in a heterodox way of his own than such critics admit, and unquestionably attached great importance to some sort of objective, higher, supernatural order. The ideas of God, immortality, and salvation meant something more to him than mere symbols for a purely monistic, this-worldly humanism, though they could not, of course, mean to him what they mean to the Christian believer. Certainly he never thought of the story of Faust as being finished with his physical death, and it has already been argued that he must from the outset have planned to show him in one way or another as being saved.

Goethe has carefully devised the situation at the moment of Faust's death in such a way that Faust's salvation appears at least possible, but by no means certain. He has shown that he is "sich des rechten Weges wohl bewusst," but he has also lost his wager. The issue between him and Mephisto hangs in the balance, and something further must supervene to decide it. This alone makes the idea that the drama could be regarded as finished at this juncture untenable. The two scenes, "Grablegung" and "Bergschluchten," in which Faust's salvation is presented, raise many problems of chronology and interpretation. One thing we can be certain of, on grounds of contents and to a lesser extent of style, is that they were not written in the form in which we know them before 1825. Another thing we can also be certain of is that they were preceded by substantial fragments, or even by one or two provisionally worked out entire scenes, which must have been written as early as 1800 or 1801, and that the great bulk of this already existing material was incorporated in the final text. There are only two passages, both in "Bergschluchten," of which it matters much whether they were written at the earlier or the later date: the eight lines embodying what might be called the formula of Faust's salvation, "Gerettet ist das edle Glied/ Der Geisterwelt vom Bösen etc." (Delivered is the noble member of the spiritual world from evil), and the grand finale in which Gretchen is reunited with Faust and the whole work terminates in a hymn exalting "das Ewig-Weibliche" (the Eternal Feminine). These passages are of the greatest structural importance, and it makes a considerable difference whether they belong to Goethe's original conception or were only, as is often assumed, more or less casual afterthoughts of the years 1825–1831. If they indeed, as is here maintained, belonged to Goethe's original conception, they are more likely than any other passages in the two final scenes to have been written in 1800 or 1801, rather than in 1825 or later. The question is whether the objective evidence we have, which is unfortunately very meagre and indefinite, points to the earlier or later date for their composition.

It is almost universally assumed that "Bergschluchten" was an entirely new conception of December, 1830, and that there was nothing corresponding to it in Goethe's earlier plans or the "völliger Schluss" of March, 1825. One important point is that this scene differs strikingly in style from the rest of *Faust* and from almost everything else that Goethe wrote. So far, however, as its style points to one period rather than another of his development, it makes the impression of belonging to his latest phase, to his old age, which is still, it should be noted, quite as compatible with its having been given its final form in 1825 as with its not having been written at all till 1830 or 1831. Staiger, from whom we unfortunately find ourselves compelled to differ on this whole issue, writes: "Nun sträubt sich aber unser Gefühl hartnäckig dagegen anzunehmen, der überirdische Ausgang sei . . . bereits in Goethes mittleren Jahren entstanden. Denn sprachlich scheinen die Verse ganz dem höheren Alter anzugehören" (But our feeling stubbornly refuses to admit that the celestial termination was already written in Goethe's middle years. For stylistically the verses seem to belong to his advanced old age).[38] The question is, however, *which* verses? It is true enough that the bulk of the scene displays the characteristics of Goethe's latest style; but it is not true of the two passages we have singled out as of such great structural importance for the entire drama. Stylistically the scene is not so uniform that we can be sure it does not incorporate some passages from the earlier phase, 1800–1801. That is a possibility that is hardly ever considered. There is nothing about the construction of the scene—a loose series of monologues and choruses with very little action or dialogue to give it anything more than a general continuity of theme —which would suggest that it must all have been written at the same time. Such a form allows fullest scope for transpositions, interpolations, omissions, and for the combining of older with newer work. Even the criterion of style is not reliable. What is felt as being characteristic of Goethe's old age in this scene is above all the use of staccato, predominantly dactylic, two-beat verses with cumulative rhymes, which entail a certain curious stylization of the syntax and word-order. Goethe evidently regarded this type of verse and diction as appropriate for distinguishing the "mystical" from the mundane sphere, and that is why we find it here. But he had used it already in just the same way, with the same effect, and from the same motive as early as 1798 in the not altogether satisfactory choral Easter songs in *Faust I*. In view of those choral songs it is quite conceivable that even the bulk of "Bergschluchten" may have been written as early as 1800–1801, and that its linguistic and prosodic peculiarities may be determined simply by the mystical, pseudo-Catholic theme, and not by Goethe's age at the time of composition.

The earliest definite record we have of Goethe's plans for the conclusion of *Faust* is the phrase in *Paralipomenon I*, which we have dated about June 20, 1797: "Epilog im Chaos auf dem Weg zur Hölle" (Epilogue in Chaos on the way to Hell). The word "Epilog" here can certainly not mean, as is sometimes assumed, a valedictory speech addressed to the audience by one of the players, any more than the word "Prolog" in the title of the "Prolog im Himmel" means an introductory speech addressed to the audience by one of the players. What Goethe must have envisaged is a short scene in which Faust's soul would have been rescued from Mephisto at the eleventh hour by some celestial agent or agents, most probably by the apotheosized Gretchen, accompanied or not accompanied by a throng of saints or angels; it may well have been intended that she should appear at this point as a kind of avatar of the Virgin Mary, as the "madre di tutti i santi." We can assume that the scene "Grablegung" in the final text preserves the essential idea and outlines of this projected "Epilog im Chaos," which must, if our argumentation is sound, have belonged to Goethe's early Frankfort plans. It will be seen that Gretchen, although she does not appear amongst the angels in "Grablegung," has an important share in the device by which they rescue Faust's soul from Mephisto. The detailed scheme, completed by July 5, 1797, fairly certainly provided for an "Epilog im Himmel," either in addition to or in place of this projected "Epilog im Chaos." *Paralipomena* 194, 195, and 196, which consist of outline drafts for "Grablegung" and "Bergschluchten," although they are to be dated about February, 1825, probably go back to the 1797 scheme.

On August 3, 1815, Goethe said to Boisserée in reply to a question about the conclusion of *Faust*: "Das sage ich nicht, darf es nicht sagen, aber es ist auch schon fertig, und sehr gut und grandios geraten, aus der besten Zeit" (I shall not tell you that, I must not tell you about it, but it too is already finished and has come out very well and grandiosely, from the best period).[39] By "aus der besten Zeit" it is universally agreed that Goethe can only mean the time before Schiller's death, and other considerations narrow it down to about 1800–1801. But what exactly is Goethe here referring to as having been written about 1800–1801, and as being "sehr gut und grandios geraten"? The contention of Hertz that only *Paralipomena* 91–96 (which were not incorporated in the final text) can be intended,[40] is not tenable. Staiger gives two different answers to the question. First of all he says: "Mit dem 'Ende' ist höchst wahrscheinlich der irdische Ausgang Fausts gemeint" (By the end in all probability the earthly termination of Faust's life is intended),[41] which is to say, the scene "Grosser Vorhof des Palasts." But later he points to "Grablegung" and says of it: "das ist der 'grandios und gut geratene' Schluss 'aus der besten Zeit,' den Goethe im Gespräch mit Sulpiz Boisserée erwähnt" (This is the "grandiose and felicitous" ending "from the best period" which Goethe once mentions in conversation with Sulpiz Boisserée).[42] But "Grablegung," at least in the form in which we know it, lacks finality. It still contains no emphatic, resonant pronouncement on Faust's salvation, and it terminates with a monologue in which Mephisto gives vent to his exasperation and sense of grievance. Altogether, this scene is in the first place Mephisto's scene; 180 of the 240 verses it contains are spoken by him and he has the last word:

> Und hat mit diesem kindisch-tollen Ding
> Der Klugerfahrene sich beschäftigt,
> So ist fürwahr die Torheit nicht gering,
> Die seiner sich am Schluss bemächtigt.*

If this was ever intended to be the conclusion of the *Faust* drama, it was a lame, disappointing conclusion, in which one cannot imagine Goethe ever taking the satisfaction and pride expressed in his conversation with Boisserée.

"Grablegung" is in the first place a comic scene. The macabre humour not only occupies by far the greater space in it; it is qualitatively better than the earnest, lyrical element, which remains subordinated to it. Mephisto is waiting for Faust's soul to leave the dead body, and summons a multitude of grotesque devils, who bring the Jaws of Hell onto the stage with them and assist him in his vigil. Then suddenly a throng of angels descends and pelts the devils with roses, which turn into flames in their fiery breath. These flames, being celestial in origin, cause the devils great discomfort and drive them to flight. But they are also flames of love, and Mephisto, who holds out longest, is seized with paederastic lust after the angels. When he is driven back from the grave, as covered with boils as Job, the angels seize Faust's "Unsterbliches" (immortal part)—that is to say, his "Entelechy"—and fly up to Heaven with it. This excellent though often scabrous humour is what makes the liveliest impression in the scene, while of the choruses sung by the angels only the second one, "Rosen, ihr blendenden . . ." (Roses, you dazzling ones . . .) lingers in the memory as genuinely fine lyric, representative of Goethe at his best. Now is it conceivable that Goethe ever contemplated concluding his *Faust* on a note of farcical, scurrilous humour? The scene is certainly excellent in its own grotesque way and where it stands, in the penultimate position; and it is quite possible that most of it was written, as Staiger sug-

---

* And if one who is clever and experienced / Busies himself with this childish, crazy thing, / Then the folly is indeed not slight / Which in the end overcomes him.

gests, about 1800 or 1801. But it would have been quite unfit to stand at the end, and there is nothing "grandiose" about it, nor is there intended to be. Whatever Goethe was referring to in his conversation with Boisserée in 1815, it cannot have been "Grablegung" as we now know it. It might at most have been "Grablegung" in an earlier form, including some of the passages which now stand in "Bergschluchten" and ending on a solemn instead of a flippant note.

That the "grandiose" conclusion of *Faust* about which Goethe spoke to Boisserée in 1815 could, as some have suggested and as Staiger also seems to think possible, have been the scene showing Faust's death is ruled out by the inconclusiveness of that scene. The objections to the view that it was "Grablegung" have been seen to be even greater. The only possibilities that remain are that it never really existed at all and that Goethe was only indulging in a little wishful thinking; or that it was after all judged unsuitable and rejected *in toto* and that nothing of it has survived; or that it was later incorporated in "Bergschluchten." The two first of these possibilities can be ruled out. The epithet "grandiose" applies to "Bergschluchten," especially to the final section of it, as it could never apply to "Grablegung."

We can be fairly certain, however, that "Bergschluchten" was not yet in existence as a whole in its final form in 1815. This emerges from Goethe's letter to K. E. Schubarth of November 3, 1820: "Auch den Ausgang haben Sie richtig gefühlt. Mephistopheles darf seine Wette nur halb gewinnen, und wenn die halbe Schuld auf Faust ruhen bleibt, so tritt das Begnadigungsrecht des alten Herrn zugleich herein, zum heitersten Schluss des Ganzen" (You have also shown a right feeling for the end. Mephisto can only half win his wager, and if half the guilt rests with Faust, the Old Gentleman's (that is, God's) prerogative of mercy at once intervenes and brings the whole matter to the happiest of conclusions). This means that Goethe had up to 1820 still not abandoned the idea of making the final scene a good deal nearer in construction to the "Prolog im Himmel" than "Bergschluchten" actually is.[43] God the Lord was to have appeared again and formally pronounced judgement in Faust's favour. There is no reason for supposing that this plan was already worked out in the concluding scene about which Goethe spoke to Boisserée. It is more likely that Goethe from 1797 onward—and probably from a much earlier date onward—planned in any case to bring in the Virgin Mary and Gretchen at the end, and that God the Lord was only intended to appear as well as them, not instead of them. Some such reappearance of God the Lord at the end seemed to be demanded on grounds of symmetry, consistency, and logic by the "Prolog im Himmel," whether it appealed specially to Goethe's own feelings and imagination or not. Actually it did not appeal in the least to his feelings and imagination, which inclined very much more to some kind of vision of the Virgin Mary or Gretchen, such as he had probably conceived of long before the idea of the "Prolog im Himmel"occurred to him in 1797. In the end his feelings and imagination triumphed over his sense of what the strict logic of the situation demanded. The reason he gave to Friedrich Forster for not concluding *Faust* exactly on the lines prescribed in the "Prolog im Himmel" was: "Das wäre ja Aufklärung. Faust endet als Greis, und im Greisenalter werden wir Mystiker" (But that would have been rationalism. Faust ends as an old man, and in old age we become mystics).[44] Up to February 1825, however, to judge from *Paralipomena* 194 and 195, Goethe seems to have thought still of bringing in, in addition to the appearance of the Virgin Mary, something in the nature of a formal trial of Faust before a Court of Appeal, in which Mephisto would have been the appellant and Christ the judge. But there are no traces of his ever having taken any serious steps to carry out this plan, and he must already have abandoned it when he wrote in his diary on March 13, 1825, about two and a half weeks after he had resumed work on *Faust*: "An Faust den Schluss fernerhin redigiert" (The end of Faust further revised). The "völliger Schluss" which he referred to in May, 1827, as being "schon längst fertig" can only have been this "Schluss" which he was revising in March, 1825, and there must have been a certain resonant finality about it. Staiger is, however, of the opinion that Goethe probably meant by the "völliger Schluss" Mephisto's monologue at the conclusion of "Grablegung," and that he came "erst später auf den Gedanken, den himmlischen Aufstieg folgen zu lassen" (he only later thought of following this up with the ascent into Heaven).[45] We have seen what serious objections there are to this view of Staiger's. The entry in Goethe's diary of December, 1830: "Abschluss des Faust und Mundum desselben" (Termination of Faust and a fair copy of it) is evidence that the "völliger Schluss" of March, 1825, must have been revised and in all likelihood extensively amplified about that date. The question is, whether "Bergschluchten" was only first thought of in December, 1830, as is usually assumed and as Staiger explicitly declares, or whether, as we would maintain, the essential idea of it and some of the most important passages in it had by then already been in existence for some time and needed only to be further worked out and perhaps given a new scenic setting. There are good reasons for supposing that there was originally one single scene, corresponding to the "Epilog im Chaos auf dem Weg zur Hölle" envisaged in Paralipomenon I, in the place of "Grablegung" and "Bergschluchten" as we now know them, and that "Berg-schluchten" arose through Goethe's detaching from this scene the passages with a character of solemn finality, giving them a new set-ting and so making something independent out of them. Whether he did this in March, 1825, or not till December, 1830, cannot be decided and does not greatly matter.

"Bergschluchten" turns upon the mysteries of love, identified with the Eternal Feminine, which Mephisto, as the devil, is incapa-ble of comprehending, and which Faust, the Promethean repre-sentative of the Eternal Masculine, had been only imperfectly capable of comprehending or experiencing, as appears in his re-lationships to Gretchen and Helena. It is characteristic of Goethe that he makes no sharp distinction between "Eros," which was celebrated at the conclusion of the "Klassische Walpurgisnacht" as having "begun all things," and Christian "Caritas," or between the love of the sexes and the love of God. The holy anchorites, *Pater ecstaticus*, *Pater profundus*, and *Pater seraphicus*, who have their cells high up in a wild, desolate mountain region, sing the praises of love in its various manifestations. They are passed by a number of souls of innocent boys who have died soon after their birth and are now flying heavenward. These are followed by the angels bearing Faust's "Unsterbliches." They first sing together the verses containing the formula for Faust's salvation, then the "younger" and the "more perfect" angels sing separately. The

younger angels exult over the strategem by which they have tricked
Mephisto and his devils out of Mephisto's soul, much like a gang
of mischievous schoolboys after a successful rag. This song of
theirs is chiefly interesting because of what it tells us about the
origin of the roses with which they had pelted the devils:

> Jene Rosen aus den Händen
> Liebend-heiliger Büsserinnen
> Halfen uns den Sieg gewinnen . . .*

The importance of this is that one of these "liebend-heiligen Büs-
serinnen" turns out to have been Gretchen; she is indeed, from
the point of view of the drama, the one who counts most, or even
the only one who really counts. That is to say, *Gretchen is decisively instrumental in the actual deliverance of Faust's soul from
Mephisto.* We are once more forced to differ from Staiger who,
in accordance with his late dating of the conception of "Bergschluchten," says of this correspondence: "Als die *Grablegung*
geschrieben wurde, war dies kaum die Meinung. Sonst hätte Goethe
wenigstens im Vorbeigehen darauf hingewiesen" (This can hardly
have been intended when "Interment" was written, as otherwise
Goethe would, at least in passing, have drawn attention to it).[46]
But Goethe quite deliberately refrained from drawing attention to
such hidden correspondences in *Faust*, especially in the second
part; that belonged to his avowed policy of "Hineingeheimnissen,"
and of setting posterity riddles to guess ("aufzuraten"), as he puts
it in his letter to Zelter of January 4, 1831. The song of the "vol-
lendeteren Engel" takes us beyond the earlier, too trite distinction
between the "zwei Seelen" in Faust's breast; those two souls are
here seen to be indistinguishably welded together in an organic
unity, and we learn also that something is still wanting to complete
Faust's salvation—namely, that the earthly element should be
eradicated; only the "eternal Love" from above can accomplish this:

> Uns bleibt ein Erdenrest
> Zu tragen peinlich,
> Und wär' er von Asbest,

---

* Those roses from the hands / Of loving, penitent women, / Helped us to
gain the victory.

> Er ist nicht reinlich.
> Wenn starke Geisteskraft
> Die Elemente
> An sich herangerafft,
> Kein Engel trennte
> Geeinte Zwienatur
> Der innigen beiden,
> Die ewige Liebe nur
> Vermag's zu scheiden.*

The angels hand Faust's immortal part over to the souls of the innocent boys, who begin to unwind him out of his cocoon.

At this point the Virgin Mary, as *Mater Gloriosa*, is seen approaching from above, accompanied by a throng of holy, penitent women, and is hailed by one of the anchorites, Doktor Marianus, as "Göttern ebenbürtig" (equal of the gods)—a theologically indefensible phrase which had also been earlier applied to Helena, and which indicates how far Goethe is from taking the Catholic concepts he here employs seriously in their orthodox sense. The scene moves imperceptibly towards the celestial plane. After three representative penitent women have addressed their intercessions for Gretchen to the Mater Gloriosa, Gretchen herself, nestling against Faust, sings:

> Neige, neige,
> Du Ohnegleiche,
> Du Strahlenreiche,
> Dein Antlitz gnädig meinem Glück!
> Der früh Geliebte,
> Nicht mehr Getrübte,
> Er kommt zurück.†

It has already been pointed out how these verses link up with

---

* To carry earthly remains / Is still offensive to us; / Even if they were of asbestos, / They are not cleanly. / When the strong power of the spirit / Has once drawn the elements to cleave to it, / No angel could separate / The united double nature / Of the ardent pair. / Only Eternal Love / Can divide it.

† Bend, bend, / Thou incomparable one, / Thou who aboundest in radiancy, / Thy countenance in grace to my happiness. / The early loved one, / Now no longer overcast, / Has come back to me.

Gretchen's prayer to the Mater Dolorosa in the scene "Zwinger" of the *Urfaust*.[47] Faust's immortal part has by now grown to celestial proportions and freed itself from "jedem Erdenband" (every earthly fetter). An activity is assigned to him in Heaven: he is to educate the innocent boys on the strength of the earthly experience which he has and of which they have been deprived by their early death. Gretchen addresses one more petition to the Mater Gloriosa: that she may be permitted to initiate Faust into the mysteries of the heavenly existence:

> Vergönne mir, ihn zu belehren,
> Noch blendet ihn der neue Tag.‡

The Mater Gloriosa grants this in the only words she utters throughout the scene, words which closely link up Faust's salvation with that of Gretchen:

> Komm! hebe dich zu höhern Sphären!
> Wenn er dich ahnet, folgt er nach.*

It is almost as though Gretchen had postponed her own salvation until Faust should have joined her. The scene concludes with the famous words, sung by the *Chorus Mysticus*:

> Alles Vergängliche
> Ist nur ein Gleichnis;
> Das Unzulängliche,
> Hier wird's Ereignis;
> Das Unbeschreibliche,
> Hier ist's getan;
> Das Ewig-Weibliche
> Zieht uns hinan.†

It is significant that Faust himself does not speak a word throughout the scene. Goethe could not have put any words into Faust's mouth here, without explicitly raising the question of whether he repents or not, and he evidently preferred to leave it to the reader

---

‡ Grant to me that I may instruct him; / The new daylight still dazzles him.
* Come! ascend to higher spheres, / Feeling where thou art, he will follow.
† Everything transient / Is but a symbol; / The unattainable / Here is realized; / The indescribable / Here is accomplished; / The Eternal Feminine / Draws us upward.

to answer that particular, not unimportant, question for himself, in accordance with his own views and his own intelligence.

"Bergschluchten" really is grandiose and has the qualities of a genuine finale which "Grosser Vorhof" and "Grablegung" lack, and are meant to lack. Whether one likes it or not is another question. Some object to it as too Catholic, others object to it for having anything Christian about it at all. Some are shocked by it as an arbitrary, irreverent, and ironical travesty of Christian beliefs. Some find it too idealistic, some too facilely optimistic. Others find something sentimental, nebulous, obscure, or absurd about it, and it has often been parodied, notably by F. T. Vischer and Nietzsche. Probably those who wholeheartedly like it are in the minority. The question for us, however, is whether this scene was in Goethe's own eyes a necessary, integral part of the *Faust* drama, without which it would not have been complete, and as such belonged to his plans in one form or another from an early date, or whether it was only a not strictly relevant afterthought of 1830 or 1831. The latter view is maintained by a majority of critics including Staiger, who says that the final scene "ganz für sich besteht" (stands quite by itself),[48] and also argues: "Mit keiner Silbe hatte [Goethe] Fausts Entrückung in höhere Sphären begründet" (Goethe had not with a single syllable paved the way for Faust's translation into higher spheres).[49] There are, however, it could be maintained, quite a number of indications that this is ultimately to be Faust's destiny. It is implied by the "Prolog im Himmel" and more than just implied in the scene "Nacht" by his premature desire "Auf neuer Bahn den Äther zu durchdringen/ Zu neuen Sphären reiner Tätigkeit" (To penetrate the ether on a new path to new spheres of pure activity) by turning his back upon the "holde Erdensonne" (the beauteous sun of this world) in suicide; and it is implied also by his declaration in the "Spaziergang vor dem Tor" that his nobler soul aspires "gewaltsam vom Dust zu den Gefilden hoher Ahnen" (vehemently from the dust/ To the domains of its lofty forebears). It is hinted at in Gretchen's words just before her execution: "Wir sehn uns wieder!" and by the vision Faust has of her at the beginning of Act IV of the second part: "die holde Form . . . erhebt sich in den Äther hin/ Und zieht das Beste meines Innern mit sich fort" (The gracious form mounts up into the ether,/ Bearing along with it what is best in my inmost being). Schelling, we saw, was, on the strength only of his reading of *Faust, ein Fragment,* confident that Faust would be "in höhere Sphären erhoben."[50] Faust is never so totally committed to this life and this world that the sense of his celestial "Urquell" is unrenewably extinguished in him. We know too that Goethe, impatient though he usually was with other people's convictions about the soul's immortality and the other world, particularly with orthodox Christian convictions, himself firmly believed in a selective immortality based on the idea of "entelechy." We recall once more his declaration of 1818 that "man, however the earth attracts him . . . feels deeply and clearly within himself that he is a citizen of the spiritual domain."[51] All these considerations make it probable that something corresponding to "Bergschluchten" formed from the outset a part of his Faust plans.

Gundolf characteristically deplores "Bergschluchten" as a dilution, almost a betrayal of the autonomous, heroic greatness of Faust:

> Dass die Erlösung Fausts durch das Ewig-Weibliche, durch die All-Liebe erfolgt, ist in der Fausthandlung, ja im Faustproblem selbst nicht angelegt, widerspricht der Haltung und Gesinnung des titanischen und prometheischen Menschen, ist keine immanente Lösung des Strebens und Werdens, und biegt sogar den Sinn des Prologs im Himmel um. Man hätte erwartet, dass Gott Vater, der Weltschöpfer und Weltrichter, das Urteil über die schöpferische Seele fällen würde. Das Ewig-Weibliche, mag es in Goethes Gesamtleben eine der grossen Potenzen sein, kommt im Faust einigermassen ex machina.*[52]

---

* That the salvation of Faust is brought about through the Eternal Feminine, through Universal Love, is not grounded in the action of the *Faust* drama itself or, for that matter, in the Faust problem; it is inconsistent with the attitude and mentality of the titanic and Promethean man, it is not an immanent solution to striving and becoming, and it even distorts the meaning of the "Prologue in Heaven." It was to be expected that God the Father, the Creator and Judge of the world, would pass judgment on the creative soul. Although the Eternal Feminine may be one of the great forces in Goethe's life, it emerges in *Faust* more or less as a *dea ex machina*.

Gundolf assumes here that the Titanic and Promethean principle of "striving and becoming" is posited absolutely in *Faust*, without considering the possibility that it may all along be envisaged in a relationship of dialectical polarity to the no less important, though seldom explicitly presented or evoked, opposite principle of the Eternal Feminine, or in other words that "Bergschluchten" only expresses at last more openly and directly a criticism and correction of the excesses and deficiencies of Faust which is *implied* throughout the two parts of the drama, most forcibly in the Gretchen and the Philemon and Baucis episodes. This would mean that there is no "Lösung" immanent in striving and becoming as such, and that if there is to be any solution for them at all, it must ultimately be a transcendental one. That is a view we are not prepared for from the pantheist Goethe, who often speaks so impatiently of the idea of an "extramundane" God. But where the last religious and ethical issues are concerned, as they are in *Faust*, Goethe's pantheism could and did expand to transcendental or quasi-transcendental, theistic horizons. He himself wrote to Jacobi on January 6, 1813:

> Ich für mich kann, bei den mannigfaltigen Richtungen meines Wesens, nicht an einer Denkweise genug haben; als Dichter und Künstler bin ich Polytheist, Pantheist hingegen als Naturforscher, und eins so entschieden als das andre. Bedarf ich eines Gottes für meine Persönlichkeit, als sittlicher Mensch, so ist dafür auch gesorgt.†

The Eternal Feminine is then less of a *dea ex machina* than Gundolf asserts; it is all along present in the background as the complementary opposite of Faust's ruthlessness. The God of the "Prolog im Himmel" on the other hand really is something of a *deus ex machina*, and would have been so still more, if he had reappeared at the end.

Barker Fairley voices a similar criticism to Gundolf's, but in more circumspect, discriminating, and temperate terms:

---

† I for my part cannot, in view of the diverse tendencies of my nature, be satisfied with one mode of thinking alone; as a poet and artist I am a polytheist; as a scientist, on the other hand, I am a pantheist, the one as emphatically as the other. If I need a God for my personality as a moral being, that is a requirement which is also provided for.

It is only at the very last, when the poem is surging up from earth to heaven, that there is any hint of a deeper reconciliation . . . Goethe is thinking of that which must be given, and without which the striving is of no avail. But we cannot honestly say that this deep wisdom grows out of the poem; it grows rather out of the other side of Goethe's mind which Faust is incapable of expressing. If we wish to understand what *das Ewig-Weibliche* and the attitude of acceptance meant to him, we have to go outside *Faust* and read the rest of his poetry and read it long. It is as if at the eleventh hour *Faust* was trying to capitalize what it had not earnt or mastered. We can imagine that it is on its way to mastering it.[53]

While it may be admitted that the Eternal Feminine does not "grow out of" *Faust*, we can say that it is what *Faust* is all along working up to, and that the drama therefore does not so much "try to capitalize what it had not earnt or mastered" as find itself merged in it.

Goethe himself said to Eckermann on June 6, 1831 that the "Schlüssel zu Fausts Rettung" (key to Faust's redemption) is contained in the eight verses sung by the angels in "Bergschluchten."

> Gerettet ist das edle Glied
> Der Geisterwelt vom Bosen,
> Wer immer strebend sich bemüht,
> Den können wir erlösen.
> Und hat an ihm die Liebe gar
> Von oben teilgenommen,
> Begegnet ihm die selige Schar
> Mit herzlichem Willkommen.*

There has been endless dispute about the true meaning of this passage. The problem is that Faust's salvation is made here to depend not on one factor alone, but on two quite distinct ones:

---

* Delivered is the noble member / Of the spiritual world from evil: / Him who ever strives and toils / We can save. / And if, in addition to this, the love from above / Has concerned itself for him, / The host of the blessed / Will encounter him with a hearty welcome.

on his own "Streben" and on the "Liebe von oben"; and it remains
unclear which, if either, is the more important of the two, or how
they are related to one another. The German word "gar," which
seems to mediate between them and which can be translated either
as "in addition to" or as "even," only further obscures this issue,
instead of clarifying it. As it is often used expletively in poetry and
in everyday conversation, and here has to serve as a rhyme-word,
it need not have any particular significance one way or the other.
But if it has any particular significance, it is still difficult to decide
whether it implies that the "Liebe von oben" is simply a natural
consequence of Faust's "Streben," and therefore merely supple-
ments it as a means to his salvation, or whether it is before all
human striving, independent of it, and operates perhaps even to
some extent in spite of it. In other words: Is Faust saved through
his own unaided striving alone, because of what he is and has done?
Or is he saved by the divine mercy and grace, in spite of what he
is and has done? Is his salvation to be conceived of on fundamentally anti-Christian lines, as the insistence on the sufficiency of his
"Streben" suggests, or—after all—on more or less Christian lines,
as the insistence on the "Liebe von oben" suggests? If his striving
alone is sufficient for his salvation, why is there any mention at all
of the "Liebe von oben" as having concerned itself for him? If
the love from above is the decisive factor, why is so much made of
Faust's striving, which appears to have so little that is divine about
it, either in its aims or in its results?

A certain analogy can be seen between these questions and the
ancient dispute over salvation through "good works" or through
"faith" which began with St. Paul and St. James and has agitated
the Christian world intermittently ever since, most spectacularly
in the writings of Luther. But there is nothing at all of "good
works" in any possible sense of the term about Faust's striving, nor
does "faith" enter into it, unless the nebulous issue of "saying Yes
or saying No to Life," raised by Faust's great pessimistic curse on
all existence and by his optimistic dying vision, is to be dignified
with that name. What makes the problem still more complex, or
vague, is that the concepts of sin and guilt are here kept entirely
in the background, just as there had been only the shadowiest
mention of them in the agreement between the Lord and Mephisto

and no mention of them at all in that between Faust and Mephisto. All that had mattered then, in the "Prolog im Himmel" and in the Pact scene, had been apparently, that Faust's activity should not "erschlaffen," that he should not lie down upon a "Faulbett"; and it seems still to be all that matters now—that he should be one "der sich immer strebend bemüht." In the song of the "vollendetere Engel," which follows almost immediately upon the formula of salvation, the question of guilt and sin is, however, obliquely referred to, when Faust's "Unsterbliches" is described as "nicht reinlich." It might appear as though Faust's salvation were a process in two stages: first the actual delivery of his soul from Mephisto by the angels, the sole condition of which is that he has "striven and toiled," and secondly the purging away of the earthly baseness still inherent in it, which can only be performed by the "ewige Liebe von oben," represented by the Mater Gloriosa and Gretchen. But we have seen that the love from above plays an essential part in the first stage of this twofold process too. One consequence of Faust's soul keeping silent throughout "Bergschluchten" is that the repentance he had never felt or expressed on earth still remains unexpressed on his entry into the heavenly existence. That is something that is evidently not required of him, as it is of Gretchen, who does all the repenting that is needed for him as well as for herself. One seeks in vain in "Bergschluchten" for any express indication that Faust has been "forgiven," or that he himself or anybody else regards him as requiring forgiveness. His salvation is not then salvation from "sin," but from earthly limitations and the imperfections occasioned by them. He is so much redeemed as reconditioned. Daur designates Goethe's idea of salvation here felicitously enough as "Befreiung von dem irdisch unvollkommenen Lebensstoff" (Deliverance from the earthly, material substratum of life and its imperfections),[54] and Emrich calls it a purely natural, rejuvenating "Umartung von Leib und Seele" (reconstitution of body and soul).[55] Again Emrich says: "Nichts anderes als Selbstoffenbarung ursprünglichster Jugend ist Fausts Eingehen in den Himmel." (Faust's entry into Heaven is nothing but the self-revelation of the most pristine youthfulness).[56]

Interpretations of the end of *Faust* necessarily tend to fall into three main categories.

There are those who see Faust's guilt as real and heavy, and in itself deserving of damnation; and according to them, he is saved only through the divine mercy and grace that he has done little or nothing to merit. This is the more or less Christian line of interpretation, which has come to dominate during the last thirty years or so, and it is sometimes adopted by critics who have little use for orthodox Christian tradition, but accept in a modified, humanistic, or idealistic form the ethical standards of Christianity. The difficulty for such critics is to explain the words: "Wer immer strebend sich bemüht,/ Den können wir erlösen." It is more or less on such lines as these that *Faust* is interpreted by Burdach, Rickert, Böhm, Barker Fairley, and Beutler, amongst others. Rickert writes: "Die Engel fügen noch ein Erlösungsmotiv *hinzu* . . . Schon das Wort 'gar' . . . weist auf eine Steigerung gegenüber Fausts eigener Tätigkeit hin. Das bedeutet . . . : blosse *Gerechtigkeit*, die Faust wegen seiner Verdienste erlöst, genügt in diesem Falle nicht. Das wäre "Aufklärung", würde Goethe sagen. Daher muss die Liebe als Gnade hinzukommen" (The angels *add* a further ground for Faust's salvation. The word "gar" alone points to something that goes beyond Faust's own activity. That means: mere justice, which saves Faust because of his *deserts*, does not suffice in this case. That would be "rationalism," Goethe might have said. Therefore love must supervene as grace).[57]

There are those who think that Faust's guilt, though real, is not so heavy as to merit damnation, because he himself has expiated it and outgrown it in his development towards nobler and more altruistic aims. He has undergone a steady upward progress and thereby overcome his own Faustian lawlessness. The double formula of Faust's salvation causes these interpreters no difficulties. Their line of interpretation can be called "Pelagian." As a representative of them Spranger may be cited: "Die Lösung des Faust . . . liegt in den zwei sich ergänzenden Kräften: im unablässigen *Streben*, und in der entgegenkommenden, Gnade und Verzeihung spendenden Liebe" (The solution of Faust lies in the two complementary forces: in the ceaseless striving and in the love which meets it half way, bestowing grace and forgiveness).[58]

There are those for whom Faust's guilt is not real guilt at all, because he is so great as to be above guilt. It would indeed be guilt in a lesser man, but Faust is beyond good and evil; ordinary laws do not apply to him. Genius counts as much in the eyes of God as righteousness or holiness—some would say, far more. This can be called the "Faustian" line of interpretation. Its difficulty is to explain away the "Liebe von oben." It flourished during the final decades of the last century and the first decades of the present one, and would probably flourish still, but for the shock given to the human mind by National Socialism and its concentration camps. It is interesting to note that Nietzsche, to whom this school of interpretation owes so much, was too irritated by the "Liebe von oben" and "das Ewig-Weibliche" to see Faust as his followers do. One of its representatives, Gundolf, writes:

> Das Ewig-Weibliche gilt aber ursprünglich gar nicht der Erlösung Fausts, des strebenden Titanen, sondern der Erlösung Gretchens, der liebenden Sünderin . . . Dass aber Goethe selbst noch eine ausdrückliche begriffsmässige Motivierung der Gretchen-artigen Erlösungsform für Faust nötig gefunden hat, zeigt die . . . fast als entschuldigende Moral wirkende Strophe, womit die Engel Fausts Unsterbliches emportragen: "Und hat an ihm die Liebe gar/ Von oben teilgenommen." Die Liebe von oben wird hier als ein Überschuss über das zur Erlösung Fausts genügende, ihm selbst immanente Prinzip empfunden und bezeichnet.*[59]

Gundolf goes on to deplore Goethe's "Verwischung und Vermischung des faustischen Erlösungsproblems" (blurring and adulterating of the problem of Faust's salvation). Korff finds an ingenious

---

* The Eternal Feminine, however, applies originally not at all to the salvation of Faust, the striving Titan, but to the salvation of Gretchen, the sinful woman. But that Goethe felt the need for some additional, explicit, abstract motivation of this Gretchen-like form of salvation, is shown by the strophe with which the angels bear Faust's immortal part upward and which makes the impression almost of a moral apology: "And if the love from above has concerned itself for him," The love from above is here felt and designated as something superadded to the already sufficient principle of salvation immanent in Faust himself.

way of fitting the "Liebe von oben" into an extremely Faustian interpretation:

> Und diese Erhebung [Fausts in den Himmel] bedeutet also keineswegs die Begnadigung eines Sünders, der von Rechts verdammt werden müsste—das wäre christliche Theologie— sondern durchaus einen Akt der *Gerechtigkeit,* auf den der Mensch nach einer so schweren Prüfung *Anspruch* hätte, wenn Gott von sich aus nicht darüber hinausginge und in Liebe gar denjenigen zu sich emporhöbe, der so seiner Menschenidee entsprochen hat . . . *Faust kommt nicht als armer Sünder, sondern als Götterliebling in den Himmel.**⁶⁰

What Korff means by God's "Menschenidee" emerges in another particularly Nietzschean passage:

> Denn man muss sich philosophisch eingestehen, dass ein selbstverständlicher Egoismus allerdings die natürliche Form noch ungebrochenen Lebens ist. . . . Fast ohne es zu merken, ja beinah guten Gewissens opfert eine solche Persönlichkeit alles andere ihrer Selbstvollendung auf und überrennt im blinden Drang die Grenzen, die diesem ihrem Ziel im Wege stehen. . . . Das beginnt mit Gretchen. . . . Grosse Persönlichkeiten verschlingen die kleineren, das ist das Gesetz der Natur. Und ihr unethisches Verhalten besteht nur darin, dass sie zwangsläufig diesem ihrem Naturgesetz gehorchen, ohne sich durch ihre auch vorhandenen moralischen Affekte daran hindern zu lassen. . . . Und glaubt man an Selbstvollendung als den natürlichen und gewollten Sinn des Lebens, so muss man glauben an das höhere Recht auch alles dessen, was sie möglich macht. *Opfer sind keine Gegengründe* . . . Ein grossartiges Menschenleben vermag es darum, Opfer zu

---

* And this elevation of Faust's soul to Heaven does not mean the pardoning of a sinner who ought strictly speaking to be damned—that would be Christian theology—but simply an act of *justice,* to which man would have a *right* after so hard a trial, if God himself did not go beyond that, even raising to himself in *love* the one who had so much come up to his idea of what man should be. *Faust does not come into Heaven as a miserable sinner, but as a favourite of the gods.*

verantworten, die ein kleineres moralisch erdrücken müssten. Das ist der unausgesprochene, aber gelebte Glaube jenes übermoralischen Idealismus, dessen höhere Gültigkeit wir voraussetzen müssen, wenn wir Fausts Rechtfertigung vor Gott verstehen wollen.†[61]

One point is to be noted in connexion with what we have called the "Faustian" line of interpretation. Those who deplore the "Liebe von oben" as a regrettable lapse into other-worldliness which spoils the essentially this-worldly point of *Faust,* and would therefore explain it away as being merely an inorganic afterthought of 1830, should take into consideration that the fundamental idea of the salvation strophe is expressed already, in the review of spring, 1827, quoted above (p. 326). The words applied here to Faust and Gretchen and their love: "ein Verhältnis, das nur durch *einen Hauch von oben, der sich zu dem natürlichen Gefühl des Rechten und Guten gesellte, für die Ewigkeit gerettet werden konnte*," are almost like a paraphrase or commentary on the salvation strophe, which must, if our argumentation is correct, then already have been in existence certainly since 1825 and, very probably, since 1801. The "Hauch von oben" in the 1827 review and the "Liebe von oben" in the salvation strophe stand after all in a line with the "Stimme von oben" in the 1798 version of the "Kerker" scene. There is moreover an interesting textual indication that the salvation strophe may well, before it found its present position,

† For one must on philosophical grounds admit that an unquestioning egoism is indeed the natural form of still unbroken life. Almost without noticing it, nay almost with a good conscience such a personality sacrifices everything to its self-perfection and tramples down all barriers in its way to this goal. This begins with Gretchen. Great personalities devour the lesser ones, that is a law of nature. And their unethical conduct consists only in their being compelled to obey the law of their own natures, without allowing themselves to be restrained by the moral feelings which they too possess. And if one believes in self-perfection as the natural, intended meaning of life, one must also believe in the higher right of everything that makes it possible. That others have to be sacrificed in the process does not invalidate it. A magnificent human life can therefore answer for sacrifices which would be bound to crush a smaller one morally. That is the belief, expressed not in words, but in living facts, of that supra-moral idealism the higher validity of which we must postulate, if we would understand Faust's justification before God.

have formed a part of "Grablegung" and been sung by the angels immediately after they had snatched Faust's "Unsterbliches" from Mephisto, and when they were beginning to fly heavenward with it. The close parallel between the first line of that strophe: "Gerettet ist das edle Glied," and the scurrilous words with which Mephisto ascertains that the angelic flames of love have done no irreparable damage to his diabolical vitals: "*Gerettet sind die edlen Teufelsteile,*" can hardly be accidental. Goethe may very well originally have conceived of this phrase as a characteristically obscene Mephistophelian travesty of the angels' proclamation of Faust's deliverance, and then later, in justified apprehension that such ribaldry would be too prejudicial to the earnest purport of the salvation strophe, have thought it wiser to transfer that strophe to another, later scene, where the correspondence between it and Mephisto's gibe would no longer be conspicuous.

The Christian, the Pelagian, and the Faustian types of interpretation recur in infinite shades and variations in conjunction with an endless diversity of critical reservations and metaphysical, psychological, and political postulates. But if we ask which of them is right, the only answer is that none of them is in itself so indefensible as to be quite wrong. For all three the strongest supporting evidence can be found not only within the *Faust* drama itself, but also in the rest of Goethe's work and in his many epistolary and conversational utterances. The best case may perhaps be made out for the Pelagian view, which can appeal to Goethe's well-known Pelagian declaration in Book VIII of *Dichtung und Wahrheit,* and to the Lord's description of Faust as "ein guter Mensch." But apart from the discrepancy between what Goethe says of Faust's "immer höhere und reinere Tätigkeit bis ans Ende" and what we actually find in the drama, there is something dissatisfying about a mere fifty-fifty conclusion. Only the salvation of a Faust who strictly speaking deserves to be damned is interesting enough to be worth presenting poetically, whether he owes his salvation to the grace and mercy of a God conceived on more or less Christian lines, or to the enthusiastic approval of a God conceived on very different lines, as the supreme patron of genius and flamboyant personalities rather than of the poor in heart. There is after all more to be said in favour of both the other types of interpretation, irreconcilable though they are with one another, than in favour of the Pelagian type. As a specimen of the ample evidence that could be advanced in support of the Christian interpretation of Faust's salvation, Goethe's words eleven days before his death to Eckermann may here be quoted: "Möge . . . der menschliche Geist sich erweitern wie er will, über die Hoheit und sittliche Kultur des Christentums, wie es in den Evangelien schimmert und leuchtet, wird er nie hinauskommen" (However much the human mind may expand, it will never get beyond the loftiness and ethical culture of Christianity, as it gleams and shines in the gospels). As a specimen of the ample evidence that could be advanced in support of the "Faustian" interpretation of Faust's salvation, Goethe's ribald poem on Napoleon of 1814 or 1815 may here be quoted:

> Am Jüngsten Tag, vor Gottes Thron
> Stand endlich Held Napoleon.
> Der Teufel hielt ein grosses Register
> Gegen denselben und seine Geschwister,
> War ein wundersam verruchtes Wesen;
> Satan fing an, es abzulesen.

> Gott Vater, oder Gott der Sohn,
> Einer von beiden sprach vom Thron,
> Wenn nicht etwa gar der Heilige Geist
> Das Wort genommen allermeist:

> "Wiederhols nicht vor göttlichen Ohren!
> Du sprichst wie die deutschen Professoren.
> Wir wissen alles, mach es kurz!
> Am Jüngsten Tag ists nur ein. . . .
> Getraust du dich, ihn anzugreifen,
> So magst du ihn nach der Hölle schleifen."*

* At the Last Day before God's throne / Stood finally the hero Napoleon. / The Devil had kept a great register / Against him and his brothers and sisters; / It chronicled some queer, disgraceful goings-on; / Satan began to read it out. / God the Father or God the Son, / One of the two spoke from the throne, / If it was not the Holy Ghost itself / That had most to say: / "Don't repeat it before our divine ears! / You speak like the German professors. / We know all about it, cut it short! / At the Last Day it is only a f—t. / If you dare to attack him, / Then you are at liberty to cart him off to hell."

In these casually improvised verses the theme of the salvation or damnation of a Faustian personality whom Goethe greatly revered is dealt with in an exuberant, unguarded, absolutely characteristic manner. They reveal something of what we may well suppose to have been Goethe's attitude towards the salvation of Faust himself.

In fact the strophe embodying the formula of Faust's salvation is completely ambiguous, and all three possible lines of interpretation are equally defensible and equally exceptionable. It reflects, as does indeed the *Faust* drama in its totality, the lifelong tension between Goethe's conviction that Christianity is eternally rooted in human nature and its penury, and his conviction that the misdemeanours of such great men as Napoleon, Faust, or himself count for nothing in the eyes of God. This was a matter in which Goethe wanted to have it both ways. In "Bergschluchten" and particularly in the salvation strophe he aimed at a higher synthesis between these opposed views. But such a higher synthesis is not possible. What resulted instead was an ambiguous set of nebulous and somewhat rhetorical phrases, which can be made to mean almost anything and look too much like a halfhearted Pelagian compromise. What is essential and arresting alike about the Christian and the Faustian impulse was largely obliterated in the process.

This dualism is to be observed in Goethe as early as 1772 and accompanies him then, constantly modified in form and emphasis, but never in essence, throughout his life. The tension between the two poles appears at its minimum in *Iphigenie* with its classical humanism, at its maximum in *Faust*. What Goethe wanted was—to put it crudely for the sake of clarity—that a God, who had still not quite lost his identity with the God of Christianity, should treat him as an exception because of his genius, should say to him: "Of course, all this doesn't apply to *you*." Such thoughts Werther has, when his heart tells him that he has not been given to the Son, because the Father desires to keep him for himself, and when he imagines the Father benevolently reuniting him with Lotte in Heaven. So it is that Faust comes into a Heaven that is still meant to be recognizably a kind of Christian Heaven and is there reunited with Gretchen, without ever having to humble himself, to repent and confess his sins, to ask or accept forgiveness. Though the conception was not worked out till very much later, it bears all the marks of having originated in Goethe's Storm and Stress years.

Goethe attached great importance—and certainly not on merely opportunistic grounds—to the final scene of *Faust* being acceptable for Christian readers. This emerges from what he said on June 6, 1831, to Eckermann about the possibility of interpreting the salvation formula in a Christian sense:

> In diesen Versen ist der Schlüssel zu Fausts Rettung enthalten: in Faust selber eine immer höhere und reinere Tätigkeit bis ans Ende, und von oben die ihm zu Hilfe kommende ewige Liebe. *Es steht dies mit unserer religiösen Vorstellung durchaus in Harmonie,* nach welcher wir nicht bloss durch eigene Kraft selig werden, sondern durch die hinzukommende göttliche Gnade.*

Goethe's anxiety not to offend Christian sensibilities unduly may have been in part responsible for his abandoning the plan to bring God the Father and Christ on to the stage in the final scene, and for the way in which some of the most important issues are veiled over or evaded. It was an insoluble task, however, to write on such themes equally acceptably for the Christian and the non-Christian reader, even if one felt oneself to be, at one and the same time, "ein dezidierter Nichtchrist" (a decided non-Christian)[62] and perhaps the only living "Christ, wie Christus ihn haben wollte" (the only living Christian as Christ wanted him to be).[63]

It is one of the constantly repeated commonplaces of Goethe criticism that Faust is meant to be the "representative of humanity"—in fact, a kind of Everyman. It is also usually asserted that this was not Goethe's original intention, but a revolutionary new idea first introduced with the writing of the "Prolog im Himmel," Faust having before only been thought of as an exceptional individual. Thus Scheithauer writes of the Prologue: "Faust . . . rückt damit auf eine höhere Stufe als bisher, er wird Vertreter des Menschen überhaupt" (with this Faust is promoted to a still higher

---

* These verses contain the key to Faust's redemption: in Faust himself an ever higher and purer activity right to the end, and from above the eternal love that comes to his aid. *This is quite in harmony with our religious ideas,* according to which we are saved not by our own powers alone, but through the supervening divine grace.

level than before; he becomes the representative of all mankind).[64] Actually we know from Luden's conversation with Goethe of August, 1806, that long before the publication of the "Prolog im Himmel" Schelling and his circle, who had nothing but *Faust, ein Fragment* to go by, were already declaring Faust to be "der Repräsentant der Menschheit (the representative of humanity).[65] This view is expressed in the extremest form by Grumach, who, as we saw, would date the "Prolog im Himmel" about 1769. He says of it, "dass der Herr und Mephisto hier nicht über Fausts Schicksal verhandeln, sondern über das Schicksal der Menschheit (that the Lord and Mephisto are here not discussing the fate of Faust, but the fate of man),[66] and again: "Faust sollte ein Spiel werden von der neuen Versuchung Adams, von dem letzten vernichtenden Anschlag Luzifers gegen den Menschen, der durch Christus gerettet wird" (Faust was meant to be a drama about the new temptation of Adam, about Mephisto's last deadly plot against man, who is rescued by Christ).[67] These interpretations have, however, not remained unchallenged. They are particularly penetratingly criticized by Karl Wolff, who writes amongst other things: "Das meiste von dem, was Faust begegnet, liegt völlig ausserhalb des Kreises, der das Feld der Erfahrungen gewöhnlicher Sterblicher darstellt" (Most of what happens to Faust lies completely outside the circle within which the experiences of ordinary mortals are confined).[68] Of course even the most exceptional individual, once he is shown standing between God and the Devil, takes on a certain representative character and appears as a kind of Everyman. In this sense, but in this sense only, Faust can be seen as representative of humanity; but the idea that he was ever meant to be a new kind of Adam, whose salvation was to bring about that of the entire human race, is quite untenable. The whole point is that he is saved in a different way from the general run of mankind, because he differs so much from them. The elements in the "Prolog im Himmel" that are appealed to as showing that Faust is intended to represent all humanity are merely incidental and of secondary importance. They arise out of Goethe's special problem of bringing Faust and Mephisto together, and the question, how far Faust is or is not representative of mankind in general, is only apparently involved. Goethe could not begin abruptly with the transactions between God and Mephisto over Faust, which were really what mattered to him; he had in some way to work up to them, to provide some plausible motivation for them. The theme of humanity in general is given a special twist, so that it may provide a suitable opening for the Lord to raise the particular case of Faust. At every other point in the drama the distance and difference between Faust and ordinary humanity are emphasized. Goethe himself said to Eckermann on January 10, 1825: "Faust ist ein so seltsames Individuum, dass nur wenige Menschen seine inneren Zustände nachempfinden können" (Faust is so strange an individual that only few people can enter into his state of mind).

Faust is often referred to as the "Bible of Modern Man." But the man for whom Faust can still serve as a bible is hardly any longer modern. It is a work that has begun to date, as those of Homer, Dante, and Shakespeare, and some of Goethe's other works, do not date. It sums up the ideals, aspirations, and hopes of an epoch of the human mind that is over and never likely to return. There can be few people left now who would acclaim it with Daur as "das kühnste Menschenbild, das je geschaffen wurde" (the most audacious image of man that was ever created).[69] We have been too alarmed and disillusioned by crude, misguided attempts to put the ideal of the Faustian superman into practice during our own lifetimes, and we are having to struggle too hard to uphold far more modest traditional ideals of human culture against the dangers of collectivization and mechanization. It is symptomatic of this development that criticism now tends to see in Faust only a warning example, whereas he was clearly meant also and even more to be a figure held up for sympathy, admiration, and emulation. Only by keeping both these opposed aspects of the drama simultaneously before our minds can we hope to understand it.

The nearest Goethe ever came to making an explicit statement about the conception at the back of *Faust* was when he said to Eckermann on May 6, 1827: ". . . dass der Teufel die Wette verliert und dass ein aus schweren Verirrungen immerfort zum Bessern aufstrebender Mensch zu *erlösen* sei, das ist zwar ein wirksamer, manches erklärender guter Gedanke, aber es ist keine *Idee*, die dem Ganzen und jeder einzelnen Szene im besonderen zugrunde liege" (that the devil loses the wager and that a man for ever striving up-

ward from grave aberrations to what is better can be *saved* is indeed
a good, efficacious thought which explains much, but it is not an
idea that underlies the whole work and each individual scene in
particular).

In our attempts to find out what, if anything, holds the vast and
heterogeneous *Faust* drama together, it is this conception of Faust's
salvation that we have arrived at. We came to the conclusion that
this conception is as old as the beginnings of *Faust* and that it was
only modified in comparatively inessential respects during the sixty
succeeding years. From this it arose that there are far fewer inconsistencies in *Faust* than is usually supposed and that it is in fact as
consistent as there is any need for it to be in view of its dreamlike,
fantastic character. We would, however, in conclusion dissociate
ourselves no less from those who claim a strict philosophical unity
for *Faust* than from those who deny it any unity at all. The conception of Faust's salvation only holds the work together loosely,
and Goethe has brought in much of the greatest value and interest
which has little or no bearing upon it—for example, the "Klassische
Walpurgisnacht" and the Helen of Troy episode. But Goethe could
not thus have brought such a welter of multifarious motifs, themes,
and incidents into the work unless he had had the conception not
only of Faust's personality (which is curiously unstable), but also
of his destiny as a string to thread them on (to use his own image),
or, to use the perhaps even more felicitous image of Schiller, as a
hoop to bind them together.

Ultimately it is with the imagination, not with the understanding
that such a work as *Faust* must be approached. The utmost that the
critic, who has to address himself to the understanding, can hope
to achieve, is to create more favourable conditions for the imagination to operate in, by clearing away some of the purely textual and
interpretative hindrances that obstruct it. But at the end of all his
exertions he must repeat to himself Goethe's own words of warning: "Der Faust ist doch ganz etwas Inkommensurables, und alle
Versuche, ihn dem Verstande näher zu bringen, sind vergeblich"
(*Faust* is after all something quite incommensurable, and all attempts to bring it nearer to the understanding are in vain).[70]

Notes

GOETHE'S WORKS are referred to by their titles and by the numbers or headings of the divisions into which they fall, so that the passage in question can easily be traced in any of the standard editions. On the same grounds his letters are referred to simply by the dates and the names of the addressees, and his conversational utterances by the dates and names of the interlocutors by whom the conversations in question were recorded. Publications on Goethe are, after the first citation, referred to by the author's name or a short title and page numbers; more detailed information about them is given in the Bibliography. The Faust Paralipomena are quoted according to the numbering given in the still unsuperseded great *Sophien-Ausgabe*— Volumes 14, 15, and 16, of *Goethes Werke* (Weimar, 1887/1888).

Chapter 1 (pp. 1–19)

1. Compare E. M. Butler's *The Myth of the Magus*, passim.
2. Conversation with H. Voss, Feb. 24, 1805.
3. Compare Hans Henning, "Faust als historische Gestalt."
4. Compare Ludwig Kahn, *Literatur und Glaubenskrise* (Stuttgart, 1964), pp. 59 ff.; and Erich Heller, *The Artist's Journey*, pp. 8 ff.
5. Compare Crabb Robinson's conversations with Goethe of August 13/19, 1829.
6. H. Schneider, *Urfaust?* p. 9.
7. Heine's circumstantial account in the "Erläuterungen" to his own *Der Doktor Faust* of two performances by strolling players of the old popular Faust drama, which he claimed to have seen some twenty-five years previously (about 1821) in villages near Hamburg and Hanover, can be disregarded as merely fictitious.

8. Pniower, *Goethes Faust*, pp. 15–16.
9. H. Schneider, p. 12.
10. H. Schneider, p. 97.
11. Hefele, *Goethes Faust*, p. 41.
12. *Tages- und Jahreshefte* (Bis 1780).
13. Burdach, "Das religiöse Problem," p. 37.
14. "Vorwort" to *Dichtung und Wahrheit*.

Chapter 2 (pp. 20–38)

1. Oskar Seidlin, "Ist das Vorspiel?"
2. Momme Mommsen, "Zur Entstehung und Datierung."
3. *Rede zum Schäkespearstag* (Oct., 1772).
4. *Italienische Reise*, III (dated March 1, 1788). For the authenticity of this letter, see above, p. 40.
5. H. G. Gräf, *Goethe über seine Dichtungen*.
6. Conversation with Eckermann, Feb. 13, 1831.

Chapter 3 (pp. 39–91)

1. On the question whether Goethe did any work on *Faust* between Oct., 1775, and Feb., 1788, see above, p. 146.
2. See n. 4 to chap. 2.
3. Scherer, *Aus Goethes Frühzeit*, p. 78.
4. Scherer, *Aufsätze über Goethe*, p. 321.
5. Roethe, "Die Entstehung des Urfaust," p. 50.
6. Grumach, *Faustiana*, pp. 259–273.
7. Roethe, p. 61.
8. Roethe, p. 64.
9. Roethe, p. 78.
10. Roethe, p. 91.
11. The scenes of the *Urfaust* bear no numbers or titles. They are here referred to by the titles which Goethe later gave to them. Faust's dialogue with Wagner is treated as part of the first scene, not as a scene by itself. The seventeenth scene ("Valentin") is incomplete, consisting of two still unconnected fragments, which in some reprints are treated as separate scenes.
12. Petsch, "Zur Chronologie des Faust," p. 219.
13. *Dichtung und Wahrheit*, Book VII.
14. Compare Schneider, pp. 21 ff.
15. Roethe, p. 73.
16. Compare Hefele, p. 113.
17. Letter to Frau von Stein, March 20, 1782.

18. Scherer, *Aufsätze über Goethe*, p. 318.
19. Roethe, pp. 91–92.
20. Letter to Schiller of May 4, 1798.
21. H. Schneider, pp. 84–85.
22. Burger, *Das Kräftespiel*, p. 144.
23. Hans Albert Maier, "Goethes Phantasiearbeit," p. 142.
24. In the *Goethejahrbuch* VII (1886), attention was drawn to an anecdote, recorded by Pfitzer in a note to his second chapter, about a girl called Amee who is seduced by a certain young student, Apion, and kills her child with the help of the maid Caride, both of them being beheaded for this crime two years later. This story has nothing to do with Faust, and all the circumstances are quite different from those of Goethe's Gretchen tragedy.
25. Beutler, "Der Frankfurter Faust," p. 603.
26. Beutler, pp. 673–675.
27. Beutler, p. 599.
28. Compare *Goethes amtliche Schriften* (Schriften der Jahre 1776–1786), ed. W. Flach (Weimar, 1950), p. 251.
29. Thomas Mann misleadingly puts these words of Vogel's into Goethe's own mouth in his *Lotte in Weimar* (Stockholm, 1939), p. 344.
30. Beutler, p. 603.
31. Beutler, p. 604.
32. H. Schneider, pp. 64–65.
33. H. Schneider, p. 83.
34. Staiger, *Goethe*, I, p. 207.
35. Burdach, "Das religiöse Problem," p. 35.
36. Maier, p. 128. Maier here uses the words "philologisch" and "Philologe," in accordance with normal German practice, to denote *literary*, not exclusively *linguistic* scholarship.
37. See above, p. 43.
38. H. Schneider, p. 32.
39. Gräf, p. 16.
40. Gräf, p. 161.
41. *Jahrbuch der Goethe-Gesellschaft*, XIV (1928), p. 80.
42. H. Spiess, "Neue Beobachtungen," pp. 91–92.
43. Conversation with Eckermann of Feb. 10, 1829.
44. Hanna Fischer-Lamberg, "Zur Datierung der ältesten Szenen des Urfaust," p. 389.
45. Minor, *Goethes Faust*, I, p. 3.
46. Letter to Limprecht, April 13, 1770.
47. Max Morris, *Der junge Goethe*, II, p. 103.
48. Morris, II, p. 103.
49. Enders, *Die Katastrophe in Goethes Faust*, p. 79.
50. Agnes Bartscherer, *Paracelsus, Paracelsisten und Goethes Faust*, p. 27.
51. Bartscherer, p. 31.

52. Compare above, p. 56.
53. Burger, p. 157.
54. H. Schneider, pp. 21–25.
55. Burdach, "Das religiöse Problem," p. 33.
56. Schuchardt, "Die ältesten Teile des Urfaust," p. 474.
57. Maier, p. 130.

Chapter 4 (pp. 92–109)

1. Maier, pp. 133–134.
2. *Italienische Reise*, III (dated Feb. 2, 1788).
3. Roethe, p. 50.
4. Letter to Schiller of June 24, 1797.
5. Compare above, p. 22.
6. Compare Max Morris, "Mephistopheles," p. 181.
7. Maier, p. 137.
8. Roethe, p. 65.
9. Scherer, *Aus Goethes Frühzeit*, p. 81.
10. Enders, p. 22.
11. Roethe, p. 65.
12. Beutler, p. 601 and p. 684.
13. Burger, p. 166.
14. Günther Müller, *Kleine Goethebiographie*, p. 59.
15. H. Schneider, p. 70.
16. Fischer-Lamberg, p. 388.
17. Scherer, *Aus Goethes Frühzeit*, p. 78.
18. Scherer, *Aufsätze über Goethe*, p. 301.
19. Scherer, *Aufsätze über Goethe*, p. 305.
20. Scherer, *Aus Goethes Frühzeit*, p. 80.
21. See above, p. 54.
22. Beutler, p. 684.
23. See Spiess, p. 80, and Krogmann, *Goethes Urfaust*, p. 157.
24. Compare above, p. 40.

Chapter 5 (pp. 110–178)

1. Scherer, *Aufsätze über Goethe*, p. 315.
2. Scherer, p. 321.
3. Scherer, p. 324.
4. See above, p. 75.
5. H. Schneider, p. 76.
6. Barker Fairley, *A Study of Goethe*, p. 20.
7. Fischer-Lamberg, p. 404.

8. It used to be maintained that the "sage" here alluded to is Herder and that Goethe had in mind a particular passage in one of Herder's works, which he did not read till 1774. It is now, however, generally recognized that the words in question only reproduce an idea found everywhere in cabbalistic and mystical writers. Herder's indirect influence on Goethe's *Faust* was certainly very important; but it is unwarrantable to identify Herder either with Faust or with Mephisto, as some interpreters still do.

9. Compare E. C. Mason, "Goethes Erdgeist und das Pathos des Irdischen," passim.

10. Roethe, p. 84.

11. Bartscherer, pp. 87–95.

12. Grumach, "Prolog und Epilog," pp. 95–100.

13. Bartscherer, p. 88.

14. Goebel, *Goethes Quelle für die Erdgeistszene*, p. 2.

15. Goebel, Max Morris, Grumach, and others have tried with varying success to find sources or analogies for this curious notion of "sucking" amongst the cabbalistic writers. It is more important, however, that this was a favourite conception and word of the youthful Goethe. Thus in 1771, in the original *Götz von Berlichingen*, Adelheid is spoken of as having "sucked her husband to death" with poison, and Götz himself, just before he dies, longs "once more to suck the air of freedom into himself." In 1774, Werther says that he has "sucked strength and the balm of life into his heart" from Lotte's kiss. The poem *On the Lake* of June, 1775, begins: "I suck nourishment from the world through my navel-string." That Faust has "sucked at the sphere" of the Spirit of Earth fits in, of course, with his desire "to grasp the breasts of infinite nature." Compare Wilkinson and Willoughby, *Goethe, Poet and Thinker*, pp. 102–103.

16. "Aus Herder's Nachlass," published by H. D. Irmscher in *Euphorion*, Vol. LIV, 1960, p. 288. My thanks are due to Dr. Hugh B. Nisbet for drawing my attention to this recently discovered Herder manuscript.

17. Niejahr, *Kritische Untersuchungen*, pp. 279 ff.

18. This is in the *Requiem* for the Prince de Ligne of 1815, where the Spirit of Earth appears amongst other allegorical figures as a personification of war and violence, who practises "destruction as a building up."

19. Kurt Wollf, *Fausts Erlösung*, p. 48.

20. Muschg, *Tragische Literaturgeschichte*, 2nd ed. (Berne, 1953), p. 57.

21. F. J. Schneider, *Goethes Satyros und der Urfaust*, p. 25.

22. Grumach, "Prolog und Epilog," p. 98.

23. Roethe, p. 82.

24. F. J. Schneider, p. 26.

25. Max Morris, "Mephistopheles," p. 181.

26. For Herder's conception of a "Gott" or "Genius" of the Earth compare above, p. 134. Herder took over the idea of an Erdgeist from Goethe in the 1780's, in his *Ideen*.

27. Schiller's letter to Goethe of June 23, 1797.

28. Galatians v: 17.
29. Letter to Lavater of Feb. 22, 1776.
30. Friedrich und Scheithauer, *Kommentar zu Goethes Faust*, p. 187.
31. W. Böhm, *Goethes Faust in neuer Deutung*, p. 23.
32. Karl Wollf, p. 50.
33. Minor, I, p. 224.
34. Minor, I, p. 224.
35. Maier, p. 134.
36. Maier, p. 136.
37. Maier, p. 136.
38. Grumach, "Prolog und Epilog," p. 103.
39. Grumach, "Prolog und Epilog," pp. 103–105.
40. Grumach, "Prolog und Epilog," pp. 87–88.
41. This theory of H. Schneider's was anticipated by Petsch in 1926 in his "Zur Chronologie des Faust," p. 228.
42. H. Schneider, p. 71.
43. H. Schneider, p. 72.
44. H. Schneider, p. 75.
45. H. Schneider, p. 92.
46. H. Schneider, p. 74.
47. Scherer, *Aus Goethes Frühzeit*, p. 81.
48. Enders, p. 15.
49. Amongst the limitations to the devil's powers specially insisted on by Le Sage in his *Diable Boîteux* (1707) and by Defoe in his *Political History of the Devil* (1726) is this very one of not being able to release prisoners. In reply to the question of Don Cléofas: "What, haven't you the power to release a man from prison?" Le Sage's Devil on Two Sticks says: "Certainly I have not. . . . If you had read the *Enchiridion* or Albertus Magnus, you would know that neither I nor my brethren can set prisoners at liberty."
50. The quite exceptional use of the word *Schalk* to designate "ein Frauenzimmer, das einer Person, von der es abhängt, durch Gleichgültigkeit, Kälte und Zurückhaltung das Leben sauer macht," by Sinclair in *Die guten Weiber* (1800) has certainly no bearing on its application to Mephisto by the Lord in the "Prolog im Himmel," as Momme Mommsen would have us believe. ("Zur Entstehung und Datierung" pp. 320–321). Goethe undoubtedly understands the word here in what Sinclair himself defines as its "gewöhnlichen Sinn"—that is to say, as meaning "eine Person, die mit Heiterkeit und Schadenfreude jemand einen Possen spielt." Grumach has demonstrated that the "Prolog im Himmel" cannot possibly have been written later than spring, 1798. See above, p. 265.
51. Compare E. C. Mason, *Goethe's Sense of Evil* (Publications of the English Goethe Society, 1964), pp. 1–53.
52. II Corinthians iv: 4.
53. Minor, I, p. 377.
54. Compare above, p. 138.

55. It may be noted that even in the 1725 German Faust chapbook, Faust asks Mephistophilis "whether the devils too hope to be saved."
56. Maier, p. 135.

Chapter 6 (pp. 179–186)

1. Compare above, pp. 85–86.
2. Compare above, pp. 23–26.
3. Böhm, *Faust der Nichtfaustische*, p. 79.
4. Böhm, *Faust in neuer Deutung*, p. 16.
5. Böhm, *Faust in neuer Deutung*, p. 23.
6. Böhm, *Faust in neuer Deutung*, pp. 25–27.
7. Wollf, p. 167.
8. The name of the university town in which Faust lives is nowhere given, but it can, in accordance with the Faust tradition, be assumed to be Wittenberg, or possibly Mainz. The only scene in *Faust I* which can be assigned by name to a particular locality is the "Auerbachs Keller" in Leipzig.
9. Compare above, pp. 85–86.
10. Compare above, pp. 58–60.
11. Compare above, p. 50 and p. 172.
12. Minor, I, p. 129.

Chapter 7 (pp. 187–245)

1. Compare above, pp. 64–74.
2. Roethe, p. 70.
3. Hefele, p. 28.
4. Krogmann, "Zum Ursprung der Gretchentragödie," p. 197.
5. *Dichtung und Wahrheit*, Book XIV.
6. Compare above, p. 66.
7. Conversation with Kanzler von Müller of Dec. 17, 1824.
8. Letter of Nov. 7, 1767 to Behrisch.
9. Schneider, p. 84.
10. Compare above, p. 7.
11. The scene "Ein Gartenhäuschen" is to be regarded as an immediate continuation of the preceding scene, "Garten," and therefore as not constituting a separate meeting between Faust and Gretchen.
12. Calvin Thomas, *Goethe's Faust*, I, pp. lxii–lxiii.
13. Daur, *Faust und der Teufel*, pp. 104–105 and pp. 486–487.
14. H. Schneider, p. 69.
15. Bartscherer, p. 47.
16. Wollf, p. 171.
17. See Burger, p. 175.

18. Compare E. C. Mason, "The Paths and Powers of Mephistopheles," passim.
19. Wollf, p. 95.
20. Rickert, *Goethes Faust*, p. 226.
21. Scherer, *Aufsätze über Goethe*, pp. 334–335.
22. Max Morris, *Der junge Goethe*, VI, pp. 532–533.
23. *Wilhelm Meisters Lehrjahre*, IV, ch. 14.
24. *Wilhelm Meisters Lehrjahre*, IV, ch. 16.
25. Ronald Gray, "Goethe's Faust Part I," *Cambridge Quarterly*, I (Spring, 1966), pp. 130–131.
26. For Goethe's later modification of this phrase see above, p. 258.
27. Daur, p. 367.
28. Thomas Mann, "Über Goethes Faust," p. 704.
29. See above, p. 161.
30. Burger, pp. 162–163.
31. Burger, p. 175.
32. See *Der junge Goethe*, VI, p. 337.
33. Roethe, p. 70.
34. Burger, p. 159.
35. H. Schneider, pp. 89–90.
36. Roethe, p. 52.
37. Roethe, p. 66.
38. Roethe, p. 56.
39. Roethe, p. 56.
40. Köster, "Besprechung von Minors Faust," p. 74.
41. Hertz, "Zu Goethes römischem Faustplan," p. 403.
42. Hertz, p. 403.
43. Hertz, p. 404.
44. Schelling, *Philosophie der Kunst* (1802–1803), published in *Sämmtliche Werke* I, 5. Band in 1859; p. 732.
45. Sarauw, *Entstehungsgeschichte des Goetheschen Faust*, p. 74.
46. Burdach, "Faust und die Sorge," p. 55.
47. Minor, I, p. 236.
48. Enders, p. 35.
49. Roethe, pp. 56–66.
50. Beutler, p. 638.
51. Compare E. C. Mason, "Wir sehen uns wieder!" *Literaturwissenschaftliches Jahrbuch der Görres-Gesellschaft*, VI (1965), pp. 79–109.
52. Hertz, pp. 383–427.
53. Conversation with C. F. John of May 2, 1812.

Chapter 8 (pp. 246–260)

1. Letter to Herzog Carl August of Feb. 16, 1788.
2. Hertz, p. 416.

3. Hertz, p. 410.
4. Hertz, p. 408.
5. Hertz, p. 405.
6. Hertz, p. 404.
7. Hertz, p. 384.
8. Compare above, p. 30 and p. 40.
9. Compare above, p. 40.
10. Compare above, pp. 228–229.
11. Compare above, p. 190 and pp. 208–209.
12. Hans Jaeger, "The Wald und Höhle Monologue in Faust," p. 397.
13. Jaeger, p. 398.
14. Scherer proposes the characteristic and entirely superfluous theory that these lines must have been written very much earlier than the rest of the scene, in the days of the *Urfaust*, and for a different context. He finds them inconsistent with the tone of the rest of the scene, asserting that there are "far more realistic elements in them than are otherwise employed in this scene," and thinks that Goethe only "sandwiched them in here because he did not after all want to have to throw them away altogether" (*Aus Goethes Frühzeit*, p. 105).
15. Max Morris, "Mephistopheles," pp. 166–167.
16. Sarauw, p. 18.

Chapter 9 (pp. 261–312)

1. Tieck, quoted by Düntzer in his *Einleitung* to *Faust* in the D.N.L. edition of Goethe's works, Vol. XII, p. xx.
2. Schiller's letter to Goethe of Nov. 29, 1794.
3. Letter to Schiller of Dec. 2, 1794.
4. Pniower, pp. 44–53.
5. Compare above, p. 24.
6. Compare above, p. 263.
7. Grumach, "Prolog und Epilog," p. 70.
8. Grumach, "Prolog und Epilog," p. 81.
9. Friedrich and Scheithauer, p. 124.
10. Grumach, "Prolog und Epilog," p. 101.
11. Conversation with Eckermann of June 6, 1831.
12. Compare above, pp. 147–148.
13. *Wilhelm Meisters Lehrjahre*, Book VIII, ch. 5.
14. Max Kommerell, "Faust und die Sorge," *Goethe-Kalender des Hochstifts* (1939), p. 128.
15. Scherer, *Aufsätze über Goethe*, p. 332.
16. Staiger, II, p. 331.
17. Conversation with Eckermann of April 18, 1827.
18. Compare above, p. 177.
19. Compare above, pp. 21–26.

20. Grumach, "Prolog und Epilog," p. 71.
21. Compare above, p. 22 and p. 28.
22. Grumach, "Prolog und Epilog," pp. 74–77.
23. Compare above, pp. 92–94.
24. Compare above, p. 174.
25. Scherer, *Aufsätze über Goethe*, p. 336.
26. Compare above, p. 252.
27. Compare above, pp. 282–284.
28. Compare on these questions Julius Burghold's *Die Faustwetten und ihre scheinbaren Widersprüche.*
29. Scherer, *Aufsätze über Goethe*, p. 332.
30. Compare above, pp. 200–202, 207 and 219.
31. Enders, p. 54.
32. Compare above, p. 61.
33. Compare above, pp. 349 ff.
34. Compare above, pp. 21, 28, 286.

Chapter 10 (pp. 313–376)

1. Emrich, *Symbolik des Faust II*, p. 12.
2. Emrich, p. 50.
3. Emrich, p. 54.
4. Emrich, p. 60.
5. Emrich, p. 66.
6. Emrich, p. 19.
7. Heller, "Faust's Damnation," p. 36.
8. From an unutilized preface for "Helena," dated June 10, 1826, and reprinted by Pniower, p. 183.
9. Gräf, p. 586.
10. From the review of Hinrich's *Das Wesen der antiken Tragödie*, reprinted by Pniower, p. 183.
11. Grotthus, *Probleme und Charakterköpfe* (1897). Quoted by Hans Schwerte in *Faust und das Faustische*, p. 183.
12. Emrich, p. 400.
13. Staiger, III, p. 435.
14. Staiger, III, pp. 434–435.
15. Conversation with Eckermann of May 29, 1831.
16. Burdach, "Faust und die Sorge," p. 51.
17. Burdach, p. 49.
18. Daur, *Faust und der Teufel*, pp. 322–323.
19. Staiger, III. p. 435.
20. Burdach, "Das religiöse Problem," p. 25.
21. A. R. Hohlfeld, in his "Die Entstehung des Faust-Manuskripts von 1825–26," p. 303, challenges the generally accepted view that Goethe did not give this speech its final form till January, 1832.

22. Hohlfeld, pp. 285 ff.
23. Staiger, III, pp. 424–425.
24. Emrich, *Symbolik des Faust II*, p. 368.
25. Emrich, p. 418.
26. Emrich, p. 471.
27. Emrich, p. 403.
28. Emrich, p. 393.
29. Emrich, p. 398.
30. Emrich, p. 393.
31. Emrich, p. 400.
32. Emrich, p. 393.
33. Compare Daur, p. 467, on Hermann Türck.
34. Böhm, *Faust der Nichtfaustische*, p. 74.
35. See above, p. 269.
36. Diary entry, reprinted by Gräf, p. 605.
37. Korff, *Faustischer Glaube*, pp. 127–128.
38. Staiger, III, p. 425.
39. Gräf, p. 215.
40. Hertz, "Zur Entstehungsgeschichte von Faust II, Akt 5," *Euphorion*, XXXIII (1932), p. 276.
41. Staiger, III, p. 423.
42. Staiger, III, p. 451.
43. Joachim Müller in his *Prolog und Epilog zu Goethes Faustdichtung*, pp. 13–15, argues that there is the closest correspondence both in purport and in composition between the "Prolog im Himmel" and "Bergschluchten."
44. Compare Pniower, p. 287. The date of the conversation is unfortunately unknown. It must have been in the late 1820's.
45. Staiger, III, p. 426.
46. Staiger, III, p. 461.
47. See above, pp. 237–238.
48. Staiger, III, p. 426.
49. Staiger, III, pp. 452–453.
50. See above, p. 229.
51. See above, p. 177.
52. F. Gundolf, *Goethe*, p. 781.
53. Barker Fairley, *Goethe as Revealed in His Poetry*, p. 119.
54. Daur, p. 358.
55. Emrich, p. 412.
56. Emrich, p. 409.
57. Rickert, p. 483.
58. Spranger, *Goethes Weltanschauung*, p. 50.
59. Gundolf, pp. 781–782.
60. Korff, p. 151.
61. Korff, pp. 162–165.
62. See above, p. 241.
63. Conversation with Kanzler von Müller of April 7, 1830.

64. Friedrich und Scheithauer, p. 128. Compare also Joachim Müller, pp. 10–11.
65. Gräf, p. 135.
66. Grumach, "Prolog und Epilog," p. 69.
67. Grumach, p. 107.
68. Karl Wollf, p. 228.
69. Daur, p. 371.
70. Conversation with Eckermann of January 3, 1830.

Selected Bibliography

ON NO WORK of world literature, not even on *Hamlet,* has so much been published as on Goethe's *Faust.* What is given below is only an unclassified list in alphabetical order of the books and articles actually quoted within the present study, supplemented with a few others which, although not referred to by name in the text, have been useful or stimulating. Amongst the many sound commentated editions of *Faust* now in print that of Trunz—Volume III of the *Hamburger Ausgabe* of *Goethes Werke*—may be specially recommended. There, as also in the *Kommentar zu Goethes Faust* of Friedrich und Scheithauer (see below), good classified selective bibliographies will be found.

In cases where the page references in the Notes are from later reprints of the books or articles in question, the date of the original publication is given in parentheses, in addition to the bibliographical particulars of the edition actually utilized.

Atkins, Stuart. *Goethe's Faust.* A literary analysis. Harvard, 1958.

Bartscherer, Agnes. *Paracelsus, Paracelsisten und Goethes Faust.* Dortmund, 1911.

Beutler, Ernst. *"Der Frankfurter Faust," Jahrbuch des Freien Deutschen Hochstifts.* Frankfurt, 1940. (Amongst other publications.)

Böhm, Wilhelm. *Faust der Nichtfaustische.* Halle, 1933.

———. *Goethes Faust in neuer Deutung.* Köln, 1949.

Boenigk, Otto von. *Das Urbild von Goethes Gretchen.* Greifswald, 1914.

Burdach, Konrad. "Faust und die Sorge," *Deutsche Vierteljahres-schrift für Literaturwissenschaft und Geistesgeschichte*, I (1923), pp. 1–60.

——. "*Das religiöse Problem in Goethes Faust*," *Euphorion*, XXXIII (1932), 1–83.

Burger, Heinz Otto. "Motiv, Konzeption, Idee—das Kräftespiel in der Entwicklung von Goethes Faust," in *Dasein heisst eine Rolle spielen*. München, 1963. (First published in 1942.)

Burghold, Julius. "Die Faustwetten und ihre scheinbaren Widersprüche," *Goethe-Jahrbuch*, XLIII (1913), 64–82.

Butler, E. M. *The Myth of the Magus*. Cambridge, 1948. (Amongst other publications.)

Collins, J. *Über Goethes Faust in seiner ältesten Gestalt*. Giessen, 1893.

Daur, Albert. *Faust und der Teufel*. Heidelberg, 1950.

Emrich, Wilhelm. *Die Symbolik des Faust II*. Berlin, 1943; 3rd edition: Berlin, 1964.

——. "Symbolinterpretation und Mythenforschung," *Euphorion*, XLVII (1953), 38–67.

Enders, Carl. *Die Katastrophe in Goethes Faust*. Dortmund, 1905.

Fairley, Barker. *Goethe*. London and Toronto, 1932.

——. *Goethe as Revealed in His Poetry*. London and Toronto, 1932.

——. *A Study of Goethe*. Oxford, 1947. (Amongst other publications.)

Fischer, Kuno. *Goethes Faust*. Stuttgart, 1878.

Fischer-Lamberg, Hanna. "Zur Datierung der ältesten Szenen des Urfaust," *Zeitschrift für deutsche Philologie*, LXXVI (1957), 379–408.

Friedrich, Theodor. (See Scheithauer.)

Gillies, Alexander. *Goethe's Faust, an Interpretation*. Oxford, 1957.

Goebel, Julius. "Goethes Quelle fur die Erdgeistszene," *Journal of English and Germanic Philology*, VII (Illinois: 1909), 1–17.

Gräf, Hans Gerhard. *Goethe über seine Dichtungen*, 2. Theil, 2. Band. Frankfurt, 1904.

Grauffunder, P. "Der Erdgeist und Mephisto in Goethes Faust," *Preussische Jahrbücher*, LXVIII (1891), 700–725.

Gray, Ronald. *Goethe the Alchemist*. Cambridge, 1952.

————. "Goethe's Faust Part I," *Cambridge Quarterly*, I (Spring, 1966).

Grimm, Herman. *Das Leben Goethes*. Berlin, 1877.

Grotthuss, J. E. Freiherr v. "Faust," in *Probleme und Charakterköpfe*. Stuttgart, 1897.

Grumach, Ernst. "Prolog und Epilog im Faustplan von 1797," *Goethe-Jahrbuch*, 1952–1953, pp. 63–107. (Amongst other publications.)

————. *Faustiana, Beiträge zur Faust-Forschung*. Berlin, 1959.

Gundolf, Friedrich. *Goethe*. Berlin, 1916.

Hefele, Herman. *Goethes Faust*. Stuttgart, 1931.

Heller, Erich. "Faust's Damnation," in *The Artist's Journey into the Interior*. New York, 1965.

Henning, Hans. "Faust als historische Gestalt," *Goethe-Jahrbuch*, 1959, pp. 107–139.

Hertz. "Zu Goethes römischem Faust-Plan," *Euphorion*, XXXI (1930), 387–427.

————. "Zur Entstehungsgeschichte von Faust II, Akt 5," *Euphorion*, XXXIII (1932).

Heusler, Andreas. "Goethes Verskunst," *Deutsche Vierteljahresschrift für Literaturwissenschaft und Geistesgeschichte*, III (1925), 462–482.

Hohlfeld, A. R. (Amongst other publications.) "Die Entstehung des Faust-Manuskripts von 1825/26, *Euphorion*, XLIX (1955), 283–304.

Jaeger, Hans. "The Wald und Höhle Monologue in Faust," *Monatshefte für den deutschen Unterricht*, XLI (Wisconsin: 1949), 395–402.

Kahn, Ludwig. *Literatur und Glaubenkrise*. Stuttgart, 1964.

Klett, Ada M. *Der Streit um Faust II seit 1900*. Jena, 1939.

Kommerell, Max. "Faust und die Sorge," *Goethe-Kalender des Hochstifts* (1939).

Korff, H. A. *Faustischer Glaube*. Leipzig, 1938. (Amongst other publications.)

Köster, Albert. "Review of Minor's *Faust*," in *Anzeiger für deutsches Altertum und deutsche Literatur*, XXVIII (1902), 72–80.

Krogmann, Willy. "Zum Ursprung der Gretchentragödie," *Germanisch-Romanische Monatschrift*, XVII (1929), 193–204.

——. *Goethes Urfaust*. Berlin, 1933.

Maier, Hans Albert. "Goethes Phantasiearbeit am Fauststoff im Jahre 1771," *P.M.L.A.*, LXVII (1952), 125–146.

Mann, Thomas. "Über Goethes Faust," in *Adel des Geistes*. Stockholm, 1945. (First published, 1938.)

Mason, E. C. "Mephistos Wege und Gewalt," also in *Exzentrische Bahnen*. Göttingen, 1963. (First published in English, 1962.)

——. "Goethes Erdgeist und das Pathos des Irdischen," in *Exzentrische Bahnen*. Gottingen, 1963. (First published in English, 1960.)

——. *Goethe's Sense of Evil*. Publications of the English Goethe Society, 1965.

——. "Wir schen uns wieder!" *Literaturwissenschaftliches Jahrbuch der Görres-Gesellschaft*, VI (1965), 79–109.

May, Kurt. *Faust II. Teil, In der Sprachform gedeutet*. Berlin, 1936.

Minor, J. *Goethes Faust, Entstehungsgeschichte und Erklärung*. Stuttgart, 1901.

Mommsen, Momme. "Zur Entstehung und Datierung einiger Faustszenen um 1800," *Euphorion*, XLVII (1953), 295–330.

Morris, Max. *Goethe-Studien*. Berlin, 1897/1898. (Amongst other publications.)

——. "Swedenborg im Faust," *Euphorion*, VI (1899), 491 ff.

——. "Mephistopheles," *Goethe-Jahrbuch*, XXII (1901), 151–191; and XXIII (1902), 139–176.

——. *Der junge Goethe*. 6 vols. Leipzig, 1909–1912.

Müller, Günther. *Kleine Goethe-Biographie*. Bonn, 1947.

Müller, Joachim. *Prolog und Epilog in Goethes Faustdichtung*. Berlin, 1964. (Amongst other publications.)

Niejahr, Johannes, "Kritische Untersuchungen zu Goethes Faust," *Euphorion*, IV (1897), 272–287 & 489–508.

Petsch, Robert. "Zur Chronologie des Faust," *Euphorion*, XXVII (1926), 207–222. (Amongst other publications.)

Pniower, Otto. *Goethes Faust : Zeugnisse und Excurse zu seiner Entstehungsgeschichte*. Berlin, 1899. (Amongst other publications.)

Rickert, Heinrich. *Goethes Faust*. Tübingen, 1932.

Roethe, Gustav. "Die Entstehung des Urfaust," in *Goethe—Gesammelte Vorträge und Aufsätze*. Berlin, 1932. (First published, 1920.)

Sarauw, Chr. *Entstehungsgeschichte des Goetheschen Faust.* Copenhagen, 1918.

Scheithauer, Lothar J. Revised edition of Theodor Friedrich's *Kommentar zu Goethes Faust.* Stuttgart, 1959.

Scherer, Wilhelm. *Aus Goethes Frühzeit.* Strasburg, 1879.

———. *Aufsätze über Goethe.* Berlin, 1886.

Schneider, F. J. *Goethes Satyros und der Urfaust.* Halle, 1949.

Schneider, Hermann. *Urfaust?* Tübingen, 1949.

Schuchardt, G. "Die ältesten Teile des Urfaust," *Zeitschrift für deutsche Philologie,* LI (1926), 465–475.

Schwerte, Hans. *Faust und das Faustische, Ein Kapitel deutscher Ideologie.* Stuttgart, 1962.

Seidlin, Oskar. "Ist das Vorspiel auf dem Theater ein Vorspiel zum Faust?" in *Von Goethe zu Thomas Mann.* Göttingen, 1963. (First published in English in 1949.)

Seuffert, Bernhard. "Die älteste Szene von Goethes Faust," *Vierteljahresschrift für Literaturgeschichte,* IV (1891), 339 ff.

Spiess, Heinrich. "Neue Beobachtungen und Gedanken über die Entstehungsgeschichte des Urfaust und des Fragments," *Jahrbuch der Goethe-Gesellschaft,* XXI (1935), 63–107.

Spranger, Eduard. *Goethes Weltanschauung.* Leipzig, undated (after 1932).

Staiger, Emil. *Goethe.* 3 vols. Zürich, 1952/1956/1959.

Strehlke, Fr. *Wörterbuch zu Goethes Faust.* Stuttgart, 1891.

Thomas, Calvin. *Faust Part I.* Boston, 1892.

Türck, Hermann. *Eine neue Faust-Erklärung.* Berlin, 1901.

Wehnert. "Gottvater, Erdgeist und Mephisto," *Zeitschrift für den deutschen Unterricht,* XX (1908), 758–768.

Weisse, Christian Hermann. *Kritik und Erläuterung des Goetheschen Faust.* Leipzig (?), 1837.

Wilkinson, Elizabeth M., and Willoughby, L. A. *Goethe, Poet and Thinker.* London, 1962. (Amongst other publications.)

Witkowski, Georg. *Das Leben Goethes.* Berlin, 1932. (Amongst other publications.)

Wollf, Karl. *Fausts Erlösung.* Nürnberg, 1949.

Ziegler, Theobald. Responsible for the final sections of Albert Bielschowski's *Goethe, sein Leben und seine Werke,* Volume II. München, 1903.

Indexes

Devil: could not be conjured up as such by Faust, 120, 124, 293, 295; works the bellows of nature, 162; H. A. Maier on, 167–168; extent of his powers, 173, 382 n. 49; possible salvation of, 176, 383 n. 55. *See also* Mephisto

Devoutness, Gretchen's, 211–212, 214

Dialectic, as natural mode of Goethe's experience: partly responsible for supposed contradictions in *Faust*, 37; of this-worldliness and other-worldliness, 177–178, 274–275, 301. *See also* Antithesis; Dualism; Paradoxicality; Polarity

"Diese Widersprüche . . . disparater zu machen" (These contradictions . . . should be made more disparate): interpretation of this phrase in Paralipomenon I, 269–270, 274, 280

Discontent, essential characteristic of Faust: 137, 253, 275, 280–281. *See also* Insatiability of Faust's nature

"Disputation" scene, projected, 290, 299–300

Divine element in human nature, 160, 161–162

Documentation of Goethe's work on *Faust*: defective, for all its amplitude, 35

Dornburg conversation of April 1818, 177, 284, 361

Drama, the dramatic: *Faust* a drama with "epical" qualities, 251; dramatic character of *Faust II* denied by Emrich, 315–316. *See also* Theatre

Dream-world, *Faust* conceived of as being enacted in a: thence its incoherencies and supposed inconsistencies, 27, 97, 278, 376; Gretchen action assimilated to, 202; *Helena-tragödie* a dream within a dream, 324

Dualism of Goethe's nature, mirrored in *Faust*: of action and contemplation, 142; fundamental dualisms in *Faust*, 158–159, 269–270; in respect of nature and love, 221; of extreme individualism and esoteric Christianity, 241–245 *passim*; in respect of Christianity, 372–373. *See also* Antithesis; Polarity; Synthesis

"Du gleichst dem Geist, den du begreifst," 168, 306

Earth and Earthiness, this-worldly connotations of, 149–156 *passim*

Earth-spirits in traditional, folklore sense, 135–136, 295

Eckermann. *See* Riemer and Eckermann

"Ein guter Mensch in seinem dunklen Drange" (A good man in his obscure impulse), 281–282

Elements: earth as one of the four, 133, 136, 154; Faust assumes that Mephisto may be a spirit of one of them, 295; Faust's struggle against, 330, 343, 344; Mephisto claims them as his allies, 341; felt as offensive by the "more perfect" angels, 358

Emancipation, spiritual: Gretchen incapable of, 216; possible and desirable only for the gifted, exceptional individual, 241

Emrich, Wilhelm (critic): on differences between *Faust I* and *Faust II*, 314–316; condones Faust's treatment of Philemon and Baucis, 334; on Faust's dying vision, 345–347; on Faust's salvation, 365

Enders, Carl (critic): on dating of *Trüber Tag. Feld*, 100, 101, 106; on Goethe's Shakespearean epoch,

B. Index to Scenes of Faust

C. *Index to Other Works of Goethe*